# ON THE

# MOVE

# ON THE
# MOVE

### MOBILITY IN THE MODERN WESTERN WORLD

## TIM CRESSWELL

**Routledge**
Taylor & Francis Group
New York  London

Routledge is an imprint of the
Taylor & Francis Group, an informa business

Published in 2006 by
Routledge
Taylor & Francis Group
270 Madison Avenue
New York, NY 10016

Published in Great Britain by
Routledge
Taylor & Francis Group
2 Park Square
Milton Park, Abingdon
Oxon OX14 4RN

Printed in the United States of America on acid-free paper
10 9 8 7 6 5 4 3 2 1

International Standard Book Number-10: 0-415-95256-5 (Softcover)
International Standard Book Number-13: 978-0-415-95256-9 (Softcover)
Library of Congress Card Number 2005031472

---

**Library of Congress Cataloging-in-Publication Data**

---

Cresswell, Tim.
  On the move : mobility in the modern Western world / by Tim Cresswell.
     p. cm.
  Includes bibliographical references and index.
  ISBN-13: 978-0-415-95255-2 (hardback)
  ISBN-13: 978-0-415-95256-9 (pbk. )
  1. Movement (Philosophy) I. Title.

B105.M65C74 2006
304.801--dc22                                                                                    2005031472

---

Taylor & Francis Group
is the Academic Division of Informa plc.

Visit the Taylor & Francis Web site at
http://www.taylorandfrancis.com

and the Routledge Web site at
http://www.routledge-ny.com

*To Mum and Dad*

# Contents

# Acknowledgments

This book is the product of many years of thinking about mobility, dating back to an undergraduate dissertation on "Metaphors of Mobility in the Lyrics of Bob Dylan" (1986)—a dissertation I had to justify to the head of the geography department at University College London, who was a sceptical geomorphologist. This was expanded in my master's thesis at Wisconsin (1988) on the topic of "Go-egraphy: Metaphors of Mobility in American Popular Culture." So thanks are due to all those people who let me get away with it, and especially those who encouraged me to think about mobility—particularly Peter Jackson. My Ph.D. on transgression was not directly about mobility, but as I was rewriting it into the book *In Place/Out of Place* (1996), I was constantly struck by the emergence of mobility as a theme both in the empirical material and (as metaphor) in the theoretical reading. Perhaps this is obvious. After all, transgression involves displacement, the moving between in place and out of place. Graffiti moved along the subway lines of New York; travelers moved toward and around Stonehenge just as the nomads and travelers of theoretical resistance moved across the pages of theorists such as Bahktin and de Certeau. Mobility seemed, at first glance, to fit quite snugly alongside transgression and resistance as concepts. Clearly, though, there are forms of mobility that are neither transgressive nor resistant—the flows of the transnational business community and of the capital that travels with them are examples of this. It is clear that there are also examples of resistance that involve not moving, staying put, resisting dominant flows and motions. It was at that point that I decided to write this book.

Since 1996 mobility has emerged as an important cross-disciplinary research agenda referred to as the *mobility turn* and the *new mobilities paradigm.* I have been lucky enough to develop these ideas as this interest developed. I have been helped by many people and institutions. I have been fortunate enough to learn from the astonishing work of a number of postgraduate students over the last few years, including Brian Hoskins, Peter Adey, Joanne Maddern, and Gareth Hoskins. Colleagues at Lampeter and Aberystwyth have also made significant input as well as providing much-needed encouragement and support. These include Ulf Strohmayer, David Atkinson, Chris Philo, Rhys Jones, Mark Whitehead, Luke Desforges, Deborah Dixon, Martin Jones, Robert Dodgshon, Mark Goodwin, and Peter Merriman. I am also grateful to a number of other people who have read and commented on various parts of this book, including David Delaney, Nick Blomley, Ginette Verstraete, John Urry, and Caren Kaplan. I am particularly grateful to those who have shared with me their thoughts on aspects of mobility as I have traveled to gather material for this book. These include Ed Soja, Leon Deben, Donna Houston, and Ginette Verstraete. Aspects of this research have been presented at seminars and conferences at Louisiana State University; Dartmouth College; University of North Carolina, Chapel Hill; University of California, Davis; University of California, Los Angeles; University of Vermont; Middlebury College; University of Illinois, Urbana-Champaign; University of Hull; University College, London; University of Southampton; and The Centre for Mobilities Research, Lancaster. I am grateful to the hosts and participants at each of these for their comments and friendly critiques. Special mention should be made of a number of meetings around the theme of mobility at Leeds, Amsterdam, Lancaster, Illinois, and the University of Wales. I learned a great deal during a weeklong sojourn hosted by the Institut pour la Ville en Mouvement in Cerisy, Normandy. During 2003 I was fortunate to spend a semester as a visiting scholar attached to the Global Migrations program at Hampshire College, Massachusetts. Many thanks to Myrna Breitbart and Kim Chang for their hospitality and encouragement.

Parts of this book have been or will be published in different form in *New Formations, Cultural Geographies*, and *Gender, Place and Culture* as well as in the edited collections; *Space and Social Theory* and *Les Sens du Mouvement*. Many thanks to the editors and anonymous reviewers for their helpful comments.

Over the last four years I have used the resources of many libraries and special collections, and owe a lot to numerous librarians and archivists who have been extremely helpful. These places include: Stephens College, New Jersey; Purdue University; the Bancroft Library, Berkeley; the New York University Library; the Schlesinger Library at Harvard; Smith College Special Collections; the library of the Imperial Society for Teachers of

Dancing, London; the National Library of Wales, Amsterdam Municipal Archives; New York Public Library, and the Special Collections Department at the University of Chicago. I am also grateful for the people who talked to me during my groping attempts at ethnography, particularly the Bus Riders Union of Los Angeles, the inhabitants and taxi drivers of Schiphol Airport, and Jan Bentham and Paul Mijksenaar.

I am grateful to David McBride at Routledge for encouraging me to write this book. None of this would have been likely without the support of the Economic and Social Research Council, which awarded me a two-year fellowship (grant number R000271264). I also benefited from small grants from the British Academy and the University of Wales, Aberystwyth. Finally, I am eternally grateful for the help, support, and love of Carol, Owen, Sam, and Madison Jennings, without whom . . . nothing.

## CHAPTER 1

# The Production of Mobilities:
# An Interpretive Framework

Moving your hand, walking, dancing, exercising, driving to work, moving home, going on holiday, marching, running away, immigrating, traveling, exploring, attending conferences. All of these are forms of mobility but they rarely enter each other's orbit in social and cultural enquiry. The slippery and intangible nature of mobility makes it an elusive object of study. Yet study it we must for mobility is central to what it is to be human. It is a fundamental geographical facet of existence and, as such, provides a rich terrain from which narratives—and, indeed, ideologies—can be, and have been, constructed. From the first kicks of a newborn baby to the travels of international business people, mobility is everywhere. Mobility, it seems, is also ubiquitous in the pages of academia. It plays a central role in discussions of the body and society.[1] It courses through contemporary theorizations of the city.[2] Culture, we are told, no longer sits in places, but is hybrid, dynamic—more about routes than roots.[3] The social is no longer seen as bound by "societies," but as caught up in a complex array of twenty-first century mobilities.[4] Philosophy and social theory look to the end of sedentarism and the rise of foundationless nomadism.[5] Finally, but perhaps most importantly, mobility bears a number of meanings that circulate widely in the modern Western world. Mobility as progress, as freedom, as opportunity, and as modernity, sit side by side with mobility as shiftlessness, as deviance, and as resistance. Mobility, then, is more central to both the world and our understanding of it than ever before. And yet mobility itself, and what it means, remains unspecified. It is a kind of blank space that stands as an alternative to place, boundedness, foundations, and stability. This space needs examining, and that is the purpose of this book. With this in mind, it explores the geographical imaginations that lie behind mobilization in a diverse array of contexts. It investigates the ways in which mobilities have been given meaning within contexts of social and cultural power. How, in other words, mobility has emerged as an object of knowledge in a range of practices from physiology to international law, dance notation to architecture, and simultaneously, how imaginations of mobility have informed judgments about people and their practices over the last several centuries in the Western world. In order to provide an interpretive framework for these explorations it is first necessary to start, as it were, at the beginning.

## Movement and Mobility

Let us begin with a basic signifier of mobility—getting from point A to point B.

A--------------------------->B

Mobility involves a displacement—the act of moving between locations. These locations may be towns or cities, or they may be points a few centimeters apart. This is the simplest understanding of mobility as it appears on maps of movements. In classic migration theory, for instance, the choice of whether or not to move would be the result of so-called *push* and *pull* factors in A and B, respectively. The content of the line between them would remain unexplored. The cumulative effects of these movements are also what remain taken for granted in more recent social theory where movement is coded as *travel*, *nomadism*, *routes*, or *lines of flight*. This line is a good starting point for such an exploration. I want to explore the content of the line that links A to B, to unpack it, to make sure it is not taken for granted.

The movements of people (and things) all over the world and at all scales are, after all, full of meaning. They are also products and producers of power. I want to make an analytical distinction here between movement and mobility. For the purposes of my argument, let us say that *movement* can be thought of as abstracted mobility (mobility abstracted from contexts of power). Movement, therefore, describes the idea of an act of displacement that allows people to move between locations (usually given as point A and point B in abstract and positivist discussions of migration). Movement is the general fact of displacement before the type, strategies, and social implications of that movement are considered.

We can think of movement, then, as the dynamic equivalent of location in abstract space—contentless, apparently natural, and devoid of meaning, history, and ideology. The critiques of abstract space and location are well known.[6] Movement, as the dynamic equivalent of location, has not been given the same attention. If movement is the dynamic equivalent of location, then mobility is the dynamic equivalent of *place*. Place is a word we use in all manner of contexts in theoretical expositions and in everyday life. Within geographical theory and philosophy it has come to signify meaningful segments of space—locations imbued with meaning and power.[7] A place is a center of meaning—we become attached to it, we fight over it and exclude people from it—we experience it. The same cannot be said of location. Why geographers have not subjected mobility to the same scrutiny as the more allegedly fixed and bounded categories of space, time, territory, and landscape is curious. I have frequently heard commentators at conferences talk of the rise of mobility in the modern world as the "end of geography." I presume they do not mean the discipline, but even so, such a statement is thought provoking. What is not "geographical" (both in real world and disciplinary terms) about things and people on the move? Why is geography equated with fixity and stasis? Mobility is just as spatial—as geographical—and just as central to the human experience of the world, as place.

In this book, mobility as socially produced motion is understood through three relational moments. First, when talking of human mobility, we are talking about mobility as a brute fact—something that is potentially observable, a thing in the world, an empirical reality. This is the mobility measured and analyzed by modelers, migration theorists, and transport planners. It is the mobility captured by high-powered computer hardware and software in sports science labs or animation studios. It is the motion tracked by closed circuit television and biometric systems in airports and elsewhere. Here mobility comes closest to pure motion and is at its most abstract. Second, there are ideas about mobility that are conveyed through a diverse array of representational strategies ranging from film to law, medicine to photography, literature to philosophy. These representations of mobility capture and make sense of it through the production of meanings that are frequently ideological. Mobility means this. Mobility means that. Thus the brute fact of getting from A to B becomes synonymous with freedom, with transgression, with creativity, with life itself. Third, mobility is practiced, it is experienced, it is embodied. Mobility is a way of being in the world. The way we walk, for instance, says much about us. We may be in love, we may be happy, we may be burdened and sad. We inhabit mobility differently according to our mood. Human mobility is an irreducibly embodied experience. Our feet may hurt as we walk, the wind might blow in our face, we may not be able to sleep as we fly from New York to London. Often how we experience mobility and the ways we move are intimately connected to meanings given to mobility through representation. Similarly, representations of mobility are based on ways in which mobility is practiced and embodied. As David Delaney has written, "human mobility implicates *both* physical bodies moving through material landscapes *and* categorical figures moving through representational spaces."[8] Mobile people are never simply *people*—they are dancers and pedestrians, drivers and athletes, refugees and citizens, tourists or businesspeople, men and women. This book is about the interface between mobile physical bodies on the one hand, and the represented mobilities on the other. To understand mobility without recourse to representation on the one hand or the material corporeality on the other is, I would argue, to miss the point.

## Movement, Time, and Space

Movement is made up of time and space. It is the spatialization of time and temporalization of space. Any consideration of movement (and mobility) that does not take time *and* space into account is missing an important facet. Time and space, as Kant reminded us, are the fundamental axes around which life revolves—the most basic forms of classification. Certainly any material object has to have coordinates in time and space. Movement, as the displacement of an object from A to B, involves a passage of time and, simultaneously, a traversal of space. Time and space, however, cannot be simply taken for granted in the consideration of movement. Time and space are both the context for movement (the environment of possibility for movement to occur) and a product of movement. Moving people and objects are agents in the production of time and space. Perhaps the most well-known formulation of this is *time–space compression*—the effective shrinking of the globe by ever-increasing mobility at speed enabled by innovations in transportation and communications technology. Thus Marx was able to write of the annihilation of space by time. The success of railroad technology in the nineteenth century and the new modes of mobility that it enabled meant that things were, for all practical purposes, a lot closer.[9] While the abstract idea of movement is composed of equally abstract notions of absolute time and space, the notion of mobility I want to propose here, as a thoroughly social facet of life imbued with meaning and power, is composed of elements of social time and social space.

The question of the social production of space and time has received sustained attention in the social sciences and humanities in recent years.[10]

While space has been produced through the division of the world into functional spaces (the processes of mapping and geometry, the classification of space as property, and the delineations of planners), time has become regulated and standardized as clock time, as the time of the time-table and the daily schedule. Both time and space, it has been argued, have been taken out of the world of nature and immediate experience and placed, instead, in the world of abstraction—abstraction ruled, for the most part, by the demands of trade and capital, but also by various forms of patriarchy, colonialism, and imperialism.[11]

Clearly this process of the social production of abstract time and space has implications for the understanding of movement and mobility. Mobility, as a social product, does not exist in an abstract world of absolute time and space, but is a meaningful world of social space and social time. Mobility is also part of the process of the social production of time and space. Consider the story of the railroad as an example. Wolfgang Schivelbusch has described how the invention of the railroad and its rapid spread across the surface of the globe forced a fundamental rethinking of space. Distances were practically shrunk as it became possible to travel farther in a shorter time. The metropolis was conversely allowed to expand into the new suburbs as it became possible to travel farther between work and home. Indeed work and home became functionally separate spaces because of the new modes of mobility. As more and more people traveled at new speeds in trains, a new panoramic perception of space (as seen from the train window) emerged. For the first time it was possible to see the world as a continuous blur. Even the earliest English trains at a mere 20 to 30 miles per hour were three times faster than a coach. The effect was noted at the time in the *Quarterly Review*:

> For instance, supposing that railroads . . . were to be suddenly established all over England, the whole population would, speaking metaphorically, at once advance en masse, and place their chairs nearer to the fireside of their metropolis by two thirds of the time which now separates them from it; they would also sit nearer to one another by two-thirds of the time which now respectively alienated them. If the rate were to be repeated; our harbours, our dockyards, our towns, the whole of our rural population, would again not only draw nearer to each other by two-thirds, but all would proportionally approach the national hearth. As distances were thus annihilated, the surface of our country would, as it were, shrivel in size until it became not much bigger than one immense city.[12]

Finally the new modes of mobility enabled by the railroad reduced the distinctiveness of places—their *auras*. Without effective mobility over long distances at high speed, places served as local and unique markets selling their own products, which were tied to seasonal production. Transportation changed these products into commodities, as goods began to lose their spatial presence and became instead products of an increasingly expansive market.[13] At the same time it became possible to visit these places as tourists—another factor, some have argued, in the erosion of local distinctiveness.

The railroad also deprived localities of their own time. In 1870 a traveler from Washington, D.C. to San Francisco would have passed through over two hundred *time zones*. Every town had their own time, tied more or less to the position of the sun in the sky. This system worked until the building of the transcontinental railroad (1869); the increased speed of the railroad made this dangerous as it became possible for two trains to be in the same time and space with potentially fatal consequences. On November 18, 1883, the railroad enforced four uniform time zones in the United States. In 1884 this was expanded to the globe with the designation of Greenwich as the prime meridian and the division of the world into twenty-four time zones. Time, thanks to the railroad, was increasingly rationalized, mechanized, and timetabled as people accustomed themselves to tickets, labels, luggage, clocks, timetables, and uniforms. As Ralph Harrington has put it, "The passengers were as much a component of the great railway machine as the tracks and trains, and just as all the movements of the mechanical components had to be controlled if the machine was to operate effectively, so the behaviour of the human traveller had to be regulated with mechanical efficiency."[14] Clearly, then, mobility is not just a function of time and space, but an agent in their production. While the movement of the train (from Paris to Lyon, say) occurs in abstract, absolute space and time, it plays a central role in the production of social time and space. Here, movement becomes mobility.

## Ideology, Scale, and Mobility

Mobility seems a chaotic thing—chaotic in the sense that moving things are often chaotic in the way we experience them. Stationary, sedentary life, on the other hand, is hard to see as chaos. Some might say that little of interest can be said about what links the movement of blood in the body and movement of jet planes around the globe. The fact of movement, skeptics might suggest, is both obvious and uninteresting. What connects mobility at the scale of the body to mobility at other scales is *meaning*. Stories about mobility, stories that are frequently ideological, connect blood cells to street patterns, reproduction to space travel. Movement is rarely just movement; it carries with it the burden of meaning and it is this meaning that jumps scales. It is this issue of meaning that remains absent from accounts of mobility in general, and because it remains absent, important connections are not made. Writing on mobility remains either very specific (about commuter patterns, migrations, or dance for instance) or maddeningly abstract—the kind of work that talks of points A and B. Connections need to be made between the determinedly different approaches applied to the different facets of human mobility listed above. I am inspired here by Daniel Miller, who in an entirely different context, wrote that it was his belief that, "in the present the social sciences would benefit considerably from any theory that managed to clarify connections between features of our world that too often seem like isolated fragments whose simultaneous existence is no more than fortuitous."[15] As Miller points out, this is a dangerously unfashionable enterprise in the post-poststructural world we move in, but one that nonetheless needs to be attempted if we are to avoid simply telling stories to each other with no relevance beyond their own confines. My aim, then, is to provide a way of thinking that traces some of the processes that run through the different accounts of human mobility at different scales, and ties them into a single logic without negating the very important differences between them.

Some examples might help. Consider the flow of blood through the body and the circulation of traffic in the city. Richard Sennett has described the revolution in images of the body that came with the publication of William Harvey's *De motu cordis* in 1628.[16] It was in this text that Harvey announced his discovery that the heart pumps blood through the arteries around the body—blood which is then returned to the heart by the veins. He had discovered the body's circulation system. In so doing he prompted others to see the body in similar ways. Thus, Thomas Willis began to suggest the presence of the nervous system. "The mechanical movement in the body, nervous movements as well as the movements of blood, created a more secular understanding of the body in contesting the ancient notion that the soul (the *anima*) is the source of life's energy."[17] Now it was not the soul that energized life in the body, but the blood. Blood was, for Harvey, "life itself." Clearly, Harvey's discovery had momentous implications for the study of the body and for the history of human medicine, but its implications were much wider than that. Ideas about mobility in the sphere of the body were quickly translated into areas such as economics and city planning.

Health came to be associated with *circulation*. Just as the blood circulated through the body, so air circulated through the city. City managers and planners in the eighteenth century began to clean dirt off the streets and instigated the construction of intricate sewer systems. Road surfaces, previously constructed from pebbles, were made smooth through the use of flagstones.[18] Urban planners and architects sought to maximize flow and movement. Words such as *artery* and *vein* began to appear in the texts of the new urbanists. They believed that blockages created bad health in the urban body. As Alain Corbin has put it, "Harvey's discovery and his model of the circulation of the blood created the requirement that air, water, and [waste] products also be kept in a state of movement."[19] Thus the meaning of blood circulating through the human body became the guiding metaphor for L'Enfant's plan for Washington, DC.

Textbook descriptions of the reproductive system are remarkable for the way they give meaning to bodily processes in ways the status of *textbook* would normally deny. Emily Martin has shown how the process of menstruation has, for many years, been described in terms of failure using words such as degenerate, decline, lack, and deteriorate. She compares this to the language used to describe male reproductive physiology in a popular textbook: "The mechanisms which guide the *remarkable* cellular transformation from spermatid to mature sperm remain uncertain. . . . Perhaps the most *amazing* characteristic of spermatogenesis is its *sheer magnitude*: the normal human male may manufacture several hundred million sperm per day."[20] This kind of language of achievement is extended into what was, until recently, the dominant way of thinking about human fertilization—the act of a mobile sperm cell penetrating an immobile egg. The mobility of the sperm cell was equated with agency. Martin reports the way physiology texts described the way the egg "drifts" and "is transported," while the sperm "deliver" their genes to the egg after a journey of considerable "velocity" propelled by "strong" tails. Ejaculation "propels the semen into the deepest recesses of the vagina" where the sperm are aided by "energy" so that with a "whiplashlike movement and strong lurches" they finally "burrow through the egg coat," and "penetrate" it. The egg, in other words, is passive and the sperm is active. The sperm does things and the egg has things done to it.[21] It is only recently that the language has changed and the active role of the egg in selecting a sperm has been acknowledged. Or, as Gerald and Helen Schatten, wrote in 1983,

> The classic account, current for centuries, has emphasised the sperm's performance and relegated to the egg the supporting rôle of sleeping beauty. The egg is central to this drama to be sure, but it is as passive a character as the Brothers Grimm's Princess. Now, it is becoming clear that the egg is not merely a large yoke-filled sphere into which the sperm burrows to endow new life. Rather, recent research suggests the almost heretical view that sperm and egg are mutually active partners.[22]

So here, in the body, the sperm's mobility is coded as masculine and active, while the egg is passive, relatively immobile, and feminine.

Such ideological codings of mobility in the body are not bound by the body's walls. These meanings, like those Harvey attached to blood, travel and jump scales. In a remarkable instance of the geopolitics of mobility, the American space agency, NASA, found itself in conflict with its Soviet counterpart as the superpowers attempted to plan a historic linkup in space in 1975 between an Apollo and Soyuz spacecraft. The linkup was seen as an important part of the process of détente during the cold war. The conflict was over the design of the docking mechanism to be used in the linkup. Orthodox docking systems used a male part and a female part. The male part was seen to be active and would penetrate the female part, which was considered passive. The male part would move and the female part would remain motionless. The metaphorical implications of this arrangement became all too apparent during the planning of the Soyuz-Apollo mission and, to put it simply, neither party wished to be penetrated. To overcome this problem, the superpowers designed a whole new androgynous docking system, which featured interlocking *capture latches* where both sides could be active or passive. Although this language is not being taken directly from human physiology textbooks, it is clear that a similar process to that which linked Harvey's blood circulation to the urban environment took place. Meanings given to mobility inside the human body—meanings with highly gendered connotations—are being translated into the politics of the space race. Mobility, here at least, means masculinity.

What these two stories show is that the bare fact of movement—the observation that things like blood and sperm, city traffic, and spacecraft move—is rarely just about getting from A to B. The line that connects them, despite its apparent immateriality, is both meaningful and laden with power.

## Historical Senses of Mobility

Mobilities need to be understood in relation to each other. As the dance scholar Norman Bryson has suggested, individual forms of mobility, such as dance, might best be understood in an expanded field of the study of structured mobilities. His call is to open up dance scholarship and consider it as one instance of socially structured human movement, where movement is made meaningful within the conventions and institutions that authorize meaning. He charts, for example, the transformation from premodern to modern forms of dance movement through the idea of abstraction and mechanization. He argues that modern dance in Paris must be understood as but one example of a complex interplay of spectacle, spectatorship, and sexuality that "figured forth, in intense and specialised form, the essential social relation of observer and observed."[23] But to thoroughly comprehend this transformation between emergent and residual senses of movement, he argues, social kinetics requires that we see a form of movement such as dance as symptomatic of wider changes in the sense of movement. The rise of abstraction and mechanization in a dance such as the Can-Can for instance, must be seen alongside changes in the work place such as Taylorism, the arrival of mass production and new forms of mechanical transport. To understand the Can-Can, then, we must "refer to other domains of movement than dance, to other social regions where movement is analysed and represented and to larger social processes that turn on the redesigning and stylization of action and gesture."[24] He proposes a new field of social kinetics. *Social kinetics* is the history of socially structured movement; it points toward the political and theoretical necessity of seeing mobility as operating within fields of power and meaning, and the crucially larger contexts of changing senses of movement.

In his essay, Bryson points toward one key transformation in the sense of movement, or as I would prefer to call it, sense of mobility. This transformation is one that can be seen to mark the advent of high modernity—a moment when mobility became increasingly regulated and regular—marked by timetables and mechanization. But this is clearly not the only transformation of senses of mobility—of socially structured movement. It is not the ambition of this book to provide a delineated and detailed account of the whole history of mobilities in the West. It is possible, however, to sketch an outline of the transformations in senses of mobility that have preceded the worlds of mobility in the modern West, which form the subject matter of this book.

## The Feudal Sense of Mobility

Mobility in European feudal society was a luxury item. The vast majority of people stayed pretty much where they were. To people who lacked transportation facilities and were, for the most part, tied to the land, movement beyond the local was feared and forbidden. In medieval Europe, people and things had their place in the great chain of being and this place was both literal and figurative. Feudal society was intensely territorial. Kings, as figures close to God, granted land to their vassals and demanded obedience in return. These new landholders could, in turn, collect tribute from those who worked on their land. The peasants, the great mass of people, were completely dependent on their lord. Just as lords existed in relations of dependency to the king, so the peasants were permanently in the debt to the lord. He was tied to both the lord and the land.[25] A laborer was referred to as *adscriptus gelbae*—attached to the soil. The right to move, such as it was, was in the hands of private entities. Masters controlled the movements of their servants, lords the mobility of their serfs, and slaveholders the travels of their slaves.[26] Zygmunt Bauman argues that the premodern world was one of security in relatively small groups of stable people. "Villagers and town dwellers alike knew most of the others they were ever likely to meet, because they had ample opportunity to watch them—to watch continuously, in all their functions and on most diverse occasions. Theirs were communities perpetuated and reproduced by mutual watching."[27] Premodern, European life, in other words, was, for Bauman, the kind of miniature version of a modern utopia where all is seen. This version of society, however, had a necessarily small scope, as "the limits of the gaze defined the size of the world in which secure life could be produced and maintained."[28] To be mobile was to exist on the margins. Wandering minstrels, troubadours, crusaders, pilgrims, and some peripatetic monks existed, for periods of time, outside of the obligations of place and roots. So-called *wandering Jews* lived outside the web of obligations and duties that marked feudalism. For this reason they were looked down upon and distrusted. As Lewis Mumford put it:

> The unattached individual during the Middle Ages was one condemned either to excommunication or to exile: close to death. To exist one had to belong to an association—a household, manor, monastery or guild. There was no security except through group protection and no freedom that did not recognize the constant obligation of a corporate life. One lived and died in the identifiable style of one's class and one's corporation.[29]

For all but a very small minority, to be mobile in the Middle Ages was to be without place, both socially and geographically. Minstrels, for instance, were thought of as lecherous and irresponsible fly-by-nights.[30] Minstrels had no obvious place in medieval life. They were neither peasants nor nobility, and they were frequently wandering through the countryside looking for employment. As people without place, their status was tenuous at best. They would dress in a way that suggested a much higher status, thanks to the generosity of the lords who employed them, and as entertainers they were free to transgress social hierarchies in ways few could get away with. Minstrels also used their footloose life to act as spies in the courts of their employer's enemies. They were frequently made scapegoats for crimes that had gone unpunished.

Jewish people were also subject to the fear and loathing of settled folk. Many Jews wandered around medieval Europe, not through choice but as a result of persecution and expulsion. Ironically, the fact that they were then made mobile led to them being distrusted across Europe for their mobility. Alongside this mobility was their involvement in commerce and the newly emergent merchant city, both of which were also objects of suspicion by the landed classes.

Of course mobility at a number of scales occurred in feudal Europe. The mobility involved in working on the land must have been relentless. It was the scale of mobility that was restricted. It was not possible to simply travel between towns, much less between nations. There were exceptions to this. Pilgrimages, warfare, and communication necessitated movement over larger distances. The *Canterbury Tales* was, after all, a tale of the road. Much has been made of the "roguish vagabonds" who took to the road at the end of the medieval period following the emancipation of the serfs across Europe. Bauman has described them as the "advanced troops or guerrilla units of post-traditional chaos."[31] In Spain these vagabonds were called *picaro*, which gave rise to the form of literature known as the *picaresque*. A classic of the period was Mateo Aleman's *Guzman de Alfrache* (1599) in which a group of beggars work out various ingenious ways to cheat the ruling elite. Luther's *Liver Vagatorum* (1529) describes twenty-eight varieties of vagabond.[32] It was these vagabonds who created the need for a new societal-level state ordering system. The vagabond was scary because of his apparent freedom to move and escape the status of *adscriptus glebae*, as well as the mutual gaze that ensured premodern order. This new movement was seen as unpredictable.[33]

## *The Early Modern Sense of Mobility*

By the sixteenth century, Europe was experiencing hitherto unheard of levels of mobility by the newly landless and all those associated with trade. The city was the one place where an increased level of mobility was acceptable. The rise of mercantile capitalism necessitated the mobility associated with trade. This commercial mobility gradually loosened the rootedness of feudal society as guilds emerged to protect commercial interests. For the first time there were associations made between freedom, mobility, and city life. "The city air makes men free" the saying went, and hand in hand with this freedom went mobility. A "new freedom of movement" Mumford wrote, "that sprang up with corporate liberties claimed by the medieval town itself."[34] Alongside this, by the late sixteenth century, English feudal order was being rapidly undone as the population grew and agriculture became more efficient, needing less bodily labor and creating new kinds of relationships to the land. Many people became disconnected from the kind of order that held life together for centuries. People were homeless and economically marginal. They were without place. These new "masterless men" were considered extremely threatening because they did not appear to be part of any recognizable form of order. Their mobility made them illegible. These were the new vagabonds—"people too listless and too numerous to be tamed and domesticated by the customary method of familiarization or incorporation."[35] Whereas medieval society had operated on the basis that every member of a community was responsible for every other (a system known as *frankpledge*) these new mobile strangers made such a system inoperable.

New types of mobility called for new forms of social surveillance and control. All manner of means were devised to achieve this. Vagabonds were branded like sheep to make them visible. Workhouses and prisons sprang up to deal with the casualties of the new vagrancy laws developed in England and France and later exported to the American colonies.[36] Gradually the disciplining role of the gaze became less mutual and more focused in the hands of the state. The control over mobility was nationalized and taken out of private hands. Whereas the only relevant scale for most people in medieval Europe was extremely local, the rise of the modern state gradually took power out of the hands of the local and created the *nation-state*. Central to this process was *poor relief*. Poor relief was the process whereby the local poor were seen to be the responsibility of the local community. In this way the mobility of the poor was managed. As European nation-states became established alongside correspondingly larger markets for goods and wage labor, landowners and local lords found their power to control mobility diminished. As labor became mobile on a national scale, so poor relief became a national issue. The scale of mobility changed for good. People could now move over a much greater range without obtaining anyone's permission. As Torpey has noted, "What we now think of as 'internal' movement—a meaningless and anachronistic notion before the development of modern states and the state system—has come to mean movement within national or 'nation-states.' Historical evidence indicates clearly that, well into the nineteenth century, people routinely regarded as 'foreign' those from the next province every bit as much as those who came from other 'countries.'"[37]

But mobility is not just about the literal movement of people; ideas about mobility in general, and what it might mean, were also changing. Science and philosophy increasingly looked to mobility as a central fact of existence that needed to be accounted for. The historical circumstances of the early seventeenth century and the success of mercantile capitalism saw transformations in the way the concept of mobility was valued. Galileo's new science had reconfigured understandings of movement. Most importantly, the idea of inertia stated that bodies would continue to move in a straight line unless deflected by an outside source. This view of moving bodies contradicted the hegemonic Aristotelian belief that things only moved in order to reach some end point—some telos. Movement to Aristotle was a result of potential already in an object that had to be fulfilled. The natural state of things was rest. To Galileo, the natural state of things was movement with rest being a mere accident.[38] As Galileo reconfigured mobility in the physical world, so William Harvey gave it new meaning in the body. In the early seventeenth century most medical experts believed that food was converted into blood in the liver, and that this blood then acted as a fuel that was used by the body. Through extensive dissection, Harvey knew this to be false. He was interested in the way blood flowed through the human body. In 1628 Harvey published *An Anatomical Study of the Movement of the Heart and of the Blood in Animals,* which explained how blood was pumped from the heart throughout the body, then returned to the heart and recirculated.[39] The discoveries of Galileo and Harvey had impacts well beyond the realms of science. They informed the political philosophy of Thomas Hobbes.

Crucially, Thomas Hobbes borrowed from Galileo's new science to place relentless movement at the heart of a philosophy of human life that equated movement with liberty. Here was a liberal conception of human mobility—as an individual form of freedom. To Hobbes, individuals were like machines that performed a kind of Brownian movement continually moving and bouncing off of each other in the pursuit of their appetites. Hobbes was also informed by the work of William Harvey. "Now vital movement is the movement of the blood," he wrote, "perpetually circulating (as hath been shown from many infallible signs and marks by Doctor Harvey the first observer of it) in the veins and arteries."[40] Life itself, Hobbes believed, was located in the movement of blood and the movement of the limbs. So whereas Aristotle had imagined a world of clearly directed and finite movements, Hobbes thought of social life as a "homogeneous swarm of incoherent, aimless perpetuations of momentum that had no capacity for growth, for fulfilment, or for rest."[41] The new world, the world of Hobbes, Galileo, and Harvey, was an infinite, restless entanglement of persistent movement. And yet in this new society, happiness itself was based on the freedom to move. Liberty was fundamentally, and for the first time, seen as unimpeded movement. In the *Leviathan* he wrote that "Liberty signifieth (properly) the absence of Opposition; (by Opposition, I mean externall Impediments of movement)."[42]

> For whatsoever is so tyed, or environed, as it cannot move, but within a certain space, which space is determined by the opposition of some externall body, we say it hath not Liberty to go further. And so all living creatures, whilest they are imprisoned, or restrained with walls, or chains; and of the water whilest it is kept

in by banks, or vessels, that otherwise would spread it selfe into a larger space, we use to say, they are not at Liberty, to move in such manner as without those externall impediments they would.[43]

The view of mobility and liberty in Hobbes is replicated two hundred years later by William Blackstone, who argued that law is derived from a heady mixture of God and physics. The most important principles of matter, he argued, are the "laws of movement, to which all moveable bodies must conform."[44] Mobility, he argued, was an absolute right of man. The right to personal liberty he defined as the power of "loco-movement" or the ability of "changing situation, or removing one's person to whatsoever place one's own inclination may direct; without imprisonment or restraint, unless by due course of law."[45]

The idea of mobility as liberty and freedom would have made little sense in feudal society. In the early modern period, as cities grew and people were displaced from the land, the practice and ideology of mobility was transformed. New mobile figures began to inhabit the landscapes of Europe. Mobility as a right accompanied the rise of the figure of the modern *citizen* who was granted the right to move at will within the bounds of the nation-state. Meanwhile, the popularity of the *grand tour*, an extended voyage around the sites of Europe taken by well-to-do young men, signaled the advent of another modern mobile figure—the *tourist*.[46] To Dean MacCannell the tourist was and is the epitome of modernity. The tourist world, he argues, depends upon the paraphernalia of modern life, on the fact of displacement as a widespread experience, and on the increasing interest in the past as distinctly premodern and marginal—a place to visit. Both citizens and tourists depend on excluded others for their identities. Citizens, allowed to move freely, depend on the noncitizens, the aliens who are not free to move in the same way. Tourists depend on the relative immobility of those who service the new leisure class—those who are stuck in the picturesque European south as well as those (mostly women in the early years) who were left at home.[47]

*Western Modernity and Mobility*

The modern individual is, above all else, a mobile human being.[48]

The explorations of mobility in this book are, for the most part, explorations of mobility in the last two hundred years in the Western world. Mobility seems self-evidently central to Western modernity. Indeed the word *modern* seems to evoke images of technological mobility—the car, the plane, the spaceship. It also signifies a world of increased movement of people on a global scale. Perhaps most importantly, though, it suggests a way of thinking in terms of mobility—a metaphysics of mobility that is distinct from what came before it.

In Britain, improvements in the road network had led to dramatic reductions in travel time by the early nineteenth century. Although still dependent on horse and coach for travel, improvements in the condition and number of roads meant that although it had taken forty-eight hours to get from London to Bristol in 1750, by 1821 it was possible to reach most of England and Wales in the same amount of time.[49] The advent of the railway with the Liverpool to Manchester line occurred in 1830. By 1860 the majority of the current rail network (and, indeed, many lines that have since been closed) was in existence. By 1910 all but the north of Scotland was within ten hours travel time of London. But it was not just speed that allowed space to be annihilated. Rail travel also included more people in the experience of travel. In 1835 around ten million individual coach journeys were made. Just ten years later, thirty million rail journeys were made. By 1870 the number had reached a staggering 336 million journeys. A similar story could be told in the United States. In 1850 the continental United States had 9,000 miles of track. By 1869 the figure had grown to 70,000. It was in 1869 that the transcontinental railroad was completed allowing relatively easy travel from coast to coast for goods and people. The railroad quickly became a symbol of national identity in the United States.[50]

Modernity is certainly a contested concept, and most commentators recognize that it has ambiguities and tensions within it.[51] As Miles Ogborn writes, "Its periodisation, geographies, characteristics and promise all remain elusive."[52] Arguments about the nature of modernity revolve around notions of newness, artificiality, order, reason, democracy, technology, and chaos. All of these are bound up in a general idea that something happened at some point in the past when life before that point could be called premodern. Few terms in contemporary social theory signify so much and so many terms that are apparently in opposition to each other.

The tension that is central in much of this book is the tension between a spatialized ordering principle seen by many to be central to modernity, and a sense of fluidity and mobility emphasized by others. Following Foucault, many commentators have focused on the rise of surveillance and discipline in modernity.[53] The modern world, they argue, is one in which new constructions of space and time have functionalized and rationalized everyday life. Thus Henri Lefebvre notes how modern time has been abstracted and rationalized. Before modernity, he argues, time was etched into life like markings in a tree. With the coming of modernity, however, time becomes separated from life and nature and is instead a property of measurements—an abstraction.[54] James Scott's critique of *high modernity* emphasizes the spatial ordering of society. His argument is that high modernity has been characterized by a particular way of seeing, which sought to impose order on the chaos of life. The straight lines of trees in modern forestry and the grand plans of Brasilia and New Delhi are all examples of this. At the heart of the project of modernity for Scott is a process of legibility, making the chaotic and localized world of the premodern intelligible by imposing order on it—by replacing the "view from somewhere" and the kind of practical knowledge he calls *metis* with the "view from nowhere," which comes with rationality and science.[55]

Intriguingly, Scott notes in his introduction how the issue of legibility arose from another research direction entirely. He set out to "understand why the state has always seemed to be the enemy of "people who move around.""[56] As examples he cites the experience of nomads and pastoralists, gypsies, homeless people, and runaway slaves. The imposition of legibility through space, in other words, was in some way related to the lack of fixity of important marginalized groups in modern society. This sense of anxiety about mobility in modernity is far more extensive than these state reactions to the perpetually peripatetic. There is a more pervasive sense in which mobility has been a source of anxiety in modernity. Think, for example of the social theory of Georg Simmel. In the "The Metropolis and Mental Life," Simmel famously argued that modern, urban life was providing sensory overload. Traditional, rural life, he argued, had been slow and habitual, and the onset of modern urbanity, and especially the development of a money economy and clock time, meant that people were bombarded with sensations that led to an increasingly abstracted sense of self and society. Life became a matter of intellect and the "blasé attitude." This accelerated modernity was a source of both anxiety and important new freedoms as citizens became increasingly cosmopolitan.[57] This sense of anxiety prompted by modernity was also evident outside of classical sociology. In *American Nervousness*, a book popular at the end of the nineteenth century in the United States, George Beard describes the causes of a specific disease he called *neurasthenia*. Beard describes how "modern civilization" is marked by five elements "steam power, the periodical press, the telegraph, the sciences, and the mental activity of women."[58] As with Simmel, Beard looked to modern conceptions of time and the increased velocity of life to show how the capacities of the nervous system were being stretched to the breaking point.

> The perfection of clocks and the invention of watches have something to do with modern nervousness, since they compel us to be on time, and excite the habit of looking to see the exact moment, so as not to be late for trains or appointments. Before the general use of these instruments of precision in time, there was a wider

margin for all appointments, a longer period was required and prepared for, especially in travelling—coaches of the olden period were not expected to start like steamers or trains, on the instant— men judged of the time by probabilities, by looking at the sun, and needed not, as a rule, to be nervous about the loss of a moment, and had incomparably fewer experiences wherein a delay of a few moments might destroy the hopes of a lifetime.[59]

Early American sociologists at the Chicago School of Sociology also placed mobility at the center of their understanding of the world. Robert Park had studied with Simmel in Heidelberg. He inherited many of his ideas about the mobile nature of urban life. Mobility was used by Park's student, Nels Anderson, to differentiate the city from the country. The city, Anderson wrote, "is more mobile, mobility being a characteristic of its life just as stability is characteristic of rural life." Anderson goes on to compare "Main Street" (the country) to "Broadway" (the city), arguing that Main Street is marked by repetition and natural rhythms while Broadway is "cultural, being man-made, and mechanised; and being mechanised, the urban environment has a mobility of its own quite distinct from the movement of people."[60]

While commentators such as Scott have portrayed modernity as an enemy of certain kinds of mobility, others have shown how mobility has been central to the constitution of the modern. Perhaps most famously Marshall Berman adopted Marx's warning about capitalist modernity— "all that is solid melts into air"—to provide a vivid portrait of a modernity where everything was in a state of flux. "Modern environments and experiences," he writes, "cut across all boundaries of geography and ethnicity, of class and nationality, of religion and ideology: in this sense, modernity can be said to unite all mankind. But it is a paradoxical unity, a unity of disunity: it pours us all into a maelstrom of perpetual disintegration and renewal, of struggle and contradiction, of ambiguity and anguish. To be modern is to be part of a universe in which, as Marx said, 'all that is solid melts into air.'"[61] Berman's modernity is one where nothing is fixed or secure. It is chaotic and forever on the move. It is certainly a long way from Scott's rational ordering of the world through modern rationality. It is not the enemy of mobility but its friend.

This general sense of modernity as the age of mobility can be read through accounts of specific forms of mobility. We have already seen how the train journey has become metonymic for a specific kind of modernity. The more everyday experience of walking has been coded in a similar way. Walter Benjamin's account of modernity in Paris includes a multitude of references to both trains and pedestrians.[62] The *flâneur*—a figure free to stroll freely along Paris' new boulevards—has become a central figure in discussions of modernity and mobility.[63] The migrant has been given the additional burden of signifying a modern condition. John Berger's remarkable trio of novels about encroaching modernity in rural France, feature the rural-urban migrant as the central figure of modern displacement.[64] Exiled and migrant artists and writers are central to the canon of modernity. Think of Picasso. Think of Joyce.[65] Tourists, vagrants, and pilgrims have been used, metaphorically, by Zygmunt Bauman to provide a diagnosis of modernity. Indeed Bauman is one of the most forceful commentators on the incessant mobility of the modern.

> Modernity is what it is—an obsessive march forwards—not because it always wants more, but because it never gets enough; not because it grows more ambitious and adventurous, but because its adventures are bitter and its ambitions frustrated. The march must go on because any place of arrival is but a temporary station. No place is privileged, no place is better than another, as from no place the horizon is nearer than from any other.[66]

Arjun Appadurai's *Modernity at Large* also places migration right at the heart of the modern. He argues that the rupture between the premodern and the modern is founded on linked developments in media and migration. Together, he argues, they produce a new form of imagination that becomes a "constitutive feature of modern subjectivity."[67] Electronic media, he argues, have transformed preexisting worlds of communication and face-to-face conduct. Migration, when juxtaposed with the new electronic media, produces a "new order of instability in the production of modern subjectivities."[68]

> As Turkish guest workers in Germany watch Turkish films in their German flats, as Koreans in Philadelphia watch the 1988 Olympics in Seoul through satellite feeds from Korea, and as Pakistani cabdrivers in Chicago listen to cassettes of sermons recorded in mosques in Pakistan or Iran, we see moving images meeting deterritorialized viewers. These create diasporic public spheres, phenomena that confound theories that depend on the continued salience of the nation-state as the key arbiter of important social changes.[69]

Peter Taylor identifies something of this ambiguity within the analysis of modernity. The modernity of order exemplified by Scott is contrasted with the modernity of chaos exemplified by Berman. "One way in which the ambiguity of modernity operates can now be understood," writes Taylor, "Modern people and institutions devise projects which aspire to order their world but without fully appreciating that the modern world is the antithesis of order. Modernity, therefore, is a perpetual battle between makers of order and the incessant change which is the condition of modernity."[70]

It is clear, then, that mobility is central to what it is to be modern. A modern citizen is, among other things, a mobile citizen. At the same time it is equally clear that mobility has been the object of fear and suspicion, a human practice that threatens to undo many of the achievements of modern rationality and ordering. Again the development of the railway provides an illustrative case in point. Just as the railway was instrumental in ordering modern life through the production of abstract time and abstract space, so it was the source of new anxieties. As the railway historian Ralph Harrington put it, "Railways could be seen as a symbol of progress, promising economic and social betterment, democracy, energy, freedom from old restrictions, all the benefits and opportunities of the constantly circulating liberty of modern, mechanized civilization. Yet they were also associated with pollution, destruction, disaster and danger, threatening the destabilization and corruption of the social order, the vulgarization of culture, the despoliation of rural beauty, the violence, destruction and terror of the accident."[71]

One place to look for meaning in mobility is the dictionary. Indeed, the definitions given to terms like movement and mobility in the *Oxford English Dictionary* suggest something of the complexity of thinking about these terms. The word *mobility* was introduced into the English language in the seventeenth century when it was applied to persons, their bodies, limbs, and organs. It referred to a capacity to move and was used interchangeably with *movement* in natural science. In addition to these embodied and natural science uses, mobility was also used in a social sense. By the eighteenth century, the moveable and excitable crowd was known as the mobility (the *mobile vulgus,* in contrast to the nobility), later shortened to the *mob.* Meanwhile, the word movement was going through its own transformations. On the whole it was used from the seventeenth century to refer to the process and mechanics of movement, especially in terms of machines. Even older than this, however, is the idea of the movements as shitting—as "the runs." There are both embodied and abstract histories to both terms. On the whole, however, movement appears to refer to an abstract and scientific conception, while mobility is thoroughly socialized and often threatening. Both terms emerged with modernity.

We do not have to confine ourselves to dictionary definitions to see the fractured ways in which mobility has been understood. More generally, modernity has been marked by time-space compression and staggering developments in communication and transportation. At the same time, it has seen the rise of moral panics ranging from the refugee to the global terrorist. The celebrated technologies of mobility simultaneously open up the possibility of an increasingly transgressive world marked by people out of place at all scales. This is the tension that runs through the chapters in this book. Mobility is both center and margin—the lifeblood of modernity and the virus that threatens to hasten its downfall.

This brief account of changing historical senses of mobility is supposed to be indicative. I cannot hope to provide a comprehensive accounting for all the different mobilities that have occurred in the world. Clearly much has been missed. What this sketch does reveal, however, is the way ideas about, and practices of, mobility have been historically variable. The movement of people has been central to the construction of worldviews in wildly different ways. It is to this process of the production of mobilities that I now return.

## Mobility—A Critical Geosophy

This book is about how the fact of movement becomes mobility. How, in other words, movement is made meaningful, and how the resulting ideologies of mobility become implicated in the production of mobile practices. It is an exercise in critical geosophy. *Geosophy* is a term coined by J. K. Wright in 1947 to describe the geography of knowledge. Geographers, he argued, would benefit from studying the *terrae incognitae*—the unknown territories—of the modern world. These unknown territories, he argued, were no longer literal, material places. The whole world, or nearly all of it, had been charted and mapped. The *terrae incognitae* he wrote of were the worlds known and unknown by people in everyday life. The geographical knowledge of sailors, farmers, or dockworkers.[72] By *critical* geosophy, I mean an examination of the way geographical concepts structure and enable practice in the world. Specifically, this book considers the role played by mobility and, necessarily, relative immobility, in people's geographical imaginations. These imaginations, I argue, are not simply colorful mental maps confined to the world of ideas. Rather they are active participants in the world of action. They inform judges, doctors, factory managers, photographers, government officials, lawyers, airport planners, and all manner of other people with the ability to mold the world we live in. They escape the bonds of individual dreams and aspirations and become social. They become political.

Some forms of geographical imagination tread lightly on the world and remain largely individualistic or context specific. They may be personal mental maps or ways of seeing and knowing specific to limited spaces and times. Others, however, can be called deep knowledges. These knowledges play a deep and abiding structuring role in the world we live in. One example might be the division of public and private space—a form of geographical imagination that capitalist and patriarchal relations are based on. Yet it is possible to think of a world without distinctions between public and private space. Indeed, significant strands of Marxism, feminism, and anarchism have all done this. The division of public and private space, in other words, is a social construct—a product of history.

There are other elements of the geographical imagination, however, that it is not possible to abolish, even theoretically. One of these is mobility. Mobility is a fact of life. To be human, indeed, to be animal, is to have some kind of capacity for mobility. We experience the world as we move through it. Mobility is a capacity of all but the most severely disabled bodies. Unlike the division between public and private space, mobility has been with us since day one. Ubiquity, though, sometimes seems like banality. Perhaps its universal nature makes it seem uninteresting, but its universality is *precisely* what also makes it a powerful part of ideologies of one kind or another in specific times and places. Mobility, in human life, is not a local or specific condition. To talk of the social construction of mobility, or the production of mobility, is not to say that mobility itself has somehow been invented and can be made to disappear. It is not like the automobile or the novel. But neither is it like gravity or the hardness of diamonds. Automobiles and the novel have been produced by society and will one day be made redundant by society. Gravity and the hardness of diamonds existed well before society did, and no society can undo them. I argue that mobility, like place, inhabits a middle ground. It is inconceivable to think of societies anywhere without either, and yet any particular way we have of thinking about them is self-evidently socially produced. They are social productions but necessary ones. The fact that our bodies allow us to move means that the meanings, which are produced in a myriad of ways and are mapped onto mobility are all the more powerful. The ubiquity of mobility makes it possible for *particular* mobilities to be portrayed as more than particular—as fundamental, as natural. It is not possible to do this with automobiles or novels, as their historicity is obvious.

It is this status of a *necessary social production*, I argue, that makes knowledge surrounding mobility (like that surrounding other fundamental geographical concepts such as space and place) so important and so deeply implicated in the politics of the modern world. Stasis and mobility, fixity and flow, are the subjects of deep knowledges that inform any number of ways of seeing the world. For this reason, an understanding of the ways in which ideas about fixity and flow provide a profound undercurrent to thinking (which is closer to the surface of cultural life—law, medicine, activism, film, photography, planning, architecture, philosophy, and even geography itself) enacts a critical geosophy. It enables us to examine the role of geographical knowledges in the always political and always differentiated production of social life.

It is the distinction between fixity and flow that is the subject of chapter 2 in which I develop the notion of a metaphysics of fixity, place, and spatial order on the one hand, and a metaphysics of flow, mobility, and becoming on the other. The purpose of the chapter is to review a set of literatures about mobility and to show how these literatures are themselves part of a world in which fixity and flow structure action and thought in ideological ways. The chapter ends with a call for a fully developed politics of mobility that links mobilities at the scale of the body to mobilities across the globe.

Chapters 3, 4, and 5 consider the politics of bodily mobility. Chapter 3 outlines the way the photographer Eadweard Muybridge and the physiologist Etienne-Jules Marey attempted to represent mobility through the development of photographic techniques that made mobility intelligible in new ways. Chapter 4 continues this analysis through an examination of the factory-based motion-studies of Frederick Taylor and Frank and Lillian Gilbreth. I show how movement studies employed increasingly sophisticated representational strategies, not just to record the already existing movements of workers, but also to produce new, ideal kinds of movement invested with the moral glow of health, efficiency, and productivity. Chapter 5 is an account of the development of ballroom dancing in Britain in response to the proliferation of so-called *freak steps*, supposedly originating in the United States. This chapter thus unites the scale of bodily mobility considered in the two earlier chapters with a wider sense of mobility across the ocean. The development of a particularly British, and then Imperial style of dancing was developed in response to perceived American, and specifically black American, dances such as the Turkey Trot, the Shimmy, and the Jitterbug. Once again particular forms of appropriate, refined, and moral mobilities were produced at the same time as inappropriate, uncivilized, and immoral mobilities were railed against. Throughout these three chapters I argue that particular types of mobility are produced in relation to other, often allegedly pathological, mobilities that are threatening and excessive.

Chapters 6 and 7 focus on the role of mobility in the historiography and ideology of the United States. As well as being an important constituent of a national ideology of exceptionalism, mobility is shown to be central to discourses of rights, citizenship, and heritage. Chapter 6 considers the development of the right to mobility through an examination of Supreme Court cases over a one-hundred-year period, and argues that mobility as a right became central to the legal definition of the figure of the citizen. The chapter ends with a discussion of the activism of the Bus Riders Union of contemporary Los Angeles in order to suggest a progressive way in which the logic that ties mobility to citizenship and rights can be reconfigured. Chapter 7 continues the discussion of mobility and citizenship in the United States through an examination of the coding of the mobility of immigrants in the Chinese Exclusion Act of 1882 and the Peopling of America Theme Study Act of 2001. In the first case Chinese immigration was coded as a threat, and in the second it is (along with all immigration) seen to be central to what it is to be American. The final two chapters of the book focus on two very different cases of mobility in which different scales and mobility interact.

Chapter 8 looks closely at a particular journey across the Atlantic—that of two American suffrage activists on a trip to visit their activist sisters in Britain and to attend an international suffrage conference in Stockholm. It explores how the two women were enabled by a network of technologies of mobility ranging from transatlantic steamers to Thomas Cook offices. On their return to Boston, emboldened by their travels, they took to the road in an automobile as part of a new public politics labeled by the newspapers as "made in England." Chapter 9 takes a close look at a particular site for the production of mobilities—the airport. The site of the airport is important because it brings together a number of important scales of mobility under one roof. The airport, for instance, is a central metaphor for postmodern, transnational life in the writings of social and cultural theorists. In addition, it is a place designed to finely control bodily mobility in ways similar to those employed by Taylor and Gilbreth. It is a place where national and international conceptions of mobility as a right becomes a reality or a cruel trick, depending on what kind of mobile subject you are planning to become. Through an examination of Schiphol Airport in Amsterdam, I bring together the different scales and narratives of mobility that run throughout this book. The book ends with an epilogue on the politics of mobility in and around New Orleans during and following the devastating experience of Hurricane Katrina in 2005.

## CHAPTER 2

# The Metaphysics of Fixity and Flow

The purpose of this chapter is to provide a first example of the way the geographical imagination—ideas about such things as place, spatial order, and mobility—provides an underlying metaphysics that influences and informs thought and action. In later chapters we will see how areas such as law, physiology and choreography have given mobility meaning at the same time as they have been informed by preexisting meanings of mobility. This chapter is presented in the same spirit—as an exploration of the mobilization of mobility as a *root metaphor* for contemporary understandings of the world of culture and society. It is an examination, in other words, of the way a geographical imagination informs the construction of new forms of knowledge—in this case, academic knowledge. In contemporary social thought, words associated with mobility are unremittingly positive. If something can be said to be fluid, dynamic, in flux, or simply mobile, then it is seen to be progressive, exciting, and contemporary. If, on the other hand, something is said to be rooted, based on foundations, static, or bounded, then it is seen to be reactionary, dull, and of the past. This has not always been the case and this chapter explores some of this history.

It is a premise of this book that mobility, and the meanings given to it, permeates modern culture and society in the Western world. Deeply rooted ideologies of mobility are just as pervasive in contemporary social and cultural theory as they have been in the wider world of thought and action. The literature is just as much a part of this world as anything else, and so distinctions between contemporary academic thought and the world to which it is supposed to refer are, for my purposes at least, entirely unhelpful.

This chapter, then, explores the pervasive role of imaginations of mobility in the arena of social and cultural thought. It introduces two principal metaphysical ways of viewing the world: a *sedentarist metaphysics* and a *nomadic metaphysics*. Each of these revolves around understandings of mobility, spatial order, and place. The first sees mobility through the lens of place, rootedness, spatial order, and belonging. Mobility, in this formulation, is seen as morally and ideologically suspect, a by-product of a world arranged through place and spatial order. The second puts mobility first, has little time for notions of attachment to place, and revels in notions of flow, flux, and dynamism. Place is portrayed as stuck in the past, overly confining, and possibly reactionary. In both cases the moral geographies of place and mobility interact to inform ontology, epistemology, and politics as well as practice and material culture. These are very much ideas in the world. While it is clear that these ways of thinking have permeated the world we live in to influence all manner of beliefs and practices, it is equally clear that they form ends of a continuum and rarely exist in pure form. Nevertheless, these are pervasive ways of thinking that provide a bedrock for the world we live in.

## A Sedentarist Metaphysics

One of the principal ways of thinking about mobility in the modern Western world is to see it as a threat, a disorder in the system, a thing to control. This lies at the heart of James Scott's observation that modern states have preoccupied themselves with the ordering and disciplining of mobile peoples. Think of the role of the outsider in modern life—a constant source of anxiety with a whiff of "elsewhere" about her. The drifter, the shiftless, the refugee and the asylum seeker have been inscribed with immoral intent. So, too, the traveling salesman, the gypsy-traveler, and the so-called wandering Jew. These have all been portrayed as figures of mobile threat in need of straightening out and discipline.[1]

The phrase "sedentarist metaphysics" comes from the anthropologist Liisa Malkki who, in her writing on refugees, has noted a tendency to think of mobile people in ways that assume the moral and logical primacy of fixity in space and place. She argues that notions of identities rooted in the soil of home are profoundly metaphysical. In the incessant desire to divide the world up into clearly bounded territorial units, she suggests, a "sedentarist metaphysics" is produced. Her argument is t. fixed, bounded, and rooted conceptions of culture and identity are linkt to particular ways of thinking, which are themselves sedentarist. These ways of thinking then reaffirm and enable the commonsense segmenta-tion of the world into things like nations, states, countries, and places. This process is so ingrained as to be invisible. The consequences of a sedentarist metaphysics for mobile people are severe. Thinking of the world as rooted and bounded is reflected in language and social practice. Such thoughts actively territorialize identities in property, in region, in nation—in place. They simultaneously produce discourse and practice that treats mobility and displacement as pathological. This process has clearly been at work in reactions to tramps in turn-of-the-century America and gypsies in the United Kingdom. A similar process has surrounded the existence of the refugee and the asylum seeker. The following passage is taken from a post-war study of refugees cited by Malkki.

> Homelessness is a serious threat to moral behaviour. . . . At the moment the refugee crosses the frontiers of his own world, his whole moral outlook, his attitude toward the divine order of things changes. . . . [The refugees'] conduct makes it obvious that we are dealing with individuals who are basically amoral, without any sense of personal or social responsibility. . . . They no lon-ger feel themselves bound by ethical precepts which every honest citizen . . . respects. They become a menace, dangerous characters who will stop at nothing.[2]

In the first half of this chapter, I develop this idea of a sedentarist metaphysics in order to explore a number of different forms of knowledge ranging from the discipline of geography to the settlement of the mobile. In the second half, I explore the emergent nomadic metaphysics, which marks an alternative way of thinking with mobility at its center. First, consider the meanings given to mobility in spatial interaction theory (broadly positivist in outlook) and humanistic geography (informed by existentialism and phenomenology), two ways of knowing the world that are often seen as opposites. Human geogra-phy is, after all, a way of knowing the world just like law or architecture.

## Spatial Interaction Theory

In Peter Haggett's book *Locational Analysis in Human Geography* (1965), he refers to an earlier (1938) paper in which Crowe took geographers to task for their "overwheening concern with the static elements of the Earth's surface. Is progressive geography, he asked, to be solely concerned with the distribution of Homo Dormiens?"[3] Since then, mobility has moved in and out of the orbit of geographical enquiry. In many ways the study of human mobility in geography has a history as long as the discipline itself. The migrations of humanity have always been a central concern, from the ideas of origins and dispersals in Sauerian cultural geography to the contemporary concerns with hybridity and globalization.[4] To attempt to review all of it would be futile. Instead, I have selected some key moments in the history of human geography to trace the development, in the first instance, of a sedentarist metaphysics in human geography. My intention is to show how one powerful way of thinking about mobility has developed, rather than to suggest that all geographers at all times have contributed to it. I am not replicating Crowe's argument about Homo Dormiens here, but suggesting that even when mobility has been at the center of geographical attention it has been conceptualized through the lens of fixity as an ideal. My account focuses on spatial interaction theory and humanistic geography.

The general critique of spatial science, quantification, and logical positivism is well known and needn't be repeated here.[5] Instead, I focus on the specific issue of theorizations of human movement. Haggett devotes the first substantive section of *Locational Analysis* to "movement." Haggett's book played a central role in the development of spatial science. Unlike other modes of human geography, the movement of human beings played a starring role in spatial science. Transport geography and migration theory have never been so central to the discipline.[6] Some of the central sets of laws and theories in spatial science concern mobility. Spatial interaction theory is one of them. Lowe and Moryadas's book *The Geography of Movement* is one of very few books in the history of the discipline dedicated to a general understanding of movement. It is marked by the universal rationality of "rational mobile man."

> Movement occurs to the extent that people have the ability to satisfy their desires with respect to goods, services, information, or experience at some location rather than their present one, and to the extent that these other locations are capable of satisfying such desires.[7]

Mobility is also central to one of the key textbooks of the day—Abler, Adams, and Gould's *Spatial Organization: The Geographer's View of the World*. Again, mobile man is annoyingly rational.

> We can think of each migrant assigning one value to his present location and other values to places where he could be. He compares his present status with potential status elsewhere. Then he weights the different alternatives according to their distances and how risky he thinks each of them is. Finally he picks a strategy he thinks will be best for him.[8]

A by-product of this virtual rational mobility is a submersion of difference in considerations of mobility. Spatial interaction does not consider the different ways in which people are mobile or immobile, nor the relationships among them. Indeed, it is often the stated aim of law construction to make difference irrelevant. Lowe and Moryadas, for instance, insist on the importance of generalizations for understanding human movement: "hence whether a trip for medical attention, for example, is to a witch doctor or to a medical complex is totally immaterial."[9] This understanding of difference in human movement as "totally immaterial" is a function of law generation. It is repeated in the identification of so-called *ideal movements* in Abler, Adams, and Gould. The differences between ideal movements are simply differences in patterns—from an area to a line, an area to an area, or an area to a volume. Within these ideal types, differences are conflated. Thus movement from an area to a line describes water moving from a roof to a gutter and commuters moving from a suburb to a highway. Not only are differences between human movements erased, but they are made to equate to movements in nature as well.

> When water runs off a roof and into a gutter during a rainstorm the dimensions of the moves are the same as those when animals come out of the forest to drink at the river; or when commuters leave their garages for the street; or when soil is wasted through sheet erosion into ditches, gullies, and stream beds. In all cases something moves from an area to a line with least net effort expanded.[10]

This principle of least net effort is key here.[11] The basic assumption is that things (including people) don't move if they can help it. This is a notion borrowed directly from physical science. The principle of least net effort leads to movement itself being described as dysfunctional, as spatial structures, in an ideal world, are supposed to be organized in such a way as to minimize the need for movement.

Logically, movement always comes second to arrangements of space and the measurable qualities of particular locations. Spatial arrangements exist to negate movement and are produced by the constant need to reduce distances over which movement occurs. In classic migration theory, the movement is explained by the place that is being left and the place of arrival. People move because they have come to the rational decision that one place is better (in some quantifiable way) than another. The line that connects A to B is explained *by* A and B, and their relative push and pull factors.

In certain central strands of spatial science, then, there are a number of well-established (but by no means universal) assumptions about human movement: that it is a product of rationality, can be described in universal terms that negate difference, is inherently a dysfunction, and that it can be explained as a secondary characteristic of spatial arrangements and the qualities of locations. Within all of this we can see a sedentarist metaphysics at work. This is most clearly the case in the definition of movement as a dysfunction—a word that defined mobility as the other of some sense of function that is valued, at least implicitly, as a good thing.

It is not the case that all of what we now call spatial science is equally unsophisticated when it comes to mobility. Haggett's discussion of movement in *Locational Analysis* is an extended consideration of many factors in the explanation and modeling of movement. Forer's development of notions of "plastic space" emphasized how transport technologies made time and space malleable.[12] The work on migration and mobility at all scales, undertaken by Hägerstrand (and others at the Lund school) and later developed by Pred, does not repeat the logic of movement minimalization and progressively began to point to the politics of the everyday mobility patterns of men and women.[13] As Rose has pointed out, however, the time-space paths of men and women in time-geography remain annoyingly abstracted from the embodied experience of mobility or anything else.[14] Despite these caveats, it is clear that the models of mobility outlined above were central to spatial science.

One of the clearest absences in a spatial science approach is any sense of the values and meaning that get embedded in mobility. Spatial science itself is clearly unintentionally giving a certain meaning to mobility through the label of dysfunction. Insofar as difference in the experience of mobility is taken into account, it is only as something that can be subsumed under the label of cost or benefit.

## Humanistic Geography

If anyone or anything was going to take mobility seriously as a human experience outside of the rationalization of costs and benefits, it was and is humanistic geography. Within the canon of humanistic geography, however, mobility once again plays second fiddle to the overriding concern with place, and once again mobility is portrayed as a threat and dysfunction. In general terms, place, in its ideal form, is seen as a moral world, as an insurer of authentic existence, and as a center of meaning for people.[15] Mobility is often the assumed threat to the rooted, moral, authentic existence of place. We have to make assumptions about the role of mobility in humanistic geography as it is rarely approached directly as a subject. Mostly we learn of mobility through insinuation and implication.

It should be pointed out, however, that some of the richest work on mobility as a fundamental geographic constituent of our cultural geographies comes from J. B. Jackson (a key figure in the development of humanistic geography despite his extra-disciplinary status) and David Seamon. While Jackson's astute essays are positively saturated with the value of mobility in the perception and construction of the American vernacular landscape, Seamon's phenomenological construction of the life-world through bodily mobility was an important precursor to contemporary work on nonrepresentational theory.[16] Despite the work of Jackson, Seamon, and others, however, the valorization of place and the focus on Crowe's Homo Dormiens remains a central and, I argue, dominant theme in the development of a humanistic approach.

Humanistic geographers developed, in a number of ways, the thesis that geography is the study of "earth as the home of man."[17] Whether it is through literature, art, architecture, or the decoration of the favorite corner of a child's bedroom, humanism highlights the effort people have gone through in all cultures to create order and homeliness out of the apparent chaos of raw nature. Humanists insist that the concept of place is central to our understanding of the ways in which people turn nature into culture by making it their home. Indeed the warm coziness of home as a general concept rubs off on the geographic appreciation of place. Relph suggests that, "to be human is to live in a world that is filled with significant places: to be human is to have and to know your place."[18] Place, then, becomes the phenomenological starting point for geography. Place, home, and roots are described as a fundamental human need: "to have roots in a place is to have a secure point from which to look out on the world, a firm grasp of one's own position in the order of things, and a significant spiritual and psychological attachment to somewhere in particular."[19] Place is a center of meaning and field of care.

What role does mobility have in this striving for commitment? The answer is an ambivalent one. Place, Tuan argues, "is an organized world of meaning. It is essentially a static concept. If we see the world as process, constantly changing, we would not be able to develop any sense of place."[20] The world of nomads, he suggests, might include a strong sense of place as their movements often occur within a circumscribed area. "Modern man," he goes on, might be so mobile that he can never establish roots and his experience of place may be all too superficial.[21] As place is an essentially moral concept,[22] mobility and movement, insofar as they undermine attachment and commitment, are antithetical to moral worlds. By implication, mobility appears to involve a number of absences—the absence of commitment and attachment and involvement—a lack of significance. Places marked by an abundance of mobility become *placeless*. To Relph, for instance, modern tourism and superhighways play their part in the destruction of place. Before the highways, the railways were the culprits destroying authentic senses of place. Now, we might look to airports.

In much of humanistic geography, then, mobility once again appears as a dysfunction. Rather than being evidence for a non-ideal arrangement of spaces (as in spatial science), mobility is suspicious because it threatens the quite explicit moral character of place—threatening to undo it. Once again, human geography's construction of mobility is deeply marked by a sedentarist metaphysics. What is evident in both spatial science and humanistic geography is a very strong moral geography that marginalizes mobility ontologically, epistemologically, and normatively. While it was certainly not the only geography at work, it was an important, dominant strand in the discipline's deep philosophy, which united approaches as different as spatial science and humanism.

## Sedentarism and Culture

The metaphysics of sedentarism pervades modern thought. We have already seen how an imagination informed by the moral values of place, rooted-ness, and order underlies important aspects of geographical thought. It can also be found in early cultural theory both in its conservative tradition and in early forms of what is now known as cultural studies. In this section I examine the use of metaphors of mobility in the work of T. S. Eliot, Richard Hoggart, and Raymond Williams.

T. S. Eliot's *Notes Towards the Definition of Culture* is one of the key texts in the conservative Culture and Society tradition, alongside those of Matthew Arnold and F. R. Leavis.[23] Eliot advances the argument that Culture (with a big C) can be preserved only through the maintenance of class hierarchy and a strong attachment to place and region. Without the stability provided by these frameworks, he argues, chaos and anarchy will prevail. One danger Eliot saw concerned the rise of universal education.

> For there is no doubt that in our headlong rush to educate every-body, we are lowering our standards, and more and more abandoning the study of those subjects by which the essentials of our culture—or that part of it which is transmissible by education—are transmitted; destroying our ancient edifices to make ready the ground upon which the barbarian nomads of the future will encamp in mechanised caravans.[24]

The image of "barbarian nomads" in "mechanised caravans" is a chaotic metaphor of mobility. The metaphor of the nomad is clearly pejorative. In this passage the nomads are contrasted with *edifices* that are, equally clearly, positive, representing stable and rooted certainties. The nomads represent the threat of chaos brought about by the fracturing of class lines and regional loyalties. People would no longer know their place socially or geographically. This mirrors some of the observations made by Yi-Fu Tuan when he argues that "Modern man" might be so mobile that he can never establish roots, and that his experience of place may consequently be all too superficial.[25] For a conservative commentator such as Eliot, this would signal the death knell of culture—culture as roots and tradition. Eliot makes this clear in a more literal passage.

> Certainly, an individual may develop the warmest devotion to a place in which he was not born, and to a community with which he has no ancestral ties. But I think we should agree that there would be something artificial, something a little too conscious, about a community of people with strong local feeling, all of whom had come from somewhere else. . . . On the whole, it would appear to be for the best that the great majority of human beings should go on living in the place in which they were born. Family, class and local loyalty all support each other; and in one of these decays, the others will suffer also.[26]

Eliot's metaphorical nomads quickly become literal. Eliot, himself a mobile intellectual (but surely no nomad!) removed from his place of birth, sees the contours of culture as firmly attached to the contours of region. Eliot is disturbed by people who literally move, as culture, for him, depends on a lack of movement, on stability, rootedness, and continuity. People who insist on moving present problems.

> The colonization problem arises from migration. When peoples migrated across Asia and Europe in pre-historic, and early times, it was a whole tribe, or at least a wholly representative part of it, that moved together. Therefore, it was a total culture that moved. In the migrations of modern times, the emigrants have come from countries already highly civilized. . . . The people who migrated have never represented the whole of the culture of the country from which they came, or they have represented it in quite different proportions. They have transplanted themselves according to some social, religious, economic or political determination, or some peculiar mixture of these. . . . The people have taken with them only a part of the total culture in which, so long as they remained at home, they participated.[27]

Culture and home (defined as region) belong together in Eliot's mind, so the movement of people can be seen only as a problem and threat to cultural distinctiveness. So we can see that Eliot's reference to the mechanized nomads of mass education and culture is linked to beliefs about mobility and place that are far from metaphorical.

The metaphysics of sedentarism reappear in the work of Raymond Williams. This is, perhaps, surprising given Williams's leftist critique of the work of Eliot and others, and his lifelong struggle to promote more progressive and inclusive views of culture. But the moral coding of place and mobility runs deeper than ideological differences—these moral geographies act as the bedrock for remarkably consistent sets of assumptions that work across political and theoretical divides. Raymond Williams wrote in 1985, in an essay on the miners' strike:

> Yet there is the implacable logic of the social order which is now so strongly coming through: the logic of a new nomad capitalism which exploits actual places and people and then (as it suits it) moves on. Indeed the spokesmen of this new nomad capitalism have come less and less to resemble actual human beings, and more and more to look and talk like plastic nomads: offering their titles to cash at a great distance from any settled working and productive activity, . . . Back in the shadow of their operations, from the inner cities to the abandoned mining villages, real men and women know that they are facing an alien order of paper and money, which seems all powerful. It is to the lasting honour of the miners, and the women, and the old people, and all the others in the defiant communities, that they have stood up against it, and challenged its power.[28]

Williams continues his attack on rootless capitalism claiming that "we need not worry about the plastic nomads" as they will inevitably leave just as they arrived and "we" will remain "here and needing to stay here" constructing a new economic order more rooted in the particularity of place. While Eliot's nomads represent the threat of mass culture to his ideal rooted and stratified Culture, Williams's nomads are those of twentieth-century industrial capitalism, profiteers who roam the earth taking what they can and giving nothing back. While it is easier, perhaps, to sympathize with Williams's vision, the implications of the nomad metaphor are surprisingly consistent. For Williams and Eliot culture is a fairly sedentary thing, linked to the continuities of place and community. Williams's moral geographies in these passages are of real people in real places such as miners' villages and inner cities set against the plastic nomads who come and go. Place provides a consistent point of reference from which to understand the threat of the mobile. This is an example of Williams's "militant particularlism."[29]

Williams's moral geography of place and mobility is mirrored in one of the key books in early cultural studies, Richard Hoggart's *The Uses of Literacy,* in which he portrays working-class English culture as a cozy, snug, and resolutely sedentary existence. "The more we look at working class culture" he suggested, "the more surely does it appear that the core is a sense of the personal, the concrete, the local."[30] Like Williams, Hoggart appears firmly rooted in the closely knit neighbourhoods of his upbringing. All that is good about working-class culture is encapsulated in snug family living rooms with open fires and overloaded mantelpieces. Everyone knows one another, shopkeepers are polite, people help their neighbors when it snows. The watchwords here are family, community, place, and tradition.

> Unless he gets a council house, a working-class man is likely to live in his own local area, perhaps even in the house he "got the keys for" the night before his wedding, all his life. He has little call to move on if he is a general labourer, and perhaps hardly more if he is skilled, since his skill is likely to be in a trade for which several nearby works . . . provide vacancies. . . . He is more likely to change his place to work than his place of living; he belongs to a district more than to one works.[31]

Working-class life, in Hoggart's eyes, is determinedly local. Movement, when it occurs, is over a small distance and repeated as part of a routine of home, work, and the pub. T. S. Eliot would be assured that these people were staying where they were as "the speed and extent of his travel" were little changed from thirty years earlier. "The car has not reduced distance for him: the trains are no faster than they were three quarters of a century ago." In short, the working-class person undertook "very little travel except within a mile or two."[32]

Hoggart's nostalgic vision of working-class culture in northern England revolved around home and place, with travel only occurring for the occasional funeral, wedding, or trip to the seaside. This vision is underlined by Hoggart's metaphorical loathing of the bandwagon of the new "mass culture" with its "wagon loaded with its barbarians in wonderland" which "moves irresistibly forward" simply for "forwardness's sake."[33] Opposed to the snug living room of working-class culture with its glorious profusion of knickknacks is the glitzy, shallow temptation of popular music, magazines, and cheap novels. While the old working-class culture is symbolized by the coziness of the pub, the new bandwagon is symbolized by the "milk bar" with its "glaring showiness" and "odour of boiled milk" in which customers live a "myth world" taken to be American consisting of slicked-back hair and endless milkshakes. But Hoggart is still hopeful about the survival of a full and rich working-class culture. Tradition is also threatened by progressivism and the forward march of science, which is marked by "obsessive speed" which might end up putting us into a "speed-wobble."[34] Progress, to Hoggart, is a word that encapsulates the various threats to the world of home and neighborhood. Progress replaces local pubs with American milk bars.

The working-class culture that Hoggart values and admires is small in scale, close knit, and family based—it is stable and, for the most part, unchanging. The aspects of mass entertainment that Hoggart feels it is necessary to warn us against are foreign (mostly American), rapidly changing, and unattached to place. Progress implies movement, and Hoggart's repudiation of progressivism is couched as a warning against speed and its dangers. His evocation of working-class life is one of motionless continuity, and his more symbolic description of threats to it is laced with references to movement and speed. This is essentially a morality play of stability versus mobility. The forces of mass entertainment are to be prevented from opening up an Americanized "candy-floss world" of chrome and depthlessness full of barbarians (always the nomadic threat to civilization's order) of bandwagons and buses—"the hedonistic but passive barbarian who rides in a fifty-horse-power bus for threepence, to see a five-million-dollar film for one and eightpence, is not simply a social oddity; he is a portent."[35]

Despite their considerable differences in politics and philosophy, Eliot, Hoggart, and Williams are united in their respect for roots and their use of metaphors of mobility to suggest threat. Mass education, mass entertainment, and industrial capital are all painted as nomadic and alien, threatening the integrity of cozy regions, towns, and neighborhoods, within which lie the virtues of culture in all its manifestations. These writers mobilize the *nomad* in particular as a symbol of transience that disrupts the bounded value systems they have invested with moral worth. These moral geographies extend well beyond cultural theory. They mirror similar concerns in important strands of human geography and, as we shall see, in state reactions to mobile populations.

## Mobility as Social Pathology

The emergence of sociology as a discipline in the early twentieth century prompted intense speculation about the increasingly mobile world of the city. While the rural was theorized as a place of rest and rootedness—of community—the urban was a site of movement and alienation—a space of "society."[36] These ideas were developed thoroughly in the first American Department of Sociology at the University of Chicago. To Ernest Burgess, for instance, mobility was central to the morphology of the city. It was the central factor in the growth of the individual and the city, but was also the potential cause of pathology when it became detached from society— "where mobility is the greatest, and where in consequence primary controls break down completely, as in the zone of deterioration in the modern city, there develop areas of demoralization, of promiscuity, and of vice."[37] To Burgess, areas of high mobility were areas of prostitution, gangs, crime, and violence. To his student, Nels Anderson, mobility threatened to undo place and create chaos. "The mobility of the city" he wrote, "detaches and undomesticates the urban man" and "with this independence comes a loss of loyalty." This loss of loyalty imbues the city dweller with his freedom, but only "at the cost of his locus."[38]

Mobility, then, plays a central role in the work of Burgess, Robert Park, Nels Anderson, and others at the Chicago School. It is the disorder produced by mobility (among other things) that was at the heart of their view of society. It is certainly not all bad. Mobility is, after all, what separates the city from the country. Mobility is connected to civilization, progress, and freedom as well as deviance and destitution. But the mobility is still framed within a moral geography of place and locus that is constantly threatened. "Society" wrote Robert Park "is made up of independent, locomoting individuals. It is the fact of locomotion . . . that defines the very nature of society. But in order that there may be any permanence and progress in society the individuals who compose it must be located . . ."[39]

This strand of thinking about mobility as a pathological threat to society became a consistent thread in American social commentary. In 1970 the popular sociologist Alvin Toffler wrote the hugely successful *Future Shock* in which he prepared the citizens of the world for a future world of runaway mobility.[40] Here he describes a world in which everything is accelerating. Science, technology, and culture were all speeding up. In many ways this was George Beard nearly one hundred years later—Toffler appears to be breathlessly describing a late-twentieth-century version of neurasthenia. "All the old roots" he tells us "are now shaking under the hurricane impact of the accelerative thrust." In order to cope with this, people need to understand "transience."[41] Part of his diagnosis concerned places and their relation to increased and accelerated mobility. Tellingly he described the inhabitants of this world as the "new nomads." His description of their predicament was suitably apocalyptic:

> Never in history has distance meant less. Never have man's relationships with place been more numerous, fragile and temporary. Throughout the advanced technological societies, and particularly among those I have characterized as "the people of the future," commuting, travelling, and regularly relocating one's family have become second nature. Figuratively we "use up" places and dispose of them in much the same way that we dispose of Kleenex or beer cans. We are witnessing a historic decline in the significance

of place in human life. We are breeding a new race of nomads, and few suspect quite how massive, widespread and significant their migrations are.[42]

To Toffler the figure of the nomad provided the perfect metaphor for the modern person. The nomads, we learn, "are not the same kind of people as those who stay put in one place."[43] To the nomad, geographical mobility means freedom from constraint, and it is valued positively rather than being seen as a result of pressure to move. Toffler sees this everywhere—in the fact that Americans move house so often, in the love of automobiles, and in the idealism of Peace Corp activists. He recognizes the pervasive influence of sedentarism in human life. "Commitment" he writes, "takes many forms." The most important of these is "attachment to place." Indeed, "[w]e can understand the significance of mobility only if we first recognise the centrality of fixed place in the psychological architecture of traditional man."[44]

Toffler presents us with an apocalyptic vision of a world in motion. In many ways his book prefigures the writings of Augé, Virilio, and others.[45] It certainly mirrors the concerns about the threats to place that pervade the writings of humanistic geographers in the 1970s and 1980s. Toffler seems excited by this new mobile world. He provides the reader with a flood of facts and figure about the frequency and velocity of mobility undertaken by the new nomads. Its purpose is to diagnose a pathology—future shock—a sense of disorientation and overload that modern man needs to react to quickly. The prevalence of mobility in modern life is, to Toffler, most definitely a problem. In this sense, his anxieties sit snugly beside those of his sociological forebears at the Chicago School. Indeed, mobility presents itself as a problem in many of the sociological texts of the twentieth century such as William Whyte's *The Organization Man* and the Lynds' *Middletown*.[46]

## Sedentarism Made Material

If the metaphysics of sedentarism were limited to the internal scribblings of geographers, sociologists, and cultural theorists, it could be considered harmless enough. But the view of the world that attaches negative moral and ideological codings to mobility extends well beyond the ivory tower to pervade thought and practice in multiple domains of social and cultural life. Indeed, the view of mobility as threat and dysfunction in the social sciences is only a reflection of the wider world. Malkki introduces the idea with reference to the assumption that people belong in particular places— particularly to national "homes." Refugees, seen through this lens, are a worrisome moral threat. It is worth considering political, state-led reactions to other kinds of mobile people—nomads, gypsies, and the internal migrant—people without place.

## Nomads, Gypsies, Migrants

State reactions to mobile people are, of course, diverse. What is remarkable, however, is how similar reactions have been in a variety of unrelated instances. James Scott notes how the state seems to have been the enemy of mobile people in modernity. This is certainly true of some mobile people. Take the Bedouin in Libya under Italian fascism, for example. David Atkinson has described how the Sanussi tribe of about two thousand men took on the colonial Italian army in 1923. The Italians could not figure out how to govern these nomadic people. The problem for them was that guerrilla warfare is based on mobility rather than territory—the Sanussi could attack and then melt away into the desert. As the British anthropologist Evans-Pritchard put it, "the Sanussi were fighting in their own country and the Italians had to adapt themselves to the kind of fighting which seldom fails to upset the orthodox military mind. Ordinary tactics are useless against an enemy who wanders at will over the country with which he is familiar, among a population all friendly to him, and whose tactics are little more than the three guerrilla imperatives, strike suddenly, strike hard, get out quick."[47]

The Sanussi rebels were not tied to any particular conception of place-belonging, and therefore had no static space to defend. In addition, they were liable to turn up in any place at any given moment. As the Italian General Graziani put it, "(the Bedouin are) [r]ebellious against every tie of discipline, used to wandering in immense, desert territories, bold in mobility and ease of movement, and pervaded by a fascination with independence, they are always ready for war and raiding, the nomads have always resisted every governmental restraint."[48]

The Italians responded through the lens of sedentarism. They divided the desert as best they could with enormously long barbed wire fences to limit the Sanussi mobility. But they also responded by confining the nomads in concentration camps that were the epitome of rational spatial planning. Beginning in 1930, nomadic and semi-nomadic groups were put into the camps. They were kilometer-square enclosures arranged so that the inmates would set their tents up in a grid pattern with broad corridors for surveillance (see Figure 2.1). As Atkinson put it: "the camp and its barbed wire fences materialised European notions of a bounded territoriality; they finally forced the Bedouin to live within a disciplined, controlled, fixed space—in contrast to their traditional conceptions of group encampments and unfettered movement across territory."[49]

Perhaps the Italian concentration camps can be thought of as functional spaces of imprisonment ensuring the safety of Italian troops. The same cannot be said about the migrant camps constructed in California under the auspices of the Farm Security Administration (FSA) during Roosevelt's

**Figure 2.1** Tahe concentration camp at el-Abair, Rodolfo Graziani, *Pace Romana in Libia* (Milano: A. Mondadori, 1937), 272–73.

New Deal in the 1930s. Overfarming and mechanization in the southern and midwestern United States had resulted in massive soil erosion in states such as Texas, Arkansas, and Oklahoma, and poor tenant farmers were displaced from the land and forced to migrate in search of a livelihood. Many moved west, tempted by stories of California as a land of "milk and honey." When they arrived, however, they were met with the same kind of distaste and maltreatment faced by mobile people the world over. The Farm Security Administration was, by American standards, a liberal organization that sought to provide relief for these Okies and Arkies. They sent out photographers, such as Dorothea Lange, to capture the plight of the migrants so that Americans might be informed of the situation and their sympathy raised. She photographed migrants in the most appalling conditions, stuck in broken-down cars loaded with the paraphernalia of domesticity. In addition, under the orders of her employer Roy Stryker, she photographed "'Air views' of camps (from as high a spot as possible)."[50] The resulting images of the camp at Schafter, California (1938) reveal a neat rectangular plot divided into a grid and crisscrossed by broad thorough-fares (see Figure 2.2). Within each block of living space there is a laundry, toilet and cleaning facilities. It is an image of clean, rational space that stands in stark contrast to the disordered images of migrants outside of the camps. It looks remarkably like an Italian camp for the Sanussi.[51]

Dorothea Lange and FSA clearly wanted to improve the condition of the migrants. Their guiding ideology was a long way from the totalitarian fascism of Mussolini, but for both of them mobility posed a problem. The

**Figure 2.2** Dorothea Lange, Schafter, California, June 1938. FSA camp for migratory agricultural workers, Library of Congress, Washington, DC, Prints and Photographs Division, U.S. Farm Security Administration Collection.

photographs of Lange and others exist to promote the benefits of a settled existence. The vision of proper, ordered, and sedentary life is made clear by the ordered nature of the camps. It is underlined by the inscription under one of Lange's images that reads, "U.S. 101 migratory pea-pickers near Santa Monica, California, February 1936. Constant movement does not favor the development of normal relationships between citizens and community, and between employer and employee for the proper functioning of democracy."[52] Indeed, to Lange and her husband, the economist Paul Taylor, the plight of the migrants stood in sharp contrast to their Jeffersonian vision of a rural property-owning democracy firmly embedded in place. It comes as no surprise, therefore, that the dominant metaphor they use to describe the migrants is that of "erosion." Just as the dust blowing over the plains is natural erosion, so the migrants represent "human erosion." "By a curiously symbolic coincidence" they wrote "Oklahoma is the most wind-blown state in the country, its newly-broken red plains are among the worst eroded, and its farm people are among the least rooted in the soil."[53]

The photography of Lange is clearly informed by a sedentarist metaphysics, and the planning of the migrant camps is equally clearly an attempt to straighten out and make legible in space the lives of people who have been forced to move. Gypsy-travelers, on the other hand, have chosen to live a seminomadic existence. The history of the gypsies is a history of continued harassment and discrimination over centuries, due in part to their perceived mobility.[54]

In Nazi Germany, Gypsies, Jews, and gay people were murdered by the millions. Behind this genocide lay a well-developed ideology of sedentarism.[55] Gypsies, Jews, and gays were described as rootless in order to legitimate the holocaust. Nazi academics and writers built up a German mythology based on deep soil, the forest, and roots. The German character, it was claimed, was best characterized by the Black Forest with its lush trees and deep roots; Martin Heidegger, in particular, portrayed the good life through the model of a log cabin in the forest where people could live an "authentic" existence.[56] While Germany was being constructed as a rooted culture, other cultures were being located elsewhere—the city and the desert. Jewish people were symbolized as desert snakes winding around the roots of the German trees. Jews and gays were, further, associated with the city (a modern rootless and mobile space as we have seen in the work of Simmel and the Chicago School). The city, like the desert, is in Nazi mythology a space without soil, where it is impossible to develop roots. Gypsies were seen as the ultimate rootless groups in Nazi Germany, and met the same fate as the Jewish and gay people in the gas chambers.

David Sibley has described some of the reactions to Gypsies in the United Kingdom. Gypsies and other travelers have suffered hostility since medieval times when they were seen as worrisome "people without place" who had the potential to upset the place-bound order of feudalism. More recently, however, local planners have sought to make what appears to house-dwelling society as a chaotic and disordered life, legible. Gypsies, when left to their own devices, tend to camp in a circular pattern with a shared public space in the middle of their vehicles. Planners, when providing sites for the Gypsies, would completely ignore this and, in a by now familiar style, plan camps that resembled housing estates with gridlike, geometrical arrangements of plots with fenced off separate working areas and a "hygiene block."[57]

In the widely diverse contexts of colonial Libya under Italian rule, Depression era California, and postwar Britain we see strikingly similar reactions to mobile people. Their mobility is seen as a threat, and the thinking that goes into planning for them emphasizes legibility and order. The material sites provided for them are virtually interchangeable—plans of order, hygiene, and sedentary values.

## A Nomadic Metaphysics

We have seen how the moral valuation of place and roots at the expense of mobility has been a powerful ideological commitment in the modern world, which has framed the way human life, in particular instances, has been understood and managed. This sedentarist metaphysics has informed particularly powerful ways of thinking about mobile people in the twentieth century. But mobility has not always been coded as negative and threatening. There is a long-standing history of positive valuation of mobility as progress, as freedom, and as change, which runs alongside a sedentarist metaphysics. Recently, ways of thinking that emphasize mobility and flow over stasis and attachment have come to the fore. As the world has appeared to become more mobile, so thinking about the world has become *nomad thought*. In the remainder of this chapter, I explore the development of this nomad thought both in social and cultural theory and in the world of architecture. As with the first half of the chapter, the point of the exercise is not to simply review a now burgeoning literature, but to explore the role that mobility plays as a foundation for this seemingly antifoundational metaphysics.

## The Rise of Nomad Thought

It is instructive to look at some of the intellectual arenas of the contemporary social sciences to illustrate how a serious consideration of mobility is reconfiguring an array of disciplines. Sociologists have been confronted with the need to reconstruct their traditional object of study—society. An increasingly mobile world means that sociologists can no longer talk, with any degree of safety, about discrete objects called societies. Instead, sociology has been asked to shift its attention to the study of mobilities across scales and throughout the world. A sociology that focuses upon "movement, mobility, and contingent ordering, rather than upon stasis, structure and social order" involves looking at the "corporeal, imagined and virtual mobilities of people,"[58] the interactions between people and objects, the constitution of social identities through travel rather than embeddedness in societies, and the increasing importance of trans-national, global, forms of governance. In short, pretty much everything that has been at the heart of the history of sociology has changed or been made irrelevant due to an observable change in the world itself toward increasing levels of mobility.

James Clifford, Marc Augé, and others have long been calling for a similar transformation in anthropology.[59] While sociologists looks to mobility to pull apart the familiar category of society, anthropologists use the term *travel* to ask similar questions of the anthropologist's interest in *cultures* and *identities*. Culture simply carries too much of its origins in agriculture with it—particularly the idea of rootedness.

> If we rethink culture . . . in terms of travel then the organic, naturalizing bias of the term culture—seen as a rooted body that

grows, lives, dies, etc.—is questioned. Constructed and disputed historicities, sites of displacement, interference, and interaction, come more sharply into view.[60]

To think of anthropology as about travel and translation changes the focus of the discipline from the study of bounded and rooted cultures (like sociology's fixed and bounded societies) to the study of routes—the way in which identities are produced and performed through mobility or, more precisely, travel. As this travel increases, so cultures can no longer be said to be located. While place has traditionally been thought of as a fantasy of a "society anchored since time immemorial in the permanence of an intact soil"[61] such places are receding in importance and being replaced by "non-places"—sites marked by the "fleeting, the temporary and ephemeral."[62] Non-places include motorways, airports, supermarkets—sites where particular histories and traditions are not (allegedly) relevant—unrooted places marked by mobility and travel. Non-place is essentially the space of travelers. The work of anthropologists, such as Clifford and Augé, force theorists of culture to reconsider the theory and method of their disciplines. While conventionally figured places and the notion of roots demand thoughts that reflect assumed boundaries and traditions, non-places and routes demand new, mobile ways of thinking.

Cultural and literary studies have also seen a turn toward a fuller grasp of mobile worlds. Mobility and migration are seen as the markers of our time. The lived experience of exiles, migrants, and refugees is tied to the need to think nomadically. Mobile lives need nomad thought to make a new kind of sense. Often this mobility is portrayed as transgressive. Consider, for instance, the words of Edward Said:

> For surely it is one of the unhappiest characteristics of the age to have produced more refugees, migrants, displaced persons, and exiles than ever before in history, most of them as an accompaniment to and, ironically enough, as afterthoughts of great post-colonial and imperial conflicts. As the struggle for independence produced new states and new boundaries, it also produced homeless wanderers, nomads, vagrants, unassimilated to the emerging structures of institutional power, rejected by the established order for their intransigence and obdurate rebelliousness.[63]

In addition to mass migrations of mobile people (either forced or voluntary), the postmodern world includes the experiences of communication and transportation on a scale and speed hitherto unknown—the phenomenon David Harvey calls "time-space compression."[64] In this new world, a place such as the airport lounge, once seen as a reprehensible site of placelessness, becomes a contemporary symbol of flow, dynamism, and mobility. Cultural theorist Iain Chambers delights in a postmodern world that finds its ultimate expression in the international airport:

> With its shopping malls, restaurants, banks, post-offices, phones, bars, video games, television chairs and security guards, it is a miniaturised city. As a simulated metropolis it is inhabited by a community of modern nomads: a collective metaphor of cosmopolitan existence where the pleasure of travel is not only to arrive, but also not to be in any particular place.[65]

Cultural theory, to take the age we live in seriously, has to grapple with the issue of mobility. It simply doesn't make sense to think of culture as mappable in a straightforward, static way. People are no longer simply from "here" or from "there." Again, as Said has put it:

> No one today is purely one thing. Labels like Indian, or woman, or Muslim, or American are no more than starting points, which if followed into actual experience for only a moment are quickly left behind . . . No one can deny the persisting continuities of long traditions, sustained habitations, national languages, and cultural geographies, but there seems no reason except fear and prejudice to keep insisting on their separation and distinctiveness . . .[66]

Not only does the world appear to be more mobile, but our ways of knowing the world have also become more fluid. This "weak thought" or "nomad thought" is more willing to transgress the boundaries of academic disciplines, the boundaries that separate high and popular culture, and the boundaries that separate academia from the everyday world outside the ivory tower. These new kinds of thinking are symptomatic of postmodernity. In addition to (and complicit with) the willing embrace of metaphors of mobility such as the nomad and the rhizome in the analysis of society and culture, is the whole range of ways of knowing that fall under the description of antifoundational, or "weak" thought. "Social and cultural sense, then, becomes not a goal but a discourse, not a closure but a trace in an endless passage that can only aspire to temporary arrest, to a self-conscious drawing of a limit across the diverse possibilities of the world."[67]

As with sociology, anthropology, and cultural studies, geography has started to take a keen interest in the way mobility has changed both the world and our ways of knowing it. This is not entirely new. Geographers have looked at place, for instance, not as an arena of static rootedness but as an achievement of dwelling, constructed through the intricate, repeated, habitual movements of people performing "place-ballets"—the collective effect of individual bodies moving through space.[68] Similar arguments have been at the heart of structuration theory and time-geography.[69] Most fundamental, perhaps, has been the willing embrace of metaphors of mobility generated within poststructural and nonrepresentational philosophies ranging from Maurice Merleau-Ponty's phenomenology of bodily perception to Deleuze and Guatarri's rhizomatics and nomadology.[70] Mobility has become the ironic foundation for anti-essentialism, antifoundationalism and antirepresentationalism. While place, territory, and landscape all implied at least a degree of permanence and flexibility, mobility seems to offer the potential of a radical break from a sedentarist metaphysics.

A central theme of the emerging nomadic metaphysics is the equation that links mobility to forms of subaltern power. Some of the key theoretical figures in contemporary poststructuralism (broadly conceived) have posited mobility as central to the practices of transgression and resistance. These include de Certeau's celebration of the walker in the city, Said's focus on the migrant and exile, the nomad of Deleuze and Guatarri and Braidotti, the carnivalesque folk culture of Bakhtin, and Bauman's vagrant.[71] Alongside the celebration of these nomad figures there has been a focus on spaces of mobility ranging from the hybrid borderlands, to the global city, to the airport lounge.[72]

Nigel Thrift has developed the most compelling call for a mobile ontology and epistemology in geography over time. He labels a particularly (post) modern structure of feeling *mobility*.[73] Mobility, to Thrift, is a structure of feeling that emerged with modernity and has attained new characteristics as we approached the twenty-first century. The focus of his argument is on developing technologies and "machine complexes" starting with the stage coach and ending (provisionally) with the Internet. By the end of the twentieth century, developments in speed, light, and power had reached such a point that they had combined and fused with people to produce a kind of cyborg, which changed everything. Toward the end of his essay he lays out some of the consequences of this structure of feeling for human geography, one of which concerns place.

What is place in this "in-between" world? The short answer is—compromised: permanently in a state of enunciation, between addresses, always deferred. Place are "stages of intensity". Traces of movement, speed and circulation. One might read this depiction of "almost places" . . . in Baudrillardean terms as a world of third-order simulacra, where encroaching pseudo-places have finally advanced to eliminate places altogether. Or one might record places, Virilio-like, as strategic installations, fixed addresses that capture traffic. Or, finally, one might read them, . . . as frames for varying practices of space, time and speed.[74]

Gone are the implicit moral judgments of inauthenticity and lack of commitment. A sedentarist metaphysics is no longer in action. At worst this reading of mobility and place is neutral, and at best it is a positive celebration of mobile worlds. Thrift does not equate mobility to subaltern worlds of resistance. Rather he sees mobility as a mark of all of life in an increasingly speeded up world. The study of the modern world is a study of velocities and vectors. Rather than comparing mobility to place, mobilities are placed in relation to each other.

## Mobility as Becoming

Within nomadic metaphysics, mobility is linked to a world of practice, of anti-essentialism, anti-foundationalism, and resistance to established forms of ordering and discipline. Often mobility is said to be nonrepresentational or even against representation. Linking all of these, perhaps, is the idea that by focusing on mobility, flux, flow, and dynamism we can emphasize the importance of *becoming* at the expense of the already achieved—the stable and static. These links are clear in the work of a number of theorists who have all, in one way or another, placed mobility, or figures of mobility, at the heart of their intellectual and political agendas. Let us consider Michel de Certeau, Mikhail Bakhtin, and Gilles Deleuze and Felix Guattari in turn.

Michel de Certeau, in *The Practice of Everyday Life*, enjoys the nomad metaphor. For him, power is about territory and boundaries—asserting what he calls a "proper place." The weapons of the strong are *strategies*—classification, mapping, delineation, division. The strong depend on the certainty of mapping. The weak, on the other hand, are left with furtive movement to contest the territorialization of urban space. The cunning of the nomad allows pedestrians to take short cuts, to tell stories through the routes they choose. These *tactics* refuse the neat divisions and classification of the powerful and, in doing so, critique the spatialization of domination. Thus, the ordinary activities of everyday life, such as walking in the city, become acts of heroic everyday resistance. The nomad is the hero(ine).

Tactics do not "obey the laws of the place, for they are not defined or identified by it."[75] The tactic never creates or relies upon the existence of some place for its identity and power. The tactic is consigned to using the space of the powerful in cunning ways. The tactics of the weak are a form of consumption—never producing "proper places" but always using and manipulating places produced by others. The world of production is thus confronted with "an entirely different kind of production, called 'consumption,'" which is marked by "ruses," "fragmentation," "poaching," and its "quasi-invisibility"—"it shows itself not in its own products . . . but in the art of using those imposed upon it."[76] Thus the tactic is the ruse off the weak—the mobile drifting through the rationalized spaces of power. The tactic is a nomadic art—an art that will "circulate, come and go, overflow and drift over an imposed terrain like the snowy waves of the sea slipping in among the rocks and defiles of an established order."[77] De Certeau's hero(ine)s are essentially urban beings. The furtive figure of the nomad takes his/her place on the streets of the city and is the direct descendant of the modern *flâneur*.

De Certeau's mobilization of forms of mobility as against the power that comes with fixity is symptomatic of a wider move to invest mobility with subversive meanings. Consider Mikhail Bakhtin in *Rabelais and His World*. Here Bakhtin famously produced a heavily coded critique of Stalinism through a detailed interpretation of the literature of Rabelais. He describes how a carefully ordered "official" culture with its regularly scheduled rituals and feasts is opposed by the world of the marketplace, the fair, and the carnival. While official culture is symbolized by the monument, the seriousness of lent, and the classical body (smooth, finished, perfect). The culture of carnival has no monuments, it is temporary and frivolous and is symbolized by the grotesque body (fat, incomplete, in process).[78] Mobility is not an explicit concern of Bakhtin, but it plays an important implicit role. Official culture is monumental, "the truth already established," complete and eternal, while the carnivalesque is momentary, fluid, and incomplete. While the classical body is smooth and orifice free (think of a classical marble statue), the grotesque body is marked by fluid connections with the world (defecation, sex, urination, digestion, etc.). The fluidity of the grotesque body is matched by carnival and marketplace culture that is also in constant motion. "No dogma, no authoritarianism, no narrow-minded seriousness can coexist with Rabelaisian images: these images are opposed to all that is finished and polished, to all pomposity, to every ready-made outlook."[79] While the official feast "was the triumph of truth already established, the predominant truth that was put forward as eternal and indisputable"[80]—the carnivalesque—was "opposed to all that was ready-made and completed, to all pretence at immutability, [it] sought a dynamic expression; it demanded ever-changing, playful, undefined forms."[81] So while the official is rooted in the eternal and the fixed, the carnivalesque is dynamic and ever-changing. This closely mirrors de Certeau's notions of strategy (as bounded, as fixed, as proper) and tactic (as fleeting, as mobile, as everyday). There has been a tendency in geography and beyond to think about carnival in a fairly limited sense with all the temporal and spatial limits that a once yearly event implies, but

Bakhtin's notion of the carnivalesque exceeds the moment of carnival and can be found in the everyday lives of people throughout the year.[82]

It is in the complicated theorizations of Deleuze and Guattari that the nomad becomes the central figure of contemporary social theory.[83] They distinguish between the machinations of the state (royal science), which are ordered and hierarchical, and the inventions of the "war machine" (nomad science/art). While nomads are the conveyors of "vague essences" (here vague is connected to vagabond), they illustrate these distinctions with reference to journeymen (*compagnonnages*)—nomadic laborers involved in building Gothic cathedrals. Deleuze and Guattari write of the traveling laborers, building cathedrals across Europe "scattering construction sites across the land, drawing on an active and passive power (*puissance—* mobility and the strike) that was far from convenient for the State."[84] The state, in response, managed the construction of cathedrals, created divisions of labor such as mental and manual, theoretical and practical, and proceeded to govern the nomads.

> We know about the problems States have always had with jour-
> neymen's associations, or *compagnonnages*, the nomadic or itiner-
> ant bodies of the type formed by masons, carpenters, smiths etc.
> Settling, sedentarizing labor-power, regulating the movement of
> the flow of labour, assigning it channels and conduits, forming
> corporations in the sense of organisms, and, for the rest, relying
> on forced manpower recruited on the spot (corvee) or among
> indigents (charity workshops)—this has always been one of the
> principal affairs of the State, which undertook to conquer both a
> *band vagabondage* and a *body nomadism*.[85]

To Deleuze and Guattari the nomad is constituted by lines of flight rather than by points or nodes. While the migrant goes from place to place, moving with a resting place in mind, the nomad uses points and locations to define paths. While sedentary people use roads to "parcel out a closed space to people,"[86] nomadic trajectories "distribute people in open space."[87] The nomad is never reterritorialized, unlike the migrant who slips back into the ordered space of arrival. The metaphorical space of the nomad is the desert—a desert imagined as flat, smooth, and curiously isotropic. The nomad shifts across this tactile space making the most of circumstance.

The state, on the other hand, is the metaphorical enemy of the nomad, attempting to take the tactile space and enclose and bound it. It is not that the state opposes mobility, but that it wishes to control flows—to make them run through conduits. It wants to create fixed and well-directed paths for movement to flow through. Deleuze and Guattari use the nomad as a metaphor for the undisciplined—rioting, revolution, guerrilla war-fare—for all the forces that resist the fortress of state discipline. "Nomad life is an experiment in creativity and becoming, and is anti-traditional and anti-conformist in character. The postmodern nomad attempts to free itself of all roots, bonds and identities, and thereby resist the state and all normalizing powers."[88]

As with de Certeau, Deleuze and Guattari also locate their nomads in urban space (recall how Nazi ideology located Jewish people in the desert and the city). Urban space, in their lexicon, is space where "smooth space" and "striated space" play off one another in a constant dialectic tension—"the city is the smooth striated space par excellence: . . . the city is (also) the force of striation that imparts smooth space."[89] Smooth space is the space of the nomad—a horizontal space that resists and threatens the vertical striations of power. This smooth space is "sprawling temporary, shifting shantytowns of nomads and cave dwellers, scrap metal and fabric, patchwork, of which the striations of money, work, or housing are no longer even relevant."[90] The nomad moves over this smooth space while power is realized in the striated spaces of money and influence. Within the city, the two impulses are in a constant tension, with the nomads never being fully incorporated into the striated spaces of power.

Another key metaphor in the work of Deleuze and Guattari is the *rhizome*. They write of the rhizome as a liberating, dynamic entity that provides lines of escape from the confines of territorial power. The nicely ordered garden with everything in its place displeases Deleuze and Guattari; they revel instead in the constant multiplication and unmanageability of the weed/rhizome. While the classic plant (i.e., the tree) is rooted and understandable in terms of its fixity, the rhizome exists on a level plane of multiplication and differentiation. Rhizomes cannot rely on any generative principle for meaning.

> As an underground stem a rhizome is absolutely distinct from roots and radicals. Bulbs and tubers are rhizome. . . . Even some animals are rhizomorphic, when they live in packs like rats. . . . In itself the rhizome has many diverse forms, from its surface extension which ramifies in all directions to its concretions into bulbs and tubers. Or when rats move by sliding over and under one another. There is the best and worst in the rhizome: the potato, the weed, crab-grass.[91]

Just as Deleuze and Guattari took the nomad, a figure filled with threat, and transformed it into a figure of resistance, so they take the humble weed and generate a new way of thinking. Displacement ceases to be a threat and becomes a virtue (or perhaps the threat becomes a virtue).

*Nomadic Architecture*

The metaphysics of nomadism is beginning to appear everywhere. The philosophical and theoretical celebration of mobility appears prominently in contemporary architectural theory practice. Architecture is most often thought of as the creation of spaces, boundaries, senses of attachment, and contextual meaning. In *Learning from Las Vegas*, Robert Venturi and his team broke away from this formulation arguing that the landscape of Las Vegas introduced a new way of organizing space based on the view from the moving car at thirty miles per hour rather than the classical subject walking the streets. The idea of a monument as a big tall space is replaced by the low space with the big sign (the shopping mall). It is an architecture of mobility par excellence. The signs and symbols are enlarged because they need to be intelligible at speed—to the driver rather than the shopper in the medieval bazaar or the citizen in the classical city. The new landscape has a new order and it is the order of motion.[92]

Perhaps the foremost advocate of an architecture of mobility in recent years has been Bernard Tschumi, who professes a different set of priorities. "For me, architecture starts with the concept of mobility. Without mobility there is no architecture. I would go further; it is always said that architecture is static, that it is about substructures, foundations, shelter, safety. . . . Exactly the opposite is true: architecture is always in confrontation with movement, the movement of the bodies that pass through it."[93] Tschumi compares architecture to choreography as 20 to 30 percent of a building is transit space, which to him "generates" a building. Movement is more fundamental than the façade, which usually features as the focal point of buildings. In a humanist gesture he makes a biological claim for the primacy of movement as rooted in the body. An embryo's first perceptions, he tells us, are of movement, of her mother's steps and heartbeat. "Before architecture" he claims, "comes the movements of bodies in space."[94]

So architecture, to Tschumi, is not the imposition of immobile edifices and the development of deep contexts rooted in history, but the production of vectors. His architecture is centered on the provision of conditions for people to move and meet. In the Parc de la Villette in Paris, a park designed with insights from Derrida's deconstruction, Tschumi based his design on a system of points and lines that were supposed to provide a logic of mobility and flow. The park is full of walkways and overhead linear shelters to walk under. The space is not there to tell you what to do, but to provide an opportunity to move and, in doing so, make things happen. Tschumi describes how he used a system of points and lines to form a grid that allowed him to overcome the demands that were placed upon him.

These function in a way that resembles the smooth-space of Deleuze and Guattari's nomads.

> The grid, then, presented the project team with a series of dynamic oppositions. We had to design a park: the grid was antinature. We had to fulfil a number of functions: the grid was antifunctional. We had to be realists: the grid was abstract. We had to respect the local context: the grid was anticontextual. We had to be sensitive to site boundaries: the grid was infinite. We had to take into account political and economic indetermination: the grid was determinate. We had to acknowledge garden precedents: the grid had no origin, it opened onto an endless recession into prior images and signs.[95]

Similarly, in his development of Lerner Hall at Columbia University in New York, Tschumi chose to emphasize mobility as the organizing principle of space. He had to fit his ideas into a previously existing master plan in nineteenth-century neoclassical style. Two ends of his project, therefore, had to be built in brick, but in the space in between he was free to develop his own aesthetic. He connected the two brick wings with a system of ramps along which a program of "events" was organized. The ramps are encased in an envelope of glass so the movement of bodies along the ramps is completely visible from the outside. At the bottom of the auditorium he placed a nightclub and bookstore and the usual student clubs, but once again, it was movement that was central to the way he structured the space.[96]

Tschumi conceives of his architecture of flow as a break from previous architectures of symbolism and context. Contextualist architecture is architecture that is sensitive to inherited morphologies—architecture that develops an already existing sense of *place*. It is all about history and attachment. It is sedentarist in orientation. The architecture of symbolism is an architecture of representation—that is, it is designed to *mean* something. Tschumi's architecture of vectors, on the other hand, emphasized the conditions of possibility for movement, *events*, becoming. In his innovative theoretical project—*The Manhattan Transcripts*—Tschumi emphasizes the importance of moving bodies as the unregulatable subjects of space: "Movement . . . the inevitable intrusion of bodies into the controlled order of architecture." While buildings, at least in their orthodox guise, present a "precisely ordered geometry," moving bodies "carve unexpected spaces through their fluid or erratic motions." Architecture, to Tschumi, is thus "an organism passively engaged in constant intercourse with users, whose bodies rush against the carefully established rules of architectural thought."[97] Rather than using clear plans and the architectural notation of sections and perspectives, Tschumi advocates an architecture that starts from the movements of bodies. To this effect he uses elaborate dance notation as the base pattern from which to construct space. "The logic of movement notation" he writes, "suggests real corridors of space, as if the dancer has been 'carving space out of a pliable substance'; or the reverse, shaping continuous volumes, as if a whole movement has been literally solidified, 'frozen' into a permanent and massive vector."[98] In this way Tschumi makes material a nomadic metaphysics—a way of seeing, knowing, and being that is centered on movement rather than stasis. There is a strong sense of anti-ideology in Tschumi's writings on architecture. The past (the time of context and symbol) is a time of ideology, while the present—at least Tschumi's present—is ideology free. Movement, unlike context, is, not, in Tschumi's work, ideological.

## Positioning Nomad Thought—Lines of Critique

The figure of the nomad has been central to both the metaphysics of sedentarism and, clearly, the nomadic metaphysics we are exploring here. The postmodern nomad, though, is a remarkably unsocial being—unmarked by the traces of class, gender, ethnicity, sexuality, and geography. They are nomads who appear as entries on a census table, or dots on a map—abstract, dehistoricized, and undifferentiated—a mobile mass.

A recent, distinctly postmodern, book on design in New York, subtitled "Nomadic Design," aptly illustrates the vacuous generalizations to which the nomad has been subjected.[99] In the introduction to the pages of glossy photographs, the editors make the argument that New York is a nomadic city where the nomadic world of the horizontal contests the vertical skyscraper world of power and money. They suggest that in New York "everything crosses over." The pictures that make up the majority of the text focus on the design of New York, juxtaposing the work of guerrilla artist, urban graffiti campaigns, and antihomeless activism on the one hand, with the designer spaces of the Investment Banking Partnership, the Cleary, Gottlieb, Steen and Hamilton Law Offices, and the offices of Island Records. All are linked (in the editors' eyes) by their expression of nomadic desire. The book is a beautiful book that makes even homelessness appear to be aesthetically seductive. Yet to place the protests of the homeless next to the lush million dollar interiors of New York's hyperprivileged eradicates the differences between them through a philosophical and aesthetic deceit that singularly fails to point out the other, less pleasing, connections between huge private spaces of the wealthy and the colorful protests of the homeless. Here, as with other mobilizations of the nomad metaphor in recent times, little attention is paid to the historical conditions that produce specific forms of movement, which are radically different.

Janet Wolff has gone some way to contextualizing the moving subjects of postmodern discourse. She describes how these metaphors are gendered in a way that is usually unacknowledged. Her argument is that the actual practices of travel, which serve to exclude women, are reflected in the androcentric tendencies of theoretical mobility.

> [T]he problems with terms like "nomad", "maps" and "travel" is that they are not usually located, and hence (and purposely) they suggest ungrounded and unbounded movement—since the whole point is to resist selves/viewers/subjects. But the consequent suggestion of free and equal mobility is itself a deception, since we don't all have the same access to the road.[100]

The nomad figure is also "raced" in ways that are often elided. As a metaphor, the nomad repeats centuries of Western romanticization of the non-Western other. It simultaneously reproduces representational strategies of colonialism under the guise of the nonrepresentational. This strategy "allows the critic to stand outside the suspect domains of manipulation and representation; it confers a kind of immunity . . ."[101] Further, it allows Deleuze and Guattari to duck the "ethical burden of representing real, actual nomads who might eventually have something to say in response."[102] Nomads, as such, do not have a voice in the text nor do non-Western anthropologists. The view they construct is entirely Eurocentric, based on extremely dubious colonial accounts of nomads in Africa and elsewhere.

> If Deleuze and Guattari's nomad thought is in fact "arborescent," if it is rooted in and following the practices of, for example, a violently representational, colonial ethnography, while at the same time claiming to be anticolonial, antianthropological, and nonrepresentational, then it might have to be considered one of those "pseudomultiplicities" that the authors abhor.[103]

Insofar as nomadology looks to the representations of colonial anthropology for its conception of the nomad, it is a thoroughly Orientalist discourse investing the non-Western and, in this case, nonsedentary population with desire and romance. So, in addition to the critique that nomadic metaphysics is overly abstract and universalizing in its allocation of meaning to mobility, its advocates often overlook the colonial power relations that produced such images in the first place. Indeed, the use of the nomad is often nothing more than a form of imaginative neocolonialism.[104]

## Conclusions: Mobility Against Place

The purpose of this chapter has been to delineate two pervasive ways of thinking about mobility and place. The metaphysics of sedentarism and nomadism inform thought, practice, and material culture. They have political and ideological implications for the way mobility is encountered and experienced in the world. Indeed, these ways of thinking and acting run through the accounts of mobility in the chapters that follow. They are, if you like, the metanarratives of mobility that inform more specific, more local, more contextual attitudes to mobility in a range of arenas from photography to architecture, law to transportation planning.

It is a central claim of this book that neither of these approaches is particularly aware of the ideological nature of the meanings they ascribe to mobility. Politics, power, and ideology are not parts of their lexicon. They take it for granted that mobility has meanings, but are unaware of their own role in ascribing these meanings. The metaphysics of sedentarism is a way of thinking and acting that sees mobility as suspicious, as threatening, and as a problem. The mobility of others is captured, ordered, and emplaced in order to make it legible in a modern society. Mobility is experienced as *anachorism*—the spatial equivalent to *anachronism*. While anachronism is a logical category (a thing out of time), anachorism is a social and cultural category—a thing out of place or without place entirely.[105] Insofar as place is a morally resonant thing-in-the-world, mobility as anachorism is a threat to a moral world. Thus the nomads of Eliot, Hoggart, and Williams are deeply suspect—to be resisted in favor of stability and roots. The metaphysics of nomadism, on the other hand, has little time for traditional kinds of "placey place." The world is seen through the lens of mobility, flow, becoming, and change. Mobility in Deleuze and Guattari, Michel de Certeau, or in the work of Bernard Tschumi is, on the whole, positive. Place is seen as redundant, quaint, in the past—no more (or less) than the logical outcome of unique combinations of flow and velocity. While a sedentarist would see a building, for instance, as a complete whole, an edifice, a relative permanence in space and time, a nomadologist would see the building differently, perhaps as J. D. Dewsbury sees it. "[T]he building you walk through/within—what is the speed of flux that is keeping it assembled? It seems permanent . . . but it is ephemeral nonetheless: whilst you are there, it is falling down, it is just happening very slowly (hopefully)."[106] When seen through the lens of a nomadic metaphysics, everything is in motion, and stability is illusory. But just as the sedentarist point of view has a hidden politics so to does the nomadic. As the critiques of Deleuze and Guattari have shown, mobility is differentiated socially. The romanticization of the nomad, for instance, is infected with the discourse of Orientalism. It is also the outcome, historically, of deep-rooted ideas about mobility as a progressive force, as a form of relative freedom, as a break from earlier, more confined, spaces and times. In order to be able to mobilize metaphors of mobility, a preexisting set of ideas—ideas rooted in power—need to exist. Some of these ideas are the topic of this book.

## CHAPTER 3

# Capturing Mobility: Mobility and Meaning in the Photography of Eadweard Muybridge and Etienne-Jules Marey

Moving bodies fascinate not only because they (or a particular moment of their present-ness) have vanished the moment we acknowledge having apprehended them . . . The act of perceiving movement enacts its own displacement. In the act of movement, of "putting something in another place," there is the displacement of a body. In the act of interpreting movement, then, there is the displacement of a displacement.

**Heidi Gilpin[1]**

Places, landscapes, territories, and all the objects of material culture have a reassuring solidity about them. However abstract and ethereal our discussions of place (for instance) might become, we can always, in the last instance, return to ground and point to something and say "that is what I am talking about." Mobility, however, has no such presence. It is absent the moment we reflect on it. It has passed us by. It is true that there are places and landscapes of mobility—airports, roads, passages—but this is not the same as mobility itself. Maybe, on the other hand, our ways of knowing are just not mobile enough and we are stuck in a sedentarist metaphysics—a way of knowing that valorizes the apparent certainties of boundedness and rootedness over the slippery invisibility of flux and flow.[2] Liisa Malkki's conception of a sedentarist metaphysics was applied to the way mobile people, particularly refugees, have been categorized as a threat in a world ordered by fixity and place-based identity. Here I am widening this notion to think about fixity and flow on a much smaller scale—the scale of individual bodies. It is my argument that ways of conceiving of mobility itself—not just mobility between nations, regions, and places—are often informed by a desire to fix what is unfixable in order to make it knowable within a clear spatial framework. I also want to argue, however, that it is not just a case of fixity against flow, or place against mobility, but of ordering and taming mobilities by placing one against another—by producing some mobilities that are ideologically sound and others that are suspect. This chapter and the two that follow it focus on mobility at the scale of the body, for it is with the body that mobility starts. It is through the body that mobility is experienced. The body is mobility's first and last instance. This chapter focuses on the representational strategies of photography and physiology in the late nineteenth and early twentieth centuries. Chapter 4 deals with the management of mobility in the workplace and chapter 5 deals with superficially freer realm of the dance floor.

It is remarkable how central to modernity the capture of mobility has been. History is littered with attempts to enact such a capture. The snapshots of the history of abstraction I consider here (and in the next two chapters) chart the tension between the threat of actual lived and embodied motion—always potentially excessive and threatening—and the rationalized and abstracted mobility of philosophers, planners, technocrats, and others who have attempted, through representation, to make mobility functional, ordered, and in the end, knowable. This is the basic conflict that runs through the production of mobilities at the scale of the body—between mobility as a core facet at the heart of modernity, and mobility as a threat to the kind of rationality that modernity signifies.[3] In this chapter I focus on two well-known innovators in the representation of mobility, the photographer Eadweard Muybridge and the physiologist Ettiene-Jules Marey.

## Eadweard Muybridge

In the spring of 1872, a man photographed a horse. With the motion studies that resulted it was as though he was returning bodies themselves to those who craved them—not bodies as they might daily be experienced, bodies as sensations of gravity, fatigue, strength, pleasure, but bodies become weightless images, bodies dissected and reconstructed by light and machine and fantasy.[4]

A key moment in the development of modern understandings of the mobile body was the photography of Eadweard Muybridge in California. The former governor of California, Leland Stanford, hired Muybridge, an English immigrant, to photograph his horses in the spring of 1872. Stanford's aim was to own the finest stable of racehorses in the nation, and to this end he sought to understand horses "scientifically." One of the key questions of the day was whether all four feet of the horse left the ground while the horse was trotting. The answer to this question was not clear until 1876 and 1877 when Muybridge devised a mechanism to capture the movements of Stanford's horse, Occident. Muybridge was experimenting with a number of new technologies, including faster film and faster shutters. Before his famous images of consecutive moments in the motion of Occident, he had taken single images of Occident traveling at 35 feet per second in order to test the ability of the lens, shutter, and film.

To successfully take this photograph, he had to reliably utilize a shutter speed of one-thousandth of a second, a time period in which the horse did not move more than one quarter of an inch. The image was reported in the *Alta* on August 3, 1877:

> Mr. Muybridge sends us a copy of an instantaneous photograph of *'Occident'*, taken when he was trotting at a speed of 35 feet per second, or a mile in 2 minutes and 27 seconds. The negative was exposed to the light less that one-thousandth part of a second, so brief a time that the horse did not move a quarter of an inch. The photographer has made many experiments to secure the highest sensitiveness and the briefest possible exposure, and the result was a novelty in photographic art, and a delineation of speed which the eye cannot catch. . . . The negative was retouched before the photograph was printed; but we are assured the outlines are unchanged.[5]

Clearly it is something of an understatement to say that the picture of Occident had been retouched. Because the photographic image was nothing more than a vague silhouette, Muybridge only had the outline of an image. He had an artist make a picture based on the negative and then photographed the painting. The only thing that was important to Muybridge was the *shape* of the horse in motion. The details were unimportant. It is not surprising, however, that people who saw the image, which circulated in San Francisco in 1877, believed it to be a fraud.

Viewers were unimpressed at the unlikely image they saw before them. They found the picture quite illogical given the conventions of horse portraiture at the time.

To convince a skeptical public, Muybridge needed to present more than one moment in the movement of the trotting horse. Muybridge had developed the film and shutter technology to repeatedly take pictures at one-thousandth of a second and now he needed to take a series of such images in rapid succession. To do this he arranged twelve cameras in a line, each attached to an electric trigger, which was activated by a wire that was tripped by the moving object (horse and cart). Each of his twelve cameras featured a shutter made from two slides with a slit in each of them. The slides were connected to two rubber bands, which on release, moved in opposite directions. The photograph was taken in the brief moment when these slits were both in front of the lens. This elaborate technology was set up in a laboratory in Stanford's stables in Palo Alto. A white wall was built with black vertical lines marked on the wall at intervals of twenty-one inches, each with a consecutive number. This was the backdrop for the moving subject. Opposite the wall the twelve cameras were set up pointing directly at the wall. In the resulting image, the horse would appear as a silhouette against the giant rulerlike backdrop with the numbers indicating the motion (Figure 3.1). This apparatus was successfully used in 1878 and Muybridge quickly became a feature in the local, then national, then international media.

Some still couldn't quite believe what the images showed them. Traditional paintings of horses in motion almost always showed a horse with fore and hind legs symmetrical to each other like those on a rocking horse. These images seemed to have legs all over the place—images that to some where both comic and grotesque—certainly not aesthetically pleasing.

**Figure 3.1** Occident trotting, 1877, Eadweard Muybridge, courtesy of the Library of Congress.

> For the first pictures obtained by Muybridge were not believed.
> That is perhaps one of the most symptomatic features of his exper-
> iment. Even Meissonier, the great equine painter, steeped in the
> codes of representation of academic painting . . . refused for a
> time, we are told, to believe in the authenticity of the documents
> Muybridge had published. . . . Need I add that all those . . . who
> found these pictures unrealistic also found them ugly?[6]

Muybridge's images are remarkable in many ways. Most obviously they
made visible the world of motion. Photography had, for a long time, been a
technology that extracted stillness from the motion of the world or perhaps,
as Rebecca Solnit has remarked, *imposed* stillness on the world.[7] The enemy
of the camera had been the blur of speed. Muybridge's series of images
had begun the process of reanimating the world—of turning objects back
into process. "The subject of the pictures was not the images per se but the
change from one to another, the change that represented time and motion
more vividly, more urgently, than the slow motion of parades passing and
buildings rising. It was a fundamental change in the nature of photography
and of what could be represented."[8]

Rebecca Solnit connects Muybridge's groundbreaking photography to
general transformations in the sense of movement that marked the nineteenth century. When Muybridge was born in September 1830, the first
railroad was still six months away. Mobility was still firmly rooted in the
limits of nature. The speed of a horse, or water in a river, or wind in the
sails marked the limits of mobility. By the time of his death in 1904, large
portions of the world were connected by the iron web of rail, steamships
crossed the Atlantic on regular schedules, and the Wright brothers had successfully flown a powered aircraft just six months earlier. The annihilation
of time and space was a project that had overcome its principle hurdles.

Muybridge's sponsor, Leland Stanford, was also the president of the
Central Pacific Railroad, and thus played his part in the transformation of
senses of mobility. He was one of the four principle backers of the construction of the transcontinental railroad that was completed in 1869. Much of
the money that paid for his horses, and for the labor of Muybridge, came
from the development of the railroad and the transformation in the land
that surrounded it. Jonathan Crary sees a logical connection between the
development of the railroad system and the photography of Muybridge.[9] He
argues that Muybridge gave movement a "new form of legibility and rationality" through the development of innovative representational practices.[10]
Stanford, through his investment in the railroad, was a central figure in the
reduction in time and money of mobility and the "time spent in motion
from one place to another."[11] He was, in other words, deeply implicated

in transformations in the sense of mobility at the end of the nineteenth century—the process of the eradication of space by time.[12] Along with the increased speed in life came new forms of perception—new understandings of the world in terms of speed and motion. The inventions of Muybridge and others, Crary argues, meant that "visuality would coincide with the speeds and temporalities of both circulation and telecommunication."[13]

## The Epistemology of the Grid

A feature of Muybridge's photographs that is often taken for granted is the way the background is divided into equal spaces by the giant ruler he used as a background. In later photographs this became a grid. What we see in these images is the development of a "grid epistemology."[14] Grids were everywhere in America from Jefferson's land survey of 1787 to the arrangement of streets in New York or San Francisco. Grids appeared in the ledgers of accountants and in the tables of sociologists. The grid symbolized rationality and modernity—the ability to quantify and know. As Rebecca Solnit has argued, "The grid gives the work the aesthetic of science—dispassionate, orderly, coherent."[15] As well as playing the role of a modern aesthetic of order, the grid also metaphorically evoked the production of space under capitalism. In urban and rural America the imposition of a grid had made the creation of transferable property easier. Space had been made a standardized commodity abstracted from ecology and topography.[16] Richard Sennett invokes the use of the grid in urban planning as the production of "neutral space" designed to dominate and subdue the population and erase the variability of "place."[17] Just as the imposition of grids on space made the formally anarchic world legible, so the grid that forms the backdrop to Muybridge's horses makes mobility legible. But this legibility was, finally, aesthetic more than it was scientific. As John Pultz put it:

> The grids against which the figures move and the grids into which the individual frames are organized suggest a level of scientific certitude that the photographs do not have, primarily because the relationships of time and space from frame to frame are neither obvious nor specified.[18]

One possible source of Muybridge's grid was the anthropological photography of John Lamprey, who had made anthropometric studies of Malay men in 1869, which were well known at the time. Lamprey had devised a grid made out of silk threads attached to a wooden frame that acted as a measuring device for his subjects. It was through the use of this grid that Lamprey's subjects could be compared as if they were any other objects placed before the world in the interests of science. The Malayan man became a generic type framed by a grid of objectivity and universality. This grid could then be used to compare the Malayan man with other "types." This, as Huxley put it, would enable "the formation of a systematic series of photographs of the various races of men comprehended within the British Empire."[19] It was in this spirit that Lamprey developed his photometric grid system in 1869; the grid quickly became one more technique in the state's arsenal of surveillance and regulation, which increasingly allowed for the management of populations from the nineteenth century onward.[20]

The layout of Muybridge's horse studies in a series of lines and columns effectively dissociate the horse from stable coordinates in time and space. When looking at them together, the viewer is uncoupled from space. As the artist Sol LeWitt suggested in an interview with Lucy Lippard, "When space is divided up into such equal parts, a kind of negation of space takes place. All parts are given equal value and space is so systematized that it becomes least important; in the resulting inertia sequence becomes most important."[21] In one sense space is, as Crary has suggested, deleted. "It announces a vision compatible with the smooth surface of a global marketplace and its new pathways of exchange."[22] Stability becomes process. "[T]he horse, which had been for thousands of years the primary mode of vehicular movement in human societies, is symbolically dismantled into quantified and lifeless units of time and movement."[23] But looked at differently, we can see how space and time are recoded into the horse's movement. The presentation of Muybridge's photographs as a grid also produces a way of reading them as a kind of narrative. The layout proceeds from left to right and from top to bottom mimicking the written page. This leads the Western viewer, at least, to see the images as a short, concise story replicating the passage of time in the layout of space—the space of the page. So while Muybridge effectively removed Occident from "real" space, he inserted him back into a new kind of abstract space—a space of narrative legibility.

## Humans in Motion

In August 1879 Muybridge was visited at the Palo Alto estate by a selection of athletes from the local Olympic Club. This marked the beginning of Muybridge's explorations of human mobility. By then he had doubled the number of cameras in his set to twenty-four and he was taking images from all around the moving subject simultaneously. Later that year he began to take images of himself, naked, involved in a number of forms of motion such as swinging an axe and running. Soon Muybridge had collected hundreds of images of men involved in running, tumbling, fencing, wrestling, and boxing. In some images the figures were naked and in others they wore tight trunks in order, apparently, "to display as completely as possible the movements of muscles."[24] The progression of Muybridge's interests away from animals and toward people marked the beginning of the end for his relationship with Stanford who was, after all, interested in race horses. In 1881 Muybridge left Stanford's employ and embarked on a series of trips to Europe where his images were well known. By 1884 he was based at the University of Pennsylvania campus in Philadelphia. It was there he continued to capture the motion of the human body.

Muybridge's images of human motion are curious to today's viewer. They are marked by a hybrid mixture of medicine, science, and art. Muybridge had been invited to set up his equipment at the university by the artist Thomas Eakins, who had incorporated information from Muybridge's horse images into his own painting.[25] Such was the confusion about the representation of motion at the time, that he had perfectly reproduced the legs of the horse as if taken by a high-speed camera (clear and focused) while, at the same time, blurring the spokes of the wheels on a carriage being pulled by the horse. Eakins was keen to produce art informed by science, and it was for this reason that he invited Muybridge to Philadelphia.

Eakins provided models for Muybridge to photograph, but Muybridge also insisted on finding his own. Of 781 published motion studies from Philadelphia, 562 are of human figures. Many are of people engaged in what Muybridge thought of as everyday activities. Two blacksmiths, for instance, were photographed striking an anvil (Figure 3.2). Muybridge had found real blacksmiths who were willing, perhaps surprisingly given the moral climate of the time, to have their photo taken wearing nothing but a G-string. Muybridge simultaneously expected his models to act naturally and be naked or close to it.[26] As a "pure" artistic photographer he would not have been allowed to strip his subjects of their clothes, but as a "scientist" he was. It is as if the laboratory context, symbolized by the ever-present grid, gave Muybridge special license.

The politics of mobility become clear in the kinds of mobilities he considered to be "natural" for the men and women he photographed. Men are photographed involved in an array of outdoor pursuits. They throw javelins, wrestle each other, box, run, and engage in manual labor. Women, on the other hand, are shown engaging in domestic work: filling jugs, bathing, pouring tea, and dancing. Clearly these are gendered motions, which reflect both Muybridge's expectations of the kinds of motions men and women enact and the wider expectations of the place and time. The simple act of moving is burdened with meaning. As Muybridge put it, his images "embraced a large number of actions incidental to men and women in the course of their every-day life; we followed the farmer to his field and blacksmith to his anvil, the athlete to his recreation ground, and the child too

**Figure 3.2** Eadweard Muybridge, Movements, male, blacksmith, two models, hammering on an anvil, from the Collections of the University of Pennsylvania Archives, plate 374.

its nursery; the lady to her boudoir, and the laundress to her wash-tub."[27] For the most part, the men and women are naked. Occasionally Muybridge photographed women as they undressed. In one disturbing sequence, a naked woman is shown acting surprised, turning away from some invisible threat, and running away covering her face and genitals (Figure 3.3). It is difficult to think of a scientific rationale for such an image, yet the gridded background reminds us that this is a laboratory. The movements form a narrative, and the positions of the woman's body remind us of artistic conventions. In the name of abstraction, Muybridge presents us with mobility as ideology—a set of meanings about mobility that replicate the assumptions of established power about how, why, and where men and women move.

Some of the images have more than one body. Men are typically shown fighting and fencing (Figure 3.4). Women, on the other hand, enact curious interactions that come close to reflecting standard pornographic male fantasies of harems. The ever-present grid in the background only amplifies the women's status as objects. In one photograph a woman kneels and drinks from a water jar offered to her by another woman. In another, one woman disrobes another. Muybridge's notebook title for this image was "Inspecting a Slave." In Figure 3.5, one naked woman pours water over another.

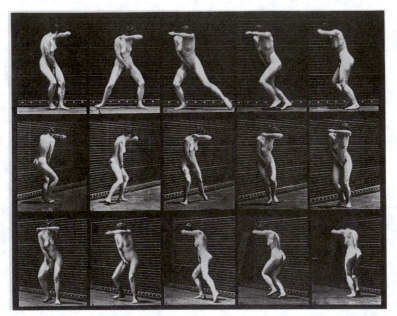

**Figure 3.3** Eadweard Muybridge, Turning around in surprise and running away, courtesy of the Kingston Museum, plate 73.

**Figure 3.4** Eadweard Muybridge, Movements, male, fencing, from the Collections of the University of Pennsylvania Archives, Plate 350.

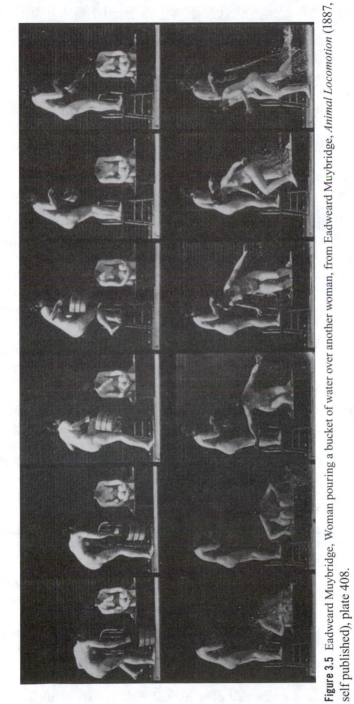

**Figure 3.5** Eadweard Muybridge, Woman pouring a bucket of water over another woman, from Eadweard Muybridge, *Animal Locomotion* (1887, self published), plate 408.

It seems unlikely that these images of naked women have the study of motion as their purpose. Pictures of men involved in boxing or fencing tend to describe them as experts or masters of particular kinds of motion. In this sense their motions can be seen to fit neatly alongside the pictures of animals in *Animal Locomotion*. Just as race horses and pigs could be seen as ideal types of their species, so these expert men, drawn from the college's athletics program, could be seen as pure examples of motion from which could be deduced a universal theorization of movement across species. It is entirely appropriate, therefore, that these pictures appeared in a book about the movement of animals. The women, on the other hand, not only participated in motions that were more likely to be drawn from art and aesthetics, they were never referred to as experts or masters of their motions.

> The female models were chosen from all classes of society. Number 1, is a widow, aged thirty-five, somewhat slender and above medium height; 3, is married, and heavily built; 4 to 13 inclusive, 15 and 19, are unmarried, of ages varying from seventeen to twenty-four; of these, 11 is slender; the others of medium height and build; 14, 16, and 93 are married; 20 is unmarried, and weighs three hundred and forty pounds. . . .
>
> The endeavor has been in all instances to select models who fairly illustrate how—in a more or less graceful or perfect manner—the movements appertaining to every-day life are performed.[28]

Here the women are described in terms of their marital status (never mentioned in the pictures of men), their build, and their level of gracefulness. They do not appear to be the masters of their own motion in the way the men are. They are instead merely representative of quotidian mobility. This seems all the more remarkable when we consider the kinds of motions the women (usually models and art students rather than athletes) are asked to perform. In her account of "Throwing Like a Girl," Iris Marion Young noted how female bodily mobility is produced in different ways from that of men. While men move in a way that involves the whole body and is open to the world, women use only parts of the body and are constantly protective of the body. So while girls throw with their arm only, boys are encouraged to put their whole body into it. While girls carry books protectively against their chests, boys carry books swinging by their side. These differences, she argues, are not simply natural, but a product of mobilities being conditioned over time. While the bodily mobility of boys and men is supposed to be transcendent, girls and women remain trapped in immanence. The act of orienting the body to its surroundings—of moving—reveals something other than a universal act of transcendence. Female bodily mobility, she argues, is inhibited and thus the mobile feminine body is less a body-subject (a term borrowed from Maurice Merleau-Ponty) and more an "object-subject."[29] Muybridge's photographs suggest this status of women as object-subjects—as married, slender, or medium height, rather than as experts or masters of their mobility.

*Pathological Mobilities*

Muybridge, as we have seen, was keen to represent what he considered to be the everyday and common. His situation at Pennsylvania, however, also allowed him to photograph the rare and unusual. Muybridge's laboratory was situated adjacent to the hospital, and some of the medical staff believed that the university could make better use of Muybridge's expertise. They believed he should photograph the diseased and pathological in order that students would be able to study mobilities that were symptoms when real live subjects were not available.

Dr. Francis X. Dercum convinced the medical authorities to allow him to take selected patients down to Muybridge's laboratory where Muybridge photographed their movements from three angles with thirty-six cameras. In one case Dercum artificially induced convulsions through hypnosis in an otherwise healthy model.

> The result is that the subjects (in this case, the patients) rather than their movement became the object of the viewer's fascination: the photographs make no attempt to hide the patient's identities, and the faces of these naked, deformed beings expressively inform their plight.[30]

Once again the gridded background signifies the status of science for the images. But here, even more than in other images, the grid brings to mind the anthropometric images of Lamprey and others. While the athletes and others who featured in the bulk of Muybridge's photographs of human motion could be anyone—indeed they were supposed to represent the everyday and commonplace—the diseased and disabled subjects of his "pathological" images are clearly coded, like Lamprey's Malayan male, as *other*. The images, like those of Lamprey, become "overt expressions of the positivist concentration of the "mathematization of empirics", and the related notion that images, like graphs, could work without text and become controlled lexical space."[31]

Most of these images are of people in the act of walking. They suffer from maladies ranging from curvature of the spine to missing limbs. As with the other images, the subjects are frequently naked. The medics hoped that Muybridge's series of images could be reanimated in a zoopraxiscope, a device Muybridge invented to show his images in rapid sequence in order to reanimate the moving subject. Students could then observe the various "pathological" mobilities. The images stand in sharp contrast to the classical perfection of his various athletes and everyday people engaged in classical and even artistic mobility. In one of his studies for the hospital, Muybridge photographed a nude 340-pound woman getting up slowly from the ground.[32] Alongside muscular men throwing javelins and naked women carrying classical vases on their heads, this must have seemed particularly strange.

The doctors who worked with Dercum were particularly fascinated by the popular work of George Beard and his book *American Nervousness*.[33] Beard had developed the diagnosis of *neurasthenia*—a condition he blamed on, among other things, the increased mobility of daily life that came with modernity. American citizens, he argued, were threatened with nervous collapse by the demands of travel (the railroad), punctuality and communication (the telegraph), and speeded-up nature of modern life. The railroad was a particular source of anxiety—for Beard at least. "Whether railway travelling is directly the cause of nervous disease is a question of not a little interest," Beard wrote, "[r]easoning deductively, without any special facts, it would seem that the molecular disturbance caused by travelling long distances, or living on trains as an employé, would have an unfavourable influence on the nervous system."[34] Mobility was once again at the center of attention, and once again the history of the railroad intersects with Muybridge's attempts to capture mobility. Dercum was a colleague of Silas Weir Mitchell, who was one off the foremost specialists in the diagnosis and treatment of neurasthenia. He prescribed rest cures for sufferers. Men and women were treated differently, however. Men were sent into the rural outdoors to pursue exercise and athletic pursuits. Women were sent to bed and confined to the home. In order to escape the bustle of the speeded up world, one half of patients were sent outdoors and the other half were sent indoors. It is curious how closely these treatments reflect Muybridge's images of men and women in motion. Indeed, it has been suggested that Muybridge's Philadelphia images are illustrating treatments for neurasthenia.[35]

Muybridge's images of mobility represent an important moment in the history of mobilities and modernity. His work marked a key innovation in the development of representational strategies to capture movement in a world that hummed with mobility and the anxieties that surrounded it. He connects the development of the transcontinental railroad to the anxieties about neurasthenia produced by it. In these images, art is combined with science with often bizarre and sometimes disturbing consequences. The ever-present grid marks the attempt at abstraction and objectivity, while the movements themselves suggest a mixture of artistic convention, private fantasy, and cultural expectations. Muybridge's pictures are marked by a tension between motion as abstract and mobility as culturally overdetermined.

The images are aesthetically uncanny because they broke the relationship between immobile representations and the mobile world people had come to expect. Photography had relied on its ability to capture the world "as it is," and here most of the world is excluded. Because of the effects of blurring, photographers had gone to great lengths to avoid any suggestion of movement in their images. Indeed, a painter could better represent motion than a photographer could. Muybridge had taken motion as the object of his study and excluded everything else. The beauty of place and landscape had been replaced by a new kind of beauty—the beauty of figures in motion against a gridded wall—the beauty of abstraction. Human eyes could not catch the intricacies of movement. They could not tell whether all four of a horse's feet left the ground when trotting, but Muybridge and his cameras could. Photography was no longer about capturing the visible but extending vision into new realms—making the invisible world of motion tangible. This revolution in the history of mobility was not all the responsibility of Muybridge, however. Even more remarkable was the work of Etienne-Jules Marey in France.

## Etienne-Jules Marey and the Moving Body

All movement is the product of two factors: time and space; to know the movement of a body is to know the series of positions which it occupies in space during a series of successive instants.

**Etienne-Jules Marey**[36]

The understanding of a movement implies a double knowledge, namely, that of space as well as that of time.

**Etienne-Jules Marey**[37]

While it is clear that Muybridge was fixated on capturing movement in photography, he had little to say about the nature of movement and mobility itself. His counterpart in France was the physiologist Etienne-Jules Marey. In contrast to Muybridge Marey wrote about the nature of movement endlessly. Movement, to Marey, was a physiological and philosophical conundrum of the highest order. Marey wanted to use the laws of thermodynamics to look at the physiology of the human body.[38]

By the middle of the nineteenth century the world was a very mobile place. This was not simply because more people were moving and new forms of transport were being rapidly developed (thanks in part to Leland Stanford), but because the world of ideas had radically destabilized the taken-for-granted boundedness of existence. Industrialists, keen to increase the output of the new machines of mass production, invested a great deal in studies of energy and motion. The more efficient a machine was, the more it could produce and the more profit could be made. To be efficient meant to maximize productivity with minimal use of energy. The goal of the industrialists was to make a *perpetual motion machine*. Such a machine would convert heat into work with full efficiency. If such a machine could be developed, it could effectively run off its own heat and engage in a perpetual cycle of heat being converted into work, which would in turn produce heat and so on. No one managed to produce such a machine, but they did come up with theories to prove its impossibility. The first law of thermodynamics states that energy can neither be created nor destroyed. The sum of mass and energy in the universe is therefore constant. In itself, this does not negate the possibility of perpetual motion, but the second law of thermodynamics does. Physicists attempting to enact a perfect conversion of heat into energy discovered that some quantity of heat always escapes into the surrounding environment and thus there is always some form of waste. This loss was equated with "disorder" in the system in question. This disorder was called *entropy*. The second law states that in all energy exchanges, if no energy enters or leaves the system, the potential energy of the state will always be less than that of the initial state. Put in simple terms, a car that has run out of petrol will not run again until more petrol (potential energy) is put in the tank.

Although these laws were born out of the limited concerns of industrial capital with machines, they quickly undergirded all kinds of endeavor. Kinematics (the science of motion) was born and scientists busied themselves studying motion and the traces of motion in objects. The whole universe, from the smallest atom to the celestial bodies, were now seen in terms of dynamism and change—a huge machine of energy and motion and transformations among them. Existence went mobile. This new interest in motion and energy led some to focus on the body as a machine in order to make it more productive—to reduce the amount of entropy in the human machine. Among those who were fascinated with human motion was Etienne-Jules Marey. The laws of thermodynamics had fed a long-standing suspicion that the body could be understood as a locus of dynamic energy subject to positivist laws.

To begin with, Marey was mostly concerned with the mobility of the body's interior. He wanted to develop a way of representing accurately the movements of the body in a graphic form. To him the body was an animate machine, like any other machine, subject to the laws of theoretical mechanics. Behind Marey's many inventions lay the full force of logical positivism.[39] If something can be made visible, it can be measured and then it can be known and laws developed. Invisible motion, once represented visually, could be codified in this way. Marey's first invention was a graph-making instrument that translated the rhythm of the pulse into a line on a smoke-blackened cylinder. This device and the graphs it produced translated movement into a new form of representation based on time and space by breaking up movement in order to analyze it. This new language of mobility became the basis of modern cardiography. Marey was able, for the first time, to represent movements from the inside of the human body, beyond the reach of the human senses, in a continuous form. The graph of the human heartbeat was a form of writing that made movement intelligible in new ways (Figure 3.6).

Time and space were joined so that a record of the human heart was not a moment in time, but an event recorded continuously by a line on a graph. This sphygmograph (1859) was quickly taken up by the French medical establishment and the royalties from it allowed Marey to set up his own private laboratory in Paris. It did not take long for Marey to become recognized not just for his new way of seeing the rhythms of the body, but also for his thesis on the elasticity of arteries. In 1868 he was made professor of the Natural History of Organised Bodies, and by 1882 he had been provided with extensive facilities for his work at the Station Physiologique in the Bois de Boulogne. Meanwhile, the discipline of French physiology had undergone an astonishing change of fortune. It was not until 1821 that physiology had its own journal and was still considered a part of anatomy

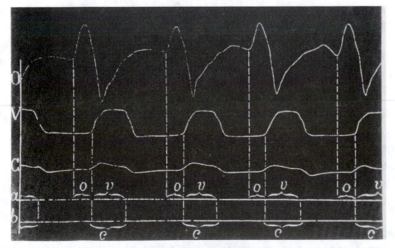

**Figure 3.6** Third cardiogram published by Marey and Chauveau in 1863. *Bulletin de l'Académie de Médecine*, 26.

until 1823. The invention of the laboratory as a scientific space played a key role in the rise of physiology. This place of vivisection and chemical and biological experimentation proliferated in France more than anywhere else, and new kinds of knowledge followed. By the middle of the century, physiology was a very important discipline in the grip of fierce debates between those who saw the body as subject to the same laws as anything else (particularly the laws of thermodynamics) and those who believed that life provided its one unique kind of vital energy. Marey was particularly anxious to overcome the inert nature of the study of physiology. Marey believed that the essence of the "animate machine" was movement, and that any form of studying such machines that did not take movement into account was misguided. What physiology needed was a graphic representation of the dynamism of the body. Physiology without graphic instruments, he said, was like "geography without maps."[40] Movement, to Marey, was far more than an interesting challenge to representation—it was the essence of existence.

In his book *Movement* (1895), Marey traces the evolution of graphic methods for tracing movement. This begins with the simple plotting of a body at a steady speed on a graph with two axes—one for time passed and one for distance traveled. He shows how such a method had been used in the nineteenth century to produce train timetables by the French engineer Ibry (Figure 3.7). In this way, train companies could chart all the movements of trains along one track in both directions in order to work out, at any point in time, where any train would be. Along the y axis would be printed the names of the stations along the track, and these would be separated by intervals proportional to the number of kilometers of track between them. The x axis is divided into hours and subdivided into ten-minute intervals. The speed of the train is thus represented by the angle of the line, with stationary trains represented by horizontal lines (taking up time but not distance). The direction of the sloping line indicated the direction in which the train was traveling.

Ibry's diagram only recorded the theoretical movement of trains. The next question for Marey was how a moving body could record its own movement. He describes the apparatus developed by the French mathematicians Morin and Poncelet in their work on improving the efficiency of waterwheels. To register the movement of a falling body, the object is attached to a needle that leaves a mark on paper attached to a revolving drum that moves at a uniform rate. The result is a parabolic curve—the graphic representation of a falling object. The problem with this device is that the movement it records is to actual scale, and it is thus useless for anything too small or too big (such as the movement of a train from

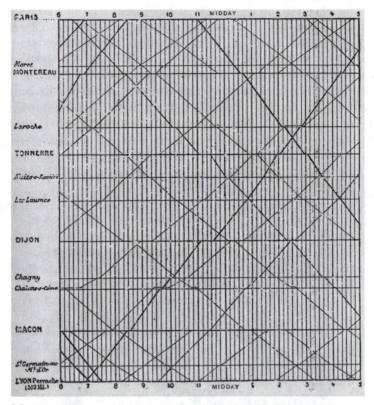

**Figure 3.7** Ibry's diagram plotting trains and their velocities (Etienne-Jules Marey and Eric Pritchard, *Movement* (New York: D. Appleton and Company, 1895), 26.

Lyon to Paris or a feeble human pulse). Marey's own invention—the sphygmograph—captured the movements of the human pulse through the use of levers with needles attached. Larger-scale movements could be correspondingly shrunk by a mechanical arrangement of wheels, as in the odograph (the direct ancestor of the odometer).

The next step in Marey's discussion of the representation of movement was to record movement without borrowing (as it were) the kinetic energy of the thing being recorded. The answer was photography:

> We saw in Chapter II that photography could reproduce the trajectory of a body moving in space; but the idea there conveyed of the successive changes in position was not sufficient to define the movement. The power to do so presupposes a knowledge of the relationship existing at any moment between the distance traversed and the time occupied. . . . if the two notions of time and space can be combined in photographic images, we have instituted

a chronophotographic method, which explains all the factors in a movement which we want to understand.[41]

To demonstrate, Marey described an image of a falling ball against a black screen, taken using one of his adapted cameras (Figure 3.8). The image reveals a series of pictures of the ball showing the position it occupies with each different exposure. "In this way" he wrote, "all the necessary elements are obtained for determining "the laws of motion."[42] This image can be analyzed by letting the distances between the images stand for time. It is thus possible to construct a time-curve of the distance covered by the ball on a standard graph. Velocity and acceleration can also be deduced. As Marey notes triumphantly, "Such chronophotographic pictures contain the two necessary elements for understanding a movement, namely, a notion of space as well as that of time."[43]

**Figure 3.8** Falling ball, Etienne-Jules Marey and Eric Pritchard, *Movement* (New York: D. Appleton and Company, 1895), 51.

Marey's belief in the essential unity of lifeless machines and living bodies centered on the unifying force of energy as a foundational idea in the understanding of everything. Energy connected all things and: "The value of a theory depends on the number of facts which it embraces: that of the unity of physical forces tends to absorb them all. From the invisible atom to the celestial body lost in space, everything is subject to motion."[44] It was this confidence in a scientific epistemology that led Marey to develop the sphygmograph, and in so doing he developed a new standard for physiological time equivalent to Greenwich Mean Time (1884). As Marta Braun has argued, it is difficult to overestimate the task Marey set for himself:

> Tracing the spatial relations (following the changes from one point in space to another through a trajectory), mapping the temporal relations (the duration of the movement, with its speed, uniformity, and variations), and finally describing the force necessary to produce the movement (which differs according to the mass of the body which is moving, its speed, and medium it moves through— all these aspects had to be made apparent if the movement was to be known.[45]

Marey's task was nothing less than to make visible the invisible, transient, and intricate world of motion. What was technically very difficult was philosophically simple. Movement was the essence of the body and therefore it was necessary to study it. To study it in a positivist manner, it had to be made available to the senses. This is what the sphygmograph did, but it was only the first step in a series of investigations of movement.

Marey's next task was to develop a way of tracing the movements of a bird's wing in flight. As with the movement of blood through the human circulatory system, such movements were invisible to the naked eye. Marey thought that a thorough understanding of bird flight would allow people to travel through the air. Before working out a way of tracing such movements, however, Marey saw Eadweard Muybridge's remarkable photographs of Occident. Leland Stanford had actually read Marey's book, *Animal Mechanism*, in 1874, which considered the various modes of animal movement including some pictures of horses galloping. It was after seeing Marey's images that Stanford asked Muybridge to photograph his horses, five years after his original work.

The resulting photographs of Occident were published in *Nature* and were seen by Marey, who immediately wrote to the editor of *Nature* in unrestrained admiration. He suggested that Muybridge might attempt to capture similar images of a bird in flight. Following that, Muybridge and Marey wrote to each other and Muybridge visited France and became something of a celebrity on the lecture circuit.

Muybridge never managed to successfully photograph a bird in flight to Marey's satisfaction, so Marey began to develop his own devices for such an endeavor. The problem for Marey was Muybridge's use of twelve cameras rather than one. Marey saw in Muybridge's images less a record of movement itself and more a series of pictures of stationary bodies that the mind translated as being in motion. Between each image many moments in time were effectively lost. This differed from Marey's graphs produced by his sphygmograph as the graph was a complete record of movement within a particular time frame. What Marey wanted was a record of movement that married the graph to the photograph, accurately capturing both time and space. To this end he invented the *fusile photographique*—a single gunlike camera with a revolving dish of film in it, which could take twelve images per second. With this he hoped to translate the imperceptible world of the mobile into a visible and permanent record.

Even at twelve images per second, however, there were still unrecorded gaps in the flow of the image. Marey wanted to get a single image within one frame that captured movement. This required multiple exposures on the same portion of film. To solve this problem he invented a new process he called chronophotography (time-writing). This involved a camera with a revolving disk between the lens and the plate. The disk had slots in it. As the disk revolved, the slots would pass the lens one after another, momentarily registering a phase of the moving subject. Each time a slot passed over the lens, a new phase of movement would be captured on the plate just next to the previous one. "He captured ongoing phases of movement and spread them over the photographic plate in an undulating pattern of overlapping segments. . . . Marey's photographs gave visible extension to the present, virtually representing a passage of time."[46] These single-frame pictures were published for the first time in *Scientific American* in 1882. Their effect was to shatter the post-Renaissance idea of the frame as representing a unity of space and time:

> Marey's photographs shattered that unity; viewers now had to unravel the successive parts of the work in order to understand they were looking not at several men moving in single file, but at a single figure successively occupying a series of positions in space. Viewers had to allow themselves to be led from one figure to another, reading the several images of the single figure as it moved through time and space. The result, a vision that goes beyond sight, was a new reality.[47]

**The Process of Abstraction**

The endeavors of Marey and Muybridge both need to be understood through the philosophy of positivism. Marey in particular was looking to extend the ability of observation in order that patterns of regularity, and eventually laws, could be established. This process of abstraction can be seen in the images he produced. In the accounts of Marey's work a great deal of emphasis is placed on the technological and scientific innovation behind the images. Relatively little is said about the images themselves. Early images tend to be of men dressed all in white walking, running, and jumping. *Demeny Walking* (1883) is a single frame shot of Marey's assistant, Demeny, moving from left to right against a black background (Figure 3.9a). The black background was important as it cut out all the unnecessary detail that might divert attention from the moving subject. Demeny was dressed in white in order to stand out and make the most of the light conditions. As Marey's technology improved, more and more details of the moving body became visible. Imagine if there were no intervals between each exposure—the picture would become a white blur and functionally useless (even if aesthetically interesting).

> Now, if we take a series of images of a man walking, the question of space becomes a most complicated one. Each image must be spread over a considerable surface if it is to show the various positions assumed by the head, arms and legs. Now the larger the space covered by the image, the smaller must be the number that can be taken on one plate without superposition and confusion.[48]

The problem for Marey was that there was still too much detail in the image and this was obscuring the thing he was seeking to understand—movement.

In order to abstract movement itself from the confusing detail of actual bodies, Marey embarked on a process by which the body was dissolved and the image of movement became progressively more abstract and disembodied. His first move was to cover half of Demeny's body in black cloth so that the camera could not see it. This produced images with less clutter. Marey was effectively reversing the main advantage the camera had been blessed with—the ability to record the visible (Figure 3.9b). By making the visible invisible the invisible ironically became more apparent. The next step was to dress the subject all in black and attach a kind of external skeleton to the outfit. The skeleton was made of metal bands and shiny buttons at the joints. The body had effectively disappeared and we are left with an abstract representation of movement (Figure 3.9c). Marey was delighted

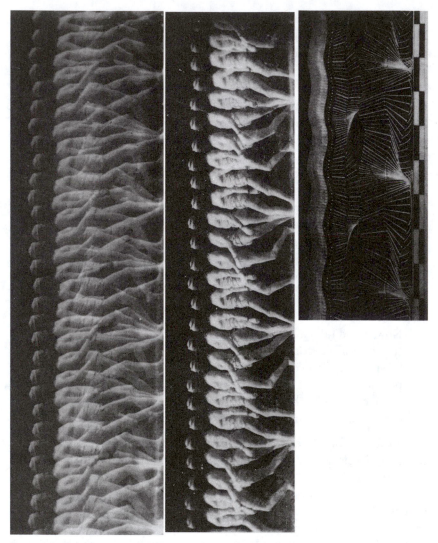

**Figure 3.9** a. Demeny walking; b. Demeny walking half obscured; c. lights only, all ©
Collège de France.

with his discovery and realized that it was now possible to massively
increase the number of exposures per second from ten to one hundred.

In geometrical photographs, thanks to the great number of the
images, the discontinuity of the phases almost entirely disap-
pears, and the actual path followed by each part of the body can be
seen represented almost as a continuous curve. These indications
are most useful in studying movement from the point of view of

dynamics, for by them the velocity as well as the acceleration of the body mass can be measured.[49]

We are left with a geometrically beautiful image of movement without bodies.

The story of the abstraction of mobility in Marey's work has been one of distilling out the essence of mobility from the messiness of actual moving bodies. Once the images of walking and jumping and running had been established, however, they became more than representations of the invisible—they became ideals. One instance of this was undertaken by Marey himself who saw his images of walking as a model to compare with other kinds of walking—pathological mobilities. In 1886 Marey started to make geometric chronophotographs of motion-impaired residents in Parisian hospitals. He had taken his technology a step further and attached small light bulbs to the joints of patients and then taken a picture of the moving light (Figure 3.10).[50] This moving light then revealed, in spatial form, the results of accidents, old age, and disease. These original experiments were extended over two years and were used to develop physiotherapy and the manufacture of prosthetic devices. These images are a far cry from Muybridge's images of motion-impaired patients in Philadelphia. While Muybridge gave us pictures of naked people moving as best they could, Marey gives us a distillation of their movement with bodies removed. In Muybridge's images it is hard to read the movement between the frames, in Marey's it is all there is. Marey's chronophotography led him to observe that "pathological movements" are "only the exaggeration—greater or lesser—of movements that are hardly apparent but that nevertheless exist in a normal state."[51] This matches the

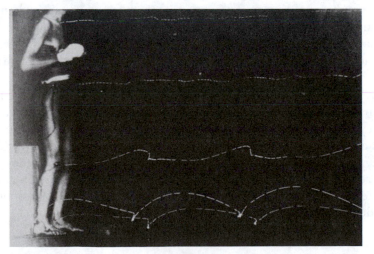

**Figure 3.10** Locomotor ataxia, 1887, © Collège de France.

position taken by the physiologist Joseph Victor Broussais, the inspiration for the positivist philosopher Comte. To Broussais and Comte, the pathological is no more than an extreme version of the normal, not, as Durkheim was to suggest, its opposite.[52]

Recall that the second law of thermodynamics stated that every transformation of energy involves entropy—a loss in energy to the environment. In the human machine, entropy was coded as fatigue. The issue of fatigue— the loss of energy—became an obsession in Europe and North America. In France, for instance, Georges Demeny (1850–1918), the subject of many of Marey's photographs, pondered on the embarrassing defeat of the French Army by the Prussians in 1870. He believed that the army was just too tired and looked for ways of regenerating an energetic fighting machine. To this end he advocated a regimented form of physical education. Demeny mobilized a medical model of deviance and degeneracy to explain the crisis. The diagnosis was one of neurasthenia (nervous exhaustion)—an overwhelming tiredness caused by the grinding life of the new metropolis. George M. Beard, you will recall, had introduced neurasthenia in his book *American Nervousness* (1881), and it was the excessive mobility of modern life that was blamed. Inventions such as the railroads, the telegraph, and steam power had massively increased the number of transactions in modern urban life and had led to neurasthenia as well as balding and early tooth decay.[53] A whole host of deviant activities including prostitution, abuse of tobacco and alcohol, crime, and madness led to mass fatigue. This fatigue needed to be reduced in order to resist widespread moral decay. Demeny used Marey's techniques to examine the movements of the army. He attached strips of lights to soldiers dressed in black and photographed the moving lights to show various forms of movement that used more energy than was required. Following this he came up with ideal ways of marching, running, jumping, and resting for the new French Army. This marked a change in the use of new understandings of mobility. Rather than just attempting to represent mobility, Demeny was using a model produced through representation to animate human bodies in new ways—to produce ideal forms of mobile practice. This link between representation and practice is key. While representation and practice are often held apart in theory and analysis, they are often intertwined in practice. Indeed, Muybridge's early images of horses were more than an attempt to win a bet, they were instruments in the training of thoroughbred racehorses. Representational strategies informed by ideas about mobility were part and parcel of the production of mobile practices—new ways of moving.

## Conclusions

If, in the act of interpreting movement, there is the displacement of a displacement, then this is a record of that process of displacement. Here, and in the rest of the book, I am attempting to develop an account of the production of mobilities in modernity. The body is just one scale that concerns me. But at this scale we can see several themes that run through other scales and thus form the basis for my own kind of abstraction—a critical theoretical account of mobility. The process of abstraction is one such theme—the process that starts with actual lived, experienced, embodied mobility and extracts from it accounts of abstract movement. This tension between abstract motion and embodied mobility is key. Intersecting this is the tension between mobility as an excess—a threat to the principles of order—and mobility as a central conduit of life in modernity. "All that is solid melts into air"—modernity is mobile. The attempted resolution of this threat is to absorb it and regulate it through the process of abstraction. Mobility is not simply against fixity (where fixity is order and mobility is chaos) but is itself in tension and internally differentiated.

The images of Muybridge and Marey are obviously about mobility. They are attempts to capture the fleeting and invisible. But what is perhaps more remarkable are the multiple ways in which their photographic exploits form parts of wider networks of an increasingly mobile world. Muybridge's images connect the world of horses and the world of trains. They enact a form of deterritorialization at the same time as they are the product of the annihilation of space by time. Marey's images provide new ways of perceiving mobility from the flow of blood to the sprinting man. At the same time they feed into the development of the moving image, the possibility of human flight, and the rationalization of marching armies. They were moments in an increasingly mobile world. But once something is set in motion, momentum takes over and, as we shall see in the next chapter, the ideas and practices of Muybridge and Marey had further travels to enact.

## CHAPTER 4

# The Production of Mobility in the Workplace and the Home

In the first decade of the twentieth century, American railroad companies were frequently in court. Few aspects of the triumphant capitalist system were more despised by the public than the railroads. They were seen to possess unreasonable monopoly powers over mobility, and they charged excessive rates for both passengers and goods. In 1910, following the merger of several eastern railroad companies and a massive increase in haulage rates, the "people's attorney," Louis Brandeis (later a Supreme Court justice), took the merged companies before the Interstate Commerce Commission in what became known as the "Eastern Rates case." Brandeis argued that the companies had increased their rates because they were inefficient. He claimed that if they knew how much things really cost by actually measuring them, using what he called "scientific management," they could save millions a day. They did not need a rate increase, he argued; they needed science and efficiency. In making his case, Brandeis used several expert witnesses including one Frank Gilbreth who stated the necessity of scientifically assessing a business. He based his testimony on the work of Frederick Taylor. The Eastern rates case was national news, and it was this event that brought the work of Frederick Taylor into the national spotlight. While his work had been well known within the business world for a few years, he had hardly been a household name. It is supremely ironic that a lawyer who was renowned for being on the side of social justice should urge a business policy based on the work of Taylor. Here he was, arguing against the injustice of one form of mobility by appealing to the work of a man who sought to inscribe a hierarchical discipline on the mobilities of the "common people" he was seeking to protect. In the case of the railroads, the freedom of mobility was being constrained by big business, while in the case of the mobile bodies of workers, Brandeis's expert witnesses were busy constraining freedom in another way. Indeed it was Brandeis who coined the term *scientific management* to describe the approach that mandated managers to precisely measure the time and resources necessary to complete a particular aspect of a business. In Brandeis's view, this would ensure that unnecessary costs would not trickle down to the customer. The Eastern Rates case marked the end of excessive railroad rates, but more importantly, it marked the advent of Taylorism.

This chapter considers the production of new kinds of bodily mobilities in the work of Frederick Taylor and Frank and Lillian Gilbreth. Their work on *motion-studies* was central to the rise of a plethora of strategies to control the mobile body—to construct meanings for particular bodies and then prescribe practices. They believed that rational and scientific analysis of the workplace could be utilized to plan forever-increasing efficiency in the world of production. This scientific management is most famously associated with Frederick Taylor and the set of practices that became known as Taylorism.[1] At the heart of his program was the transformation of learned habit—embodied habitual mobility—into a rigorous and scientifically coded abstraction of human motion. Consider Lenin's endorsement of Taylor. "The Taylor system . . . like all capitalist progress, is a combination of the subtle brutality of bourgeois exploitation and a number of its great scientific achievements in the fields of analysing mechanical motions during work, the elimination of superfluous and awkward motions, the working out of correct methods of work, the introduction of the best system of accounting and control, etc."[2] Indeed the "elimination of superfluous and awkward motions" is a central theme of this chapter and the rest of the book. A great deal of effort has been expended in the modern West toward this end.

Key to Taylorist principles were the mechanization of the human body and the production of new kinds of ruthlessly efficient mobilities. These new kinds of mobility need to be understood in relation to other kinds of mobility—mobilities that were seen as inefficient and dysfunctional in a capitalist workplace. At the heart of the project of workplace (and later homeplace) motion-studies was the specificity of the mobility that would be allowed. Superfluous and awkward motions, as in so many other arenas of modern life, were to be eliminated. In the work of Taylor and the Gilbreths we see the convergence of representational strategies, like those of Marey and Muybridge, and the production of models for ideal mobility. Representation becomes entangled with practice.

## Frederick Taylor and Time-Study

Central to Frederick Taylor's scientific management was the recording and then rearrangement of mobilities. Like Muybridge and Marey, Taylor sought to precisely record the motions of the human body. His preferred technology was the relatively unsophisticated stopwatch rather than photography. Indeed, his reliance on the stopwatch and lack of interest in advanced photographic techniques was to result in a falling out with his acolyte Frank Gilbreth. In other ways, however, Taylor went further than Muybridge and Marey. Rather than being satisfied with representing human motion, Taylor wanted to reanimate his subjects with new kinds of ideal motion. In this respect the project of scientific management reflected the efforts of Demeny to reinvigorate the French Army.

The management of mobility in what became known as the Taylor system involved more than time study—it was a complete set of coordinated planning principles with four main features: (1) centralized planning and routing of materials, (2) a systematic analysis, through time study, of every operation, (3) the detailed instructions and supervision of workers, and (4) a system of wage incentives for those who met targets. All of these were guided by the ideology of science that asserted that an objective view from above would ease conflict between capital and labor through the recognition of incontrovertible facts. A central effect of this system was the division of physical work from mental work. Taylor invented a planning department for each factory and a system of foremen to oversee specific kinds of work. As Braverman has argued Taylor sought to dissociate the labor process from the embodied skills of the workers, "the managers assume . . . the burden of gathering together all the traditional knowledge which in the past has been possessed by the workmen and then of classifying, tabulating, and reducing this knowledge to rules, laws, and formulae."[3] Brain-work would be removed from the space of the worker (the shop floor) and the body of the worker and relocated in the new planning and layout room.

At the center of this system was the fact that each job was given a particular time, and those who could work at the appropriate speed were rewarded while those who could not were penalized. Each specific job was overseen by a foreman who reported to the planning department, thus heightening the managerial control over work. Taylor took what the body knows and reproduced it as scientific laws. By watching workers and timing their every move, Taylor believed he could decipher the ideal sequence of movement and rest for the production of profit. Frederick Taylor's process of abstraction, like that of Marey, made bodies disappear and reappear. Right at the outset of his classic text *The Principles of Scientific Management*, we are confronted with bodies that move inappropriately in a practice known as *soldiering*, whereby workers in all trades deliberately work slowly in order to curtail output. "There is no question that the tendency of the average man (in all walks of life) is toward working at a slow, easy gait, and that it is only after a good deal of thought and observation on his part or as a result of example, conscience, or external pressure that he takes a more rapid pace."[4] This is Taylor's enemy and target—the lazy body with the slow and easy gait who naturally, and through association with others, slows down the output of industry. "So universal is soldiering" he wrote "that hardly a competent workman can be found in a large establishment, whether he works by the day or in piece work, contract work, or under any of the ordinary systems, who does not devote a considerable part of his time to studying just how slow he can work and still convince his employer that he is going at a good pace."[5]

Taylor's contention was that "science" could produce a different pace—a different and more efficient form of embodied mobility. He describes the process in *The Principles of Scientific Management*. The first step was the "scientific selection" of a workman to time during simple work procedures. Taylor and his team watched actual workers at Bethlehem Steel in Pennsylvania carefully for four days until they had identified four workers who could handle pig iron at the rate of 47 tons per day. "A careful study was then made of each of these men. We looked up their history as far back a practicable and thorough enquiries were made as to the character, habits, and the ambition of each of them."[6] Finally they settled on one man he calls Schmidt.

## About Schmidt

Schmidt is a highly individualized worker. He is Pennsylvania Dutch, he trots to and from work for over a mile, he values his money, saves hard, and has shown the initiative to build his own house in the time he is not at work. Taylor describes how he takes Schmidt aside and goes about convincing him to handle 47 tons of pig iron a day and be glad to do it. This involves increasing his pay from $1.15 an hour to $1.85 an hour and telling him to obey his supervisor exactly.

> you will do exactly as this man tells you to-morrow, from morning till night. When he tells you to pick up a pig and walk, you pick it up and you walk, and when he tells you to sit down and rest, you

sit down. You do that right straight through the day. And what's more, no back talk. . . . When this man tells you to walk, you walk; when he tells you to sit down, you sit down, and you don't talk back at him.[7]

Taylor admits this is "rough talk," but continues with his justification. Schmidt, we are told, is a "mentally sluggish type," and the talk is therefore appropriate. It wouldn't work, however, with educated people (such as himself) who are unsuited to heavy labor.

> Now one of the very first requirements for a man who is fit to handle pig iron as a regular occupation is that he shall be so stupid and so phlegmatic that he more nearly resembles in his mental make up the ox than any other type. The man who is mentally alert and intelligent is for this very reason entirely unsuited to what would, for him, be the grinding monotony of work of this character. Therefore the workman who is best suited to handling pig iron is unable to understand the real science of doing this class of work. He is so stupid that the word "percentage" has no meaning to him, and he must consequently be trained by a man more intelligent than himself into the habit of working in accordance with the laws of this science before he can be successful.[8]

By this point, the body and mind of Schmidt had been highly specified. He is energetic, thrifty, and incredibly stupid. He is incapable of understanding the science that is being applied to his body in order to lift his output from 12 to 47 tons a day. This increase in output is achieved by watching Schmidt closely and timing his every move. Eventually Taylor's team came to the conclusion that a first-class laborer such as Schmidt could be under load precisely 42 percent of the day and free from load the rest. The researchers "scientifically" extracted from Schmidt's laboring body a model for pig iron handling that could then be applied to others.

It is unlikely that Schmidt had any idea what a pivotal role he would play in the fortunes of Frederick Taylor or in the development of time and motion study. In 1913, following an attempt to introduce the Taylor System in Watertown Arsenal, Congress sought to put an end to Taylor's practices. Some senators believed that Taylor's methods were less than humane. Schmidt's body once again became an object of investigation. A rumor spread that Schmidt had died from overwork and exhaustion. Schmidt's real name, it turns out, was Henry Knolle (or Knoll), a Dutch immigrant. Taylor was keen to prove that he was alive and well. He wrote to General William Crozier, chief of the Bureau of Ordnance for the U.S. Army, on October 8, 1913, insisting that Knolle was fit and healthy.

It is possible, of course, that the man may have died, but I do not believe it, as he was a very tough little customer and was in the very best of health all the time I was at the Bethlehem Steel Works. His name, I think, was Henry Knolle. If the officer from your Department, stationed at Bethlehem, succeeds in finding him, and will let me know his whereabouts, I will either go up to Bethlehem myself or send someone up to persuade Knolle to allow me to have a doctor examine him and certify as to his physical condition.[9]

Crozier replied on November 26 that Knoll had been found and appeared to be a healthy 42-year-old. He claimed to have enjoyed the work and been able to earn $3 per day under the new system. He had since separated from his wife due to a drinking problem.

I rather think that this is sufficient evidence to use in connection with any statement which may be made as to Knoll's alleged death, on the floor of the House, but if you wish to go into it any further it seems that there ought to be no difficulty in having him examined by a physician, or otherwise establishing that he has not worked himself to death in unloading pig iron.[10]

Taylor was not convinced that this would be enough to disprove Knoll's early demise, and subsequently arranged to have Knoll examined by a doctor and photographed in order to "see that he is in sound and good health."[11] In late December, Taylor arranged to have a doctor visit Knolle in order to disprove the "philanthropists and trade unionists" who found Knoll's work rate "nothing short of scandalous" and were about to claim on the floor of the House that they had found Knoll "in the graveyard."[12] He arranged for Mr. Wadleigh to be provided a salary and expenses during his assessment of Knoll.

Wadleigh replied on January 3, 1914 with a report on Knoll stating that he was in good health and had experienced no problem with the workload set by Taylor. "Knoll is slow witted" the letter went on "and without much ambition. Has been a hard drinker and fond of women." Despite these character deficiencies, "Knoll makes a good appearance, dresses neatly and seems contented. He does not see why pig iron work, such as he did while on piece work, should hurt a man."[13] The report is accompanied by a certificate of good health from Dr. C. L. Johnstonbaugh of Bethlehem.

Taylor was delighted with the report but saw fit to make a few changes. In a letter of January 5, Taylor thanks Wadleigh for his work but remarks, "There is only one sentence which I would modify, if I were you, in your report, namely: at the end of page 2 you state, 'most men of his class are old men at his age.' I am very sure that the Socialists and the Member of Congress and the Trade Unionists would use this sentence to the detriment of Scientific Management. They would distort it to mean that Scientific Management made men old at 44." Taylor suggests that he omit this sentence and obligingly has the report rewritten and sent back to Wadleigh for his signature along with fifty dollars for his troubles. Clearly the mobility (or immobility) of Knolle's body had quite an impact on the history of mobilities in the workplace. First he appears as a super-human "first-class" laborer who, through his precisely controlled mobility, becomes a model for a new way of working. Much later he reappears as a central player in an argument about the legitimacy of the principles of scientific management he unwittingly brought about. His body, and specifically how it moved, became subject to the gaze of an array of "experts" ranging from Taylor to Wadleigh and Dr. Johnstonbaugh to the members of the Unites States Senate. His embodied practice was repeatedly extracted and made to stand for something else. This, needless to say, was beyond his control.

## Machine and Animal Mobilities

The predominant metaphors used in discussion of Taylor's views of worker mobility are machines and animals.[14] Antonio Gramsci, in his surprisingly upbeat accounts of the successes of Taylor and Ford, suggests that "the history of industrialism has been a continuing struggle . . . against the element of 'animality' in man."[15] To Gramsci, Taylorism was a process of transforming animals into machines. Indeed, Taylor frequently lapsed into animal metaphors—or "beast fables"—in order to explain and legitimize his methods. Schmidt is compared to an ox—a mentally sluggish type.[16] When brought before the committee investigating his methods for the House of Representatives, he continually compared workers to various forms of workhorse. When asked to define first-class laborer by the committee, Taylor made the following comparison:

> Now, what I mean by a first-class horse to haul a coal wagon is something very simple and plain. We will all agree that a good big dray horse is a "first-class" horse to haul a coal wagon. . . . If, however, you live in a small town and have a small stable of horses, in many cases you will have to use grocery-wagon horses and grocery wagons to haul coal in; and yet we all know that a grocery-wagon horse is not a "first-class" horse for hauling coal. . . . In the same way we know that a great big dray horse is not a "first-class" horse for hauling a grocery wagon, nor is a grocery-wagon horse "first class" for hauling a buggy, and so right on down the line.[17]

The worker-animal comparisons quickly became absurd when Taylor was asked what he proposed to do with men who were less than first-class laborers. Taylor responded, "Scientific Management has no place for a bird that can sing, and won't sing," to which the chairman replied, "I am not speaking about birds at all." Martha Banta has suggested that these animal metaphors are far from innocent, and that they represent an irrational and threatening excess to Taylor's rationalistic worldview. To her, the deployment of these metaphors is a form of discursive containment of any number of chaotic presences on the shop floor that needed to adjust in order to slot into his schemes of time and motion. These tales of ox, horses, and birds clash with the idea of the worker as a machine—a perfect production unit. While the mobilities of animals are irrational and threatening, the mobilities of machines are regular, rhythmic, and speedy. Taylor's enemies in Congress and in the Trade Unions were just as opposed to the machine metaphor as they were to that of animals. In the Senate hearing, for instance, Senator Martine of New Jersey declared that: "I feel that the Taylor system, so called, would tend to make a mere machine of man" and that the great majority of workers were "honest, well meaning, citizens and a benefit to the human race. . . . I believe in treating workmen as though they were human beings, and not as though they were mere machines." Stopwatches, he declared, were for horseraces.[18] What might be appropriate for animals, in other words, would not be appropriate for people.

Braverman has famously described Taylorism as a sophisticated form of de-skilling whereby the labor process is dissociated from the skills of worker. The management presume to act as the brain while the workers are mere bodies. "Thus, in the setting of antagonistic social relations, of alienated labor, hand and brain become not just separated, but divided and hostile, and the human unity of hand and brain turns into its opposite, something less than human."[19] This "less-than-human" worker is the machine or cogs in a larger machine. Taylorism thus marks the transformation of the worker from a subject into an object-machine.

Taylor's time study sought to provide a system whereby the worker's subjectivity could be controlled through the reorganization of the body in time and space. He sought to take learned habit and reproduce it as science in the positivist language of laws and mathematics. The unalienated body of the worker was seen as anarchic and threatening to bourgeois notions of respectability and rationality. Taylor wanted to rearrange these bodies and choreograph their motions to produce a new form of modern mobility where the bodies of workers were reconstituted as passive objects—machines to serve the interests of capital. Taylor, in the eyes of Mark Bahnisch, "wants to reduce the anarchy of working, to standardize the different bodily movements and bodies of different workers, to erase difference and write 'absolute uniformity' onto the actions and bodies of the workers."[20]

One realm of work Taylor discusses is bricklaying. He describes bricklaying as one of the oldest trades known to mankind and yet one that has been passed down through customary knowledge and not studied scientifically. Consequently, he argues, no major improvements have occurred for hundreds of years. Taylor's discussion of bricklaying is based on the work of Frank Gilbreth. Gilbreth went to work analyzing the task of bricklaying, Taylor tells us: "[h]e made an intensely interesting analysis and study of each movement of the bricklayer, and one after another eliminated all unnecessary movements and substituted fast for slow motions. He experimented in every minute element which in any way affects the speed and the tiring of the bricklayer."[21] Gilbreth's study revealed that the bricklayers would often step back to a pile of bricks and then forward again to the wall they were making. They would also have to bend down to pick up a brick and then straighten up to place it on the wall. By placing the bricks next to the man and at such a height that he would not have to bend down, several unnecessary movements could be saved and more bricks laid. Similarly, the observant Gilbreth noticed that bricklayers would spend a lot of their time tapping each brick to make sure that the thickness of mortar was consistent. He suggested that this was unnecessary if the mortar was more carefully applied in the first place. As a result of these observations, Taylor claimed, "Mr. Gilbreth has reduced his movements from fifteen to five, and even in one case to as low as two motions per brick."[22]

Gilbreth's application of *time-motion study* is generalized by Taylor into five general steps to be applied in any production site:

> *First.* Find, say, 10 or 15 different men (preferably in as many separate establishments and different parts of the country) who are especially skillful in doing the particular work to be analyzed.
>
> *Second.* Study the exact series of elementary operations or motions which each of these men uses in doing the work which is being investigated, as well as the implements each man uses.
>
> *Third.* Study with a stop-watch the time required to make each of these elementary movements and then select the quickest way of doing each element of the work.
>
> *Fourth.* Eliminate all false movements, slow movements, and useless movements.
>
> *Fifth.* After doing away with all unnecessary movements, collect into one series the quickest and best movements as well as the best implements.[23]

It is through this process of the abstraction of mobility from individual worker's bodies that Gilbreth and Taylor believed that "Science could provide work with a rational, objective basis. Detached from the interests of labor and capital, it could determine the optimum use of the body's energies and analyze the physiological limits of physical and mental labor."[24] By applying the methodology of "science," Taylor attempted to choreograph the assembly line so that the movements of workers were no longer their own but the product of the stopwatch and "the colonizing subjectivity of management."[25] The system he developed effectively transformed the threatening body of the lazy worker into a machine—an object that served capitalist production. The worker's body was disciplined through the construction of space and time and the division of movements within that space/time.

> The anarchic and empowered body of the worker is disciplined though inscription as a pattern on a flow chart, his body represented by equations analysing "foot pounds of energy." Science ennobles the managerial subject to calculate the bodily movements of the pig-iron handler, dividing the day into 58 percent of the time lifting a 45 pound pig and 42 percent of the time at rest. The embodied worker moves, when told, and is in stasis, when told.[26]

Taylor's aim was to negate the differences between the bodily movement of workers and create uniform motions in their place. In other words he sought to replace habitual embodied mobility with abstract motion. Taylor was quite adamant about the inability of workers to regulate their own motions. It was frequently put to him that he was only replicating what workers had been doing with their own motions for generations. He responded to this in a letter to his biographer Frank B. Copley.

> It has been contended that workmen have from time immemorial made a similar study of their own movements. No doubt this is true, but no such study as this can be called the development of a science, because the development of a science involves not only the investigation, but the formulation into rules, laws or statements, of the facts which have been investigated; and where workmen have made a study of their own movements and thereby become extremely proficient in the past, they have taken great pains not to formulate this, and write it out so that other workmen could profit by it.[27]

In lieu of worker self-regulation, it was left to Taylor to progressively break particular tasks down into a limited set of movements. In the process, labor acquired an increasingly abstract character. Each movement was assigned a quantity of time—itself a concrete abstraction. As a unit of time, the movement could then be compared to other movements expressed as a measure of time. Movements became equivalent to each other and different forms of production could be inserted into a common measure. The particular forms of production—say bricklaying and welding—may have had nothing in common other than the time taken to execute them. But as each job was broken down into movements and then into time, labor became more and more abstract. But it was not just the movements used in the immediate production process that were disciplined and abstracted. As movement involves a combination of both space and time, these contexts for movement were also regulated. As E. P. Thompson and David Harvey have brilliantly shown, time under capitalism became a concrete abstraction and the object of fierce struggle between capital and labor.[28] The working day was given a discrete length and was punctuated by bells and whistles. Workers were fined for being late. Simultaneously, space was increasingly delimited. Factories had specific points of entry and exit where workers could clock in, and which were policed by porters and timekeepers. Changing rooms acted as kinds of "airblocks" between the inside and outside. This definition process of space and time was tied to the regulation of movements both between the workplace and other places, and within the workplace itself. Workers were told when and where to work, and forms of movement that did not fit into the needs of capital were forbidden. Workers were increasingly prevented from moving between rooms. Extended use of the lavatory could result in fines. "As tasks were broken down, and as the cycle of each task became shorter," Doray writes, "the activity of labour became increasingly subject to the rate of flow of production; this provided the basis for the banalization of the labour process, and for a much stricter subordination of the activity of labour to the demands of production."[29]

This progressive abstraction of labor in and through the production of abstract movement only served to produce a scientized and quantified notion of work that was not work as experienced, but instead *virtual* work. The standardization of tasks pays no attention to the variability of raw materials or individual workers—it cannot take into account mental activity that cannot be measured by a stopwatch. These virtual tasks display a rigidity that cannot be found in the embodied experience of work. Nevertheless, the management of time and motion served to internalize ways of moving that were specified by management and became organizational norms.

## The Gilbreths

Perhaps more remarkable than the development of time studies by Taylor was the associated development of motion study by Frank and Lillian Gilbreth.[30] The Gilbreths were originally acolytes and associates of Taylor, but over time they came to believe that Taylor's claim to scientific fact was dubious at best. At the heart of their falling-out was an argument over the nature of motion. While Taylor was happy to think of motion in terms of time alone, the Gilbreths were insistent that motion involved both time and space and thus needed a spatial form of representation. To the Gilbreths, the answer was to be found in photography.

Frank was born in 1868 in rural Maine and raised by his mother. He did well at school and was admitted to MIT (Massachusetts Institute of Technology). His family needed financial support, however, and he decided to become a bricklayer instead of attending college. By 1895 he had his own subcontracting business and quickly made his name in high-speed construction work, building large buildings in dazzlingly short time periods. Frank was fascinated by bricklaying and constantly devised instruments and techniques to speed it up and reduce fatigue. One of his inventions, for instance, was a height-adjustable scaffold for bricks, which reduced the stresses on the body brought about by repetitive bending. Gilbreth attended lectures by Taylor and by 1908 they were friends.

But Gilbreth was no simple Taylor acolyte, and developed much more sophisticated ways of capturing motion for the benefit of industry. Frank Gilbreth and his wife and motion-study partner, Lillian, differed from Taylor both in terms of the tools they used to assess work and the fundamental thing they sought to assess. While Taylor used the stopwatch, the Gilbreth's developed increasingly sophisticated photographic apparatus.

For a while Gilbreth tried to convince Taylor of the importance of using photographic apparatus to accurately measure the motions of workers. In April 1912, Gilbreth wrote excitedly to Taylor informing him of his progress:

> "I have just perfected a mechanical device for taking time study by photographing the time of day in hours, minutes, tenths of minutes and hundredths of tenths of minutes. In other words I now photograph to the thousandth of a minute the time of day that each of one thousand photographs of a moving picture camera are exposed, and the actual time of any motions can be obtained by subtracting the time of day in one picture from the time of day of any other picture in the same series."

Gilbreth's excitement about his new developments was palpable. He remained polite to Taylor, stating that he did "not believe that this method will ever wholly do away with the present stopwatch method, but it will have a tremendous use in teaching certain elements of processes by exhibition of these educational films." But the precision that Gilbreth's photographic apparatus allowed was highly accurate, and he impressed this on Taylor. "You will see that this process not only enables me to take the time study to the thousandth of a minute, eliminating all error due to the human element or to differences in mental time reactions but that it also permits measuring the motion's three dimensions simultaneously."[31] By July 1912 Gilbreth was offering his invention to Taylor stating, "this process and combination of clocks and motion picture machine should really go with your great invention of time-study, and consequently if you will accept ownership of it as a present from me, or if you will undertake its control for the best interests of the great cause, I will be most happy to present it to you."[32] His invitation appears to have bemused Taylor who refused Gilbreth's offer stating, "I . . . know nothing about photography, and am therefore entirely the wrong man to follow them up properly. They should be in the hands of someone who knows at least the first elements of photography and I do not believe there is a better man for this purpose than yourself."[33]

These letters mark the beginnings of a fundamental conflict between Taylor and Gilbreth over how best to measure work. While Taylor focused on time, the Gilbreths focused on motion—the coming together of time and space. Taylor usually referred to his work as time-study, and it was only later, faced with the success of Gilbreth's methods, that he began to refer to time-motion studies. To Gilbreth the word *time* was redundant because motion clearly signified both time and space. Gilbreth resented the equation that linked Taylor to motion study as he felt that motion study was his invention. When Gilbreth read Copley's biography of Taylor he wrote furious notes in the margin whenever Taylor's name was associated with motion study. Where Copley wrote that Taylor's time study would eliminate superfluous motions, Gilbreth scribbled "Time Study will *not* eliminate superfluous motions. Taylor admitted in 1907 that he had never realized that the MOTION was the element to attack for the right method to time."[34] When Copley repeated his claim twenty pages later, Gilbreth replies: "Taylor told me in 1907 that he has never considered the motions of a worker and that our study of the motion was entirely a new idea to him and he asked me to write a book with him about it."[35]

By 1920 Gilbreth was directly criticizing Taylor's methods from within the Taylor Society, an organization he had helped to set up in the wake of the Eastern Rates case. On December 26 he presented a paper called "Time Study and Motion Study as Fundamental Factors in Planning and Control" to the New York Section of the Taylor Society.[36] In this talk he declared the principle tool of the Taylor System, the stopwatch, "absolutely worthless and also misleading so far as assisting in skill study is concerned." What is more "[i]t is unethical because it does not clearly define the subject matter of an implied contract on which the wage payment is based, and it is economically wasteful because it does not preserve the best that has been done."[37] Gilbreth described how Taylor would claim to measure averages to one ten-thousandth of a minute with only a stopwatch to help him. Whereas time study was unethical because it is often hidden and does not involve the worker, he argued, motion study would solve these problems. "*Motion study*, as here used, does not mean the kind of motion study that has been carelessly and erroneously described as being "the same as time study," or "a part of time study." Motion-study, as used here, means the science of recording motions, of which "time" is but one of scores of variables."[38] Gilbreth was concerned with the history of the anti-Taylorist activities that had marked the previous decade. As far as he was concerned, the success of motion-study depended on it being able to "live up to its claims of being a science."[39] Secretly timing workers with an instrument as imprecise as a stopwatch did not, in his view, constitute a science.

## The Gilbreth Method

Unlike Taylor, the Gilbreths were concerned with the nature of motion as a coming together of time and space. Time, alone, was not enough. In order to properly record time and space, the Gilbreth's utilized photography (and later motion pictures) alongside specially designed clocks. But behind these technological innovations was a fervent set of beliefs about motion and fatigue, which motivated the Gilbreths in a profound way. In their own minds they were leading a crusade against wasted motions in all areas of life. In their motion-study practices, Frank and Lillian Gilbreth sought to produce a new way of being through new ways of moving. This involved the reordering of space as much as the reconfiguration of motion in the human body. It also involved a revolution of the mind. As Lillian was to remark at a talk to Air Force students in a logistics class in 1959;

> What we hope when we get through, is that we have developed people who are "motion-minded," as Frank called it; people you could put in any job and in any situation who will carry their motion-mindedness with them. That is what we are hoping for as we try to put this work in the five areas of our lives: (1) what we do with ourselves, (2) what we do with our home and family, (3) what we do on our citizen job, (4) what we do on our volunteer job, and (5) what we do on our pay job.[40]

The problem for the Gilbreths was to convince people that something as apparently fleeting and immaterial as motion was as important as other, more material, inputs into the national economy. To the Gilbreths, there was "no waste of any kind in the world that equals the waste from need-less, ill-directed and ineffective motions, and their resulting unnecessary fatigue. Because this is true, there is no industrial opportunity that offers a richer return than the elimination of needless motions, and the transformation of ill-directed and ineffective motions into efficient activity."[41] Their solution to this problem of waste—motion study—was also simple in its basic premises. "Motion study consists of dividing work into the most fundamental elements possible; studying these elements separately and in relation to one another; and from these studied elements, when timed, building methods of least waste."[42] This apparent simplicity served a higher purpose than mere functionalism for the Gilbreths. While Taylor's use of the stopwatch appeared to be secretive and unethical, the clarity of motion study was wrapped in the ideological neutrality of "science"—"its fundamental principles have the exactness of scientific laws which are open to everyone. . . . We have here nothing hidden or occult or secret, like the practices of an old-time craft: we have here a science that is the result of accurately recorded, exact investigation."[43] And as motion was so basic an element of life, it could be applied to all fields—"its laws are universal."[44] Laying between the Gilbreths and their aim of reducing superfluous motions was the problem of making the motions visible and measurable.

Early on in the development of motion-study, Gilbreth took endless conventional photographs of men, particularly bricklayers, at work. As he developed his ideas, and as technology progressed, he began to use moving pictures and advanced photography apparatus. He began to use what he called a "cinematograph"—a moving picture of people at work against a background divided into regular squares—a grid (Figure 4.1). A clock would be placed so that it appeared on the image and registered the passage of time. "What better way of observing motions" he asked "than the moving picture image."[45]

A film strip or "micromotion" image would contain a series of stills of a man or woman at work, separated by fractions of a second. Sometimes the image would include the whole body and other times it would focus on particular limbs—usually hands. The resulting images of people at work are an uncanny synthesis of abstract notions of time and space. The specially designed clock measured time while the grid divided up the space just as it had in the photographs of Muybridge and Marey, but the clarity of the clock and grid were not sufficient for Gilbreth. He wanted to clarify the *motions* involved in work. To do so he attached electric lights to the moving parts he was concerned with and produced a "cyclograph"—a single-frame image produced through an extended exposure in a darkened room. All that remained visible was the path of the light. Still not satisfied, Frank Gilbreth used stereoscopic equipment to produce images in which motions could be seen in three dimensions. These images, however, did not clearly demonstrate the direction of motions. To solve this problem he used flashing lights, which lit quickly and faded slowly producing a series

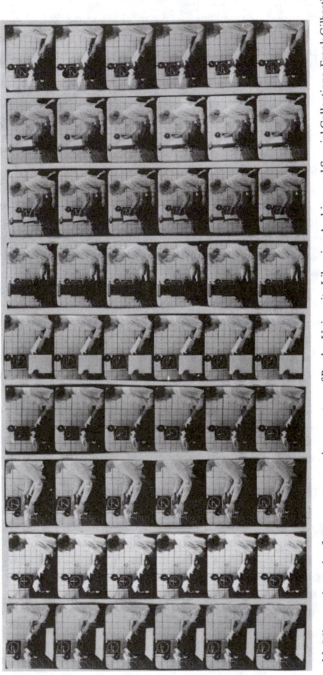

**Figure 4.1** Micromotion strip of woman at typewriter, courtesy of Purdue University Libraries, Archives and Special Collections, Frank Gilbreth Archives, NF Container 13 0031-24 NAFDR.

of light arrows rather than a continuous line. The intervals of the flashing light also revealed the dimension of time (Figure 4.2). Once a stereoscopic flashing cyclograph had been produced, Gilbreth had his assistants make wire models of the movements, complete with painted white strips replicating the flashes on the image.

The Gilbreths referred to the use of these techniques in combination as micromotion study. When Frank and his experts entered a workplace, they would examine the company records to discover which workers were the most efficient. These workers would be studied at work using the naked eye, and their surroundings would be improved so that unnecessary motions, due to the placement of tables, shelves, and other furniture, were removed. Some workers would then be selected for micromotion study, where they would be filmed at work from different angles with a fast-moving clock in full view at sixteen frames a second. Other workers would be shown how to do the task and then filmed. Then the chronocyclograph would be filmed using lights. Gilbreth found it impossible to simultaneously follow all the parts of the body at once as they moved, so he developed another innovation called the Simo (simultaneous motion) chart.

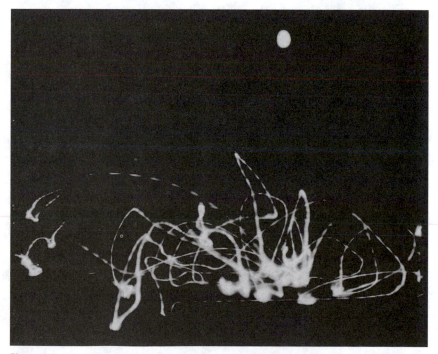

Figure 4.2 A stereoscopic flashing cyclograph of Miss MacPhail's hands folding a handkerchief, courtesy of Purdue University Libraries, Archives and Special Collections, Frank Gilbreth Archives, NF 62 0412-6 NAPTMVK4.

102 • On the Move

Using the film, Gilbreth's observers would note down the movements of each appendage and even the workers' eyes, and then map the motions out on a sheet of paper (see Figure 4.3). Simo charts for different workers would then be hung on the wall and compared. The motion-study expert would then select the best elements from each worker and

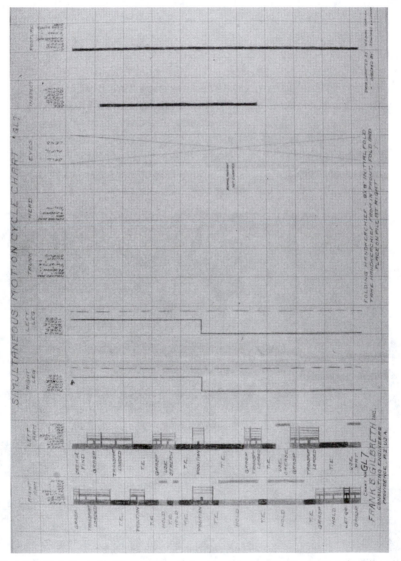

**Figure 4.3** Simultaneous Motion (Simo) chart, courtesy of Purdue University Libraries, Archives and Special Collections, Frank Gilbreth Archives, NF container 52 0297-5 NAPTMH.

combine them into what Gilbreth called the "one best way." This ideal model of motion would then be detailed on an instruction sheet and standing order, noting how the work is to be done and at what speed (see Figure. 4.4).

Gilbreth himself was particularly clear about what he hoped to achieve using this set of innovations:

> Fatigue measurement, as applied to the industries, is a new science. It is being developed though a study of the data of the activity.

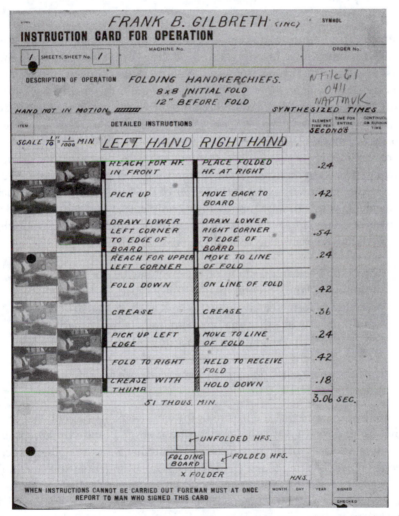

**Figure 4.4** Instruction card for folding handkerchiefs, courtesy of Purdue University Libraries, Archives and Special Collections, Frank Gilbreth Archives, NF 61 0411 NAPTMVK.

> The methods of measurement of activity are motion study, micromotion study, the cyclograph, the chronocyclograph, and the penetrating screen. Through the data derived from these, we standardize motion paths, motion habits, and all other motion variables. These enable us to test and classify, select and place, both work and workers, and to eliminate unnecessary fatigue. Through the time element we compare our various data, and finally arrive at results that enable us to standardize work and rest periods.[46]

Through this process, Gilbreth shifted the emphasis of scientific management from time to motion. The techniques of micromotion study enabled a much finer mapping and modeling of the worker's body than was possible with Taylor's stopwatch. Each task was broken into elementary motions, which Gilbreth called *therbligs* (Gilbreth spelled backwards with a minor alteration). Gilbreth claimed to have discovered seventeen of these motions, which together described the whole universe of possible workplace motions (see Figure 4.5). In micromotion study, these therbligs were separated and recombined to form the "one best way" for doing a particular task. In many ways, the designation of sixteen, and then seventeen elementary motions lies at the center of the Gilbreth enterprise. These movements, after all, were supposedly a complete set—no motion could lie outside of them. The therbligs were the units that dispelled the notion that work could be measured as time alone. As Gilbreth put it:

> The results of careful study of the peculiarities of the therbligs individually, and in combination with those that immediately precede and immediately follow, as well as those that are executed simultaneously by other anatomical members, will remove for all time any idea that scientific motion study of the behavior of workers can be accomplished with any *such obsolete device as a stop watch* or that time study and motion study are the same thing or even similar.[47]

Gilbreth was aware that the nature of these movements might be far from obvious, and took great pains to describe them.[48] Despite these repeated attempts at clarity of definition, it was clear that motion studies experts needed more coaching to tell them apart. "'Grasp' and 'hold still' and 'hold during transportation' are very much alike at times. We distinguish them by an arbitrary distinction, i.e. 'Grasp' is in the set of grasping, 'Hold' is 'Grasping' and not moving. If 'grasped' during 'transport loaded', we call it 'transport loaded'. Any other distinction would be all right, but we have found in practice that these are best."[49]

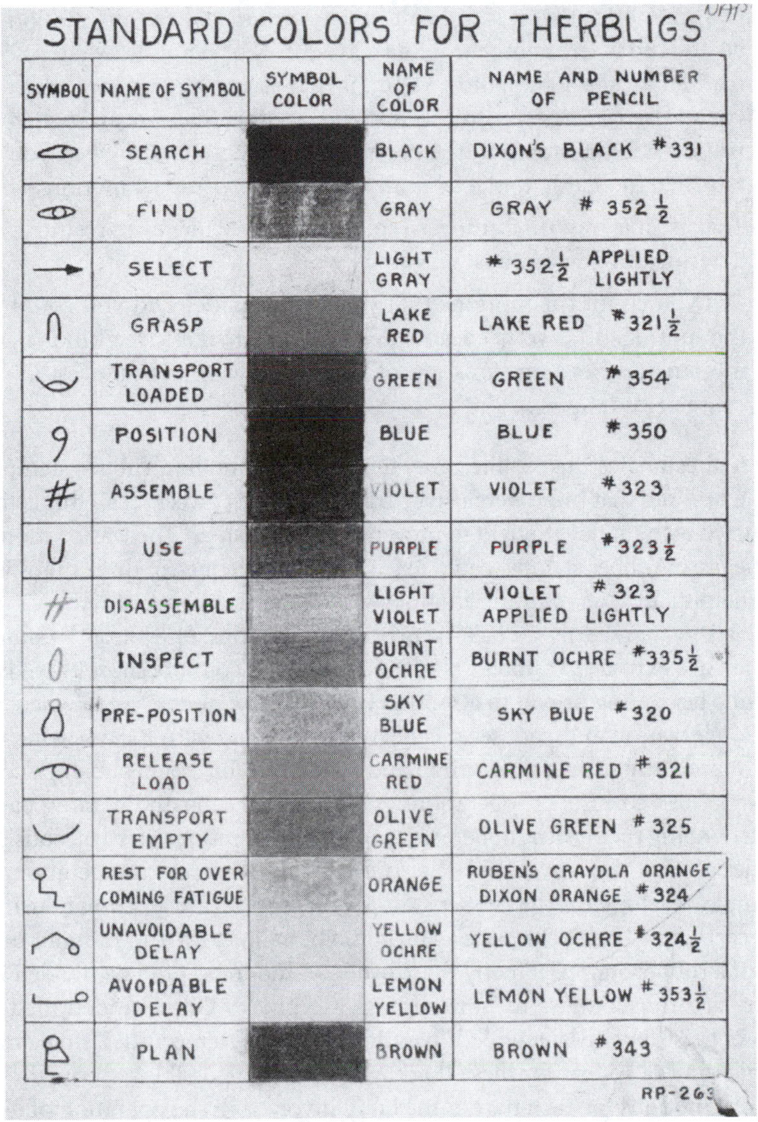

## STANDARD COLORS FOR THERBLIGS

| SYMBOL | NAME OF SYMBOL | SYMBOL COLOR | NAME OF COLOR | NAME AND NUMBER OF PENCIL |
|---|---|---|---|---|
| ⟋⟍ | SEARCH | | BLACK | DIXON'S BLACK #331 |
| ⟋⟍ | FIND | | GRAY | GRAY # 352½ |
| → | SELECT | | LIGHT GRAY | # 352½ APPLIED LIGHTLY |
| ∩ | GRASP | | LAKE RED | LAKE RED #321½ |
| ⌣ | TRANSPORT LOADED | | GREEN | GREEN # 354 |
| 9 | POSITION | | BLUE | BLUE # 350 |
| # | ASSEMBLE | | VIOLET | VIOLET #323 |
| U | USE | | PURPLE | PURPLE #323½ |
| # | DISASSEMBLE | | LIGHT VIOLET | VIOLET #323 APPLIED LIGHTLY |
| 0 | INSPECT | | BURNT OCHRE | BURNT OCHRE #335½ |
| ⍺ | PRE-POSITION | | SKY BLUE | SKY BLUE #320 |
| ⌒ | RELEASE LOAD | | CARMINE RED | CARMINE RED #321 |
| ⌣ | TRANSPORT EMPTY | | OLIVE GREEN | OLIVE GREEN #325 |
| ⌐ | REST FOR OVER COMING FATIGUE | | ORANGE | RUBEN'S CRAYDLA ORANGE DIXON ORANGE #324 |
| ⌒ | UNAVOIDABLE DELAY | | YELLOW OCHRE | YELLOW OCHRE #324½ |
| ⌐ | AVOIDABLE DELAY | | LEMON YELLOW | LEMON YELLOW #353½ |
| ᛒ | PLAN | | BROWN | BROWN #343 |

RP-263

**Figure 4.5** Standard colors for therbligs, courtesy of Purdue University Libraries, Archives and Special Collections, Frank Gilbreth Archives, NF Container 45 0265-20 NAPTM.

In his lectures to potential motion-study experts, Frank Gilbreth would engage in elaborate demonstrations of the difficulties of measuring motions. In one instance, he considers the actions of stamping a pad of paper with a rubber stamp.

Did you notice that it is difficult in determining where one motion begins and where another motion leaves off? For example, when you reached for the stamp, did you count that as one motion and when you carried the stamp to the ink pad another motion and when you carried the stamp to the paper another motion and when you returned the stamp to the table another motion—Total 4 motions—

That is one way of counting motions but it will never result in determining the one best way to do work.

Did you count the motions that your head made? Did you count the motions that your eyes made? The eyes make three kinds of motions and eye motions are of great importance because they cause great fatigue . . .[50]

Gilbreth estimates that, at the time, there were 10 million rubber stamps in active use, and that these were used 1 trillion times per week. If all this activity occurred without due thought to movement, he insisted, "The wasted motions in the use of rubber stamps would reach to the moon once in three months."[51]

The difficulty of counting motions was recognized by Gilbreth. Motion, after all, is marked by its lack of precise boundaries. "[M]otions" Gilbreth wrote, "are extremely difficult if not impossible to count because there is no definite beginning or end to a motion or distinct boundary as to where one motion leaves off and another one begins."[52] Starting with a day's work, Gilbreth gradually breaks down time and space into its smallest components. A day's work consists of "operations" such as "handling and reading papers and stamping them with rubber stamps." These operations, in turn, consist of "cycles of work" or "any complete portion or subdivision of an operation. For example, reaching for the rubber stamp, grasping it, transporting it, using it and carrying it back to its place again could be called a cycle of motions of the use of a rubber stamp." Finally these cycles of motions could be divided into their "natural subdivisions," or therbligs. Originally Gilbreth identified sixteen of these, but he later added "planning" as the seventeenth. Using a mnemonic symbol system for these therbligs, it became possible to write down a cycle of motions for each part of the body involved in the operation of using a rubber stamp—the hands and the eyes.[53] Gilbreth also impressed upon his students the importance of thirty-five essential "principles of motion economy," examples of which included using the fewest motions possible for a given result (principle 11) and the necessity of arranging motions to "build rhythm and automaticity into the operation" (principle 16).[54]

## Mobility as Habit

It is worth pausing to consider notions of *habit*, which are central to the endeavors of the Gilbreths. Frank Gilbreth was well aware of the power of habitual embodied movement. Habit—the kind of unreflective, nonrepresentational intentionality discussed by Merleau-Ponty, Bourdieu, and others was both his enemy and his friend.[55] It was his clear aim to rid workers of bad engrained habits—sometimes, as with bricklaying, the result of hundreds of years of experience—and replace them with good habits. In other words, the Gilbreths wanted to mould human movement at the level of habit, below the radar of consciousness. To accomplish this though, a painful dislocation had to occur between the rejection of old habits and the arrival of new ones.

Consider bricklaying. Bricklaying, Gilbreth argues "has passed through all the eras of history, it has been practiced by nations barbarous and civilized, and was therefore in a condition supposed to be perfection before we applied motion study to it, and revolutionized it."[56] This long history, in Gilbreth's mind, had led to a kind of rule-of-thumb method of laying bricks that varied from place to place and even bricklayer to bricklayer. Bricklaying had been developed as a secretive craft passed down from those who know to those who don't. Motion study, as a scientific form of analysis, would find the one best way to lay bricks. Standing in the way, though, was habit. "Not only do habitual motions become fixed," he wrote "but also the previous experience of the bricklayer is often the cause of his making *too many motions,* i.e., unnecessary motions. He seldom, if ever, has been rigidly trained to use a certain number of different motions."[57]

Among the "superfluous" and "unnecessary" motions Gilbreth observed in bricklayers was the tendency for workers to spin bricks around to see which side was the smoothest in order to even out the irregularities of uneven bricks. In addition, the bricklayers would tap bricks into the mortar several times lightly rather than with one brisk tap. Finally, the bricklayer would almost always pick up dropped mortar in order to avoid waste. The mortar, Gilbreth asserted, was not as valuable as the motions necessary to save it. The problem was that all of these motions had become automatic and habitual.

> Nearly all often-repeated motions become automatic. This is especially true of motions that require no careful supervision of mind or eye.
>
> The automaticity of motions is of great assistance to the worker whose training and methods conform to standardized motions. This fact makes it necessary to have the apprentice taught the right motions first, last and always.[58]

Automatic motion and habit were a constant source of fascination to the Gilbreths. One of the basic principles Frank Gilbreth insisted on was that workers should be taught initially to work as fast as possible rather than focus on quality of work. Working slowly in order to improve quality, he argued, led to bad habits. "You cannot get output with least fatigue unless you have habit. You cannot get habit on a different speed than what you are supposed to work."[59] In other words, you had to start at the speed you would eventually be expected to work at in order to develop the appropriate habitual mobility. Gilbreth would often describe experiments where he would get a worker to work deliberately slowly in order to show the influence of habit. While working at a handkerchief factory, he instructed a handkerchief folder to fold slowly: "You say to the girl, 'Fold slowly.' It has become so automatic that she cannot fold slowly. She has sub-station brains in her fingers."[60]

One of the principle purposes of the cyclograph technique was to establish what good habitual mobility looked like: "We find that the cyclographs of experts in all lines show smooth curves. These indicate well established habits, ease and the grace that comes from perfect control."[61] The wire models Gilbreth had constructed were used as aids in instilling good motion habits in workers. Gilbreth was confronted with the familiar dilemma of representing human mobility in order to make it amenable to regulation through science. A letter from one of the motion experts hired by Gilbreth to introduce his system into a factory makes the connection between the tangibility of motion in the wire models and the importance of teaching good mobility habits.

> I recommend that a young man, who is a pupil in motion study, should make several wire models in order to divest himself of the idea of vagueness and etherealness of motions, to learn what to see, and to realise that elementary motions are as definite conceptions and objects as the iron or brass shapes that are to be fashioned into the finished product.[62]

The Gilbreths were obviously heartened by the reported success of their methods and subsequently wrote a paper on the motion models expressing the importance of making motion tangible in order to encourage good habits. "It is extremely difficult to demonstrate to the average person the reality and value, and especially the money value, of an intangible thing. The motion model makes this value apparent and impressive. It makes tangible the fact that time is money, and that an unnecessary motion is money lost forever."[63] To the beginner the motion model would represent a finished product—a standard: "Through its use he can see what he has to do, learn about it through his eye, follow the wire with his fingers, and thus accustom his muscles to the activity that they are expected to perform."[64]

Indeed the focus on habit meshes well with more recent concerns of postphenomenological theories of practice. The movements of our body, or even parts of our body, are fundamental to who we are and who we have been trained to be. While phenomenological philosophers taught us that our movements are the basic ways we relate to the world, more recent theorists of the body have shown how these movements are the product and also the producer of our social position.[65] The mobile body is made meaningful and simultaneously makes meaning. It does so in the context of social and power relations that are systematically asymmetrical. The Gilbreths aimed to make the body's mobility meaningful through making people inhabit an abstraction (to make abstraction into experience, into a habit)—a durable way of being.

It is through this process of the abstraction of mobility from individual worker's bodies that Gilbreth believed he could choreograph the factory so that the movements of workers were no longer their own but the product of the stopwatch, the camera, and the intentions of management.[66] The system Frank and Lillian developed sought to transform the threatening body of the lazy worker into a machine—an object that served capitalist production. The worker's body was disciplined through the construction of space and time and the division of movements within that space/time. The aim of motion study was to negate the differences between the bodily movements of workers and create uniform motions in their place. In other words, he sought to replace unalienated mobility with abstract motion through a process of editing that excluded excessive and superfluous mobility.

## Organizing Aaron

There is certainly no figure like Schmidt in Frank Gilbreth's notes and writings. On the whole, Gilbreth seems more respectful of the workers in the factories where he worked. He liked to involve the workers in the technology that was being applied to them, and he worked through their involvement and gentle persuasion. They were regularly given lectures about what motion study involved, and were shown movies Gilbreth had made of some of them at work. In one factory Gilbreth set up his micromotion equipment in a so-called *betterment room*, which was separate from the shop floor. People who participated in his experiments were paid bonuses for their involvement.[67] In the Gilbreth archives there are many apparently pointless images of workers goofing around in one of Gilbreth's gridded rooms. They are pulling faces and smiling. Gilbreth enrolled the workers in his project, convincing them that his work was in their best interest—not by increasing output, but by decreasing fatigue. Gilbreth, unlike Taylor, was well aware that the translation of bad mobility habits into good ones was potentially painful for the workers concerned. In his lectures to motion-study students he made this clear.

> We have this terrible thing ahead of us. We are making this person do an old job a new way. We come in with a conscious air of being smarter than anyone else. . . . In the final analysis we are going to set a task on an unskilled man, and expect him to do more work, and after that task has been achieved in a reasonable time he is going to continue and bring that time down. You are going to upset his skill.[68]

In another instance Gilbreth relates the experience of entering a handkerchief factory to produce the best way of folding handkerchiefs with the least possible movements.

> One fold is to make a large handkerchief fit a small box. Another is to show you the initial in the corner. These are the principle folds. Most of the forty five girls work on these two folds. How would you tackle the problem of showing girls who had worked anywhere from three months to twenty five years folding handkerchiefs how to do it? Everybody is looking at you. You never bought a handkerchief in your life. Your wife bought them for you. You did not know how handkerchiefs should be folded. It really seems almost impossible that a person from outside could come in and show them how to do it.[69]

Despite a certain uneasiness on the part of Gilbreth and his willingness to enroll the workers in his projects, some of his practices and those of his associates must have seemed bizarre and overbearing. Indeed Gilbreth, like Taylor, did meet with fairly considerable resistance to his methods on several occasions. In 1919, for instance, messenger boys at Pierce Arrow Automobile Company threatened to strike unless Gilbreth fulfilled his promise to promote those who successfully utilized his system. He disbanded them. In 1924 workers at the American Radiator Company in Buffalo downed tools and refused to be studied by Gilbreth's assistants. As a result, Gilbreth's contract was revoked.[70]

These accounts of worker resistance to having their mobilities reconfigured are relatively well known. What is less well known is the interaction between Gilbreth's assistants and individual workers on the shop floor. Take the story of Aaron, for instance. We do not know much about Aaron. He is one of the workers who formal history frequently leaves unrecorded. He does appear several times in letters from one of Gilbreth's motion managers, Mr. S. Edgar Whitaker, who had been sent to implement the Taylor System at the New England Butt Company in Rhode Island.

On July 4, 1912 Whitaker wrote to Gilbreth about the state of the toilets:

> I find the toilets and urinals in quite an untidy condition, presumably through lack of proper attention. I have spent a good part of the day, trying to determine a practical method of cleaning the closets, without an excess of hard labor. I recommend the issuance of a standing order, providing that the care of the toilet rooms be assigned to a definite person and that daily the bowls shall be swabbed out on the inside with a cloth using one circular motion, and then flushed, and that twice a week the outside shall be wiped over with a moist cloth.[71]

Letters such as this reveal the incredible detail of Gilbreth's motion study. In an ideal world, the whole factory and everyone in it would be subject to scrutiny. In practice, Gilbreth was never allowed to institute motion study in the upper echelons of company hierarchy. Although he tried, he was never allowed to train the motions of managers, but janitors were fair game and it was with them that Whitaker went about his business. Motion study could come up with a way to clean a toilet efficiently. It took Whitaker less than a week. A letter of July 10th read, "[a]s a result of our investigation, one man has been assigned the work of thoroughly cleaning the bowls of the toilets by the use of Dutch Cleanser, both inside and outside. I will prepare a Standing Order providing for daily inspection and attention to the toilets, using as few motions as possible."[72] Once the toilets were sorted out and some valuable motions had been saved, Whitaker turned his attention to the more general duties of the janitor.

> Under the present arrangement, a waste basket is carried around by the care-taker (Aaron) and the contents of the various waste baskets are emptied into it; then the basket is taken down cellar and the contents are dumped over the coal in front of the boilers. The papers scatter all over the coal and the space is untidy; the shovelling of papers into the fire with the coal is a mental worry and annoyance to the fireman; often he shovels several times to get a piece of paper into the fire; and worst of all, the fire is unnecessarily cooled by having the fire-door open a needlessly long time. . . .

> A new arrangement went into effect to-day. Aaron takes a burlap bag with him on his rounds; the opening is big enough to take in the top of the basket which is turned upside down so that the contents of the basket drop into the bag; Aaron takes the bag to the boiler-room and empties it into a barrel that is specially painted and stencilled "Paper" in black letters. . . .

> I am gradually working out a definite time-table for Aaron.[73]

Reading these letters the reader has to feel sorry for Aaron. The archive only records Whitaker's version of events, but it is possible to imagine what this must have seemed like to Aaron. He was probably a recent immigrant who traveled across the Atlantic from eastern Europe. He had secured a job as a caretaker in a factory that made machines to braid laces, embroidery material, and other fabrics. Minding his own business, he would clean up after the workers and managers, emptying their bins and wiping their toilets. It was hardly the American Dream but it paid a wage and kept him busy. And then Whitaker arrives and tells him to clean toilets using only two swipes. This annoying intruder with his stopwatch and notepad follows him around for weeks. Every little motion is recorded and he is presented with timetables and instruction cards. He is not Taylor's Schmidt, but he must have felt equally put upon. Whitaker's letters to Gilbreth continue (he was nothing if not thorough in his reporting). Aaron appears again in a letter of July 17:

> This morning I was in the factory at 6.40 to make a study of the sort of work done by Aaron from the time he comes in until 11 O'clock and his way of doing it. From what I have seen, I regard it as a joke that he should spend 3 hours in sweeping and dusting the offices on the three floors. He works at a disadvantage a good part of the time. He does some things that another person should do. . . . His way of collecting the waste paper a room at a time results in a good many unnecessary steps. He starts in on the first floor, collects waste paper in a basket, sweeps and dusts, goes to the boiler room, some 200 feet distant to empty his waste paper basket, fills the ice water tank, cleans and dusts the toilet rooms, lavatories and toilets, then goes to the Supt's. office on the second floor and goes through a similar performance, then takes the drafting room and omits and Planning room. It is now after 9 o'clock.[74]

On July 19 we hear that Aaron has made a record of cleaning 225 panes of glass in an hour of window washing, but this is not good enough, as a letter of July 30 makes clear:

> When I come across Aaron in window washing, I find he is not working under satisfactory conditions. As an instance of what I mean, in the assembly room he was doing the necessary carpenter work in loosening up the windows so that they would slide up and down easily. Most of the upper sashes were stuck fast. I shall have to devise ways to eliminate as far as possible all these hindrances.
>
> I enclose a chart regarding window washing.[75]

Aaron's attitude to Whitaker may have been one of bemused incredulity for a while, but the constant new instructions and unremitting observation must have begun to annoy him. Whitaker's letters begin to contain a note of exasperation with his increasingly argumentative janitor.

> I was with Aaron at 6 o'clock this morning and pushed him through his morning sweeping and dusting tasks by 8.15 instead of his usual hour of 9.30. He is a foreigner and does not readily understand what he is told, and likes or has a natural tendency to argue matters. If one is very patient, I think he can be taught to do all necessary work using the right motions in an hour and a half.[76]

This is the last we hear of the unfortunate Aaron. On October 16 Whitaker writes ominously that he has "turned over the window washing to Mr. Shipley. He should easily increase the rate to 450 panes per hour under standard conditions." Perhaps Aaron was sacked, perhaps he was simply allocated different and equally tedious work. We will never know.

## Lillian Gilbreth and Domestic Mobility

Frank Gilbreth's wife, business partner and coauthor Lillian Gilbreth probably contributed more to motion study than he did. She coauthored many of the books that have only his name on the cover. When her name does appear, it is with initials only, indicating the degraded position of women in business and engineering at the turn of the century.[77] Frank died in 1924 and Lillian made the decision, along with her eleven children, to continue their work on motion study. Lillian lived until 1972 and continued to give lectures right up to her death. Immediately after Frank's death, however, she could not find work in factories. The contracts that had been given to Gilbreth, Inc. were canceled. Two engineering clubs that had invited L. M. Gilbreth to speak withdrew their invitations when they discovered she was a woman. In addition, she was discouraged from joining the American Society of Mechanical Engineers. These were still seen as masculine spaces and Lillian, regardless of her expertise, was not welcome.

Lillian's solution to this problem was to make her gender work for her by applying motion study to the home. Just as Frank had produced disciplined mobile bodies in the workplace, so Lillian would work on the more ambiguous spaces of women's work. From the office typewriter to the department store to the domestic kitchen, Lillian sought to extend the scope of rational motion. As Laurel Graham has written:

These extensions claimed women's work practices as a new terrain on which to cultivate discipline: new professions arose to realign women's bodies, tools, spaces and thoughts with the particular demands of twentieth century political and economic contexts. Together, these new efforts provided the first pieces of an emerging disciplinary network forming around women to integrate them with a rationalized society.[78]

Household engineering was an increasingly important part of American domestic life. By the 1920s, households had fewer and fewer servants due to restrictions on immigration and employment opportunities elsewhere. Middle-class women had to run their own households.[79] Homes were spaces in transformation as water, electricity, and gas were provided cheaply and reliably for the first time.[80] All kinds of appliances came on the market promising to save housewives time and energy.[81] Ironically, as Ruth Cowan has argued, these appliances invariably led to the creation of more work for the middle-class woman at home.

Just as Taylor had an enemy in the body of the soldiering worker, so the new world of domestic science found its target in the body of the traditional household worker. The traditional housewife was consistently represented as haphazard and chaotic in her lack of planning and random motions. Science and technology were given as the answer to the problem of the chaotic housewife. The late nineteenth century had been marked by the cult of domesticity, which firmly linked the household and the housewife to morality.[82] By the 1920s the new domestic scientists were gently pulling this cult apart and replacing it with a new set of associations between morality and modernity. The nineteenth-century homemaker was becoming the twentieth-century home manager.[83]

Christine Frederick instigated the quest for rationality and efficiency in the home in 1913 in her book *The New Housekeeping*. This book introduced Taylor's notion of scientific management to the home, arguing that women were driven to their careers by irrational domestic space constructed through habit and tradition rather than science. As early as 1916, Lillian Gilbreth had thought about motions in the kitchen and how they might be saved.[84] In addition, Lillian and Frank had institutionalized scientific management in their own home, where they had to order the motions of eleven children. Indeed, their life was later turned into a novel, *Cheaper by the Dozen,* which later became a stage play and film. In a 1930 speech, Lillian Gilbreth reflected on this experience.

> We considered our time too valuable to be devoted to actual labor in the home. We were executives. So we worked out a plan

for the running of our house, adopting charts and a maintenance and follow-up system as is used in factories. When one
of the children took a bath or brushed his teeth we made a cross
on a chart. Household tasks were divided between the children.
We had three rows of hooks, one marked "jobs to be done", one
marked "jobs being done" and a third marked "jobs completed"
with tags which were moved from hook to hook to indicate the
progress of a task. [85]

The observation that Frank and Lillian's time was "too valuable" for work in
the home reflects the ideological division of manual labor and "brain work"
institutionalized in Taylorized factory space. It was quite clear to Frank,
when working on factory motion, that he was selling his expertise to the
owners and managers of factories. These people would not hire Lillian, so
she had to find new clients—people to whom she could sell her expertise.
Women in the home were both management and labor, and were unlikely to
pay Lillian to impose motion study on themselves. Neither could motions be
accounted for in any strict sense as domestic labor did not produce profits.
Lillian's solution was to work within the new cultural forces of advertising
and consumer marketing for the scientific household. She began to write
for suddenly popular magazines such as *Ladies Home Journal* and was soon
selling her expertise to manufacturers of kitchens and appliances. Lillian's
work was as much about consumption as it was about production, and
increasingly it was women at home who were seen as the ideal consumers.[86]

By 1926, two years after Frank's death, Lillian had begun to conduct
motion-study experiments on activities such as making beds and setting
tables. She utilized many of the technologies and representational strategies
developed with Frank for factory work. When she turned her attention to
dishwashing, she discovered that a homemaker could reduce the annual
walking distance for this task from 26 miles to 9 miles. By the late 1920s, her
attention was firmly fixed on kitchens.[87] By 1930 Lillian had established herself
as leading figure in the use of scientific management in the home. She was
hired by the Brooklyn Borough Gas Company to design a kitchen for display
at the Exposition of Women's Arts and Industries. The result was called the
Kitchen Practical and was taken up by the New York Herald Tribune Institute
as a model for its instructions on how to plan a scientific and efficient kitchen
(Figure 4.6). The importance of motion study to the kitchen was made clear
in a poem Lillian wrote that was displayed on the wall of the kitchen.

*"My All-Electric Kitchen "*
    With power at my finger-tips—

**Figure 4.6** The Kitchen Practical as exhibited by the Brooklyn Borough Gas Company, courtesy of Purdue University Libraries, Archives and Special Collections, Frank Gilbreth Archives.

I work whene'er I please
With shortest motions, space and time
Efficiency and Ease
Here skill and satisfaction
Can have an equal part
The active mind, the busy hand
The happy-singing heart.[88]

Because the household manager was both manager and worker, it was not possible to separate the measurement of motion from its enactment. Lillian therefore gave women the knowledge to police their own motions in order to produce the perfect kitchen. In her notes accompanying the Kitchen Practical, she suggests that women draw a floor plan with a scale of a one-half inch to a foot, and include each piece of equipment at the same scale on the plan. The kitchen planner should also have a pair of compasses that were set (to scale) to the length of the worker's reach. Once these were available, the planner/worker/manager was instructed to make a process chart of her own actions in the process of baking. Baking was chosen because it was seen to provide the most satisfactory expression of "the homemaker's desire to create something which would contribute to the pleasure and wellbeing of her family."[89]

To make the process chart, Lillian suggests listing all the operations necessary in the "get ready," the "do it," and the "clean up" phases of the task in the correct order and assigning them a number which could then be connected with lines denoting movement. By this process a chart would show:

1. The total number of operations performed.
2. How many of these required walking.
3. Whether or not the smooth progress of the work was being constantly interfered with by having to move from place to place.[90]

The next step in producing the Kitchen Practical was to construct a string chart on the assembled plan. A pin was placed on each of the work stations used, and these were connected by string following the order of the numbers in the process chart. The string could then be removed and measured to reveal the total distance walked in the preparation of the perfect cake. The kitchen planner could test several possible kitchen plans in this way and hang the resultant strings next to each other showing graphically the amount of movement necessary in each layout. Lillian used several recipes to demonstrate this process. Making coffee cake she managed to reduce the distance traveled from 143 feet in a typical kitchen to 24 feet in the new kitchen. The measurements for the more complicated lemon meringue pie were 224 feet and 92 feet.[91]

The secret to Lillian's Kitchen Practical was the invention of the *circular workplace*, which involved arranging the key pieces of equipment in the kitchen within the radius of the worker's reach. Literature accompanying the Kitchen Practical suggests that utilizing Lillian's circular workplace would "eliminate all the unnecessary motions."

> The arrangement in the Institute kitchen has been given a practical test by which it has proved that this plan had cut almost in half the number of motions required in preparing any given dish, and has reduced to less than one-sixth the amount of walking required. The Institute is not opposed to walking and exercise for the woman of the family—far from it! But we do maintain that she should take that exercise in the open air, rather than in a treadmill round of refrigerator to sink, to stove and back again.[92]

This circular workplace was the original version of what is now known as the *kitchen triangle*. Kitchens all over the Western world are designed according to the simple spatial arrangement of food storage (refrigerator), cooking (hob, oven), and cleaning (sink) in a convenient triangle. In large part this is thanks to Lillian Gilbreth's desire to save us unnecessary motions in the kitchen. It also freed up time in which other tasks could be achieved. In one pamphlet produced by the Brooklyn Borough Gas Company they suggest that "every housewife study her stove to see exactly what she does on it, the time involved, and the delay periods when she could do something else, and try to utilize these periods."[93]

Models of the Kitchen Practical and other arrangements were made available for potential customers to walk through and explore, complete with Brooklyn Borough Gas Company advertising and products. Leaflets demonstrated the efficiency of motion achieved through Gilbreth's ingenuity with diagrams representing the walking patterns of typical housewives engaged in various forms of baking in, first, a "typically haphazard kitchen" and, second, the Kitchen Practical (Figure 4.7).

One element of the Kitchen Practical was another invention of Gilbreth's—the management desk. The desk was seen as a crucial part of a Gilbreth kitchen—a place where work could be planned. Just as Taylor and Frank Gilbreth institutionalized a planning space in the factory for "brain work," so the home could have its Gilbreth desk. Indeed, the literature explaining the desk tells us, "The new Gilbreth Management Desk might well be called the General Business Headquarters of the Household Manager." The desk featured an electric clock that guaranteed "constant,

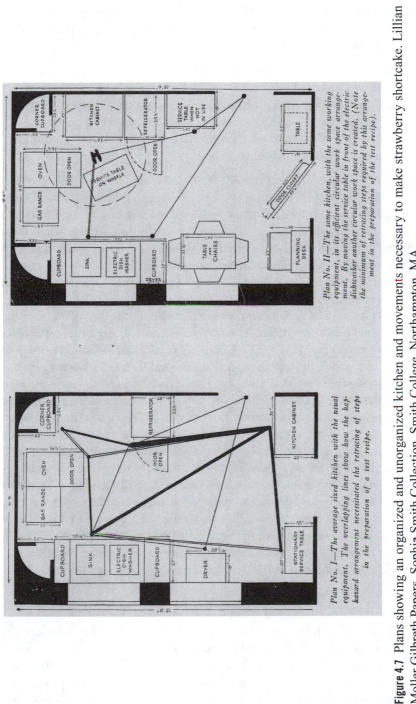

Plan No. I—The average sized kitchen with the usual equipment. The overlapping lines show how the haphazard arrangement necessitated the retracing of steps in the preparation of a test recipe.

Plan No. II—The same kitchen, with the same working equipment, in its efficient circular work space arrangement. By moving the service table in front of the electric dishwasher another circular work space is created. (Note the minimum of retracing steps required by this arrangement in the preparation of the test recipe).

**Figure 4.7** Plans showing an organized and unorganized kitchen and movements necessary to make strawberry shortcake. Lillian Moller Gilbreth Papers, Sophia Smith Collection, Smith College, Northampton, MA.

accurate time." On opening the desk, the household manager would see a radio, a typewriter, a telephone, and an adding machine, all surrounded by useful books for handy hints.

> Immediately at hand, in compartments at right and left, are located the household money budget and the visible charts containing comprehensive information on food, marketing, cooking, cleaning, health, education, finance and many other important subjects. And, in two near drawers on either side, we find cards of a complete household filing system.[94]

Behind this remarkable array of devices and spaces is an equally remarkable philosophy of motion and efficiency that reaches the heights of moral fervor. "Order is Heaven's first law," the brochure tells us, before informing us that the desk will bring you nearer to Heaven by establishing *order*. Most importantly: "Unnecessary steps are eliminated. . . . unnecessary fatigue is banished." With the Gilbreth Management Desk, "You sail over a smooth sea, over a well charted course. You save your strength, your money and your peace of mind."

Mobility and its rationalization are coded in a number of ways in the development of the Kitchen Practical. Efficiency, order, and rationality are the central principles. The Kitchen Practical is definitely a *modern* kitchen with the full force of modernity behind it. Previous arrangements are described as irrational and haphazard. But the production of modern mobilities in the kitchen is also about happiness. Lillian Gilbreth invented the concept of "happiness minutes"—her way of describing the time saved by carefully reducing motions at home in order to create "time-out for happiness." Finally, the new mobilities are seen as healthy. Along with Frank she had long ago recoded motion study as fatigue study in a way that neatly sidestepped the accusations of inhumanity leveled at Taylor by unions and Congress. Rather than motions being reordered for the purposes of increased production, they were described as saving workers, and later domestic workers, from fatigue and illness. To reorder motions in the home was rational, pleasurable, and healthy. Modernity, mobility, and morality are combined in the space of the home.[95]

## Conclusion

To Lillian Gilbreth, and her husband, motions needed to be saved. On the face of it, the story of Lillian and Frank Gilbreth, as well as that of Frederick Taylor, is not so much a story of the production of mobilities, but one of the eradication of mobilities—those considered superfluous to the production of steel, handkerchiefs, or lemon meringue pies. Yet behind this reduction in motions was the sense that new ways of moving—modern and efficient ways—would be cultivated. Not only would these new movements be efficient, they would be moral. New moral geographies of mobility were produced in the kitchen as well as the factory. As Laurel Graham has brilliantly argued, the production of ideal mobilities in the kitchen were part and parcel of an overall strategy to allow power to circulate in new ways. Women, like workers, were being invested with a new form of productive power rather than simply being denied power.[96] The regulation of time and motion were the key central pivot of the projects of Taylor and the Gilbreths. Their representational strategies sought to make the bodies of workers in the factory and the home intelligible in new ways. Once they could be made intelligible, they could be rearranged at the level of habit. Modernity was making its mark at the level of the habitual through the rearrangement of motion and the redesign of space to produce the Gilbreths' goal of the one best way to do things. Following Foucault we can see this as a move from authoritarianism to enrollment. Women, as Graham points out, were being enrolled into the new consumer society through the play of bodies, spaces and objects, networks and minds, which were reorganized in order to allow power to circulate. This rearrangement enacted by Lillian Gilbreth, the makers of the new model kitchen, and the wider world of the consumer society, created new associations between an array of materials, practices, and bodies in the home. New kinds of objects, such as the refrigerator and the Gilbreth desk as well as the kitchen as a whole, and new kinds of spaces (the work triangle, the planning office) were connected by useful and efficient motions and new mentalities in which modern efficiency became a moral cause. The rational assemblage of spaces, objects, and motions had to reflect concepts and ideologies. Gilbreth's Kitchen Practical linked material practices of motion to notions of happiness, satisfaction, and health through the intermediaries of Gilbreth herself, the New York Herald Tribune Institute, the Brooklyn Borough Gas Company, and the products that filled the kitchen. The study of motion enacted by Lillian Gilbreth marks a logical progression from Taylor timing the unfortunate Schmidt to see how he could most efficiently transport pig iron during the working day. But work was not the only realm of life being transformed by the drive to produce more regulated mobilities. In chapter 5 we will see how a similar process was enacted in the world of dance.

## CHAPTER 5

# "You Cannot Shake That Shimmie Here": Producing Mobility on the Dance Floor

The history of the eradication of superfluous motion in modernity came to the fore at a meeting in the late afternoon of Wednesday, May 12, 1920, at the Grafton Galleries in London. Two hundred dance teachers from around Britain met to discuss the condition of dance—particularly ballroom dance—in London and the provinces. The meeting had been called by the editor of the Dancing Times, Philip Richardson, who in his *History of Ballroom Dancing* recalled that: "It seemed highly desirable to me, as editor of the *Dancing Times*, that something should be done to call a halt to freakish dancing before it became something worse."[1] In this chapter I explore the processes of standardization of movement in ballroom dancing that preceded and followed this meeting. The movement of dance seems, at first glance, to inhabit a different world from the movement of work. Work appears to be the realm of unfreedom and constraint, while dance is often thought of as a realm of freedom, pleasure, and play.[2] Dance is an activity associated with free time—the weekend, the night. But it is not as simple as this. The history of dance, like the history of work, reveals the operations of an array of disciplinary practices and deep-rooted ideologies of mobility. In this chapter, then, we will see how ballroom dancing became enmeshed in beliefs about appropriate and inappropriate mobility. In particular we will see how the development of ballroom dancing is founded on its own constitutive outside—the dance of African- and Latin-American cultures. Mobility, as in the preceding chapters, is not set against place or immobility, but against other, disreputable forms of mobility. This chapter traces the process by which ballroom dancing in Britain and the commonwealth was produced in relation to the dance of clubs in Britain and the Americas. The dancing body that emerges at the end of the process is surely one that experiences pleasure, but one that, nonetheless, embodies a complex process of exclusion and othering. As with the examples of Taylor and the Gilbreths, it is an account of the production of correct movement.

The process of the production of mobilities on the dance floor involves a number of representational practices. The first revolves around the designation of certain kinds of dance movements as "degenerate" and "freakish" through a process of locating them within particular normative geographical understandings. These steps, such as the shimmy and the turkey-trot are variously located in Africa, in Latin America, and in the United States. Further, they are described as originating in particular kinds of clubs and spaces associated with jazz music and black cultures. By locating these movements in these spaces, the moves were encoded as necessarily suspicious and disreputable. The second representational strategy considered here is the production of "appropriate" or "correct" movement through forms of classification that sought to create universally accepted dance forms suitable for "the right kind of people." Throughout this process, correct movements were encoded in relation to the "freak steps" of supposedly foreign cultures. What the dance teachers of early–twentieth-century Britain were seeking to do was produce dance, shorn of its supposedly seedy origins, which was policeable and teachable according to set universal agreements about what the movements of dance should look like. In so doing they produced an aesthetics of ideal mobility.

## Dance and Mobility

Dance, like mobility in general, has been and continues to be an object of struggle in modernity and postmodernity. Attempts have been made to channel threatening mobilities into acceptable conduits. As we shall see, the graceful steps of ballroom dance are no exception. Recent developments in dance scholarship have seen an increasingly productive engagement with other moves in cultural studies.[3] If scholars elsewhere, the argument goes, have developed sophisticated ways of reading texts both written and visual, why not do the same for bodily movement? Dancers and choreographers have, after all, played a central role in making sense of movement in modern times. In the early nineteenth century, Francois Delsarte sought to develop a logical system of expressive movement through the careful observation of people as they moved, going so far as to visit morgues around mines following a disaster in order to see how the "bereaved betrayed their grief." Similarly, he would hide in bushes and watch children at play and take note of differences in the ways they moved. "[W]ith cold scientific detachment he peered at humanity unconsciously registering its emotions and made copious notes."[4] He divided the body into three zones (head, torso and arms, lower trunk and legs) and subdivided each into three. From this he generated nine laws of gesture and three major codes of movement referred to as opposition, parallelism, and succession. A similar attempt to codify the universe of movement was made by the Swiss choreographer Emile Jacques-Dalcroze, who developed a set of bodily exercises (eurythmics) to generate rhythmic awareness in musicians, dancers, and others. Perhaps the most far-reaching attempt to codify movement in dance, though, was produced by Rudolf von Laban.

Laban was one of the most important figures in the production of corporeal mobility in the early- and mid-twentieth century. It was Laban who developed a system of representing the mobility of dancers (a writing of mobility), since called Labanotation, and used almost universally in notating dance. Laban was born in 1879 in Bratislava. Following an early interest in architecture he turned his attention to choreography. He made his name as the Director of Movement at the Berlin State Opera. His relationship with the Nazis was a difficult one, and he eventually had to leave Germany for Britain. Once there, he continued with his choreography and took his ideas about movement into the workplace as part of the war effort, in order to boost British industrial output. In this period he worked with the British industrialist F. C. Lawrence to develop the Laban-Lawrence Industrial Rhythm. Like Marey and the Gilbreths, the philosophy of mobility was at the heart of his enterprise.

Laban's work with Lawrence closely mirrored the work of the Gilbreths in the United States. Like the Gilbreths he believed that motion was at the heart of factory output, and like the Gilbreths he theorized mobility in relation to the problematics of effort and fatigue. Additionally, Laban and Lawrence were pioneers in the use of cinematic technology in the workplace. Key to Laban's approach to bodily movements was the observation that how people move reflects something of their inner self. As Laban put it: "[t]he main bulk of movement and dance expression consists of motor elements, which can be freely combined to reveal something about the inner state of the moving person."[5] As with Marey, Laban believed that movement was a key philosophical nut to crack. Its importance was fundamental. "Movement in itself is the language in which our highest and most fundamental inspirations are expressed" he wrote, "[w]e have forgotten too much of this language. Movement fills our whole working time, no matter in what kind of work we are engaged. It seems quite an unimportant subordinate if our work consists mainly of thinking, writing, speaking, or any other so-called mental activity. But dealing with such a subordinate may be quite a tricky business."[6] Motion, to Laban, was "visible everywhere in the whole universe, permeated all the sciences and practical fields of application, thus building an almost inextricable network of common interest in its study."[7] To make any sense of this movement, however, it was first necessary to produce a form of notation that could account for the universe of bodily movements. Like Gilbreth's systems of therbligs, Laban devised a complicated scheme of symbols through which movement could be written, just as music could be written. His notation system is used around the world in dance instruction.

Laban was also fascinated with the automatic or habitual nature of much movement. It was during World War II that Laban used his expertise in dance movement to help the British war effort by increasing productivity in factories through motion study. It was in the factory that habitual movement became the object of his curiosity. "Many movements" he wrote "are, however, done without the investigations and guidance of a conscious decision. In the automatic repetitive movements used so frequently in industry, the worker does not think of the motive, or even the effect of his movements, he simply performs them in the right order after having taken the decision to do the work."[8] In Laban's work, then, the world of work and the world of dance come together. Despite the observation of movement's universality, however, his consideration of movement in the workplace is just as marked by ideologies of mobility as any other. Take his assessment of the gendered nature of movement at work for instance.

> It had been assumed that operating a machine for drilling holes into medium-sized logs, involving little weight-lifting and the simple handling of a few clamps and switches, was not difficult and might well prove suitable for a girl. What had been left out of consideration was that the job was very straightforward, requiring direct and angular movements. The space effort to be used thereby does not correspond with the natural nimbleness and flexibility of feminine effort. Our argument was that unless a girl could be found who had a masculine flow of movement, the job had better be left to a man or boy.[9]

In this analysis the purified world of movement becomes encoded with gender and the politics of mobility take over.

It is just this politics of mobility—the way in which movement becomes socially encoded—that has been the object of recent work in dance theory.

Jane Desmond, for instance, has argued for a formalist reading of dance movement. "While most scholars have spent years developing analytic skills for reading and understanding verbal forms of communication" she writes, "rarely have we worked equally hard to develop an ability to analyze visual, rhythmic, or gestural forms. As cultural critics, we must become movement literate."[10] Desmond is keen to see bodily movement taken seriously as a primary social text, as it is through bodily movement, she argues, that we enact our place in society. She reveals how a number of dancing bodies enact particular gendered, ethnic, and class positions in society. For instance, the history of the tango is one that "traces the development of movement styles from the dockside neighborhoods of Buenos Aires to the salons of Paris before returning, newly 'respectable' from across the Atlantic to the drawing rooms of the upper-class portions of the Argentine population."[11] Such migrations and appropriations reveal a great deal about the social construction of race, gender, and class. In the tango, and in other dance forms, movements that originate in working-class and subordinate populations and places become "polished" as they make their way upward though a social and spatial hierarchy. An important part of this civilizing process is the abolition or toning down of overtly sexual components. She charts a history of white musicians and dancers toning down dance forms that included "sharp pelvis thrusts" in association with stepping and hopping movements, which accompany a percussive beat. In addition, both men and women would perform pelvic grinds with bent knees and spread legs. In these movements there are, in Desmond's analysis, striking similarities with West African dance where "pelvic articulation features prominently along with polyrhythmic relationships between stepping patterns in the feet and concurrent arm gestures."[12] While many of the stepping patterns remained in white versions of black music and dance, she suggests, the pelvic thrusting and rotating was attenuated. In Desmond's view, the transformation of these movements marked a change from black music and dance to a more general youth culture.

Indeed, as Mark Franko has argued, dance is rarely pure and "visceral" but mediated though a net of social relations.[13] Mediation enlivens rather than nullifies the experience of dance. Far from being immediate and unmediated, dance is refracted though the lenses of society and power. Just as dance mediates issues of race, it also mediates existing normative ideals of gender.[14] Take this description of ballet from Sue Foster:

> And these two bodies, because of their distinctly gendered behavior, dance out a specific kind of relationship between masculine and feminine. They do more than create an alert, assertive, solicitous manliness and gracious, agile, vibrant womanliness. Their

repeated rushes of desire—the horizontal attraction of bodies, the vertical fusion of bodies—do more than create unified sculptural wholes that emblematize the perfect union of male and female roles. *He* and *she* do not participate equally in their choreographic coming together. *She* and *he* do not carry equal valance. *She* is persistently put forward, the object of his adoration. *She* never reaches out and grabs him but is only ever impelled towards him, arms streaming behind in order to signal her possession by a greater force.[15]

It is clear that bodily movement, in some instances at least, is implicated in the reproduction of meaning and power.

These approaches to dance suggest that bodily movement exists in the context of social and cultural worlds in which various forms of power are at play. As dance scholar Helen Thomas has suggested, dance needs to be treated as a form of cultural knowledge, and as such is "an appropriate area of socio-cultural inquiry. However, the concern is not simply to read the dance codes, but also to understand the context in order to be able to ask *how* does the movement mean?"[16] Indeed, much work in the anthropology of dance has sought to look at the ways in which context makes bodily movement meaningful in dance—how, in other words, the social and cultural context of dance provides the conditions under which bodily movement can be creative.[17] I have chosen in this chapter, and in the book more generally, to explore bodily mobility within a relational interpretive framework that includes issues of meaning, representation, and ideology as integral to the process of understanding mobility.[18] This contrasts with recent work, which has explored: "the ways in which the world is emergent from a range of spatial processes whose power is not dependent upon their crossing a threshold of contemplative cognition."[19] One of the aims of this book is to insist on the continuing importance of seeing bodily mobility within larger social, cultural, and geographical worlds, which continue to ascribe meaning to mobility and prescribe practice in particular ways.

In the remainder of this chapter I examine some key moments in the history of ballroom dancing in order to illustrate how mobilities are produced in relation to other mobilities within particular contexts of meaning-making that enable and constrain particular practices of mobility. It delineates the geographical coding of movement types as correct and appropriate on the one hand and dangerous and threatening on the other.

## Degenerate Dancing and Freak Steps

The social and cultural context of ballroom dance in the 1920s needs to be understood in the wider context of dance and music at the time. The role of professional dance instructors was becoming more influential, and a plethora of schools and institutions formed to take advantage of the yearly dance crazes that swept over Britain, normally from the United States. Dancing had never been more popular. Many of the dances that were popular were quite intricate and thus the role of the teacher became more prominent. Dance instructors sought to capitalize on the immense popularity of dancing and at the same time make dance "respectable."[20] It was in this context that the gathering at the Grafton Galleries in 1920 occurred.

In fact, the idea for the meeting was not Richardson's but that of the American dancer Monsieur Maurice, who had written to the *Dancing Times* earlier in the year.

Dear Mr. Richardson

Since being in London I have been wondering whether it would not be possible for me to carry out some arrangements of the same sort as I carried out in New York.

I was very anxious in some way to standardise ballroom dancing, so that the same standard should prevail in all good class dancing places and ballrooms. In order to do this I got together the other leading dancing teachers of New York, and we held a conference, and came to mutual agreement how the foxtrot, two-step, waltz and tango should be danced correctly, so as to avoid the ungraceful and undignified forms of dancing, which were gradually creeping into both public and private dances.

Would it be possible to arrange to do something of the sort here?

Maurice goes on to describe his horror at the "strange dippings and twirlings and eccentricities" that he sees as prevalent on the trans-Atlantic dance floors, and declares the necessity of getting together in an attempt to stamp these movements out. "Could you, as Editor of "*The Dancing Times*," arrange for a conference to be held amongst the first-class dancing teachers of London, so that we could talk this matter over and mutually help each other?"[21] At the foot of the letter Richardson suggests that this might be a good idea and asks for people to write in declaring an interest. He soon had enough replies to call the meeting at the Grafton Galleries.

Richardson chaired the meeting. He began with a stirring speech about the increasingly irregular nature of social dancing in the British Isles. He warned of increasing liberalism on the dance floor:

Just as in the big world there had been a struggle against despotic autocracy so in the dancing world had there been a revolt against the autocracy of the Victorian dancing master and the formal dances of the last generation. Unfortunately just as in the big world the struggle for liberty had on occasions gone to extremes and in places developed into bolshevism, so in the ballroom there had been a tendency towards an artistic bolshevism.[22]

The floor was then given to Monsieur Maurice. He railed against the current state of dance, blaming it on the influence of jazz music and the dubious new dance steps that had found their way into "decent places." He pointed out that such music and such dance originated in the clubs of African Americans, and therefore had a necessarily prurient significance. Jazz music, he said, was only played in third- or fourth-rate places, and its lack of melody and rhythm was responsible for much bad dancing. Monsieur Maurice and his dancing partner, Miss Leonora Hughes, then proceeded to demonstrate good steps and, to the delight of the *Morning Post* and the *Daily Mail*, whose reporters were on hand, bad ones (see Figure 5.1). Following this exhibition the dancing partners left to perform at the Piccadilly Hotel, and a number of eminent dancers and teachers of dance joined in a heated discussion in which Mr. Edward Scott, a well-known writer on dance, appealed for the suppression of ragtime.[23] Eventually, Scott moved the first resolution: "That the teachers present agree to do their very best to stamp out freak steps particularly dips and steps in which the feet are

**Figure 5.1** Steps the Teachers wish to abolish, *Daily Mail* photo reproduced in the *Dancing Times*, June 1920.

raised high off the ground and also side steps and pauses which impeded the progress of those who may be following."[24]

The resolution was carried unanimously. The second resolution formed a committee to decide what the recognized steps of each dance should be. At an October meeting the committee (headed by Richardson) presented the fruits of their labor. The approved dances were as follows:

| | | |
|---|---|---|
| One-Step | *Pas marché* | |
| | *Chassé* | |
| Foxtrot | Foxtrot Walk (one step to two beats) | |
| | *Chassé* | |
| | Three-step | |
| Tango | *Paseo* | *Marche Argentina* |
| | *Corte* | *Carré* |
| | | *Huit* |

There are many movements that met with the disapproval of the various bodies that sought to regulate ballroom dancing. The very first resolution had called for the abolition of freak steps such as dips and pauses. One that proved particularly upsetting was the shimmy—a small sideways movement accompanied by vigorous shaking of the hips and shoulders—which had found its way into up-tempo versions of the foxtrot.

One writer in the *Dancing Times* reports how Parisians believed it was connected to the word *chemise* but the explanation, he writes, "will not bear repeating in the chaste columns of the DANCING TIMES."[25] In fact, the origins of the shimmy in the United States can be traced to the performer Gilda Gray, who would move her shoulders when she sang to reveal small glimpses of the chemise she wore as part of her outfit. According to one account, around 1918 someone asked her what she called her dance to which she replied "I'm shaking my chemise, that's what I am doing."[26] Indeed, by 1918, singers such as Mae West were singing songs with shimmy in the title such as "Everybody Shimmies Now," and the dance was part of popular stage performances such as the Ziegfeld Follies. By 1919 the capacity of the shimmy to outrage was acknowledged in the song "You Cannot Shake That Shimmie Here." Given how long it takes popular dance forms to reach commercial spaces it is likely that people were dancing the shimmy long before 1918. Indeed, the word *shimmy* turns up in a 1908 song, "The Bullfrog Hop." As is often the case with forms of music and dance that are hybrid, a search for origins reveals many contradictory claims depending on where the observer thinks one dance ends and the other begins. One suggestion is that the shimmy is derived from a Nigerian dance called the *Shika* brought to the United States by slaves. Another claims it comes from

Haiti. What seems to be universally believed is that the dance originates in African-American culture. Whatever its origins, by the middle of the twentieth century the word shimmy had migrated out of dance vocabulary to denote all kinds of unwanted and potentially dangerous movements—particularly the abnormal wobbling of automobile wheels at high speed. Indeed, one dictionary definition of the verb shimmy states that it means "to vibrate or wobble abnormally."[27] So a form of bodily movement emerging from the hybrid culture of African Americans came to be used as a general term for "abnormal" movement.

Richardson recalls the effect the shimmy, and the accompanying jazz music, had on dance in the early 1920s: "The presence of the shimmy, the quickening of the tempo and hectic jazz music all combined to place the smooth foxtrot, which had been slowly developing, in grave peril. There was much freak dancing to be seen and freak variations, such as the tickle-toe, were tried."[28] A June 1921 editorial in the *Dancing Times* reports on the decision of the dancers at the May 8 meeting to outlaw the shimmy.

> The genuine "Shimmy," with its shaking limbs and shoulders, is horrible, and offends, and should not be permitted, but if the dancer likes to do a certain foot variation of the foxtrot which has come to be known as the "shimmy" let him do it. It is useless the teachers saying they won't have it; if the public want it they will help themselves. The teachers would be doing far more useful service if they would put their heads together and evolve some very harmless variation and suggest that it should take that form.[29]

Another report on the shimmy in Paris made a similar comment:

> M. Achard, manager of the Colisée Club . . . thinks its history is, and will be, exactly that of the tango. Sprung from low haunts, it has become a rage, and will gradually lose its eccentricities . . . until in the very near future dancers who stick to the shimmy in its original form will be regarded with curiosity and disdain. He thinks that in its perfected form it will prove to be quite a good dance.[30]

Note how this description of the shimmy combines a logic of exclusion and inclusion. These moves were not simply banned, but incorporated and smoothed out. The shimmy was not the only kind of movement that was treated in this way. The Charleston is another example of a dance that outraged the British dance fraternity before Victor Silvester and his colleagues enacted their process of refinement.

> The disadvantage of the Charleston from our point of view was the nuisance value of its vigourous kicking action—people were

continually getting their legs bruised and thousands of women's stockings were laddered. So in the Imperial Society we produced a simpler and more graceful version known as the flat Charleston which soon replaced the original.[31]

Richardson was well aware that some of the dances that appeared on the official list of acceptable dance forms had previously been deemed "degenerate." The tango is the classic example of the supposed "refinement" of a dance form from the Americas via Paris. This is how Richardson records the tango craze of 1910 to 1914.

> Like many other dances of to-day it was brought about by the slave trade and the consequent introduction of negro folk rhythms into Latin America, particularly into Cuba. Here as Mr. Cyril Rice wrote in 1931: "The barbaric and novel rhythms of the plantations combined with the musical tradition of the Creoles to evolve the Cuban styles of which the habanera, taking its name from the city of Havana, is the most conspicuous example."[32]

These "negro folk rhythms" made their way from Havana to Buenos Aires where they entered all manner of disreputable places. "Here in the drinking shops and bordellos of La Boca and ill famed Barrio de las Ranas seamen and gauchos from the 'camp' competed for the favours of half-Indian habituées. . . . Becoming acquainted with the harbanera rhythm in the Port, as they called the capital city, they immediately adopted it and from it created their insidious tango."[33] Tango, in Richardson's account, was a dance that emerged in marginal space—liminal zones of license where the normal rules of acceptable conduct no longer held sway.[34] These spaces of liminality, from the perspective of an English dance instructor, ranged from the whole of the Western hemisphere, to Latin America, to the particular ports and bordellos of Havana and Buenos Airies. Even in Argentina, Richardson tells us, tango was frowned upon. It took a trans-Atlantic voyage to Paris for it to be "shorn of all its objectionable features,"[35] before returning to the acceptable ballrooms of Buenos Aires. It appeared in a report in the *Dancing Times* in 1911, and by 1912 it was featured in the musical *Sunshine Girl* in London's West End.[36] Even at that stage, the pages of the London press were full of outrage about the tango's sexual suggestiveness. It is all the more remarkable, therefore, that it should feature on a very short list of acceptable dances drawn up following the meeting of 1920.

At the center of debates about dance and its alleged degeneration was the Imperial Society of Teachers of Dancing (ISTD). There was no single body that represented dancing teachers in Britain by the 1920s, but the ISTD was certainly the largest and most influential. Much of its efforts were directed to ballet, but it also included members who taught social dancing. The ISTD was the result of a previous meeting of two hundred dance teachers in the summer of 1904 at the Medici Rooms of the Hotel Cecil in Covent Garden. At that time anyone could teach dance, and there were no recognized qualifications for teachers. Dancing was a key ingredient of the social lives of fashionable society, and the teachers who met at the Medici Rooms were keen to keep their dances out of the hands and feet of people who were not of the "right background." At this meeting it was agreed that teachers of dance needed an organization to protect their interests and regulate teaching standards. As a result, the ISTD was founded on 25 July 1904 with, R. M. Crompton, a ballroom teacher from Soho, elected as president. The stated purpose of the new body was the creation of a uniform method of teaching and the encouragement of the higher education of the teacher.

The pages of the *Dance Journal*, the Imperial Society's in-house newsletter, were soon full of invectives against what was called the degeneracy of dancing.

> Bad habits are our dearest foes, and the three-score years and ten, allotted to us for discipline and growth, seem all too short a period in which to do our warfare; so the enemies are visited on the children, the battle is continued, and often many lifetimes of years are required to annihilate these stubborn adversaries. But as the generation is greater than the individual, so its bad habits are greater than the bad habits of the individual, and require a proportionally longer period to eradicate.[37]

The purpose of the ISTD, then, was to eradicate these bad habits and produce standardized and graceful steps for the nation to share. As with the work of Taylor and the Gilbreths, habit lies at the heart of the production of mobilities in ballroom dance. But despite the protestations of the dance teachers, the bad habits continued to pop up everywhere. Dance appeared, to these guardians of correct movement, to be degenerating. "Dancing now has degenerated into a mere pastime" one commentator remarked, "it is no longer an Art, and in many cases into a vulgar romp. . . . That every canon has been violated is due in a great measure to the methods by which untrained instructors have pandered to the slovenly and rough habits of those who, not having taken the trouble to learn dancing properly, introduce movements and mannerisms to disguise their own inefficiency and ignorance."[38]

Between 1908 and the meeting of 1920, many articles and letters followed up on Butterfield's outrage. Many of them were more explicit about the connections between the dance steps and their perceived lowly origins: "In the last few years some little has been done to restore to the art of dancing its pristine nobelness. Setting aside the inexplicable vogue, now happily past, of the niggers' cake-walk, we observe that the Boston is increasingly popular in drawing rooms."[39] Freak dances and freak steps, as they were called, were invariably connected to the United States, and more specifically to African-American culture. But it was not only uptight British dance instructors who made these connections. The *Dance Journal* was only too happy to report the views of Miss Margaret Chute, an American woman who joined the chorus of denunciation against the freak dances. Chute had linked dance to the evils of postimpressionism in art, decadent literature, "svelte ladies with terra-cotta hips", and "other evidence of brain kinks."

> "Ever since the American Boston and Two-step came to England," writes Miss Chute, "we have been gradually edging nearer and nearer to freak dances…At the moment the only dances that really count are the monstrous caricatures, the ungainly, unpleasant inventions best characterised as Freak Dances. . . .
>
> Anything more ungraceful, awkward, even indecent, than the contortions of most modern dancers is inconceivable. The exquisite grace has gone; the long, lilting swing in the valse is dead. We get, instead, the abominable hops, jumps, springs, and rushes of scores and freak dances and dancers."[40]

The connection between the degenerate dancing and the United States was made many times over. Often the offending movements were not only seen to be "American" but, more specifically from particular kinds of spaces in America. The following account presents a complicated, multilayered moral geography of mobility linking the United States to smart dancing establishments in London.

> The extraordinary movements and antics which are witnessed at present in modern ballrooms are giving rise to much comment and controversy as to whether what has for long been considered a graceful pastime is not rapidly degenerating into vulgar romping. "One-steps" and "glides" and "bunny-hugs" are by no means confined to the five-shilling subscription dance, but are equally familiar diversions in the drawing-rooms of Mayfair.
>
> There is no doubt that the great popularity of rag-time melody and the extraordinary suggestion that music seems to have in the way of "getting a move on"—as the Americans put it—may have

done much towards inspiring dance measures which come easily to everybody. There is no arduous tuition necessary for acquiring a "one-step" capacity. The "glide" is a stretch of the limbs, and very little more, while the "bunny hug" is—well, it is an accentuation of that closeness of contact between the arms of one dancer and the waist of an other which in Early Victorian days made the valse a forbidden dance with many respectable people.[41]

These American dances are lowly because they are both easy (not requiring the advice of dance teachers) and suggestive, accentuating closeness. Such a combination results in "vulgar romping."

This was the background to the meeting of dance teachers in 1920— more than a decade of concerns about degenerate, decadent, and freakish dancing, which was threatening to undo the carefully structured grace of the "right kind of people." In 1924 a specific branch of the Imperial Society was formed devoted to ballroom dancing.

## The Imperial Society, Victor Silvester, and the Codification of Ballroom Dancing

The origins of the ballroom branch owe everything to Richardson. Following the 1920 meeting, he was approached by ballroom teachers to decide how to judge increasingly popular dance competitions and what should be allowed. Richardson was worried about there being a profusion of dance societies, as this would mitigate against uniformity, so he asked the ISTD to form a ballroom branch. In a 1921 editorial in the *Dancing Times*, Richardson was already suggesting the increased need for standardization of dance movements: "My suggestion that the Imperial Society should tackle the very big subject of remodelling the ballroom technique and phraseology has been adopted, and the Council of the Society are now hard at work on a task that is proving bigger than was at first thought."[42] The future president of the Imperial Society, Victor Silvester, called the advent of the ballroom branch in 1924, "an event which has had as great an influence on ballroom dancing as did the founding of the Académe Royale by Louis XIV of France on the ballet."[43] Silvester himself was one of the founding members of the ballroom branch of the ISTD, and was its president between 1945 and 1958.

It did not take long for the ballroom branch to set about its business. Within a year it had set out a syllabus for ballroom dancing that included knowledge of music, carriage of the body, and four dance forms that were all inscribed in the *Dance Journal*. The ISTD certified teachers to teach these dances and they were soon being demonstrated across England and Wales. In his autobiography, Silvester recalled the situation he faced in 1924 when the branch was set up. It was, in his mind, chaotic:

> For instance, there were men who held a girl by her finger-tips with the other hand very low on her waist line. There were others who placed one hand between the girl's shoulder-blades and stretched her arm to its full length. Some men would embrace a girl in a bear-like hug so that she could barely breath, much less dance. Then there were others who held their partners too far away from them.[44]

To confront this chaos, Silvester and his colleagues worked tirelessly to develop their holy grail of standardization.

> We spent hours discussing basic principles—the correct hold and such finer points as body sway, contrary body movement and footwork—all of which we put down on paper.

> We decided the most suitable figures for the different rhythms, and we laid down what was good and bad form.

> Then, to ensure that our code of ballroom procedure and behaviour became widely known, we incorporated it in a syllabus for a teachers' examination which prospective members of the branch had to pass before they could be admitted.[45]

To Silvester the codification of ballroom dancing was a ten-year project, and indeed it took a little more than that to produce the definitive charts and terminology that would set what was to be called the "English" style in stone. In 1936 he published an alphabetical list of definitions of technical terms used in ballroom dancing. In the same year, the *Dance Journal* featured handy pull out charts, developed by Silvester, for all the approved dances (see Figure 5.2).

But Silvester's talents were not limited to dance instruction, and his ambitions went well beyond the confines of the Imperial Society. Silvester was also a musician and had become increasingly annoyed by the music of dance bands in London and beyond. While Silvester and his colleagues had been busy codifying dance, bandleaders had continued to experiment musically, especially with jazz. As early as 1920, not long after the fateful meeting at Grafton Galleries, a writer to the *Dancing Times* made a plea for a standardized tempo in dance music:

> Dear Sir,—In connection with the movement for uniformity in dance work, may I plead for a standardisation of tempo for all

Further copies of these novel, informative and concise dance charts, printed on stout paper, can be obtained from the Secretary, I.S.T.D. Please state whether Quickstep, Tango, Slow Foxtrot, or Waltz is desired.

Price 6*d*. per chart post free.

# DANCE CHARTS

COPYRIGHTED BY

## Victor Silvester

S. = A slow st[illegible] beat).
Q. = A quick step (½ beat).
R.F. = Right foot.
L.F. = Left foot.
R. = Right. P.P. = Promenade position.
L. = Left. L.O.D. = Line of Dance.
C.B.M. = Contrary body movement.
C.B.M.P. = Contrary body movement position.

*Supplement to the Dance Journal, June, 1936.*

## TANGO

| NAME OF FIGURE. | NO. OF STEPS. | NO. OF BARS. | SLOWS AND QUICKS. | CONTRARY BODY MOVEMENT OR C.B.M.P. | BODY SWAYS. | RISE AND FALL. | AMOUNT OF TURN. | ALIGNMENT (GENTLEMAN—LADY CONTRA). | REMARKS. |
|---|---|---|---|---|---|---|---|---|---|
| WALK - - | 1 | ½ | S. | C.B.M.P. on L.F. forward and R.F. backward. | Nil. | Nil. | — | Begin facing diag. to centre. | The Walk should be curved inwards slightly. |
| PROGRESSIVE SIDE STEP. | 3 | 1 | Q.Q.S. | 1.3. | Nil. | Nil. | Nil or a slight turn to L. | Begin and finish facing approx. diag. to centre. | 2nd step to side but slightly back. Lady opposite. |
| BASIC REVERSE TURN | 6 | 2 | Q.Q.S.Q.Q. S. | 1.4. | Nil. | Nil. | ¼ of a turn to L. on 1.2.3. No turn or a ⅛ turn to L. on 4.5.6. | Begin facing diag. to centre. Take 4th step back into L.O.D. Finish with back to L.O.D. or facing wall. | The figure is not used in full—only in parts. |
| OPEN REVERSE TURN | 6 | 2 | Q.Q.S.Q.Q. S. | 1.4. (If partner is outside on 3 and 6, then on 1.3.4.6.) | Nil. | Nil. | Approx. ⅜ of a turn to L. | Begin facing diag. to centre. Take 4th step back into L.O.D. Finish facing diag. to wall. | Alternative ending—4.5.6. of Basic Reverse Turn. |
| PROGRESSIVE SIDE STEP REVERSE TURN | 11 | 4 | Q.Q.S.S.Q. Q.S.S.Q.Q.S. | 1.3.8.9.11. | Nil. | Nil. | ¼ of a turn to L. on 1.2.3. No turn on 4.5.6.7. ⅛ of a turn to L. on 8.9.10.11. | Begin facing diag. to centre. Take 5th, 6th, 7th, 8th steps back into L.O.D. Finish facing diag. to wall or facing L.O.D. | Alternative ending after the Rock—4.5.6. of Basic Reverse Turn. |
| NATURAL TURN | 6 | 2 | S.Q.Q.S.Q.Q. | Man on 2. Lady 2 and 5. | Nil. | Nil. | If finished with a Promenade, 1 full turn to R. If finished with Back Corté approx. 1¼ turns to R. | Begin facing wall. 4th step back to L.O.D. Finish facing wall for Promenade. Finish back into L.O.D. for Back Corté. | On 5.6. man should twist on ball of R.F. and heel of L.F. |
| CLOSED PROMENADE | 4 | 1½ | S.Q.Q.S. | 2. | Nil. | Nil. | Nil. | Face wall (approx.) throughout. | 1 and 2 should be the longest steps, 3—short to side and slightly in advance. Lady opposite. |
| OPEN PROMENADE (Old version) | 4 | 1½ | S.Q.Q.S. | 2. | Nil. | Nil. | Approx. ⅛ of a turn to L. on 3. | Begin facing (approx.) to wall. Finish facing diagonally to wall. | 1 and 2 should be the longest steps. |
| OPEN PROMENADE (Finishing outside). | 4 | 1½ | S.Q.Q.S. | 2.4. | Nil. | Nil. | Man—nil. Lady—approx. ¼ turn to L. on 2. | Face wall (approx.) throughout. | 1, 2 and 4 should be the longest steps. 3 short. |
| BACK CORTE - | 4 | 1½ | S.Q.Q.S. | 2. | Nil. | Nil. | ⅛ or a ¼ turn to L. on 2. | Begin back into L.O.D. Finish with back diag. to centre or facing wall. | 1 and 2 should be the longest steps. 3—short to side and slightly in advance. Lady opposite. |
| ROCK L.R.L. - | 3 | 1 | Q.Q.S. | Nil. | Nil. | Nil. | Nil. | Taken back into L.O.D. | |
| ROCK R.L.R. - | 3 | 1 | Q.Q.S. | Retained throughout on 1.2.3. | Nil. | Nil. | Nil. | Taken back into L.O.D. | — |
| ROCK TURN - | 7 | 2½ | S.Q.Q.S.Q. Q.S. | 1.5. (very slight on 1.) | Nil. | Nil. | ⅜ turn to R. on 1.2.3.4. ⅜ of a turn to L. on 5.6.7. | Begin facing diag. to wall. Take 5th step back diag. to centre. Finish facing wall. | — |
| NATURAL PROMENADE TURN | 4 | 1½ | S.Q.Q.S. | 2.4. | Nil. | Nil. | Best used on corners. ⅜ of a turn to R. | Begin facing (approx.) to wall. Finish facing (approx.) to next wall. | — |

**Figure 5.2** The dance chart of the tango by Victor Silvester, *Dance Journal*, 1936.

dance measures. At present, one set of people will dance the foxtrots and one-steps quickly, another will make them moderate time, and from a playing point of view, you never feel quite safe unless you know your people well.

We all know the rhythm, spirit, and tempo of, say, a minuet. It has one and only tempo. Surely all other dance movements should have their one original dancing time and speed.—I am, dear Sir, yours faithfully.[46]

This plea did not fall on deaf ears. The Imperial Society soon busied itself with the issue of tempo in dance numbers. On July 14, 1929 another conference of teachers was held in the Queen's Hotel on Leicester Square. There it was agreed that the standardization of dances needed to make them as simple as possible, and that part of that simplification process was the designation of suitable speeds for each dance. Silvester, as a leading figure of the ballroom branch, was right at the center of the process described by Philip Richardson. "After full experiments had been made" he wrote, "the most suitable speeds at which these dances should be played were agreed upon, and it was hoped that all bands will help to make the way of the dancer easier by adhering to these speeds."[47]

It was decided, following the necessary experiments that the standard tempos should be as follows:

Quickstep... 54–56 bars per minute
Valse..........36–38
Foxtrot........38–42
Tango.........30–32
Yale Blues....30–34

The Imperial Society was apparently unsuccessful in policing these new tempos, as six years later Silvester wrote an opinion piece on just this issue in the *Dance Journal*. Here he argued that broadcasting in particular had ruined the production of dance music.

Until a few years ago a dance-band was a band to dance to, and the music played was always rendered at the correct *tempo* for dancing purposes. But to-day this is not the case. Unfortunately for the many dancing enthusiasts . . . there are a greater number of listeners who prefer to enjoy their dance music while reclining in an armchair, rather than exert themselves and enjoy the greater benefits, both physical and mental, which can be derived from actually dancing to rhythmical music.[48]

Because of the preponderance of these armchair listeners, Silvester argued, bandleaders took too many liberties with standard dance forms like the foxtrot, and played them at "every conceivable speed" making them difficult to dance to. Silvester had already worked out the solution to this problem—he set out to record his own records for dancing in a format he labeled "strict-tempo." He had been having trouble with record company directors who complained that records made for dance were invariably the worst sellers because they were simply uninteresting to listen to: "In other words," Silvester wrote, "a non-crooning number with good melodious syncopation throughout, had a small sale compared with one in which some female wailed: 'Yo-doe-de-o-doe, I've lost my beau!' "[49]

Fortunately for Silvester the anonymous company director was wrong, and Silvester, with his dance band, went on to make many strict-tempo records from 1935 onward. To date, more than 75 million have been sold. Beginning in April 1937, Silvester and Orchestra featured in more than 6,500 broadcasts for BBC Radio, including 130 during the war. Later, the Victor Silvester Television Dancing Club ran for seventeen years. His success was central to the success of the Imperial Society which, as a result of the standardization and codification of dance, managed to spread the so-called English, or Imperial, style throughout the world.

Silvester's strict tempo music stood in stark contrast to jazz music. Just as the ISTD ballroom dancing code had emerged in opposition to African-American dance, so strict tempo was opposed to jazz. Jazz and ragtime had appeared for years in the pages of the dance journals as a wildly chaotic and primitive form of music associated, like the shimmy and cakewalk, with lowly places in the ghettoes of New York City and elsewhere. It was Monsieur Maurice who had reminded the collected dance teachers at the Grafton Galleries in 1920 that "jazz music was confined to third or fourth rate places." Another well-known dancer of the time, Mrs. Vernon Castle, was quoted by Richardson as writing in 1918: "It is difficult to define jazz. The nigger bands at home jazz a tune: that is to say they slur the notes, they syncopate, and each instrument puts in a number of fancy bits of its own. In the States we dance to jazz music, but there are no fixed steps for it. We get our new dances from the Barbary Coast. They reach New York in a very primitive condition and have to be toned down before they can be used in the ballroom."[50]

Jazz was described in an American ballroom magazine as "Strict rhythm without melody. The jazz bands take popular tunes and rag them to death to make jazz. Beats are added as often as the delicacy of the player's ear will permit. There are many half notes or less, and many long-drawn wavering notes. It is an attempt to reproduce the marvellous syncopation of the African jungle."[51] The efforts of Silvester and others to produce a toned-down form of jazz with a strict rhythm did not stand in isolation. Instead they can be seen as part of a wider context in which forms of popular culture, and particularly music, were seen as American and in need of toning down. Imported jazz music had been the principle ingredient of so-called Rhythm Clubs, which had sprung up around Britain. The music was referred to as "hot" jazz and the audience was predominantly male, middle-class suburban young people. The vast majority of people, particularly those who might be described as working class, favored British commercial music that toned down jazz music in much the same way as American forms of dance had been transformed by the Imperial Society. As Jack Hylton wrote in 1929 about American "hot" music: "it has not appealed to the public. Before it can be played here it must be modified, given the British touch, which Americans and other foreigners never understand. Symphonic syncopation, which I feel proud to have developed in this country, is pre-eminently British. In the dance-hall or on the gramophone record alike, it makes a subtle appeal to our British temperament."[52]

The British style of dance music was marked by less spontaneity and more formal orchestration. This music was gentler and cooler and, it might be added, whiter.

The relationship between the Imperial Society and so-called degenerate dancing was not straightforward. A cursory reading of the dance journals of the time might suggest a simple form of disgust at freak steps originating in the lowly dance halls of African Americans. But as is often the case, disgust was tinged with desire. Dances such as the waltz, foxtrot, and tango—the first dances to be deemed acceptable by the society—had all, at one time or another, been deemed dangerous and unacceptable. Now the Boston, the cakewalk, the turkey-trot, the jitterbug, the shimmy, and others were all going through a similar process.

The Imperial Society and Victor Silvester enacted, over several decades, the codification of social dancing in Britain and beyond. The development of correct steps, the abolition of unnecessary ones, the production of accepted terminology and handy dance charts, were all part of this process. So were the production of syllabi for teachers and the awarding of bronze, silver, and gold awards to students. Finally, the policing of tempo and production of strict-tempo music by Silvester capped the process that began in the Grafton Galleries in 1920. All of this regulation occurred throughout the United Kingdom, and later the commonwealth, at a local level in dance schools that were opened in cities throughout the nation, where dance instructors, who had passed examinations set by the Imperial Society, would operate. Needless to say this process was not all encompassing. As James Nott has noted, "[a]mong those who did not learn, there was resentment at the new-found seriousness of some dancers and some dance halls. As a result it became possible to distinguish between two quite separate and opposed groups of dancers, as the *Oxford Magazine* noted in 1929: 'Ballroom dancing appeals to thousands upon thousands . . . its followers form two great camps, those who learn to dance, and that quite appreciable number who dance without learning.'"[53] Indeed, Nott argues, the attention to detail brought about by the Imperial Society deterred many thousands from entering the "right kind of places" where ballroom dance took place. They were made to feel awkward and embarrassed by their lack of technical expertise. The organization Mecca, which ran a circuit of dance halls across the United Kingdom, had no lofty ambitions to civilize dancers but simply wanted to make money from the popularity of dance. Partly in response to the efforts of the Imperial Society and others, they introduced easy group dances such as the Lambeth Walk and the Palais Glide in the 1930s in order to allow people to overcome any hesitation they might feel about joining in.

## The Aesthetics of Correct Movement

The aims of this chapter have been, first, to show how forms of "correct" and "appropriate" movement are produced in relation to "inappropriate" forms of movement through a complicated representational process and, second, to reveal the normative geographies that are at play in this process. In this account of the codification and regulation of ballroom dancing, so-called *correct* forms of ballroom dance were produced through two principal forms of representation—one that sought to locate freak or "degenerate" movements in particular moral geographies, and another that sought to produce new movements through such things as dance charts and strict tempo. First, degenerate dance steps such as the shimmy were firmly located in *other* places. These places included Africa, Latin America, the United States, the American South, and New York at one level, and so-called third- or fourth-rate places, such as jazz clubs, at another. Particular kinds of movements and rhythms—the microgeography of bodily mobility—were thus coded as being from elsewhere and not British. There was a very definite sense that forms of movement revealed national belonging. Consider the following account, which appeared at the time.

> In my books I have described or alluded to the tango as an *alien* dance, because, in its original form, the movements are wholly at variance with British tradition. The action of the limbs and movements employed in waltzing are, on the contrary, essentially British. If you would test this, watch closely any good Highland dancer—native, I mean—in the Sword Dance. You will note that between the points and hilts of the crossed weapons he executes what is practically a *waltz turn*. And this has been done for two

or three thousand years—at least, so long as the Highlander has carried a sword.[54]

Of course it wasn't simply places that located particular forms of movement in a moral lexicon. The vast majority of the descriptions were also racialized in a way that went hand in hand with the moral economy of place. Dances such as the shimmy, but also the cakewalk, the turkey trot, the bunny hug, and endless other dance forms were seen as essentially black forms of dance, variously described as simple, primitive, barbaric, eccentric, and hectic, among other descriptors.

The solution to these freak steps, proposed and enacted by the ISTD, was to produce their own coded set of appropriate movements, which were seen as universal in their applicability. There is certainly an air of high modernity about the rigorous codification of dance in charts, in strict tempo calculations, and in the definition of what is acceptable. This is only amplified by the terms used to describe British, or imperial, ballroom dancing at its finest. These include, graceful, dignified, uniform, and lilting. The accent of uniformity and universality indicate the truly imperial ambitions of Silvester and his colleagues. It was the variability of dance forms that they really could not put up with. Within both the reactions to "degenerate dancing" and the codification of "correct" movements, there is clearly an aesthetics of mobility at work. While offensive movements are described as exaggerated, out of time, too fast, or too physical (lifting off the ground for instance), the movements proposed by the ISTD were rhythmically regular, constrained, smooth, and predictable. Again, these denotations more or less mapped onto spaces such as the Americas on the one hand, and Britain on the other. Indeed, the connection is often made between regular, codified dance and the success of British dancers, including Silvester, in international competition. As one popular account of ballroom dancing put it: "As a result [of standardization], English ballroom dancers had the advantage of being taught a well-defined style which, for various reasons, led to success in international competitions. The style became known as the English Style, or Imperial Style (after the name of the Society which, through its analysis of technique and innovation, described the basic steps)."[55] Silvester makes a similar point when he credited the ISTD with making the "technique of ballroom dancing . . . as precise as that of ballet." It was for this reason, he continues that "the English Style" had become so popular around the world.[56] Richardson is, if anything, more assertive of the central role of the ISTD in the world of dancing claiming, "it was the teachers of England who first analysed the crude steps, reduced order out of chaos and evolved that modern technique which has made the English Style paramount over three fifths of the globe."[57] As Richardson notes with pride, the English style, thanks mainly to the efforts of Silvester, spread quickly to places such as Denmark and Germany. English dancers, including Silvester, won international competitions thanks, in part, to the establishment of a set of universal rules known as "English." Just as the corporeal mobilities of dance moved across the Atlantic to Britain, so Britain, in turn, exported new forms of codified mobility to the rest of the world.

The way in which correct and appropriate mobility is described, and its constitution in relation to other forms of dance, mirrors many of the themes that run through chapters two and three. Gilbreth, for instance, combined a focus on efficiency of effort with an aesthetic appreciation of smoothness and rhythm in his chronophotographic images of people at work. "We find that the cyclographs of experts in all lines show smooth curves, . . . [t]hese indicate well established habits, ease and the grace that comes from perfect control."[58] Consider also Gilbreth's discussion of brick-laying as the product of hundreds of years of unconsidered habit leading to massive variation of movements between bricklayers. In place of this, he sought to establish one-best-way—a regular, predictable, and teachable arrangement of motion. Like Gilbreth, Taylor, Muybridge, and Marey, the ISTD and Silvester mingled the exactitude of science with a normative aesthetics of mobility that equated smoothness and rhythm with the best way to do things while variation, jerkiness, exaggeration, and irregularity were encoded as dysfunctional and undesirable.

While this chapter has considered the representation and encoding of dance in the early twentieth century, it is not my argument that such strategies were entirely successful, nor that the outcomes were entirely negative. As recent accounts of nonrepresentational theory have pointed out, there is a whole world beyond the kind of account I have produced—a world of effect where representations and practices are both mobilized in order to produce a world where power may not be able to intrude. As McCormack has put it, a world of the *processually enactive* where the "styles and modes of performative moving and relating" are more important than "sets of codified rules."[59] Reading the pages of the dance journals from the 1920s, two things are quite clear. First, regardless of the attempts of the ISTD and Silvester, many people continued to dance outrageously in the clubs of London and the provinces, much to the disgust of the learned dance teachers. Second, even those who were trained in appropriate ways of moving experienced a significant and abiding sense of pleasure in the process. To diminish this sense of pleasure would have been foolhardy. But this pleasure was also surely not simply a pleasure derived from a world beyond power, but pleasure that was, in part, a result of the representational strategies at work in the Imperial Society. Power is not simply about control and regulation through denial, but about the production of pleasure itself. As Bourdieu, among others, was eager to show, it is exactly the process of the internalization of the social in the body that produces the strongest adherence to established norms. This adherence is at its most successful when it is experienced as pleasure.[60] This has not been a beguilingly simple story of representation as denial and repression on the one hand, and bodily movement as pure play on the other hand. The story that arose from the endeavors of the Imperial Society, I suggest, shows both how representational strategies produce often pleasurable bodily mobility, and how bodily movements are part of the play of representational power. For this reason it is important to see the kinds of representational worlds that have been constructed around and through dance, and to provide an account of some of the normative geographies that provided a basis for such worlds.

## CHAPTER 6

# Mobility, Rights, and Citizenship
## in the United States

In 1865 Mr. Crandall, a Nevada stagecoach operator, transported his passengers across state lines. In 1939 Fred Edwards left California for Texas to pick up his out-of-work brother-in-law, Frank Duncan, and bring him back to California. In 1958 Rockwell Kent, an artist and member of the Communist Party, attempted to visit the World Council of Peace in Helsinki. In 1964 six white men harassed a number of anonymous black men living in Athens, Georgia, to such a degree that they found it impossible to leave home. In 1966, nineteen-year-old Vivian Shapiro left Massachusetts with her child to live with her mother in Hartford, Connecticut. None of these people knew each other, but their practices of mobility (or attempted mobility) became linked through a process of legal reasoning about the status of mobility as a right in the United States. Courts make decisions based on previous decisions through the process of precedent. Thus, Crandall's story came to bear on Edwards's story, and Edwards's story on Kent's story, and so on. In previous chapters we have seen how mobilities are produced through forms of abstraction such as photography, motion studies, and choreographies. In this chapter we explore other forms of abstraction—law, rights, and citizenship—in order to see how mobilities are produced in the courtroom. In order to do this, let us return to the second of our stories, that of Duncan and Edwards.

In November of 1941, nine men found themselves arguing over whether the mobility of people could be equated with the mobility of oranges. These were not philosophers but judges—the judges who sat on the Supreme Court of the United States of America. They had been presented with the following chain of events. In December 1939, Fred Edwards left his home in Marysville, California, and drove to Spur, Texas, with the intention of bringing back his wife's brother, Frank Duncan, a citizen of the United States and resident of Texas. They left Spur on New Year's Day in an old jalopy and reentered California on January 3, reaching Marysville on January 5. Duncan remained unemployed for ten days before getting relief from the Farm Security Administration. The movements of Edwards and Duncan were far from exceptional. Migration into California from Texas, Arkansas, Oklahoma, and other states to the east had been the subject of varying degrees of moral panic since the late 1920s. Migrants, known as Okies and Arkies, had moved to California in order to get promised work in the new agribusiness centers of the California valleys following the dust storms of the Great Plains. By the time Duncan entered California, migration had mostly switched to people looking for work in the defense industry. It was in the defense industry that Duncan was finally employed—in a chemical plant in Pittsburgh, California. What made Duncan's trip special was that it led to his story, and that of his brother-in-law, being told in the Supreme Court. On February 17, 1940, Fred Edwards was convicted in the justice's court of Marysville township, county of Yuba, of a violation of section 2615 of the Welfare and Institutions Code of the State of California. The section read:

> Every person, firm or corporation, or officer or agent thereof that brings or assists in bringing into the State any indigent person who is not a resident of the State, knowing him to be an indigent person, is guilty of a misdemeanor.[1]

The case was taken to the Superior Court of the State of California on June 26, 1940 where the judgment was upheld. Edwards then petitioned for an appeal in the Supreme Court of the United States, where he was represented by Samuel Slaff of the American Civil Liberties Union.

Oral arguments were made before the Supreme Court on April 28 and 29, 1941 and again on October 21, 1941. The Court gave its judgment on November 24. The question before the Court was whether section 2615 of the Welfare and Institutions Code of California violated the Federal Constitution. "The Court was asked to answer the question whether, in a nation which protects the free movement across State lines of the products of its fields, factories, and mines, an employable citizen of that nation did not enjoy the same freedom of movement accorded to articles of commerce."[2]

Eventually the Supreme Court rejected California's statute with three different opinions that nicely illustrate the always differentiated politics of mobility. Justice Byrnes argued that the statute was an unconstitutional burden on interstate commerce. His judgment was based on Article 1, section 8, of the Constitution, which delegates to Congress the authority to regulate interstate commerce. Byrnes believed that the transportation of persons across state borders constituted commerce, and that the California statute represented an unconstitutional barrier on interstate commerce. Justice Byrnes's legal judgment was that Duncan was protected because his mobility was comparable to any other mobility that might constitute commerce—indigents were no different from oranges, farm machinery, or capital.

Justice Douglas, concurring, wanted to widen the terms on which the statue was unconstitutional. "I am of the opinion," he wrote, "that the right of persons to move freely from State to State occupies a more protected position in our constitutional system than does the movement of cattle, fruit, steel and coal across state lines."[3] The right to move, he argued was protected not by interstate commerce law, but by the privileges and immunities clause of the 14th Amendment to the Constitution. Douglas referred to an earlier case, *Crandall vs. Nevada* (1865), in supporting his judgment that the right to move freely between states was a national citizenship issue. The right to move from place to place according to inclination was, in the view of Douglas, an attribute of personal liberty protected by the 14th Amendment. Placing an impediment on personal mobility would, therefore, result in a dilution of the rights of national citizenship and an impairment of the principles of equality.

The final concurring opinion came from Justice Jackson, who further differentiated mobilities in his judgment. He not only found a different logic for defending Duncan's mobility, but he explicitly denied the legitimacy of Byrnes's commerce defense. "The migrations of a human being, of who it is charged that he possesses nothing that can be sold and has no wherewithal to buy," he argued, "do not fit easily into my notions as to what is commerce. To hold that the measure of his rights is the commerce clause is likely to result eventually either in distorting the commercial law or in denaturing human rights."[4] Jackson's argument instead looked to the fact of Duncan's U.S. citizenship—a fact that made it impossible for states to abridge his immunities and privileges, which included mobility. Jackson did not stop there, though. He argued, contra Douglas, that the right to mobility, which constituted part of citizenship, was in fact limited. He pointed out, for instance, that states were able to prevent movement of fugitives from justice and people likely to cause contagion. The crux of the issue, for Jackson, was whether or not there was something characteristic of being an indigent that could provide a legal basis for curtailing interstate mobility. His conclusion was that:

> "Indigence" in itself is neither a source of rights nor a basis for denying them. The mere state of being without funds is a neutral fact—constitutionally an irrelevance, like race, creed, or color.[5]

In the case of *Edwards v. California*, the Supreme Court justices made decisions based on differences and similarities between forms of mobility. In the course of three judgments, the journey of Duncan and Edwards was compared, in legal terms, to that of oranges, a bus full of people leaving Nevada, disease, and unnamed fugitives from justice. While Justice Byrnes ruled against California based on perceived similarities between commerce of goods and movement of people, others concurred by stating that the mobility of people was uniquely protected by the 14th Amendment and was not analogous to commerce. It was further argued that indigence was not a human characteristic that could be used to prevent mobility, unlike criminality or disease.

This story of Edwards and Duncan demonstrates that human movement is made meaningful in social and cultural contexts—in this case, in a court of law. It also indicates the crucial nature of perceived and actual differences between forms of mobility. It mattered to Duncan that his mobility was not seen as the same as a fugitive, and was seen to be the same as an article of commerce. If his mobility were like that of a fugitive, it would have been deemed reasonable to prevent it. If his mobility was like an orange, or indeed a citizen (as the Court decided it was), then it was deemed unreasonable for the state of California to prevent it. The differentiation of mobilities in a cultural context has material consequences and produces, in part, the terrain upon which further mobility takes place. The Supreme Court, and law in general, are sites through which mobility, as a sociocultural resource, is produced and distributed.

The law, then, is an influential site for the production of meanings for mobility, as well as the practices of mobility that such meanings authorize or prohibit. Legal documents, legislation, and courts of law themselves are all entangled in the production of mobilities. Mobilities are produced both in the sense that meanings are ascribed to mobility through the construction of categories, such as *citizen* and *fugitive*, and in the sense that the actual ability to move is legislated and backed up by the threat of force.

In this chapter, I focus on the concept of mobility as a *right of citizenship* and the way in which this right has been produced within the legal system in the United States. I focus on the United States because it is here that mobility as a right—as a geographical indicator of *freedom*—has been most forcefully intertwined with the very notion of what it is to be a national *citizen*—to be American. The chapter is divided into four substantive sections. The first considers a number of Supreme Court cases in the United States, both before and after the *Edwards* case. The purpose of this review is to show how judges have ascribed meaning to corporeal mobility by attaching it to the notion of citizenship through discussion of mobility as a *right* of citizenship. Once this link has been established, the second section considers the notion of citizenship in more detail to show that the kind of mobility attached to the citizen is produced through the simultaneous production of the noncitizen. The third section considers the idea of rights. As citizens are, in the classic liberal formulation, bearers of rights and one of these rights is the right to move, the notion of rights needs further examination. Here I argue that the right to mobility has constructed a particular notion of mobility that presents itself as universal, when it is, in fact, particular. The first three sections of the chapter thus establish the production of particular meanings for mobility alongside the entangled notions of citizenship and rights. The final section looks to a different kind of arena for the production of meanings for mobility and mobile practices. This is the arena of urban politics surrounding the provision of public transport in Los Angeles. While human mobility is undoubtedly an empirical reality marked by difference, it is equally undoubtedly tied to notions of social justice, which have been curiously absent from much of the debate within the mobility turn. As David Delaney has put it, "it is through mobility: as permitted, coerced or prohibited, that justice and injustice may be concretely realized—in the flesh."[6] What the activities of the Bus Riders Union in Los Angeles point toward is a revised and expanded notion of mobility rights and thus citizenship.

## Mobility, Rights, and Citizenship in the Supreme Court

While the right to mobility is enshrined in constitutional documents as diverse as the Magna Carta, the Canadian Charter of Rights and Freedoms, and the Universal Declaration of Human Rights, it is not a formal constitutional right in the United States. This is somewhat surprising given that the ideology of America as uniquely mobile is a very powerful one. Commentators from Tocqueville to Baudrillard have argued that the culture, society, and economy of the United States are marked by exceptional mobility.[7] How then has a right to mobility been negotiated in the American context? The *Edwards* case is but one example of legal arguments over the right to mobility. As an important Supreme Court judgment, it is necessarily tied to a number of other cases that come before and after it, and form parts of the construction of a legal argument about mobility. Let us consider some of these cases beginning with *Crandall v. Nevada* (1865), cited by Justice Douglas 76 years later in the *Edwards* case.

### Crandall v. Nevada (1865)

In 1865 Crandall, an operator of stagecoaches into and out of Nevada, was arrested for refusing to report the number of passengers using his coaches and, furthermore, refusing to pay a one dollar tax imposed by the Nevada state government on all passengers leaving the state by all forms of public transport. Crandall took the state government to court arguing that the law was unconstitutional. The local court overruled his objection, and the case was taken to the Nevada Supreme Court, which also found that the tax was, indeed, constitutional. The case then found its way to the United States Supreme Court. Key to the argument was that the movement of people could not seriously be thought of as "export." The lawyer for the state of Nevada at the Supreme Court argued that:

> The law in question is not in conflict with that clause of the Constitution of the United States, which provides that 'no State shall, without the consent of Congress, lay any imposts or duties on imports or exports,' &c. Persons carried out of a State are not "exports" within the meaning of this clause. An export is a "thing exported," not a person.[8]

In the U.S. Supreme Court, Justice Clifford argued that the tax was unconstitutional simply on the basis that "the State legislature cannot impose any such burden upon commerce among the several States."[9] The majority opinion, however, sidestepped the issue of whether or not people could be considered "exports." Justice Miller argued that there was a particular relationship between the federal government and the people—that is the citizens—of the United States. These citizens needed to be able to travel throughout the country in order to be citizens. They might need, for instance, to cross the country in order to participate in active service in wartime. They might, equally, need to travel to Washington in order to petition it for a change in the law. In other words, the Court argued that to be a citizen you needed to have the ability to travel—to be mobile.

*Kent v. Dulles (1958)*

In April 1958 the Supreme Court heard the case of Rockwell Kent, a well-known artist and a citizen of the United States who wanted to attend the meeting of the "World Council of Peace" in Helsinki as well as visit England. Kent was informed by the director of the passport office that his request for a passport had been denied by the secretary of state on the grounds that he was a communist and adhered to the Communist Party line. He was told that he could attend a hearing on the issue, but that he would have to sign an affidavit as to whether he was then, or ever had been, a communist. Kent refused to sign the affidavit on the grounds that it was unconstitutional to make such a demand as the only pertinent fact was that he was a citizen of the United States and therefore had a right to travel. The Court was asked if the Executive's Passport Department could defer or refuse the issuance of passports to citizens suspected of being communists or of traveling abroad to further communist causes. The Court upheld Kent's appeal by declaring the right to travel an unalienable right of citizenship. Justice Douglas wrote:

> The right to travel is a part of the "liberty" of which the citizen cannot be deprived without due process of law under the Fifth Amendment. So much is conceded by the Solicitor General. In Anglo-Saxon law that right was emerging at least as early as the Magna Carta. . . . Freedom of movement across frontiers in either direction, and inside frontiers as well, was a part of our heritage. Travel abroad, like travel within the country, may be necessary for a livelihood. It may be as close to the heart of the individual as the choice of what he eats, or wears, or reads. Freedom of movement is basic in our scheme of values.[10]

Douglas refers to the work of the legal historian Zechariah Chafee, who wrote: "Our nation has thrived on the principle that, outside areas of plainly harmful conduct, every American is left to shape his own life as he thinks best, do what he pleases, go where he pleases."[11] Douglas continues: "Freedom to travel is, indeed, an important aspect of the citizen's "liberty." We need not decide the extent to which it can be curtailed. We are first concerned with the extent, if any, to which Congress has authorized its curtailment."[12] The Court decided, by a majority of five to four, that the secretary of state was not authorized to place arbitrary limitations on the issuance of passports, as this would impede mobility, and mobility was a central facet of citizenship. The dissenting judgment, written by Justice Clarke, argued that the secretary of state did, in fact, have the capacity to refuse a passport to those who might threaten national security, and that members of the Communist Party might be included in this category. The dissenting justices referred to a paper by Louis L. Jaffe:

> The criterion here is the defense of the country from external enemies. It is asserted that the precedents of "war" have no relevance to "peace." But the critical consideration is defense against an external enemy; and communication abroad between our citizens and the enemy cannot by its nature be controlled by the usual criminal process. The facts in a particular case as to the citizen's intention are inevitably speculative: all is to be done after the bird has flown. Now our Congress and the Administration have concluded that the Communist International is a foreign and domestic enemy. We deal with its domestic aspect by criminal process; we would seem justified in dealing with its external aspect by exit control. If an avowed Communist is going abroad, it may be assumed that he will take counsel there with his fellows, will arrange for the steady and dependable flow of cash and information, and do his bit to promote the purposes of the "conspiracy."[13]

They argued, in other words, that there were limits to the rights of citizens to travel, which were set by the *purpose* of travel. If a citizen was a communist, then he or she might promote the "conspiracy" and thus his or her right to mobility could be abridged.

## United States v. Guest (1966)

In early 1964, in Athens, Georgia, six white men embarked on an extended conspiracy of harassment against unnamed black citizens of the United States.

> It was a part of the plan and purpose of the conspiracy that its objects be achieved by various means, including the following: 1. By shooting Negroes; 2. By beating Negroes; 3. By killing Negroes; 4. By damaging and destroying property of Negroes; 5. By pursuing Negroes in automobiles and threatening them with guns; 6. By making telephone calls to Negroes to threaten their lives, property, and persons, and by making such threats in person; 7. By going in disguise on the highway and on the premises of other persons; 8. By causing the arrest of Negroes by means of false reports that such Negroes had committed criminal acts; and 9. By burning crosses at night in public view.[14]

The defendants argued in Georgia's district court that the indictment did not charge an offense under the laws of the United States, and that the court therefore had no authority to hear the case. The district court sustained this motion and dismissed the indictment as to all defendants.

The United States federal government took these men to the Supreme Court in order to argue that their activities denied the black men, who were subjected to these activities, a number of rights and privileges secured to them by the Constitution and laws of the United States, including, "[t]he right to travel freely to and from the State of Georgia and to use highway facilities and other instrumentalities of interstate commerce within the State of Georgia."[15] Justice Stewart delivered the opinion of the Supreme Court. In a complicated decision, Stewart reflected on the fourth paragraph of the indictment, which stated that the defendants "conspired to injure, oppress, threaten, and intimidate Negro citizens of the United States in the free exercise and enjoyment of: "The right to travel freely to and from the State of Georgia and to use highway facilities and other instrumentalities of interstate commerce within the State of Georgia."[16] Citing *Crandall v. Nevada*, Stewart insisted that, "The District Court was in error in dismissing the indictment as to this paragraph. The constitutional right to travel from one State to another, and necessarily to use the highways and other instrumentalities of interstate commerce in doing so, occupies a position fundamental to the concept of our Federal Union. It is a right that has been firmly established and repeatedly recognized."[17] Stewart notes that the right to travel has no explicit role in the constitution. "The reason," he goes on to say, "is that a right so elementary was conceived from the beginning to be a necessary concomitant of the stronger Union the Constitution created. In any event, freedom to travel throughout the United States has long been recognized as a basic right under the Constitution."[18] Given that the right to travel has no place in the Constitution, it is somewhat surprising that Stewart could assert this so confidently. Indeed, he acknowledges uncertainty about the source of such a right. "Although there have been recurring differences in emphasis within the Court as to the source of the constitutional right of interstate travel, there is no need here to canvass those differences further. All have agreed that the right exists. Its explicit recognition as one of the federal rights protected by what is now 18 U.S.C. 241 goes back at least as far as 1904. . . . We reaffirm it now."[19]

In a separate opinion, Justice Harlan provides a long and considered essay on the possible sources of a right to travel in American legal history. He notes how the majority decision rested on Title 18, Part 1, Chapter 13, Section 241 of the U.S. Legal Code (U.S.C. 241)—a law designed to punish conspiracy against the exercise of federal rights secured by the Constitution or laws of the United States. A right to travel, Harlan notes, cannot be found in either U.S.C. 241 nor in any other law of the United States.

While he concurs that legal precedent (in *Crandall v. Nevada, Edwards v. California*, and elsewhere) had established a right to travel between states free from *government* interference, there was no law protecting people from *private* interference. Harlan sees a right to travel as having three main possible sources in American legal history. The first is the idea of mobility as a specific right of *citizenship* protected by the Privileges and Immunities Clause of the Constitution. This he traces back to opinions delivered as early as 1825 in *Corfield v. Coryell* in which the Court addressed the question of what constituted the privileges and immunities of citizens. The Court stated that it confined these "expressions to those privileges and immunities which are, in their nature, fundamental" including "The right of a citizen of one state to pass through, or to reside in any other state, for purposes of trade, agriculture, professional pursuits or otherwise."[20] It was this argument that held sway in *Crandall v. Nevada* in which, as we have seen, citizenship rights took precedent over rights of commerce. Harlan notes, however, that the right to travel as a citizen was a right specifically protected against the interference by the state of Nevada and, by implication, any state. The right to travel protected by *Crandall*, Harlan argues, was "seen as a method of breaking down state provincialism, and facilitating the creation of a true federal union."[21]

Harlan then turns to the argument that a right to move is based on the commerce clause of the U.S. Constitution. Referencing both *Crandall* and *Edwards*, Harlan demonstrates how successive Courts had insisted on a close connection between freedom of commerce and travel "as principles of our federal union."[22] Again, however, he insists that these judgments have concerned *state* interference with the right to move and not with private interference. Finally, citing *Kent v. Dulles*, Harlan suggests that perhaps the right to mobility can be seen in due process terms. In *Kent v. Dulles*, the Court had argued that "The right to travel is a part of the 'liberty' of which the citizen cannot be deprived without due process of law under the Fifth Amendment."[23] Citing Zechariah Chafee he argues that mobility is not something that can be taken away by the national government without due process of the law. "And unreasonable restraints by the national government on mobility can be upset by the Due Process Clause in the Fifth Amendment. . . . Thus the 'liberty' of all human beings which cannot be taken away without due process of the law includes liberty of speech, press, assembly, religion, and also liberty of movement."[24] Once again Harlan points out that due process is concerned solely with government action and does not apply to *United States v. Guest*. In short, Harlan dissents from the majority opinion insofar as the case in question concerned private actions impeding the mobility of others. In his opinion, *United States v. Guest* set a legal precedent by asserting that the right to travel is protected from private interference—a precedent he was unable to support.

## Shapiro v. Thompson (1969)

In June 1966, Vivian Marie Thompson, a nineteen-year-old single mother who was pregnant with her second child, moved from Dorchester, Massachusetts, to Hartford, Connecticut, to live with her mother, a resident of Hartford. In August she moved again into her own apartment. Because of her pregnancy, she was unable to work or enter a work training program. She applied for assistance to the program for Aid to Families with Dependent Children (AFDC). Her application for assistance, filed in August, was denied in November on the grounds she had not lived in the state for a year before her application was filed. The Connecticut Welfare Department was invoking 17-2d of the Connecticut General Statutes. Vivian Thompson took the Welfare Department to the district court where the judges, with a vote of two to one, declared the statute unconstitutional. The majority judges declared that the waiting period was unconstitutional because it "has a chilling effect on the right to travel."[25]

Connecticut appealed this decision to the Supreme Court, which came to a decision on April 21, 1969. The Connecticut court judgment was upheld. Justice Brennan, in his majority decision, argued that the residence requirements served to create two classes of needy people, "indistinguishable from each other except that one is composed of residents who have resided a year or more, and the second of residents who have resided less than a year, in the jurisdiction." The basic needs of food and shelter would then depend on this difference. Brennan made it clear that the reason for the statute was to discourage the poor and needy from entering Connecticut.

> But the purpose of inhibiting migration by needy persons into the State is constitutionally impermissible. This Court long ago recognized that the nature of our Federal Union and our constitutional concepts of personal liberty unite to require that all citizens be free to travel throughout the length and breadth of our land uninhibited by statutes, rules, or regulations which unreasonably burden or restrict this movement. It suffices that, as JUSTICE STEWART said for the Court in United States v. Guest, 383 U.S. 745 (1966): "The constitutional right to travel from one State to another . . . occupies a position fundamental to the concept of our Federal Union. It is a right that has been firmly established and repeatedly recognized."[26]

But, as we have seen, this "right" to mobility is not explicitly mentioned in the Constitution. Brennan cites a number of earlier cases in which the right to mobility was grounded in various parts of the Constitution, including the Privileges and Immunities Clause, the Fourteenth Amendment, and the Commerce Clause. The concurring opinions of *Edwards v. California* were cited as well as *Crandall v. Nevada*. In a dissenting opinion Justice Harlan, probably despairing at the fact that no one seemed to have paid any attention to his long report in *United States v. Guest*, found the notion of the right to mobility as fundamental to be strange, writing, "I must reiterate that I know of nothing which entitles this Court to pick out particular human activities, characterize them as 'fundamental,' and give them added protection."[27] Justice Stewart, in concurring with the majority statement, takes issue with Harlan on this. The Court, Stewart argues, "simply recognizes, as it must, an established constitutional right, and gives to that right no less protection than the Constitution itself demands. . . . As we made clear in Guest, it is a right broadly assertable against private interference as well as governmental action. Like the right of association . . . it is a virtually unconditional personal right, guaranteed by the Constitution to us all."[28]

These Supreme Court cases from *Crandall v. Nevada* in 1865 to *Shapiro v. Thompson* in 1969 form just over one hundred years of legal reasoning with case piling on case. There is surely no better example of the literary idea of intertextuality than that provided by legal reasoning. Each text can only be understood in relation to the ones that came before it. Indeed, since 1969, the production of mobilities within the law has continued in the United States, and Crandall's avoidance of transit tax and Edward's transportation of an "indigent" into California continue to exert an influence on the constitution of meanings for, and practices of, mobility within the United States.[29]

Just as Marey and Muybridge constituted mobility through representation, and just as Victor Silvester legislated against the shimmy by rationalizing and universalizing dance instruction, so Supreme Court justices produce mobilities. These legal cases ascribe meanings to particular instances of mobile practice. This mobility is the mobility of a citizen; that mobility is a form of commerce. The mobility of communists, fugitives, or diseased people might be curtailed. As a producer of meaning, the courts have few equals. These meanings tend to stick and become the basis of the material authorization of practice. This is social production at its most literal.[30] Law both acts on the basis of presumed geographies and produces geographies in the process. These include geographies of mobility.

## Mobility and Citizenship

What these cases show is that the idea of mobility, as a key geographical component of concepts such as liberty and citizenship, has formed a taken-for-granted backdrop to legal rulings in the United States where some judges (with Harlan a notable exception) have argued that mobility is a "fundamental" or "virtually unconditional" aspect of liberty and citizenship despite the lack of formal protection in the Constitution. Members of the Court have also suggested at various times that different meanings might be assigned to mobility depending on the circumstances. The references to fugitives, disease vectors, and communists foreground the limits to mobility as a right of citizenship.

The legal production of mobility in the United States has predominantly revolved around two practices of mobility: citizenship and commerce. The arguments over whether indigents entering California could be compared to oranges were about whether this form of mobility was a form of commerce or a form of citizenship. In either case, the mobility was deemed legitimate. Similarly, the tax on passengers imposed by Nevada would be unconstitutional if it either imposed limits on interstate commerce or impeded the ability of Nevada citizens to be full-fledged American citizens. But what if mobility practices were neither citizenship practices nor practices of commerce? Citizenship is defined by noncitizenship. Indeed, there are all kinds of mobile practices that were unprotected by the association between mobility and citizenship (or commerce). One example is the Chinese Exclusion Act of 1882, which forbade the travel of Chinese immigrants (noncitizens) into the United States (see chapter 7 for more on this). Another involves the numerous *tramp laws* introduced in the United States following 1876.[31] As with preceding cases of mobility in this book, "good" and "appropriate" forms of mobility are opposed to mobilities that threatened to undo established spatial order (the nation, the neighborhood, etc.). One correct way to practice mobility is as a citizen. The mobility of citizens, as Justice Harlan notes in his consideration of the right to travel in *United States v. Guest*, is "historically seen as a method of breaking down state provincialism, and facilitating the creation of true federal union."[32] The geographical imagination at play here assumes the moral space of the nation and attaches citizenship mobilities to it. Consider the contrast between this line of reasoning and the blunt preamble to the Chinese Exclusion Act of 1882: "Whereas, in the opinion of the Government of the United States the coming of Chinese laborers to this country endangers the good order of certain localities within the territory thereof..." Here the mobility of Chinese immigrants is also connected to a moral geography of "certain localities" whose "good order" is threatened. As citizenship has already been established as a category of personhood requiring the ability to move, it was necessary to disconnect citizenship from the mobility of the immigrants. As the act draws to a close, this is made clear: "hereafter no State court or court of the United States shall admit Chinese to citizenship; and all laws in conflict with this act are hereby repealed." Consider also the tramp law of Connecticut from 1902, which states, "all transient persons who rove about from place to place begging, and all vagrants, living without labor or visible means of support, who stroll the country without lawful occasion, shall be deemed tramps."[33] Laws such as this had been passed throughout the United States following the first tramp law of 1876 in New Jersey. All of them defined tramps as a particularly mobile social type, and it was this mobility (enabled by the newly constructed national railroad system), which was threatening to local forms of order. Section 1337 of the Connecticut code, for instance, stated that "Any act of begging, or vagrancy, by any person not a resident of this state, shall be *prima facie* evidence that such a person is a tramp." And if you were a tramp, the consequences were severe. In some states tramps could be hired out to the highest bidder or sold into servitude for a year. Legal codes in the United States (as well as those in France, Britain, and elsewhere) effectively produced a whole new class of criminals whose criminality was rooted in their threatening mobility.[34] While the legal construction of the Chinese immigrant was clearly and explicitly *about* citizenship as a formal category, the legal construction of the tramp was not. Recent work on citizenship, however, has suggested an expanded definition of what constitutes a citizen. The restriction of tramp mobility clearly disconnected a formal citizenship right from a group of people who effectively became "shadow citizens" through the denial of a particular kind of right to mobility.

Both the Chinese immigrant and the tramp practiced mobility, but in doing so they were deemed to be practicing something other than citizenship. Both external and internal mobilities were presented as threats to the good order of particular kinds of spaces, which had been invested with moral (and legal) worth. Citizenship was thus the "correct" way to practice mobility. This form of practicing citizenship—through mobility—needs to be understood in relation to those forms of mobility that fall outside of citizenship. Indeed, the evocation of citizenship in all of these cases contains within it the absence of the noncitizen—the figure who makes citizens make sense.[35] In his book *Being Political*, the citizenship scholar Engin Isin makes exactly this point. While it is commonplace to note that ancient forms of citizenship in the polis *excluded* groups such as women and slaves, Isin argues that it was not exclusion that was at play.

The logic of exclusion assumes that the categories of strangers and outsiders, such as women, slaves, peasants, metics, immigrants, refugees and clients, preexisted citizenship and that, once defined, it excluded them. The logic of exclusion presupposes that the excluding and excluded are conceived as irreconcilable; that the excluded is perceived in purely negative terms, having no property of its own, but merely expressing the absence of the properties of the other; that these properties are essential; that the properties of the excluded are experienced as strange, hidden, frightful, or menacing; that the properties of the other; and the exclusion itself . . . is actuated socially.[36]

This logic of exclusion can be contrasted with a logic of othering, where "otherness as a condition of citizenship assumes that in fact citizenship and its alterity always emerged simultaneously in a dialogical manner and constituted each other" thus "slaves were not simply excluded from citizenship, but made citizenship possible by their very formulation."[37] Citizens require the production of others to be possible, and the definition of citizen carries around the noncitizen or the shadow citizen as part of its constitution.

So what does this say about the meaning of mobility in the constitution of the citizen figure? Part of the answer is the development of a similar logic for mobility—a logic I have developed throughout this book. Positive evaluations of mobility exist, not through the exclusion of negative ones but in a necessarily relational mode—a logic of alterity where "pathological" mobilities are coproduced alongside and intertwined with those mobilities defined as central to this or that identity. In terms of citizenship, the Supreme Court produced notions of mobile citizens as ideal types—autonomous individualized agents who, through their motion, helped to produce the nation itself. But the unspoken Others here are the differently mobile—the immigrant or the tramp—who make citizenship mobility special. Consider also the numerous forms of mobility that are continually hindered as people inhabit shadow citizen identities. Think of Arab-Americans stopped at airport immigration, Hispanic-Americans in the fields of American agri-business or African-Americans "driving while black". All of these are American citizens but do not quite match the model of citizenship that is left unsaid—white, male, wealthy, able bodied. The form of mobility discussed in the Supreme Court for over a century is wrapped around notions of *fundamental rights* and the citizen to produce an abstract figure whose specificity is left unsaid.

## The Critique of Rights

While the first section of this chapter established a formal connection in U.S. law between mobility and the category of citizen, and the second opened up the question of citizenship to critical scrutiny, this section explores the idea of rights, which in the classic formulation, are things held by citizens. To be a citizen is, among other things, to be a bearer of rights. One of those rights in the American context is the right to mobility.

At one level, a right is a formal legal category. If a right exists in law then an infringement of that right demands a legal remedy. If the right does not exist in law, then equally clearly, there can be no legal remedy.[38] But there are also broader conceptions of rights. Civil rights, for instance, may be legal or may be based on a purely moral standpoint. Legality is one aspect of a right, but using such a narrow concept would mean that we would be able to make the claim, for instance, that black people under apartheid in South Africa were enjoying basic human rights, when we would actually say the opposite—that they were being denied their rights. Here we would be using an idea of rights that is more expansive than a legal definition. Often there is a mismatch between legal rights and wider conceptions of rights as things people have by virtue of their personhood. Similarly, a narrow definition of a citizen as someone who bears legal rights within a particular legal territory is often much narrower than ideal definitions of what constitutes a citizen. Reconsidering the right to mobility as an expanded right might, therefore, go hand in hand with an expanded conception of citizenship.

Rights in any form, like migration theory or motion study, are an abstraction. They aspire toward the universal and have no regard for the particular. In this sense, they are simply yet another form of representation of mobility alongside choreography charts or time-lapse photography. Unlike these other forms of representation, however, rights play a central role in the formation of liberal democracy. The right to mobility is central to the list of rights considered, as we have seen, to be fundamental (even when not strictly legal). In fact, the list provided by Zechariah Chafee puts the right to move alongside the rights to religion, a free press, assembly and speech.[39] Indeed, the right to move is the first fundamental right in the new European Charter of Rights, and features in the formal constitutions of nations as diverse as Mexico, Canada, Japan, Germany, and Ghana. It is also identified as a universal right in Article 13 of the United Nations Universal Declaration of Human Rights (1948) which guarantees both movement within the borders of each state and the right to leave and return to a country. Mobility is the only specifically geographical right identified as fundamental in this way. There is no equivalent right to stay still or to have a place of residence, for example.

The notion of rights, as a form of legal representation and practice, has been critiqued by those on the left who find the notion of the universality of rights problematic. The claims made for rights as being fundamental or natural or universal hides the context in which rights have been produced. In "On the Jewish Question," Karl Marx called the nexus of rights and citizenship into question within the logic of historical materialism. "*Political* emancipation certainly represents a great progress" he writes, "[i]t is not, indeed, the final form of human emancipation, but it is the final form of human emancipation *within* the framework of the prevailing social order. It goes without saying that we are speaking here of real, practical emancipation."[40] Here he praises the development of liberal conceptions of liberty by noting that they are a distinct improvement on the stasis of feudalism. But, as always, he notes that they are a product of their context—the context of capitalism within the nation-state. Indeed, it is the state rather than nature that confers rights. Marx argues that rights—the rights of man—are rights for individuals rather than groups, the community, or species-being. "None of the supposed rights of man," he continues, "go beyond the egoistic man, man as he is, as a member of civil society; that is, an individual separated from the community, withdrawn into himself, wholly preoccupied with his private interest and acting in accordance with his private caprice."[41]

The legal scholar Duncan Kennedy continues the line of critique opened up by Marx when he reminds us:

> Rights talk was the language of the group—the white male bourgeoisie—that cracked open and reconstituted the feudal and then mercantilist orders of Western Europe, and did it in the name of Reason. The mediating power of the language, based on the presupposition of fact/value and law/politics distinctions and on the universal and factoid character of rights, was a part of the armory of this group, along with the street barricade, the newspaper, and the new model family.[42]

Central to the problem with rights talk, though, is the way in which rights are represented as universal and abstract or fundamental. This process of reification lets rights stand in for events and practices that are, in fact, determinedly *particular*. To subsume each and every act of human mobility within a framework of rights serves to reproduce the isotropic plane of other forms of abstraction discussed in earlier chapters. The equation of human mobility with that of exports, for instance, hides the specificity of

Frank Edwards's movement into California with all the undoubted trials
that such a trip involved. Perhaps even stranger is the judgment in *United
States v. Guest* that six white men could be prosecuted for restricting the
rights of black men to move when, in fact, they had conspired to shoot,
beat, kill, and threaten them as well as destroy their property. All of this,
and all the pain and fear involved, get reduced to a commonality—the
infringement of a right to move. To speak of such acts merely or solely
as an infringement of abstract rights is to mischaracterize the kinds of
practices at play. The legal scholar Mark Tushnet makes exactly this point
though a different example:

> When I march to oppose United States intervention in Central
> America I am "exercising a right" to be sure, but I am also, and
> more importantly, being together with friends, affiliating myself
> with strangers, with some of whom I disagree profoundly, getting
> cold, feeling alone in a crowd, and so on. It is a form of alienation
> or reification to characterize this as an instance of "exercising
> my rights." The experiences become desiccated when described
> in this way. We must insist on preserving real experiences rather
> than abstracting general rights from these experiences.[43]

By generalizing the meaning and experience of mobility through rights
talk, all mobility becomes equateable. The travels of the global businessmen are equal to those of the domestic servants who service their hotels.
The experience of the white commuter driving her SUV into work become
the same as the working-class Hispanic negotiating an inadequate public
transport system in order to get to work on time. They are all exercising a
right. When the right to move is defended as an attribute of commerce, the
movement of "indigents" is no different from the movement of exports.

One aspect of the particularity of things that makes rights talk a form of
reification is the *spatiality* of experience and practice. Rights are distinctly
spatial and this spatiality undermines the supposed universal nature of
rights. Whether it is the protection of property, the division of private and
public, the negotiation of scale or the question of mobility, rights in the
United States, Canada, or anywhere else have distinctive spatialities.[44]
Nicholas Blomley and Geraldine Pratt draw upon Michael Waltzer's claim
that liberalism enacts a "certain way of drawing the map of the social and
political world."[45] Dualisms, such as *private* and *public*, and *citizen* and
*alien*, clearly the product of liberal demarcations of space in the world,
operate to open up or close down the entitlements that come with rights.
Key to their argument, however, is the observation that the spatiality

of rights opens up possibilities for progressive challenges to established conceptions of justice in liberal societies.

> Geography can provide some strategic leverage to challenge the limitations of rights discourse and to expand the meaning of property, citizenship, of who counts as "human." Our argument, thus, has been that the politics of rights are open and can create openings and that these openings (and closures) are constructed in and through space and time.[46]

Taking geography seriously calls into question the construction of a seemingly universal conception of rights, which is in fact the production of a specific kind of geography. This point has been made by Audrey Kobayashi and Brian Ray in the Canadian context when they argue that "spatial justice" requires taking into account the uneven distribution of risk and the situation of individuals and groups "within an institutionally constructed landscape."[47] Linda Peake and Brian Ray similarly argue that social justice involves recognizing both "where people begin—gender, sexuality, race," but also where people are in the sense that their location in marginalized communities "places them at the margins of visibility for justice."[48] This critique of rights is based on the geographical critique of liberalism as blind to historical-geographical relations of power. Liberal conceptions of rights, while pretending to be universal, are based on a "fragmentation of spaces that do not necessarily reflect the realities of the uneven geographies of oppression."[49] These uneven geographies of oppression are also evident in people's differential abilities to move.

Indeed, the reality of the material production of different mobilities effectively undermines rights talk, which conceptualizes mobility within a universalist framework. The way in which rights, mobility, freedom, and citizenship have been wrapped around each other in liberal discourse has, for instance, naturalized mobility as the property of the individual, moving, able-bodied subject. One arena in which liberal conceptions of rights have been questioned is the realm of disability politics.[50] Vera Chouinard introduced the notion of "shadow citizenship"—suggesting that spaces of shadow citizenship are formed where the "law as discursively represented and law as lived are fundamentally at odds."[51] Disabled people, she argues, often inhabit these spaces. While on the one hand, they are symbolically central to liberalism's claims to universality (an imagined geography of rights that is blind to geography) they are simultaneously marginalized by the blindness of rights discourse to the particular social space of disability in Canada. Attitudes toward the mobility of the disabled need to be located within dominant discourses of mobility in Western society. Specifically, attitudes toward the disabled are framed by "sociocultural values and practices which prioritise mobile bodies or those characterised by societally defined norms of health, fitness, and independence of bodily movements." Such values and practices, "serve to alienate impaired bodies and to prioritise the movement of what one might term 'the mobile body,'"[52] The problem is that deeply rooted assumptions about mobility are based on a universal disembodied subject-citizen.

Ivan Illich has argued against the increasing speed of life and asserts that: "Men are born almost equally mobile. Their natural ability speaks for the personal liberty of each one to go wherever he or she wants to go. Citizens of a society founded on the notion of equity will demand the protection of this right against any abridgement."[53] Illich's suggestion that "men are born almost equally mobile" is of course somewhat absurd when we consider the resolute immobility of babies. Indeed, the observation that people are born equally immobile turns our focus away from mobility as a natural and fundamental right of autonomous moving subjects, and toward mobility as a social construction produced within conditions of systematically asymmetrical power relations. The idea of a right to mobility, and mobility as an attribute of citizenship, is transformed if we start from the assumption of socially produced mobility rather than mobility as an attribute of an autonomous body.

Mobility as freedom—as liberty—lies right at the heart of some of the foundational ideologies of the modern world. The claim to the universal that ideas of rights, and the right to mobility in particular makes, disguises the specificity of the conflation of liberty, freedom, citizenship, and mobility within a liberal framework. Liberty is located in individual bodies almost as an attribute of nature. These bodies are able bodies. Ivan Illich makes this clear when he develops an idea of just transportation by starting with the body—"People move well on their feet. . . . People on their feet are more or less equal. People solely dependant on their feet move on the spur of the moment, at three or four miles an hour, in any direction and to any place from which they are not legally or physically barred."[54]

But the kind of mobility that is most often equated with rights and citizenship is also disconnected from the wider network of institutions and technologies that enable and/or disable mobility. While the idea of an individuated mobile body turns the disabled into "shadow citizens," it also glosses over the differentiated production of mobilities that result from the wider material landscapes of mobility and stasis. Liberal individualism is grounded on a false basis of bodily equality, which serves as a basis for democratic justice. An alternative way of thinking about mobile bodies is to think of them as moving with the aid of a number of prosthetic devices.

For a disabled person this might be a wheelchair or a guide dog, but it might also be a public bus or train for those of us who are not formally or legally disabled. When such devices are taken into account, citizens are no longer just bodies separated from the world but thoroughly social bodies. Citizens become "prosthetic citizens." Such a citizen—unlike the universal mobile citizen—is a subject whose capacities for mobility depend on the constraints of the public sphere. Mobility, in a world in which people and things are intimately interconnected, is clearly not a capacity of individual inalienable properties of bodies, but a product of a multitude of human/ environment interfaces—a product of geography. It is this interconnection between the human body and the wider world that signals the arrival of the prosthetic subject-citizen.[55] In an insightful essay, Celeste Langan proposes an "omnibus model of rights—a model that may require abandoning the (always problematic) category of the "physically disabled" in favor of an alliance—a strategic nonessentialism, so to speak—among the (social) mobility-impaired."[56] Here the disabled pedestrian would be joined by the children dependent on their parent's car, the inner-city residents trying to negotiate run down public transport, and the people in the long lines at the Mexican border who cannot enjoy the mobility that comes with being an American citizen.

### Mobility and Spatial Justice—The Bus Riders Union[57]

In this final section of the chapter, I tie the contested notions of mobility, citizenship, and rights back together again through an examination of the campaign for a fair public transport system in Los Angeles as conducted by the Bus Riders Union. The equation that links mobility to abstractions such as citizenship and rights, has been challenged on the ground by these activists who have sought to produce countermeanings for mobility that refuse to rely on generalized, universal conceptions of mobility. The following is an account of a relatively successful campaign for a particular kind of right to mobility, which rested on the recognition of both spatial difference and the uneven production of mobilities in Los Angeles. It is an example of the fact that "the politics of rights are open and can create openings and that these openings (and closures) are constructed in and through space and time."[58] It also points toward a "stretched" conception of citizenship that has a thoroughly social mobility at its heart rather than an abstract universal motion.[59] Recent developments in citizenship theory have pointed to the importance of thinking of citizenship as being conducted in a variety of spaces outside of the formal state-space of the traditional political citizen.[60] Here I expand that concept to think about the reconfiguration of citizenship entailed by a notion of socially produced mobility.

While much that has been written about mobility recently has failed to take into account the effect of a "mobility turn" on issues of justice and possible progressive reconfigurations of citizenship and rights, the acts of a determined group of public transport activists in Los Angeles has, with some success, produced a new politics of mobility. Once again courts of law were involved in legislating mobilities, but unlike in the Supreme Court cases above, the specific modes of mobility became all important in reaching decisions that can be seen as institutionalizing *spatial justice*—a form of justice that does recognize the spatiality of rights and responsibilities.[61]

In 1994 the Los Angeles Metropolitan Transit Authority (MTA) sought to raise bus fares from $1.10 to $1.35 and eliminate a monthly pass, thus making it more difficult for poor minority bus riders to move between home and work, as well as crucial services, schools, shops, and loved ones.[62] As a result, the NAACP legal and educational defense fund filed a suit on behalf of the Labor/Community Strategy Center, the Bus Riders Union (BRU), the Southern Christian Leadership Conference, the Korean Immigrant Workers Advocates, and individual bus riders. The suit was a class action on behalf of 350,000 poor minority bus riders. The MTA was charged with violation of the 1964 Civil Rights Act. The 1964 act specifically bars government agencies that are federally funded from using those funds in a racially discriminatory manner.

The suit charged the MTA with establishing a separate and unequal mass transit system through the underprovision of money for bus routes, while planning an extraordinarily expensive light rail system that served mainly wealthy and white areas of the city. The suit claimed that the MTA intentionally discriminated against poor minority bus riders, and that their actions had a discriminatory impact on poor people of color. The bus system meanwhile catered to around half a million Latino, black, and Asian/Pacific bus riders. Eighty-one percent of bus riders were estimated to be people of color. The case presented to the court by the plaintiff's lawyers stated that:

> Although almost 94% of the MTA's riders are bus riders and 80% of them are people of color, MTA spends only 30% of its resources on buses. A typical MTA rider is a woman of color, in her twenties, with a household income under $15,000 and no car available to use in lieu of public transit, according to the MTA's own studies. In sharp contrast, the MTA spends 70% of its resources on rail, which carries only 6% of its riders and serves a disproportionately white ridership.[63]

The ridership of the established light rail system could hardly be more starkly different.

> The typical Metrolink rider is a professional with a household income of $65,000. At least 69% of the Metrolink riders on all five commuter rail lines are white; 74% are white on the Santa Clarita Line which is entirely within Los Angeles County; 80% are white on the Ventura Line which operates mostly within Los Angeles County.[64]

In the summary of evidence produced for the court, these facts of ridership are contrasted with the money invested in each system. For the 16,300 to 18,000 daily riders on the Metrolink (rail) system there were at least 18,000 riders on each of more than 20 MTA bus lines, and yet the MTA had spent $600 million to acquire right of way for the rail lines. This, combined with other operating expenses, represented a subsidy of over $21 for every rail boarding, while subsidizing each bus rider by only $1.17. In 1992 the buses carried 94% of the MTA's riders, but received less than 20% of the MTA's $2.6 billion budget. The 6 percent of riders who used the rail lines received 71% of the budget. In addition, far more was spent on security for train riders than it was for bus riders. In 1993, for instance, the MTA spent $13.5 million on security for the 94% of riders who used the buses, while spending $15.2 million on the 2.4% of rider who used the Blue line (train) alone.

While many people depend directly and indirectly on public transit for their everyday mobility in Los Angeles, the people who use it most are undoubtedly the relatively poor, people of color, women, the elderly, and the disabled. These facts, however, do not reveal the qualitative experience of mobility. Consider the experience of twenty-six-year-old Kyle, a Latina mother of two, during her average workday. In order to work at a drug prevention program, she has to be at the bus stop at 6:00 a.m. with her children, aged fourteen and five, respectively. It takes two buses to get to one school and another two buses to get to her babysitter's house. Another thirty minutes and she is at work, three hours and six buses later.[65] Stories like this are played out daily across the Los Angeles metro region.

In response to these damning facts, the MTA looked to the geography of place to make its case, responding that the train lines passed through predominantly minority areas such as Watts and thus served minority groups. The light rail Blue Line for instance, runs between downtown's Union Station and Long Beach to the south. Between downtown and Long Beach is an area of Los Angeles that has a predominantly minority population. In response, the BRU argued that the population of areas the train lines passed through was not the relevant fact. Before the Blue Line was built, the area was heavily served by buses that stopped frequently all along the corridor. Ninety-five percent of these riders were minority. The train line has far fewer stops in this mid-corridor area and the train thus serves comparatively fewer minority riders (76% in 1995). As white riders tend to travel longer distances (from one end to the other) the actual rider miles are 32% white. In the Summary of Evidence it is noted that the MTA itself agreed that the Blue Line did not serve minority communities well. In addition, the BRU pointed out that the Blue Line was built at grade (rather than being underground or elevated), and had resulted in a high number of accidents and deaths in inner-city minority communities. The line of argument presented by the MTA was dismissed by the court in light of the facts of ridership. It wasn't the area the train passed through that counted, but who was on board.

The immediate outcome of the suit was for Judge Terry Hatter of the federal district court in Los Angeles to issue a restraining order against the MTA, forbidding them from raising fares and cutting the bus pass scheme. Following this and a second hearing, the court reaffirmed the restraining order and entered a preliminary injunction preventing the MTA from raising fares and eliminating monthly bus passes. The court declared that the proposed fare restructuring would "cause minority bus riders substantial losses of income and mobility that, for a significant number, will result in the loss of employment and housing, and the inability to reach medical care, food sources, educational opportunities, and other basic needs of life."[66] The court further argued that the effect of the fare changes on the plaintiffs (the bus riders) in terms of hardship caused, outweighed the effects of the lack of additional resources on the MTA.

In making its decision, the court noted the contrast between the probable effects of the MTA bus fare restructuring on the one hand, and the vast amounts of money being put into light rail projects on the other. Indeed, the court heard how the MTA Operations Committee had been presented with an internally produced report documenting the inequitable service provided to areas of the city that were minority and poor due to the lack of available public funds. This occurred despite the fact that it was these very people who were most transit dependent. The report also noted how busy inner-city bus lines were routinely operating at 140% of capacity and were thus severely overcrowded.

In August 1993 the Labour/Community Strategy Center had, at an MTA board meeting, requested the MTA stop rail projects that served a predominantly nonminority ridership while simultaneously planning fare hikes for the bus system. MTA board member Villaragosa proposed that the MTA board refuse to approve a $59 million fund allocation to the

Pasadena rail project in light of the need for funding in the bus system. His suggestion was ignored and the funding for the Pasadena line was approved.

In January 1994 the chief executive officer of the MTA received a memorandum stating that fare hikes would disproportionately affect poor, minority transit users. It noted that the ridership of the buses was 80% nonwhite and poor. Six months later the MTA board approved the fare hike and elimination of a bus pass that provided unlimited bus use for $42.00 a month. A few days later the board approved spending an additional $123 million on the Pasadena light-rail project. A court date of November 19, 1996 was set. The two sides came into a legal agreement (consent decree) in early November before the case could be heard.

The consent decree obligated the MTA, over a ten-year period, to make improvement of the Los Angles bus system its first priority for funding. The consent decree ordered the MTA to cut fares, reduce overcrowding, provide services that connected the poor to centers of employment, education, and services such as health care, and implement a joint working group to oversee the implementation of the consent decree. The MTA continued to contest the consent decree, first in the Ninth Circuit Court of Appeals and then in the United States Supreme Court, which rejected MTA's request for a hearing, thereby upholding the rulings of the district court. The MTA was required to purchase 350 new buses, change diesel buses to low-emission natural gas-powered buses, and reduce crowding on 78 bus lines that carried 90% of MTA's ridership. Despite the MTA's declaration that it was in compliance with the overcrowding limit on 98% of its buses, the Bus Riders Union forced the MTA to admit that it was in fact 87% in violation of the overcrowding limit. The MTA was then forced to buy another 125 buses to meet the standards imposed by the court.

The MTA continues to avoid its responsibilities to bus riders while it spends considerable amounts of money on the light rail system. The Bus Riders Union has called for a complete moratorium on rail development until the bus system has been adequately modernized. They have been particularly opposed to the proposed extension of the Pasadena Line, arguing that it is a subsidy for the mobility of the rich. A recent flyer, distributed by the Bus Riders Union, declares that the "Pasadena Gold Line is the New Gold Rush—It Steals, Disposseses and builds a Train on the backs of Indigenous Peoples, Mexicans, Blacks and Chinese" and further that "Pasadena Gold Line is 13.7 miles, $869 million to build, 28,000 daily riders. The Vermont bus line has 45,000 daily riders who each get a subsidy of less than one dollar per ride. Can you say, Transit Racism?" The flyer also notes the irony of the attempts by one local politician to rename many of the Gold Line stations to "ethnic" names such as Mariachi Station, "Did Zapata, Fannie Lou and Emma Tenayuca really die," it asks, "so we could get ethnic theme rail stations?"

The actions of the Bus Riders Union are remarkable in that they have enacted a politics of mobility based on the recognition that different people, in different places, are differently enabled and constrained in terms of their mobility. The Pasadena Line, would, after all, provide mobility opportunities for the people the line served. The Bus Riders Union insisted on a form of spatial justice, pointing out the inequities created by the production of one form of mobility at the expense of another. To the activists it is not possible to think of mobility in the form of public transit without thinking about race. While some, principally white and suburban, areas of Los Angeles were having their modes of mobility enhanced, the vast majority of poor, nonwhite, urban areas, were having theirs reduced. In addition, the mobilities of the predominantly white, middle-class suburbanites were structurally connected to the mobilities of the people of color who traveled across the city to work, often in the houses of the suburbanites. As Burgos and Pulido point out, "it is precisely at the confluence of race and class that public transportation becomes so important: given such a high degree of spatial and social marginalization, working class people of color desperately need quality transportation to enable them to access the greatest array of work and other opportunities."[67] Burgos and Pulido note how there is a "spatial mismatch" between the location of poor people's homes and the concentration of jobs. They also note how the MTA, through its thirty-year plan, has been instrumental in producing this situation in the first place. This situation is also gendered.

> The geography of work and travel reflects the spatiality of patriarchy, structural racism, and the division of labor. Domestic workers are a case in point. Often when organizing on buses travelling to affluent suburbs such as San Fernando Valley or Pacific Palisades, organizers have encountered entire busloads of immigrant women. Once while negotiating with the MTA, a staff person expressed surprise at the overcrowding of buses going from downtown to the Valley. She said that "the rush hour traffic should be going to downtown." Another person joked, "that's your maid going to your house."[68]

The case of the Bus Riders Union is remarkable in many ways. In Los Angeles the courts instituted a form of spatial justice based on a politics of mobility. As Peake and Ray have suggested, the courts recognized both "where people begin—gender, sexuality, race" and where they are, "at the margins of visibility for justice."[69] The Bus Riders Union presented the court with a case that rested on a recognition of a kinetic hierarchy in which the mobility of individuals was based on their position as "prosthetic citizens" whose mobility potentials were not based on their own capacities as individuals, but on the urban environment as prosthesis. Perhaps this points toward what Etienne Balibar has described as the "multiple" nature of ideal universal rights—"not in the sense of being 'relative,' less than unconditional, bound to compromising, but rather in the sense of being always already beyond any simple or 'absolute' unity. Therefore a source of conflicts forever."[70] Perhaps also the coding of both mobility and rights as "universal" can be seen as an instance of what Iris Marion Young calls the "assimilationist" impulse, which seeks to render differences immaterial.[71] In this case, the successful activism of the Bus Riders Union points toward a politics of difference, which recognizes the material impact of different geographies in urban Los Angeles—a geography of difference that requires action.

The actions of the Bus Riders Union also points toward an expanded notion of the connection between mobility and citizenship. The kinds of bodies-as-citizens the BRU insists on are thoroughly marked by class, ethnicity, gender, disability, and sexuality. Among the many arguments put forward by the BRU, in both courts of law and on the street, were that mobility was structured unequally according to ethnicity, class, and gender; that public transport needed to be made accessible to the disabled; and that the Los Angeles bus system should be less polluting than it was. These were not presented as separate issues but as inextricably connected. One of the often-repeated demands of the BRU was for clean fuel buses to replace the older diesel buses. On May 26, 2000, the MTA was forced to buy 370 compressed natural gas buses despite their stated intention to buy diesel buses. The BRU argued that diesel was carcinogenic and was known to cause asthma. They refused to accept any diesel buses as a solution to the mobility problems of the transit-dependent citizen: "We refused to choose between mobility and public health. 'Diesel is death on wheels.' 'No killer buses.' 'Zero tolerance for carcinogens.'"[72] The geographer and activist Laura Pulido argued before the MTA board that there was a clear link between environmental pollution and spatially concentrated vulnerable communities who were more likely than not to include people of color and people on low wages. In other words, the conception of mobility at the heart of the political activism of the BRU was a radically expanded conception of mobility that linked the act of moving from A to B to the politics of social difference and the politics of the environment. This is mobility in an expanded field. While the MTA had previously planned public transport for a seemingly unified public, it now had to plan for a group labeled transit dependent, whose needs were different from the general public. While the Supreme Court cases reviewed in the first section of this chapter hollowed out mobility to an abstraction, the BRU consistently filled in the notion of mobility with social content, and in doing so, enriched the kind of citizen who practices mobility. The universal citizen became thoroughly geographical. No longer an individuated autonomous body, the mobile body presented by the BRU is marked as different—as transit dependent, and as connected to both the humanly created world of things (buses, roads, train tracks, etc.) and the environment. This approach to mobility necessarily calls into question equally abstract notions of both rights and citizenship.

CHAPTER 7

# Producing Immigrant Mobilities

## WITH GARETH HOSKINS

In 1970 a park ranger, Alexander Weiss, was busy checking over some old buildings on Angel Island in the San Francisco Bay. The California Department of Parks and Recreation was in the process of demolishing these buildings as they were deemed unsafe and unsightly for the increasing number of local residents who visited for a picnic and, fog permitting, views of the city skyline. Several buildings had already been bulldozed and an old wooden pier removed. As he inspected the two-story detention barracks, Weiss noticed some writings on the wall and believed them to be carvings left by Chinese immigrants once detained there for questioning. He informed his superiors at the department, but apparently they shared neither his enthusiasm for, nor belief in, the significance of the writings. The ranger eventually contacted Dr. George Araki of San Francisco State University, who along with a local photographer recorded the hundreds of poems scrawled all over the inside of the building.

The poems are written in classical Chinese and are just part of a now estimated ten thousand inscriptions by different authors, recording their feelings of frustration, confusion and sadness at having been unexpectedly detained in the building under the 1882 Chinese Exclusion Act. Here are two translated examples.

I hastened here for the sake of my stomach
And landed promptly in jail.
Imprisoned I am melancholy; even when I
eat, my heart is troubled.
They treat us Chinese badly, and feed us
yellowed greens.
My weak physique cannot take it; I am truly
miserable.[1]

The low building with three beams merely
shelters the body.
It is unbearable to relate the stories
accumulated on the Island slopes.
Wait till the day I become successful and
fulfill my wish!
I will not speak of love when I level the
immigration station.[2]

The discovery of these poems and the recognition of their cultural importance sparked widespread interest from the local Asian-American community—enough to successfully lobby for $250,000 dollars for the preservation of the site. Today, these accounts of the immigration experience have become part of the heritage landscape and deemed to be significant national treasures.

From 1910 to 1940, Angel Island operated as an immigration station and detention and quarantine headquarters for an estimated 175,000 Chinese looking to find work and residence in America. It is now in the process of becoming something else—a museum and heritage center memorializing Asian immigration into the United States. The writing on the wall, following careful preservation, has become the central focus of this new heritage space.

These inscriptions are a material part of the socio-geographical construction of Chinese immigrant mobility. The purpose of this chapter is to build on chapter 6 by taking a sustained look at the specific kind of mobility embodied in the act of immigration in the United States. As such, it continues discussion of citizenship and its constituent Others within the context of American history. Central to the chapter are two pieces of American legislation concerning the mobility of Chinese citizens to the United States, which have been key moments in the process of ascribing meaning to mobility and which have, in significant ways, played important roles in the history of these poignant poems. The first is the

Chinese Exclusion Act of 1882 and the second is the Peopling of America Theme Study Act of 2001. The first act constructed Chinese mobility as radically different and a threat to the ongoing process of American identity construction. The second act, on the other hand, seeks to incorporate the experience of the Chinese into a unifying story of the "Peopling of America," which cannot help but negate the difference that it attempts to recognize. The latter statute envisages a reworking of American history and roots in a manner befitting a society of paradox, that is, one ever more fixated on its plural identity while simultaneously living out and selling its image of a coherent bounded and concrete nation.[3] This chapter explains how, in two instances divided by 118 years, the mobility of Chinese groups into the United States has been made meaningful by the United States legislature in different ways. In effect it charts how knowledges concerning the mobility of the Chinese changed, in the late nineteenth century, from ones constructing them as a threat to the economic, social, physical, and moral order of a Eurocentric civilization, to the situation today where that mobility is given another meaning—standing as a flagship for tolerance, acceptance of difference, and achievement over adversity that all peoples in the nation can share.

As in other chapters, the focus here is on how mobility and mobile people are "geographically constructed." Paying attention to the encoding of the mobility of potential and actual Chinese immigrants highlights the role of geographical imaginations in the process of making up people. Geography is important in this story because the legislation is thoroughly embedded with moral geographies about mobility and about place, and because a particular material geography arose to support and enact the legislation. Geography is part of the discourse at all levels. As Ian Hacking has argued, it is necessary to be more literal about the process of construction. Chinese immigrants, after all, could never be anything other than a social construction.[4] To make the story interesting it is necessary to show how this construction happens both in terms of the meanings ascribed to the immigrants and the material facts of their lives.

A further central strand in the argument is the entanglement of the politics of mobility and the politics of difference. The ways in which mobility is given meaning and then enacted is intimately tied to notions of sameness and difference.[5] As we will see, the Chinese Exclusion Act was based on notions of essential difference between forms of mobility, while the Peopling of America Theme Study Act, although often ambivalent, is ultimately based on the notion of unity, totality, sameness—the idea that American national identity is marked by a common experience of mobility. In this sense the account of mobility provided here develops another theme of this book—the consistent attempt to produce abstract and universal forms of mobility, which hides the fact that such an attempt is always predicated on the definition of Other mobilities as threatening, transgressive, and abject. This chapter, then, continues the story of how mobility as a cultural resource gets to be unevenly distributed—how the raw fact of motion gets encoded with meanings and how these meanings affect practices of mobility.

## Politics, Difference, and Mobility

Jean François Lyotard in *The Postmodern Condition* (1984) described the "incredulity toward metanarratives" and the heterogeneity of language games that marks the postmodern condition.[6] This leads him to, somewhat cryptically, ask us to "wage a war on totality" as "The nineteenth and twentieth centuries have given us as much terror as we can take. We have paid a high enough price for the nostalgia of the whole and the one."[7] In discussion with Jean-Loup Thébaud, he develops this ethical and political commitment to difference in *Just Gaming*.

> . . . if one has the viewpoint of a multiplicity of language games. If one has the hypothesis that the social bond is not made up of a singular type of statement, or, if you will, of discourse, but that it is made up of several kinds of these games . . . , then it follows that, to put it quickly, social partners are caught up in pragmatics that are different from each other.[8]

Once, he argues, we have abandoned the Parsonian idea of a singular and coherent "society" and we recognize the variety of "language games" that exist side by side and in conflict with each other we must necessarily jettison the political idea of "unity" and accept multiplicity and difference.

> The picture that one can draw from this observation is precisely that of an absence of unity, an absence of totality. All of this does not make up a body. On the contrary. And the idea that I think we need today in order to make decisions in political matters cannot be the idea of the totality, or of the unity, of a body. It can only be the idea of a multiplicity or of a diversity.[9]

Lyotard admits the lack of an answer to what this new form of politics and justice might look like.

This line of questioning has been inherited by Iris Marion Young, who has consistently called for a new "politics of difference" to challenge the hegemony of modernist liberal doctrines of rights and equality.[10] Her starting point is the recognition that there always has been a politics of difference based on essentialist notions of absolute difference—"a time of caste and class, when tradition decreed that each group had its place."[11] Here social inequality was based on the hierarchical difference of people's natures. This politics of essential difference was overturned (not completely and not everywhere) by an Enlightenment project in which the use of impartial reason was central to a multitude of struggles of liberty and equality—struggles against the tyranny of irrational prejudice. Recent manifestations of this project include the fight for women's rights and the civil rights movements.

> Today in our society a few vestiges of prejudice and discrimination remain, but we are working on them, and have nearly realized the dream these Enlightenment fathers dared to propound. The state and law should express rights only in universal terms applied equally to all, and differences among persons and groups should be a purely accidental and private matter. We seek a society in which differences of race, sex, religion, and ethnicity no longer make a difference to people's rights and opportunities.[12]

Young refers to this enlightenment dream of sameness as an "assimilationist ideal"—an ideal that places equal treatment at the heart of the idea of justice. A new politics of difference, on the other hand, rejects both this view and the older politics of essential difference. Instead it argues for a liberatory self-definition of group difference—difference as not rooted in nature but in social processes. Difference as not absolute but relational. Rather than thinking of difference as distance from a norm in which some groups simply function as an "other" to a preestablished neutral group, Young asks us to conceptualize difference as simply variation defined through social process in a way that undermines the previously universalized position of privileged groups who others have been constituted as different from. So while the liberal assimilationist ideal calls for all people to be subject to the same rules and standards, the politics of difference argues that "equality as the participation and inclusion of all groups sometimes requires different treatment for oppressed and disadvantaged groups."[13] In this way, Young takes the discussion of totality and difference out of the realm of philosophy and into the domain of policy and legislation, showing how such abstractions impact the material lives of people. In this sense Young is less reticent than Lyotard and is able to give an answer to the question of how a politics based on multiplicity might work.

Returning to the theme of the role of mobility in the geographical imagination that informs legislation on and about Chinese-Americans, we can utilize some of the lessons learned from Lyotard and Young concerning the challenge to totality. The focus here is specifically on geographical ideas of sameness and difference as expressed through legislation concerning Chinese immigration. Thinking about the different ways in which mobility is given meaning and experienced (in legislation and elsewhere) leads back to a focus on the politics of mobility.

## Constructing Chinese Mobility: Act One

The mobility of migrants to the United States and the mobility of people within the nation have often been cast in a positive light as a general fact of American cultural identity.[14] While this movement has been cast as a universal experience at the heart of collective identity, it has most often referred to the mobility of white European migrants. The problem with totalities is that they often obscure the situatedness of the knowledge that is produced and claim it to be universal. This mobility—represented as general—has been placed at the heart of America's creation myth. Even this form of migrancy cannot be so simply coded. The movements of the Irish, Italians, eastern European Jews, and Germans were all, at one time or another, seen as a threat to the body politic as well as the literal human body. As they passed through Ellis Island and were squashed into the maze of tenements on New York's lower east side, they were variously seen as lazy, excitable and diseased.[15] Perhaps only Anglo mobility to the United States has escaped being coded as deviant. Over time, however, the migration of white Europeans into the United States has been celebrated and given a home in the Immigration Museum at Ellis Island. Conversely, the mobility of the Chinese to an America in the midst of depression and upheaval has more often been seen as a threat of instability, and a danger for the moral and physical well-being of established American citizens.

Indeed, both groups had common experiences of poverty and deprivation, whether in Europe or China, enough to force them to move elsewhere. The meaning subsequently given to the Europeans was largely positive— as actors in a narrative of nation building. The Chinese migration was, however, perceived and understood as a threat that warranted oppression and exclusion and required defense in the form of racially determined exclusion acts. In 1882 the Forty-Seventh Congress passed the Chinese Exclusion Act.

Preamble.

Whereas, in the opinion of the Government of the United States the coming of Chinese laborers to this country endangers the good order of certain localities within the territory thereof: Therefore,

Be it enacted by the Senate and House of Representatives of the
United States of America in Congress assembled, That from and
after the expiration of ninety days next after the passage of this
act, and until the expiration of ten years next after the passage of
this act, the coming of Chinese laborers to the United States be,
and the same is hereby, suspended; and during such suspension
it shall not be lawful for any Chinese laborer to come, or, having
so come after the expiration of said ninety days, to remain within
the United States.

Section 14. That hereafter no State court or court of the United
Sates shall admit Chinese to Citizenship; and all laws in conflict
with this act are hereby repealed.[16]

The Chinese Exclusion Act of 1882 incorporated understandings of race,
class, and mobility to define the individual as an illegitimate job seeker
denying at a stroke a wider appreciation of economic and structural relations. Other sections of the Chinese Exclusion Act further differentiate
mobilities along class and occupation lines. The coding of people as raced
is seldom free of class connotations. Section 6 reads:

That in order to the faithful execution of articles one and two
of the treaty in this act before mentioned, every Chinese person
other than a laborer who may be entitled by said treaty and this
act to come within the United States, and who shall be about to
come to the United States, shall be identified as so entitled by the
Chinese Government in each case, such identity to be evidenced
by a certificate issued under the authority of said government,
which certificate shall be in English. . . . Such certificate shall be
prima-facie evidence of the fact set forth therein, and shall be produced to the collector of customs, or his deputy, of the port in the
district in the United States at which the person named therein
shall arrive.[17]

Section 13 makes it clear that diplomats and other officers of the Chinese
Government must be able to present credentials that will be taken in lieu
of a certificate. Section 15 reads: "That the words 'Chinese laborers' whenever used in this act, shall be construed to mean both skilled and unskilled
laborers and Chinese employed in mining." The Chinese Exclusion Act
then mobilized a set of suppositions about race and class to enact strict
controls on some forms of mobility for some sorts of people. The mobility
was to be policed by a bureaucratic handling of certificates that provided
the necessary details including "name, title, or official rank, if any, the age,

height, and all physical peculiarities, former and present occupation or profession…" (Section 6). People without such certificates were prohibited from entering the United States. The act was thereby enacting a politics of mobility at a number of levels. At one level it ascribed a particular set of meanings to certain kinds of Chinese mobility based on the danger posed to "the good order of certain localities" (Section 1). On another, connected, level it was producing a new set of material institutional arrangements to police and enforce exclusion ranging from the certificates themselves to the offices and material spaces needed to enact exclusion. One of these material spaces was the detention center on Angel Island. All of this was based on the finely tuned definitions of mobility implicit in the act. These did not come out of nowhere, however. Rather they were just one part of a wider set of representations and practices directed against the Chinese.

The Chinese were the first numerically significant nonwhite group to enter the United States as free immigrants. The first wave began around 1849 after the discovery of gold in California, where their subordination was at once obvious in their reworking of gold claims abandoned by white miners and earning 12 cents an hour laying track as section hands for the Central Pacific Railroad.

Roger Daniels tells of the most dangerous part in its completion, the crossing of the Sierra Mountains in California and Nevada. Chinese laborers worked with large quantities of dynamite to blast a right of way through the rock and open up the west to the rest of the world. The conclusion of this task played a large part in forging an understanding of mobility over the next decades.

> When that road was completed at Promontory Point, Utah, perhaps ten thousand Chinese workers were discharged; most of them found their way back to San Francisco where their presence in a depressed labor market helped an existing and virulent anti-Chinese movement gain strength in the late 1860's.[18]

The formulation, policing, and challenge of numerous laws during the late nineteenth century allow a wealth of insight in to the construction of knowledges about the Chinese expressed variously as alien, inassimilable, uncivil, immoral, and unhealthy.[19] Indeed preceding the Exclusion Act of 1882, there are many attempts to not only prevent entry, but to withdraw rights for existing legitimate Chinese residents. A highly symbolic decision defining the Chinese individual as outside society occurred in 1854, for instance, when the California Supreme Court ruled in the case of *People v Hall* that the testimony of Chinese against white persons could not be accepted in court. The Page Act of 1875 focused on preventing the importation of Chinese women due to fear of prostitution and the subsequent health risk to white men.[20]

It was not only through Congress and the courts that the Chinese endured persecution based on essentialist views on what it is to be Chinese. Local organizations prevented Chinese inclusion in the mining profession and placed higher taxes on Chinese-run launderettes. Moreover, a specifically anti-Chinese section was written into California's 1879 constitution, forbidding public bodies from employing Chinese people and calling upon the legislature to protect the state from the evils and burdens arising from their presence. There are countless sources that tell of the violent treatment of Chinese communities all over the West during the late-nineteenth-century cycle of depressions, when resentment was at its peak. In 1885 the white citizens of Humbolt County evicted many Chinese people from the area after the shooting of Councilman David Kendall, allegedly by a Chinese American. A year later, Del Norte County expelled all Chinese Americans to San Francisco. Inexplicable fires broke out in the buildings of the Chinese American community. In May 1887, a fire destroyed San Jose's Chinese American community under suspicious circumstances. Newspapers on the following day noted that the fire had started in three places at once and that the water tanks were empty at the time.

What these actions reveal is the enactment of a particular kind of essentialist politics of difference in which the Chinese are categorized as a threatening other to white Americans—and particularly white American laborers. The act's careful delineation of difference is clearly part of a process of differentiation that is at the same time part of the process of social construction. Ian Hacking has argued that the term *social construction* is too often used in banal and self-evident ways. He asks us to take the process of "making up" people more literally. The processes through which discourse is made to act on its objects is more than mere words. Rather, discourses have their own geographies—their brute materialities that act on the bodies of those being constructed. The Chinese Exclusion Act requires that certificates be carried by Chinese people entering the United States. Inspectors needed to exist to check over the certificates and inspect the Chinese people for physical peculiarities. Offices were created for these inspectors with desks where the process of differentiation could be enacted. Spaces needed to be constructed where the Chinese could stand in line awaiting decisions. Courtrooms became spaces in which lawyers specializing in immigration could make carefully crafted arguments over whether a Chinese person was really a laborer or belonged to some more exalted category. In these material spaces categories came alive.

The return certificates issued to legitimate Chinese visitors to the United States preexisted any need for an American citizen to carry a passport. In this sense the use of certificates to prove identity, particularly at border points, marked the beginning of a process that linked identity to documentation. The Chinese Exclusion Act was the first attempt in American history to exclude a group of people whose bodies were known only through the documents they were forced to carry. The documentation was needed to separate those Chinese immigrants who could be classed as laborers from those who were businessmen or diplomats, for instance.[21] According to the 1882 Act, it was only newly arriving Chinese laborers who were forbidden from entering the United States. All those who had entered more than ninety days prior to the Exclusion Act could legitimately leave and enter at will, providing they could prove their identity at the border. Many second-generation immigrants were, in fact, American citizens, as anyone born in the United States could be considered a citizen.

Here we see the United States exerting a form of "remote control" where immigrants were dealt with before they even left the shore of their country of origin. This mode of controlling international migration was to become the norm in the years following World War I, where the importance of passports and visas was established.[22] During the 1892 election campaign, California Congressman Thomas Geary called for all Chinese residents in the United States to be issued a document including a photograph and registered formally. All those who would not register would then have to prove their identity in some other way. This became law and soon thereafter all Chinese residents were given a year to register and obtain an identity document. Government officials entered Chinese encampments and conducted mass registrations. By the late 1890s, the process of registration and identification was complete.

This process of categorization did not go unchallenged. As the 1882 Act distinguished between laborers, merchants, and diplomats, it was deemed impossible for any group of Chinese immigrants to exist in any category outside of these three legal figures. The categories brought different consequences with them. If you were deemed a laborer, then you could be detained at Angel Island and sent back to China. If you were a merchant or a diplomat, you were allowed to enter. The distinction between laborer and merchant became a subject of legal argument in a number of court cases. One case in which the definition of a Chinese immigrant came to the fore following the 1882 Act was *Fing Yue Ting v. U.S.* Fing Yue Ting was found without a registration certificate as demanded by the Geary amendment of 1892. His attorney argued that the registration system violated a number of rights including his right to due process and the Eighth Amendment's prohibition of cruel and unusual punishment. In order to make the argument that their client had "rights," they had to establish that he was something other than an alien. An alien, after all, does not carry the same rights as a citizen. The attorneys argued that Fing Yue Ting was, in fact, a *denizen*—a kind of local citizen whose identity was attached to a territory at the subnational level. The Supreme Court rejected this argument. They argued that Fing Yue Ting was an *alien* and aliens did not have rights, so the Constitution did not apply. The *denizen* simply did not exist. Three judges, however, were persuaded that the figure of the *denizen* did represent an important and real category that fell within the scope of the Bill of Rights. Unfortunately for Ting they lost the argument and he was deported.[23] If it had been decided that Ting was some species of citizen, his mobility would have been seen as part of his bundle of rights. As he was deemed an alien, his mobility was deemed unlawful and he was, in fact, sentenced to two kinds of coerced mobility, first during his time at hard labor and second in the process of deportation.

At other times in the decades following 1882 various other categorical problems emerged as attorneys argued that their defendants fell outside of the category of laborer. The 1882 Act, for instance, did not specify how it applied to women and children who were neither laborers nor merchants. It was not until 1890 that the Supreme Court decided that both would be ascribed the category given to their husband/father. Other disputes centered on a number of vocations such as traveling salesman, fisherman, and peddler. In the years following the 1882 Act, it was tightened up on several occasions to close these perceived loopholes in the law. The definition of *merchant* was one area that had proved difficult. In a 1884 revision of the act, this was dealt with in the following manner: "the word 'merchant' was defined to exclude hucksters, peddlers and fishermen engaged in drying and shipping fish; the traveler's certificate must state where he proposed to travel and his financial standing; the certificates of identification from the Chinese Government must be verified as to facts and visaed by the United States diplomatic officer at the port of departure, [in order] to be *prima facie* evidence of right to reentry."[24] Once again, remote control of immigration began to emerge.

This elaborate and expensive system of registration, including the documents, the officials who policed them, and the granting of visas at a distance were all part of what John Torpey, in his history of the passport, has called the state monopolization of the *legitimate means of movement*, a process that involves:

a number of mutually reinforcing aspects: the (gradual) definition
of states everywhere—at least from the point of view of the international system—as "national" (i.e. as "nation-states" comprising
members understood as nationals); the codification of laws establishing which types of persons may move within or cross their
borders, and determining how, when, and where they may do so;
the stimulation of the worldwide development of techniques for
uniquely and unambiguously identifying each and every person
on the face of the globe, from birth to death; the construction of
bureaucracies designed to implement this regime of identification
and to scrutinize persons and documents in order to verify
identities; and the creation of a body of legal norms designed to
adjudicate claims by individuals to entry into particular spaces
and territories.[25]

In many ways then, the implementation of identity documents in order
to police the Chinese Exclusion Act of 1882 marked one of the earliest
moments in the development of a worldwide system for producing and
limiting mobilities on a global scale.

Clearly then, the construction of Chinese mobility to and in the United
States enacted by the Chinese Exclusion Act was founded on a meticu-
lous definition of a series of *differences*—between Chinese and American,
between citizen and alien, between merchant and laborer. The elaborate
infrastructure produced to monitor and define these differences and the
mobilities they engendered necessitated a certain geography built on the
implicit and explicit moral geography of mobility. Perhaps the most obvious material geographic component of this discourse of difference was
the detention center at Angel Island where tens of thousands of Chinese
people were incarcerated while they awaited decisions over whether they
were leaving or arriving.

## (Re)constructing Chinese-American Mobility: Act Two

With such a regrettable past, it is no wonder that totalizing historical narratives have written the Chinese out of American space, and no surprise that
heritage sites have typically directed our gaze away from the experience of
minority groups. Today, a postmodern culture with the legitimacy it affords
to marginalized groups and their alternative voices can combine with a
renewed fascination for history and roots to readdress this imbalance.

Just as earlier essentialized views of difference were inscribed in the
legislation of the Chinese Exclusion Act, so more recent cultural currents
have been expressed in legislation. On July 27, 2000, the 106th Congress

sat for a second reading of a bill, that they subsequently approved, which set out a strategy to reassess and then rework the entire social history of North America. The Peopling of America Theme Study Act, Bill S.2478, would work to:

> Direct the secretary of the Interior to conduct a theme study on the peopling of America to provide a basis for identifying, interpreting and preserving sites related to the migration, immigration and settling of America.[26]

The statute seeks to rework knowledge about the roots of America by directing investigation on mobility to show how the continent was populated. The broad term *The Peopling of America* is defined in section two of this act as characterized by:

> i. The movement of groups of people across external and internal boundaries of the United States and territories of the United States and
> ii. The interactions of those groups with each other and with other populations.[27]

This bill was cowritten, sponsored, and put to the house by Senator Daniel Akaka, representative of Hawaii, and the first native Hawaiian voted to Congress. Akaka's political career has been dominated by the task of communicating the role played by Asian Americans in the growth of the nation. With this new statute, the United States' success and the spiritual, intellectual, cultural, political, and economic strength of its national fabric is attributed to pluralism—its embracing and accommodation of diversity. This is how Senator Akaka promoted his bill in a press release before it was presented to the house.

> Americans are all *travelers* from other regions, continents and islands. We need a better understanding of this *coherent and unifying theme* in America. This is the source of our nation's greatest strength.

> Looking back, we understand that our history, and our very national character, is defined by the grand entangled process of people to and across the American landscape—through exploration, colonization, the slave trade, traditional immigration, or internal migration—that gave rise to the rich interactions that make the American experience unique.[28]

The bill's purpose therefore, is to develop a system of knowledge about mobility, use it to rewrite the history of the nation, and particularly the

West, and foster a new inclusive identity for the American nation that all can share. It intends to highlight the power of the nation through a wider understanding of the positive contributions made by diverse and marginal groups; it is a success story using minorities as its tool. Those minorities who were once excluded from the story of America are now at the forefront of demonstrating its strength.

Interpretation of the bill is not straightforward. Perhaps as a reflection of Akaka's ambiguous position as a representative of the Asian-American community and as an agent of the state, the text of the bill and supporting statements constantly shift from a recognition of difference and diversity to unified statements of American mobile identity. In the above quotation, for instance, we hear of the clearly differentiated mobilities of "exploration, colonization, the slave trade, traditional immigration, or internal migration." This is preceded however by statements about "*our* national character" and followed by the unifying tag of "*the* American experience." According to the bill, the very exceptional and distinctive nature of Americans is that they have all experienced mobility within and across national boundaries and have been formed with all the "positive" attributes of diversity—social, cultural, ethnic, and racial—that the experience of mobility brings. However, despite its will to promote inclusion and celebrate diversity, the bill constantly slips from acknowledgment of difference to the valorization of universal mobility. Textually, the mobilities of Americans are stripped of their peculiarities to reduce mobility to the simple act of movement, which is the essential core of a unified "American experience."

Here, as Steven Hoelscher has noted, the state's need to recognize diversity is at odds with the necessity for incorporation into a coherent national identity. He has called into question the appropriateness of a strategy that reflects diversity and cultural pluralism by containing them within universal themes or unifying narratives. Is it possible to achieve unity in diversity? What kind of polyethnic culture can we appreciate while pursuing integration within a secular nation-state? Can any such intention avoid rendering difference as simply symbolic and inconsequential?[29]

The framework of this act provides for funding, preservation, and education that effectively claims all stories of movement for a universal national trait of success—a success that is to be emphasized and celebrated. The Theme Study Act valorizes travel and renders the vast differences in experience between Chinese and other immigrant groups as secondary to the prime importance of the unified experience of movement. When looking at the particular context that groups entering Ellis Island and groups entering Angel Island encountered through their mobility, we see how different the types of mobility and meanings construed from them actually are. To look carefully at the experiences of those entering America via Ellis Island (even if only in retrospect and despite much that was degrading about the process of entry) is to witness one set of meanings defining mobility as positive—a civilizing force over nature where the homesteader migrates west and eventually defines America. The difficulties encountered by the incoming Chinese, on the other hand, because of their mobility, their differing reasons for moving, and how their mobility was perceived (i.e., as strangers from a different shore, aliens) can only be falsely equated with the experiences of earlier European immigrants who, after all, were retrospectively written into the metanarratives of American history.

Bonnie Honig in *Democracy and the Foreigner* argues for the key role of the foreigner as Other in the constitution of American democracy.[30] "The myth of an immigrant America," she writes, "depicts the foreigner as a supplement to the nation, an agent of national reenchantment that might rescue the regime from corruption and return it to first principles."[31] Immigrants, for instance, serve to reassure the poor of the possibility of success from humble beginnings. In another formulation, "the liberal consenting immigrant addresses the need of a disaffected citizenry to experience its regime as choice-worthy, to see it through the eyes of still-enchanted newcomers whose choice to come here also just happens to reenact liberalism's own cleaned-up Sinai scene: its fictive foundation in individual acts of uncoerced consent."[32] But as well as being seen as positive, the foreigner's mobility is also seen as a threat. Honig describes how American politics and culture are simultaneously xenophobic and xenophilic. The foreigner is unsettling because she always brings into question the presumed unity of a national identity. America both identifies itself as a nation of foreigners and attempts to constantly control and discipline them. This ambivalence, Ali Behdad suggests, is a "space of contestation where concepts of nationality as citizenship and state as sovereignty can be re-articulated and re-affirmed."[33] The fact of American xenophilia—the idea of the United States as an immigrant nation—only serves to make perceived failure and difference all the more disturbing. While some immigrants are described as what Honig calls "supercitizens"—citizens who heroically surpass all that is expected of them in the face of adversity—most can only fail. Thus, Honig asks, "deploying the supercitizen immigrant on behalf of a national ideal, do these xenophiles feed the fire they mean to fight?"[34] The relation between the (appropriately mobile) supercitizen and the (threateningly mobile) Other is described in the following way:

> the iconic good immigrant—the supercitizen—who upholds American liberal democracy is not accidentally or coincidentally partnered with the iconic bad immigrant who threatens to tear it down. . . . The co-presence in American political culture of xenophilia and xenophobia comes right out of America's

fundamental liberal commitments, which map a normatively and materially privileged normative citizenship onto an idealized immigrant trajectory to membership.[35]

Honig's diagnosis of the way the foreigner is simultaneously mobilized for the purposes of national citizenship *and* seen as deeply unsettling for liberal definitions of the citizen recalls Isin's discussion of the process of alterity at work in the notion of the citizen.[36] The foreigner as citizen simultaneously produces the foreigner as threat.

The threatening mobility of the immigrant plays an important role in the constitution of the citizen. As Lisa Lowe puts it:

> Insofar as the legal definition and political concept of the citizen enfranchises the subject who inhabits the national public sphere, the concept of the abstract citizen—each formally equivalent, one to the other—is defined by the negation of the material conditions of work and the inequalities of the property system. In the United States, not only class but also the historically sedimented particularities of race, national origin, locality, and embodiment remain largely invisible within the political sphere. In this sense, the legal and political forms of the nation have required a national culture in the integration of the differentiated people and social spaces that make up "America," a national culture, broadly cast yet singularly engaging, that can inspire diverse individuals to identify with the national project.[37]

Mobility, in the Peopling of America Theme Study Act, is a unifying force. While the Chinese Exclusion Act was predicated on a finely tuned production of difference, the Peopling Act is predicated on a negation of difference. Mobility here is a national story—inspiring (in Lisa Lowe's terms) diverse individuals to identify with a national project. Just as the Chinese Exclusion Act necessitated moral geographies of difference, so the new Peopling Act necessitates moral geographies of commonality—geographies in which a virtual unified mobility is produced.

## An Ongoing Story

> Groups experiencing cultural imperialism have found themselves objectified and marked with a devalued essence from the outside, by a dominant culture they are excluded from making. The assertion of a positive sense of group difference by these groups is emancipatory because it reclaims the definition of the group by the group, as a creation and construction, rather than a given essence.
>
> **Iris Marion Young**[38]

On the basis of the Theme Study authorized by the Peopling of America Act, the secretary of the interior will identify and recommend for designation new historic landmarks and encourage the nomination of other properties to the National Register of Historic Places. Section 4B reads:

> The purpose of the theme study shall be to identify regions, areas, trails, districts, communities, sites, buildings, structures, objects, organizations, societies and cultures that best illustrate and commemorate key events or decisions affecting the peopling of America and can provide a basis for the interpretation of the peopling of America that has shaped the culture and society of the United States.[39]

It is thus mandated that sites that help to tell the story of migration should be preserved and interpreted as such. For instance, at Angel Island the Civil War camp used as Army Barracks, detention center, Japanese prisoner of war building, and immigration processing station is now used for a museum communicating the story of the peopling of America. Indeed, funding for the Angel Island museum has a specific aim. The secretary of the interior, as instructed by the Department of Parks and Leisure, seeks to build on a migrational account of nation building of American roots rather than on the specific history of Chinese exclusion and its associated racist legislation. Importantly, the funding released as part of the Peopling of America Act requires the reworking of the Angel Island story from one that is, in part, a bounded history of specific Chinese exclusion to one that gets universalized and incorporated into a larger picture of American history.

Whether this happens is an open question. What we can see, however, is that the place was originally the product of a very particular discourse about mobility and difference, which finely differentiated mobilities along race and class lines. The place was an embodiment of the Chinese Exclusion Act—a necessary material part of the sociogeographical construction of Chinese mobility as *different,* as *threatening.* What is emerging on the same site is the embodiment of a very different conception of mobility—the idea that mobility is a *central and unifying* experience for Americans.

Angel Island is in the process of becoming a site that tells a story that all Americans can share. Through a delicate balancing act between unity and difference, which in the end prioritizes unity over difference, a generalized mobility is given value and the places that are taken to symbolize it will be preserved with a message that is intentionally abstract. It is based on a set of knowledges about the American people being travelers, a social construction directed by the Senate's new bill, which will shape how we interpret and value the past. Here a politics of sameness with a specific, historically rooted view of mobility is operationalized. Quite another view was in evidence in 1882 when the Exclusion Act was framed and in 1910 when the barracks on Angel Island opened for business.

Back in 1910 the Chinese individual's arrival at Angel Island was immediately labeled, categorized, and given meaning using xenophobic knowledges that had previously been developed within the host society—knowledges rooted in understandings of appropriate and inappropriate mobility. His or her arrival signified not a visitor, a worker, or a new arrival that could share in the money and myth of the Promised Land, but the identity of threat, alien, outsider, and risk to the health and economic welfare of the local families, the state of California, and the country as a whole. To use the text of the Exclusion Act, "the coming of Chinese laborers to this country endanger[ed] the good order of certain localities . . ." One moral geography of mobility revolves around a banal imagination of totalizing, superorganic, mobility, while the other rests on notions of essentialized difference where one mobility has to be carefully distinguished from another.

These two points in history should not be read as a simple linear and progressive transformation from one imagining of American mobility to another. In 1882 a mythology of American national mobility was already well established in notions of the frontier and of manifest destiny. It had been used to boost the construction of the very railroads that Chinese immigrants had been instrumental in building. As the act assuring the future of Angel Island was assured, the idea of racialized and differentiated mobility is still very real.

Think of the situation in which some new arrivals to California recently found themselves, barred by Proposition 187 from receiving free health care and public schooling.

PROPOSED LAW SECTION 1. Findings and Declaration.

The People of California find and declare as follows:

That they have suffered and are suffering economic hardship caused by the presence of illegal aliens in this state. That they have suffered and are suffering personal injury and damage caused by the criminal conduct of illegal aliens in this state. That they have a right to the protection of their government from any person or persons entering this country unlawfully.

Therefore, the People of California declare their intention to provide for cooperation between their agencies of state and local government with the federal government, and to establish a system of required notification by and between such agencies to prevent illegal aliens in the United States from receiving benefits or public services in the State of California.[40]

So whether immigrants were the Chinese of the late nineteenth century American West or recent arrivals from Latin America to the state of California, the method employed to make sense of and then react to these individuals is the same. A discursive definitional tool is used to differentiate mobilities in order to project sociopolitical meanings onto bodies and produce the characters *alien* or *citizen* as a frame of reference for action. In this process, the state imposes meaning on the movement of the individual, which is then deemed legitimate or not. Such meaning is always political and derived from questionable knowledges of health, class, race, and gender. Significantly, enforcement proceeds through abstract generalizations attaching attributes to the individual by their association with an imagined group. At the same time, such an individual becomes isolated as a body, understood as different, even alien, to the extent that constitutional rights and moral obligation do not apply. Labeled as nonpersons they are left to reside outside the generally accepted boundaries of justice and welfare provision.

Like a postmodern novel, this story has many endings. This chapter has considered the socio-geographical construction of Chinese immigrants to the United States through two pieces of legislation. Both of these texts touch the place where this story began—Angel Island. The discourse surrounding current attempts to make a prison into a museum is deeply strategic—designed to gather funds to memorialize a previously hidden set of histories. This plays on notions of totality to make the case for funds and preservation. These texts resonate with still more texts—a whole history of American historiography that places mobility at the center of an overarching sense of Americanness. Mobility, after all, was at the center of appeals to America's sense of manifest destiny. In addition, it was the mobility of "civilization" moving west that was at the heart of historiographic accounts of the American frontier. Americans have been portrayed as restless, mobile people, differentiating them ideologically from the sedimented rootedness of a stagnant and corrupt Europe.[41] The iconography of Americans as practitioners of mobility has been played out again and again in novels (Kerouac, Steinberg), on film (numerous westerns, road movies), and in popular music (Springsteen, Dylan, Waits). Akaka's reference to everyone being travelers is already established in the minds of many as it is part of the mythology of the nation. Similarly, the older text—the 1882 Act—played on preestablished notions of the Chinese and the alleged threat they posed to the good order of localities.

The universalizing discourse of mobility might not be the one that gets played out on Angel Island though. It is possible, after all, that the museum will become a space that does reveal its process of production. Perhaps it will become a site where the kind of politics of difference proposed by Iris Young intersects with heritage to clearly and unequivocally display the earlier politics of (essential) difference that produced it in the first place. If nothing else, the words of an anonymous Chinese immigrant detained at Angel Island will be there for all to see, problematizing any simple celebration of American mobility: "I will not speak of love when I level the immigration station."

## CHAPTER 8

# Mobilizing the Movement: Entangled Mobilities in the Suffrage Politics of Florence Luscomb and Margaret Foley, 1911–1915

In October 1911 a cartoon appeared in the pages of the *Boston Post* (see Figure 8.1). It showed an apparent race between a number of suffragists in one car and candidate for governor of Massachusetts, a Mr. Frothingham, in the other. At one point the women are referred to as *shemales* by a passing tramp being paid by a shady politico to puncture the womens' tires. At another point the cartoonist suggests that perhaps the suffrage campaigner and the candidate for governor could get together, seeing as Frothingham is a bachelor. Finally, Frothingham takes to the sky in an airplane to outpace the chasing suffragists. How might we interpret such a cartoon?

First, we should know that the cartoon refers to the *suffrage auto tour* being carried out by Margaret Foley, Florence Luscomb, and a number of other suffrage campaigners. This was a new tactic for the suffrage movement, in New England at least, and it was certainly part of a radical transformation of suffrage tactics from predominantly private meetings to public campaigning. Second, we should be aware that the sight of women

**Figure 8.1** Cartoon from the *Boston Post*, October 12, 1911.

driving cars was still highly unusual in 1911 in the United States. They were considered too uncomfortable and difficult to fix for women. Indeed, manufacturers had been making especially slow electric cars that did not involve the indignity of starting with a cumbersome crank handle at the front of the car.[1] The early history of the automobile was thoroughly entwined with the construction and defense of particular visions of masculinity. Mechanical prowess, the control of space, ideas of sexual conquest, and the feeling of power that comes from being in control of one's destiny were all wrapped up in the automobile. This was reflected in ownership figures. In 1915, for instance, only 9.1 percent of car owners in the state of Maryland were women.[2]

Third, the cartoon is indicative of the prevailing sense of mobility that formed the context for the women's travels. The move from automobile to airplane reflects the fascinatingly novel role that flight had in the second decade of the twentieth century. The Wright Brothers had made their first flight only a dozen years earlier, and the vast majority of people had never seen an airplane. The cartoon also plays on the widespread mobile trope of the car chase. The Hollywood movie industry at the time was dominated by the slapstick comedy of Mack Sennett and the Keystone Cops. These movies featured endless car chases, often deliberately speeded up by the undercranking of the camera during production.[3] The car chase, in other words, was an image that many readers of the *Boston Post* were likely to relate to. These elements of the cartoon—the aeroplane and the car chase—were both components of an emergent sense of mobility in 1911.

The cartoon thus combines some familiar elements of popular culture with the unfamiliar notion of women in cars to suggest that there is something strange and amusing about this particular kind of mobility. The suggestion that the women are shemales, and that one of them should perhaps marry the prospective governor, underlines the gendering of mobility—the way in which particular forms of mobility are coded as masculine. The suggested marriage is perhaps an attempt to bring the roving woman back home and to make her make sense again—put her in her place. Just like the sideways step of the shimmy, the mobile practice of the women in their cars produced a certain amount of anxiety in some observers, who invested particular arrangements of space and people with moral and ideological worth. The cartoon, and other commentary at the time, encoded these mobilities as pathological.

In this chapter I examine the link between the experience of mobility and the politics of women's suffrage in the United States through an account of the travels (both the car trips featured in the cartoon and a trip to Europe that inspired them to pursue such tactics) of American suffrage campaigners Margaret Foley and Florence Luscomb. In this chapter and the next we will see how mobilities exist in relation to each other, and how ways of moving have quite specific characteristics depending on who is moving and the social and cultural space that is being moved through. These connections are also reminiscent of the micro-mobilities of the dancing body in 1920s London being a result of much larger trans-Atlantic mobilities of the dance forms themselves. By reading mobility carefully we can avoid easy metaphors and be clearer about the politics of getting from

A to B. These two chapters also bring into sharper focus the interrelations among moving human bodies and the various technologies of mobility that surround them. We saw in chapter 6 how the mobility of the bus riders in Los Angeles was a product of specific configurations of people and things. Here this notion of the prosthetic subject is taken in a different direction. But like the account of the Bus Riders Union, this chapter and the one that follows will focus clearly on the actual practices of people moving and the things that enable/disable that movement.

My principal argument in this chapter is that the mobile practices of Luscomb and Foley reflected and contributed to the changing spatial practice of Boston's suffrage movement in particular and, more generally, the reconfiguration of moral geographies of gender in the early part of the twentieth century. Importantly, these mobilities were not simply intentional acts of human movement, but were the combined product of the two suffragists, feminist ideas, and objects such as ships, cars, and books. Luscomb and Foley enacted a personal journey that opened up new spatial possibilities for them. Simultaneously, they represent part of a wider transformation of the spatiality of women's experience in Boston at the time.

The history of the suffrage movement's progression from private to public space is well known.[4] Less well known is the way a number of mobilities were entangled in the production of this shift. Mobility of all kinds was an important part of a transformation in the geography of expectations that surrounded men and women. Feminist research has recently provided a cautionary note to the emergence of a nomadic metaphysics. Rather than submitting to a generalized turn to mobility in order to call a metaphysics of fixity and sedentarism into question, feminists have consistently argued that mobility is a gendered activity that is often more available to men than it is to women.[5] Additionally, feminists and others have recognized that even when women are moving, their movements may be experienced very differently from those of men. These observations range from the different experiences of the journey to work, to the gendered experience of walking the street in Paris or New York, and to the role gender plays in the adventures of explorers and travelers on the one hand, and American tramps on the other.[6] Finally some feminists have pointed out that it is important to understand mobility and movement in relation to the politics of staying still, which should not always be interpreted as passivity in the face of masculine motion, but may in fact be a form of resistance.[7]

In this chapter, I develop this work by considering the gendered politics of mobility in a way that connects the movements of human gendered bodies to a variety of objects and ideas that are equally gendered. The bodies are principally those of Luscomb and Foley, the ideas are those surrounding militant suffrage tactics, and the objects are the steamship and the auto-mobile, but also include things such as books and flags. I have argued throughout this book that mobility is a social product, but to understand how it is socially produced, it is helpful to think of it as being co-produced alongside and through objects and ideas. The way people are enabled or constrained in terms of their mobile practices differs markedly according to their position in social hierarchies. The mobilities of Luscomb and Foley were not simply acts of free will; they were heavily structured by the expec-tations surrounding gender and class at the beginning of the twentieth century. Ideology and power pervade attitudes toward, and practices of, mobility. Their travels were also constrained and enabled by the different ways in which they could connect with technologies of mobility.

John Urry's recent call for a study of mobilities for the twenty-first century as part of a "sociology beyond societies" has argued that the mobility of people needs to be understood alongside the movement of ideas and things.[8] This point is not unique to the present. Similar arguments apply to the emerging mobilities of the twentieth century as experienced and practiced by Luscomb and Foley. As they traveled, ideas traveled with them. Their mobilities represent a very small part of the cross-fertilization of British and American progressive politics that occurred in the early part of the twentieth century.[9] Key to this process was the relatively new availability of new kinds of technologies of mobility ranging from steamships to automobiles to all the paraphernalia of tourism that made travel relatively comfortable. Looking at the mobile subject involves looking at the *prosthetic subject*—a subject whose capacities for mobility depend on constraints of the public sphere in which people and things are intimately interconnected.[10]

Luscomb and Foley were struggling for the vote—a simple form of poli-tics more recently usurped by the sophisticated assertion of the personal as political and the less obvious politics of gender, class, and ethnicity in everyday life.[11] It would be easy to mistake an analysis of women's suffrage as a retreat to older and simpler ideas of "women's history." By looking at the entangled mobilities of the movement, however, it becomes clear that the practice of politics writ large is deeply entwined with the rest of life.

## The Context of the Boston Suffrage Movement

As with the development of the working class, the antislavery movement and wider hybrid identities, the suffrage movement involved flows back and forth across the Atlantic.[12] The year of Luscomb and Foley's voyages at sea and on land (1911), was near the beginning of a period in which the American suffrage movement was heavily influenced by the militant tactics of the Pankhursts and their associates in England. The history of the American women's suffrage movement had largely been conducted in private spaces, in people's homes, and in hired halls and meeting places. Two suffrage organizations had dominated the women's rights debates since 1869. Susan B. Anthony and Elizabeth Stanton had formed the National Woman Suffrage Association (NWSA), and Lucy Stone, Henry Blackwell, and Julia Ward Howe had launched the more conservative American Woman Suffrage Association (AWSA). The former restricted membership to women and lobbied for the vote for women, while the latter included men and originally fought for suffrage for African-American men. The two merged in 1890 to form the National American Woman Suffrage Association.[13] The earliest victories for women's suffrage campaigns were in sparsely populated western states such as Wyoming (1869) and Utah (1870). Despite suffrage campaigns in nearly all states, very little happened in the two decades following this despite spirited speaking tours by Anthony and Stanton and campaigns across the nation. It was not until around 1910 that the suffrage movement became more militant and engaged in very public political tactics under the guidance of Stanton's daughter, Harriot Stanton Blatch, who had traveled to Britain and experienced the more public tactics of the Pankhursts.

In Boston, in particular, suffragists had been slow to move their actions out of private space and onto the streets.[14] Boston was the capital of stuffy feminism. The radical National Woman Suffrage Association was based in New York and many histories of the American suffrage movement focus on that city.[15] In Boston, women had attempted to influence legislation through formal channels, petitioning leading politicians to support their cause. In 1879 they had won a significant victory by convincing the Republican Party to support suffrage for women in elections to local school boards. The Republicans were keen to support the suffrage movement because the mostly middle-class women involved in it were seen as tools in the fight against immigrant, Catholic and working-class influence in the schools. Once this victory was won, the Republicans backed away from further support for the cause and Boston suffragists began to think of other strategies for the expansion of female suffrage. By 1900 there were three principal suffrage organizations in the city: the Massachusetts Woman Suffrage Association (MWSA), an organization dominated by the middle-class elite who were reluctant to change tactics, the College Equal Suffrage Association, and the more energetic Boston Equal Suffrage Association for Good Government. The latter organization attracted well-educated and confident outgoing women who were less afraid to upset expectations about the proper place of women. Slowly those who supported more public politics began to win the arguments. As Strom puts it:

> By 1907 the success of the Massachusetts women in rebuilding the suffrage movement had brought them to the point where they were restless. The movement seemed to have reached a hiatus, in which the convinced reinforced their own convictions. The methods of reaching women through the endorsements of prominent citizens, labor leaders, and civic-minded organizations seemed to have reached maximum efficiency.[16]

The impetus for those who preferred public action came from Britain. Some began to look to British suffragists and the more radical public tactics they favored. Emmeline Pankhurst's Women's Social and Political Union had long been interrupting political speeches and holding processions. The women's suffrage movement in England had begun at about the same time as it had in the United States (the 1860s), but had made no impact on the major political parties who had steadfastly refused to debate the issue in the House of Commons. The suffragists had tired of presenting petitions and asking potential Members of Parliament about their views. The particular idea of the "public" embodied in official politics had been a dead end. In 1903 Emmeline Pankhurst formed the Women's Social and Political Union, which quickly took the movement in a new direction. Following the removal of two of its members, Christabel Pankhurst and Annie Kenney, from a meeting with the leader of the Liberal Party, Sir Edward Grey, and their subsequent and very public mistreatment by the police, the organization sought to deliberately induce such reaction in order to bring more attention to their cause. Militant suffrage tactics were born.[17]

This was a far cry from the patient tactics in private spaces that the Boston suffragists had become accustomed to. Strom describes how in 1908, one of the leading figures of the suffrage movement in Boston, Mary Hutcheson Page, had corresponded with the British suffragettes, but was still worried about alienating the general public. The big change in tactics occurred in the spring and summer of 1909 when the Massachusetts Woman Suffrage Association decided to embark on a series of open-air speeches in the area around Boston. This was the first time that the Boston suffragists would speak to crowds who had not been invited. The first event took place on June 12 in Bedford, Massachusetts, in front of an audience of several hundred. The newspapers were happy to report the events in full. By November, members of the MWSA were selling pro-suffrage newspapers on Boston Common.

These tactics did not receive unanimous support. While many women were pro-suffrage, they did not necessarily want to change other parts of their lives. Women were strongly associated with the home in the early nineteenth century and many had no intention of becoming public spectacles.[18] There was, therefore, a split between those who wanted to make their case more public and those who were happy to continue their politics in private. Foley and Luscomb were in the former camp.

### Locating Margaret Foley and Florence Luscomb

Margaret Foley was born in 1875 in Dorchester, Massachusetts. She had grown up in a working-class Irish-American neighborhood in Roxbury, and was educated at the Girl's High School in Boston. She worked in a hat factory where she organized a union and became a board member of the Women's Trade Union League. Between 1909 and 1915 she was an activist in the Massachusetts Women's Suffrage Association. She was like a fish out of water—the only working-class (and Irish-Catholic) activist in a middle-class Protestant movement inhabiting the parlors and drawing rooms of Boston's middle classes. She was 5 feet 8 inches tall and 140 pounds and was described by the local media as a fearless warrior. Her loudness (she had taken voice training classes) and size were often highlighted as aspects of her working-class identity. One local society paper wrote that Foley "can easily manage seven feet, turn her brown hair to flame, descend like a monster of bricks and extend her mellifluous accent to megaphonics."[19] In 1911 she decided to attend the international women's suffrage convention in Stockholm and stop off on the way in England to observe the political strategy of her English sisters. It is that journey, and the auto tours she took afterward, that are the subject of this chapter. Later she continued her suffrage work in Nevada (in 1914), where she traveled around the state for two months addressing over 20,000 men and socializing with ranchers and cowboys.[20]

Foley's companion was Florence Hope Luscomb. She was born in Lowell, Massachusetts, in 1887 and died in Boston in 1985. Her mother, Hannah Skinner Luscomb, received a substantial inheritance from her mother (Florence's maternal grandmother) to raise Florence and support a variety of causes including women's suffrage. Her father, Otis, had left when Florence was only one. Florence was fortunate enough to attend a private secondary school and finally graduate from MIT after studying architecture. She was one of the first women to graduate, and continued to work as an architect until 1917. A minor figure in the history of suffrage in the United States, she nonetheless became the executive secretary of the Boston Equal Suffrage Association in 1917. She worked for the suffrage movement as a newspaper seller on Boston Common and was sent to visit Europe in 1911 with Foley. While Foley was described as loud and large, Luscomb was more likely to be described as delicate and slim. Later she held positions with the Boston League of Women Voters and the Women's International League for Peace and Freedom. She continued to be an activist in any number of struggles, including the antiwar movement during Vietnam and the Civil Rights Movement. Her travels to Europe on the suffrage cause were matched later by visits to the Soviet Union, China, and Cuba during the cold war. On several occasions her passport was temporarily confiscated.[21]

The backgrounds of Foley and Luscomb could hardly be more different. While Luscomb's archive at Harvard is quite considerable, Foley's is small. While we know a lot about Luscomb's well-documented life, we know little of what happened to Foley after 1920. Luscomb was part of "society" and Foley was on its margins. As Sarah Deutsch has argued, Luscomb and Foley were both involved in rearranging the moral geography of Boston. While the middle-class, university-educated Luscomb was transgressing the boundaries between private and public space, Foley was moving the other way. The suffrage movement in Boston was keen to reach out to the kind of people Foley represented—the Irish, Catholic, working class, and unionized. Luscomb was moving out of a middle-class geography to engage with the "public," while Foley was moving out of her working-class roots to inhabit the private spaces of the city's middle classes. While Foley was growing up in working-class neighborhoods, Luscomb was attending MIT. As Deutsch puts it, "Foley transgressed barriers more when entering the elite parlors of the suffrage leaders than when she spoke from street corners."[22] It was, perhaps, easier for Luscomb to perform in public than it was for Foley to enter the circles of the middle-class suffrage movement.

Their trip to Europe in 1911 must have been a significant moment in both of their lives, but surely more so for Foley. They were paid salaries and expenses by the Boston Equal Suffrage Association for Good Government and Massachusetts Woman Suffrage Association. The final destination was an international suffrage convention in Stockholm. They were acting as representatives and were tasked to learn from their British sisters on the way. They traveled first class.

There can be little doubt that the journey of Foley and Luscomb was a political act. Before they left Boston, local newspapers remarked on their trip and its purpose. Luscomb told the journalist: "Both of us lean toward the militant section of English suffragists. They seem to be the only ones who are accomplishing anything over there."[23] While in England they were progressively drawn into the tactics of the English suffragists they so admired. It was partly in a response to the things they learned on their European travels that they took to the roads of Massachusetts on their return to Boston.

## A Transatlantic Voyage

Paul Gilroy has noted how the ship, and the transatlantic ship in particular, serves as a symbol for his wider discussion of race and hybridity:

> The image of the ship—a living, micro-cultural, micro-political system in motion—is especially important for historical and theoretical reasons. . . . Ships immediately focus attention on the middle passage . . . on the circulation of ideas and activists as well as the movement of key cultural and political artefacts: tracts, books, gramophone records, and choirs.[24]

Clearly the specificities of the ship as an image for the "Black Atlantic" do not all translate to the suffrage movement, but the idea of this space as a micro-political and micro-cultural system as well as a way of focusing attention on the circulation of people, things, and ideas holds true. Peter Linebaugh and Paul Rediker also see the ship as a hotbed of political activity. To them the ship was both the "engine of capitalism in the wake of the bourgeois revolution in England *and* a setting for resistance."[25] It was a space of resistance because the practices of proto-working-class revolutionaries could re-form and circulate in the Atlantic world. "The ship became, if not the breeding ground of rebels, at least a meeting place where various traditions were jammed together in a forcing house of internationalism."[26] On board the ship, the Atlantic is reconfigured as a space of "interchange, circulation and transmission."[27] The following account concerns exactly such an interchange.

Foley and Luscomb boarded the steamship *Bohemian* on April 5, 1911 (see Figure 8.2). As the ship traveled east, Luscomb set about assessing the suffrage credentials of their fellow travelers, while Foley grappled with the problems of seasickness. One note from April 6 reads:

> This evening, while M reclined to settle her supper, I tramped around with a typical young English gentleman Mr. Burr, an engineer with a blond moustache, rosy cheeks and genuine guaranteed accent.[28]

By April 7, still deprived of Foley's companionship, Luscomb had spent a number of hours with Mr. Burr.

> The most entertaining acquaintance is Mr. Burr, particularly because of his novelty. He calls himself a moderate conservative,

**Figure 8.2** The SS *Bohemian.*

believes in limited suffrage for men and women alike. He is the funniest "engineer" you could imagine, spick and span, taking his afternoon tea like any gentleman in an English novel. He has traveled considerably thru America, to Africa, and but for his family he would settle down in America. (It's a great thing to meet all these English people who prefer America).[29]

Two days later the two women approached the captain concerning his views and discovered him to be an "ardent supporter" who lived next to the headquarters of the district leaders of the suffrage movement in Liverpool. Luscomb's new friend Mr. Burr succeeded in setting off a raging debate on board ship about suffrage. This was formalized and a proper debate was held on April 10.

It brought out an audience of at least 20. Shortly after three we gathered in the music saloon and soon elected Mr. Scott chairman. . . . Poor Burr then found himself suddenly and without warning thrust forward into the conspicuous position of the first speaker on the negative. That started the ball rolling. I had my say along the lines of changed conditions requiring a corresponding change in forms of govt., the woman in the home, & how it works. Jeff did her little stunt on the working woman. Then Dr Niles rose ponderously and rambled for some time, on the God given position of woman as man's helpmate,—the usual pedestal talk.[30]

And so the great debate on suffrage began hundreds of miles into the Atlantic from Boston. When it came to a vote, a Mr. Lillie (who had previously declared himself opposed to votes for women), declared he had been given food for thought and was not prepared to vote. This prompted a general decision to cancel the vote on the issue.

Then, and not till then did we realize that our meeting had lasted two hours, and that all of that English gathering had been so absorbed that they had completely forgotten their afternoon tea. That is the highest possible tribute to the success of the meeting![31]

The attempts at education did not end with the debate, however. They distributed literature and engaged individual passengers in continuous debate. Luscomb's journal (a wonderfully funny piece of literature throughout) is often biting in its descriptions of their hapless fellow travelers.

Dr Miles asked to borrow my "Hist. of Women's Rights." He returned it today, & left between the pages the most illuminating criticism. Illuminating, that is, of Dr Miles. Badly written, *misspelled*, incoherent, hypercritical.[32]

The SS *Bohemian* was clearly the "micro-political" space that Gilroy writes of. It was also, in a dignified kind of way, a place in the history of the "revolutionary Atlantic" of Linebaugh and Redicker. The travels of Luscomb and Foley on board the *Bohemian* created a space and time of debate and education featuring arguments over dinner and the lending of books. Luscomb, Foley, and the SS *Bohemian* played their small part in the Atlantic crossing of social politics in the progressive age through which so many ideas traveled to and fro between the United States and Europe.[33]

In these accounts of politics on the move we see the connected mobilities of people, ideas, and things. It is not just Foley and Luscomb who are traveling—Luscomb's book travels too. As Gilroy suggests, transatlantic travel included the mobilities of activists, ideas, and objects, such as Luscomb's copy of the *History of Women's Rights*.[34] All of these mobilities are made possible by the increasingly regularized world of time-tabled travel in the modern world, which was gradually opening up to women. Ideas such as those surrounding women's suffrage do not just diffuse of their own accord—they have specific histories and trajectories. The microgeography of the SS *Bohemian* provided the context for debate and swapping of books.

Transatlantic travel as a form of mobility was clearly a highly gendered activity in 1911. It had only been possible to cross the Atlantic in a scheduled, reliable way for about fifty years. All the ninety berths on the *Bohemian* were first class and the vast majority of passengers were men. In all the pages of Luscomb's journal, only one other woman is mentioned and she is accompanying her husband. There are no women traveling alone. Even Luscomb and Foley traveled together. All the principal figures in the suffrage debate, with the exception of Foley and Luscomb, are male. The mobile space of the ship is a masculine one oriented to business travel. Traveling aboard the *Bohemian* was not supposed to be a pleasure cruise— this was not a luxury liner like the *Queen Mary* or the *Titanic*, which followed in the interwar years—it was still simply a functional means of crossing the ocean.

## Travels in Europe

In addition to simply traveling to attend a conference or taking a transatlantic voyage, Luscomb and Foley were simultaneously involved in the mode of mobility we now know as tourism.[35] The history of tourism, as with the history of automobility, is a clearly gendered history. As Cynthia Enloe has forcefully put it: "Tourism is as much ideology as physical movement. It is a package of ideas about industrial, bureaucratic life. It is a set of presumptions about manhood, education and pleasure."[36] Tourism, she argues, is rooted in a political history of mobilities that includes business trips, exploration, and military duty. This political history is obviously one that men and women have experienced differently.[37] Clearly there was, until recently, a sense of impropriety connected with women traveling away from home for leisure purposes. The travels of Luscomb and Foley need to be understood in this context.

Luscomb's journal is also full of references to the paraphernalia and practices of tourism. The couple's travels allowed them to take in London, Paris, Brussels, the Hague, Amsterdam, Hamburg, and Copenhagen before attending the conference in Stockholm. All the trials of tourist mobility beset them. Frequent complaints concern the complexities of money, language, and food. Luscomb frequently describes their experiences in terms of traveling representations and stereotypes, such as the novels of Charles Dickens. On April 16, the day after their arrival in Liverpool, they:

stopped at a poor little shop on the way and asked for coffee and bread and butter. We were led to a little hole in the wall at the back of the shop . . . It was really Dickensesque.

After mass we took the belt line trolley car for a general view of the city. We saw many streets of brick houses, two storied, absolutely uniform, and connecting. There was little of the charm of the reputed English cottage.[38]

England, and the life of its inhabitants, are seen through mobile eyes and transplanted sensibilities. Some of their reflections read like entries in a *Rough Guide*. In Liverpool we get comments on clothing (awful), gardens (nice), and houses (too small). As with tourists everywhere, the militant couple clearly held certain expectations of authenticity in their heads while traveling around England and, later, Europe. The charming English cottage they expected to see in Liverpool never materialized, but their expectations were met the following day on the train. On April 17 on their way to London, we read that:

We passed thru pleasant rolling country with the grass all green and here and there bright yellow flowered gorse. The great numbers of sheep, the low hedges that fenced the fields, and the country cottages built of brick were the only un-American features.[39]

On April 18, following their arrival in London, the couple took the first of many bus tours in order to see standard tourist sights such as the Houses of Parliament, London Bridge, and St. Paul's Cathedral. Mr. Burr, fulfilling a promise made aboard the *Bohemian*, met up with them and gave them an auto tour of central London finishing at Frascati's restaurant, where they "ended up with real Turkish coffee, brewed on the spot by the genuine article in costume."[40] On April 30 following the advice of their *Baedeker Guide*, Luscomb and Foley took an excursion to Richmond and Kew Gardens. After stopping at several cafes, Luscomb wonders about the apparently prodigious tea consumption of the British: "It's a wonder they aren't all nervous wrecks with the perpetual tea, but they seem to be less nervous than us."[41]

The couple frequently refer to their *Baedeker Guide* when looking for place to visit, stay or eat. On April 23, for instance, they visited Hampstead Heath and used Baedeker's guide to find the Spaniard Inn (which they referred to as a "genuine English Country Inn"). The use of the *Baedeker Guide* was almost obligatory for well-to-do tourists in Europe at the turn of the century. The guides were the invention of Karl Baedeker (1801–1859), a German publisher who produced his first guide to his home city of Koblenz. Karl's son Fritz continued the business. They were the first guides to systematically provide standardized information for tourists. By the 1840s, they had become a standard technology for savvy, and wealthy, travelers. As with today's *Rough Guides* and *Lonely Planet*, the *Baedeker Guides* appeared in standardized formats designed to easily fit into a tourist's pocket. They were also regularly updated, often by Baedeker himself, who made secret journeys to check how reliable his guides were. Sights and hotels were assigned stars so that tourists could rank the places they would visit in the time they had available. As Dean MacCannell has noted, the *Baedeker Guide* exhibits a "a distinctive upper-crustiness" and "lists *only* the hotels and restaurants of "the highest class" and those of "almost equal rank."[42] Clearly, Florence and Margaret were not traveling rough. First-class cabins on the *Bohemian* and their *Baedeker Guide* in hand, they were classy tourists.

The *Baedeker Guides* were just one of the appendages that were crucial to the invention of the new tourist. The tourist was different from earlier forms of sightseer because of the whole system of sights, guidebooks, travel offices, timetables, and transport technologies that came about with modernity. Other nodes in this (relatively) new network of tourist space were the offices of Thomas Cook and American Express. On June 5 in Amsterdam the couple went to the American Express office to get advice about where to visit. On finding the office closed, they decided to try Cook's and had more luck. They met an American man there who claimed to be traveling to study "human nature" and recommended visiting the Dyke.

Thomas Cook is a central player in the establishment of a tourist industry organized internationally and efficiently to cater to a recently (in 1911) democratized tourist market. The development of mass tourism can almost be traced to 1841 when Cook began to organize cheap train travel to the seaside for working-class men.[43] Thomas Cook is also believed to have been instrumental in the marketing of tourism to women. His original forays into the field were, to some degree, the result of a letter written to him by four Lincolne sisters who wished to explore the continent in a way that would not do them dishonor.

> How could ladies, alone and unprotected, go 600 or 700 miles away from home? However, after many pros and cons, the idea gradually grew on us and we found ourselves consulting guides, hunting in guide-books, reading descriptions, making notes, and corresponding with Mr. Cook. . . . Tis true, we encountered some opposition—one friend declaring it was improper for ladies to go alone—the gentlemen thinking we were far too independent.[44]

Nineteenth-century woman was deemed to be morally suspect for indulging in mobility on the scale of international tourism.

Perhaps because of this "democratizing influence," Cook and the excursionists he encouraged were attacked as superficial, speeded-up observers, representative of a modernity that was destroying the authenticity of places across the globe and implicating them in a growing web of economic and social forces. The new tourists were derided (as they often are now) as sheep-like people carrying their red Baedeker guides in their pockets. Speed and the paraphernalia of tourist mobility were associated with superficiality.

Luscomb and Foley were clearly beneficiaries of the democratizing of travel. While traveling first class, *Baedeker Guide* in hand, they were nonetheless participating in a form of travel mostly unavailable to women only decades earlier, and still rare in 1911. The existence of Thomas Cook and American Express with their offices all over Europe enabled two women to travel independently. They provided a rationalized and reliable system of tourist organization including information, postal services, and traveler's checks, which the independent tourist could simply slot into. Meanwhile, the *Baedeker Guide* could provide standardized comparative information (measured in "stars") concerning hotels, restaurants, and sights. One recommendation in the *Baedeker Guide* took them to the Stockholm Grand Hotel:

> This is a beautiful hotel. It was only when I got into a first class hotel that I realized how really superior they are—electric lights, an elevator, velvet carpets, a telephone in my room, a large, airy room, with beautiful comfortable furniture, drawers that do not stick, a desk to write at, chairs that do not make one ache if one accidentally sits down, and a fresh little blue and white wallpaper.[45]

The Stockholm Grand Hotel had opened in 1874 and is still regarded as the epitome of luxurious travel today. Certainly Luscomb's description paints a picture of commodious modernity where elevators meet velvet curtains. Electric elevators were not installed in public buildings before the 1880s. Indeed, hotels themselves were not common until the nineteenth century. Despite the luxury of the Stockholm Grande, by July 2, the end of their trip to Stockholm, Luscomb is tired with travel. "Why," she asks, "do people travel? They leave happy homes, good food, and the folks they love for the exact opposites."

### Experiencing Urban Mobilities—The Casual Experiences of Everyday Life

Not all the travels of Luscomb and Foley were directed by the advice of Cook offices and *Baedeker Guides*. Another mode of mobility they practiced approached that of the flâneur—the mythical Parisian stroller of Baudelaire and Benjamin.[46] Sometimes this aimless wandering would occur on foot, but at other times they would hop a bus to nowhere in particular. On a cloudy May day in London, Foley and Luscomb were riding an open-top omnibus just for fun. Looking up through the clouds they saw a pale, watery disc of light. They thought it was the moon. On realizing it was the sun, and not having seen it for a while, they burst into happy song. After a while they noticed the faces of the puzzled onlookers, and in the words of Florence Luscomb:

> Thereafter we kept our eyes rigidly downcast and were hardly persuaded to raise them when we saw everyone staring at the sky. We were rewarded however, when we did pluck up courage, by the sight of a real live monoplane sailing swiftly over the city. It was the first wild aeroplane I ever saw,—all the others were of the captive, or exhibition variety,—and made one feel that they were really quite casual experiences of every day life.[47]

Traveling on buses through London or seeing airplanes overhead hardly seem noteworthy in the casual experience of the twenty-first century, but these were relatively novel experiences in 1911 and these words reflect a sense of wonder. A few months later the cartoon appeared in the *Boston Post* depicting Luscomb and Foley in a car chase that culminates in their quarry, Frothingham, taking to the air. Air travel had not become part of the casual experience Luscomb writes of, but it would not be long before it was.

Aircraft, though, were simply the most extraordinary of the various vehicles that surround and enable the women's travels in the city. On April 20 a journal entry reads:

> Then we took a bus for nowhere in particular to see what we might see. We went to Shoreditch, a dirty unattractive part of the town, thru the ever interesting crowded streets. All the buses and cars are double deckers, a grand invention, for one can see so splendidly, and get the air, from the upper story. Most of the buses are electric ones, and are very inexpensive. . . . All sorts of conveyances flourish here. Buses—horse and motor—subways, elevated, and trams, and today I saw horse cars. I thought New York was the only civilized place where they were left, but I see London is just as mediaeval.[48]

Luscomb frequently comments on forms of transportation. It is clear that the world of ships, planes, buses, and bicycles represents a new sense of movement to her. But perhaps the most obvious of the casual experiences of everyday life was walking. Walking was worthy of several long entries. Many entries are humdrum and banal, commenting on shops and observing differences in methods of locomotion:

> It is fun just to ramble around these shopping streets of the Hague. They are very narrow and twisting, but with low buildings, so the air is not shut out, and they are nicely cobbled & clean. There is very little horse traffic indeed, and the sidewalks are such tiny little things that everyone overflows into the street, and ambles along in a leisurely way in comfort and safety. A great many bicycles are in evidence.[49]

On one occasion while in London, walking suddenly opened up a whole new experience of the city. One Mr. McCormick offered to take this thrill-seeking couple for a walk on May 17. Luscomb describes him as a flaneur-like figure, poor but poetic, prowling the streets of London. McCormick, she writes:

> is a peculiar man,—a semi-invalid, a dreamer, literary, lonesome, rather poor, inclined to be gloomy . . . Yet he seems anxious to be nice to us. . . . He has prowled around the alleys and lanes of London, and sought out all sorts of out of the way literary shrines.[50]

He thought they might like to go, in his words, "off the beaten track."

> Under his guidance we penetrated spots which would otherwise have been utterly unknown to us. One goes thru a small archway and down a narrow alley, only to emerge in some unsuspected court where plane trees are growing, and even grass and flowers, and in one spot today even a pool and fountain with shrubs and ivy, and birds drinking the water. Then from some inconspicuous corner another lane leads, and turns, and divides, and goes thru gateways, and tunnels under houses, and you find yourself in another court, or propelled unexpectedly into the roaring street once more, which seemed but a moment ago leagues away. . . . It was most interesting to get this glimpse of London by paths. We saw the oldest houses in London, Staples Inn, where Dickens lived and wrote; still used today as lodgings and law offices, and the old carved and panelled hall, with stained glass windows and solemn gloom, once the grand dining hall of the Inn, now the laboring place of statisticians and computers where they delve in shadow and unreality.[51]

Walking in the city has become a favorite subject of discussion among social and cultural theorists of late.[52] The person walking through the city has become a figure inscribed with a multitude of freedoms and constraints.

The urban landscape provides a vast labyrinth of streets, sidewalks, parks, shortcuts, and alleyways, which we inhabit by walking, by getting lost, by idling away the hours. The delight that many of us feel as we stroll the spaces of Paris or New York or London has been translated into complicated fictional, poetic, filmic, and philosophical theories that tell a number of diverse and often opposing stories.

Walking has been described as a creative act that is never fully encompassed or determined by the static plans of power that the concrete spaces of the city represent. There is, perhaps, an essential freedom in walking, in traversing the city. This freedom lies in the ability of the walker to pick and choose the spaces he or she crosses, the ability to take short cuts and to refuse the directions offered by the text of the city. Walking expresses a limited and ambiguous freedom to take the geography that is given and make more personal ones in new and mobile ways. As Michel de Certeau has put it, walking creates "shadows and ambiguities" in even the most strictly ordered space.[53]

Mobility becomes human agency. While the bounded territories of planners impose structure and order on the world, the ability to move through, within, and between these spaces constitutes a kind of almost-free will on the part of the individual walker.

De Certeau's walker is a universal type—a virtual figure—and the pedestrian in the city has been made to play similarly universal roles elsewhere.[54] Such notions have been criticized for their masculinist orientation.[55] Women in the nineteenth century (and arguably even now), could not simply stroll around on their own without being noticed and gazed at by men. Despite this, there are many instances when women have ventured out into the city as pedestrians and enjoyed the freedom and exhilaration of walking the city streets. Mona Domosh has shown how women strolling the streets of New York enacted a kind of "polite politics."[56] If we return to Luscomb's account of strolling and alleyways of London we can see feelings of freedom that many claim have been denied to women. Clearly, walking the city does afford women some of the freedom associated with the male pedestrian.

Indeed, the strolling of Luscomb and Foley did occasionally become less politely political and more political in the formal sense of the word. Reading Luscomb's journal it is often easy to forget the political purpose of their peregrinations. It is possible that the highlight of their trip was participation in a suffrage march through the streets of London.

> We have sold papers on the streets of London! I was anxious to compare it with my previous experience, so spent an hour at it today. . . . My conclusions are that it is far easier work than in

Boston. That may be largely due to the fact that the ground is broken here, it is not pioneer work. Everyone knows what I am there for, they know what the paper is and what it stands for. For this reason, and because the sidewalk was not so crowded that I was not plainly visible to every passer by, there was no necessity for the exhausting shouting I found so indispensable in Boston. It is perfectly easy to stand quietly holding up a paper. I sold seven in about 3/4 of an hour, the low price (1d) making it also easier to sell them. It was great fun, one got just the same wonderfully different viewpoint of the crowd, so detached, so different from what one gets merely standing and watching them.[57]

Here Luscomb gives a clear sense of exhilaration at the ability to be part of the city crowd and yet so detached. Here she becomes a kind of politicized flâneuse.

## On the Road Again: Suffrage Auto Tours

And so we return to Luscomb and Foley's adventures on the roads of New England. In August 1911, Councilman "King Bill" Garland of Baltimore asked, "Are women too easily rattled to run automobiles?" as he tried to introduce a local ordinance to prohibit women from driving. Margaret Foley, fresh from her trip to Europe, met this suggestion with outrage. "The fact so many women in this state are operating automobiles," said Miss Foley, "and are never, as far as I know, haled before the court for reckless driving, seems to knock the story on the head. When I visited England I saw enough to show me that men are more excitable than women in every instance that would show the difference between the temperaments. . . . It is the drunken, joy-riding men that kill and maim."[58]

Automobiles became an important part of the lives of Foley and Luscomb in the years following their trip to Stockholm. They returned to Boston in August, but by October they were traveling again—from Boston out into the country by car. Once again there was a certain poetry. This time the words are Foley's, writing in the *Boston American*.

All about us it was brilliant with Autumn foliage, and the sunset sky stretching on beyond the treetops gave a splendid reflection of the vivid colouring. As the sunset faded, the full moon rose bright in the eastern sky, and all the evening we rode through a dazzling white country that seemed a part of a fairyland.[59]

After five hours of driving the car stopped for the night in North Wilbraham. The next day the journey continued to Stockbridge, sixty miles away. Poetics and politics began to merge.

> The night before it was all romance and shadows and mystery
> around us. This morning it was brisk and exhilarating, keying us
> up to do or dare anything for the sake of Votes for Women.[60]

The women passed through small manufacturing towns. Men, women, and children were leaving their homes to go to work or school. The women received curious glances. Occasionally people would line the streets and they would see looks of amazement as the women unfurled the big yellow flag of the suffrage movement. Now and then they would wave and cheer. As they entered Stockbridge the women hid the flag waiting for the right moment to unfurl it. Outside the Red Lion a crowd was gathered listening to Mr. Frothingham. He was running on the Republican ticket for the position of governor of Massachusetts. As his speech ended, Foley let loose the flag from the car and attempted to ask a question. Frothingham replied that he did not have time to answer questions as he had a strict schedule. He then got in his car as if to move away. At that point Foley began a suffrage speech to the gathered crowds. Frothingham waited and watched. There then commenced a series of meetings on the road, with the women following Frothingham around the state, heckling him and making speeches straight after him.

The race around the state became a source of much amusement in the Massachusetts media, which delighted in the sight of a car full of militant women chasing the respectable politician in his automobile. Some of the reactions are conveyed by the cartoon (Figure 8.1) at the beginning of this chapter. The car-chase image was reproduced in a newspaper report that recorded the initial confrontation of Miss Foley and Mr. Frothingham and continued:

> The race started from this point. With the Frothingham car in
> the lead and the suffragists following close behind both machines
> raced at breakneck speed to Great Barrington.[61]

Another paper reported how the suffragists were "badly bumped on the road for it was very uneven and it was necessary to maintain a high rate of speed to keep up with Frothingham." Indeed, such was the speed of the chase that the women reportedly had to take a few minutes to recover their equilibrium and fix their hats. There was a great fascination with how the automobile was being used to such great effect by Foley and crew.

While the purpose of the auto tours was clearly to raise public consciousness about suffrage issues, they also became empowering on a much more personal level. By 1915, Luscomb had been on many such tours. During a Massachusetts auto tour of 1915, the group's chauffeur,

Archie, began to give Luscomb driving lessons, and within the year she had accumulated enough miles to earn her license. Luscomb's letters to her mother during that year are full of details about her driving. As Luscomb's biographer Strom put it:

> Learning to drive was symbolic of the mastery she was feeling over her own destiny—this was a young woman who, both literally and figuratively, knew where she was going. A twenty mile trip at night over a muddy road became an opportunity to prove what she was made of and to make a point for "the class of women."[62]

Luscomb was particularly proud of her ability to deal with emergencies that were frequently part of the experience of driving rural roads in 1915. As one letter home recounts:

> Part way home it began to pour,—a drenching thunderstorm,— and then our headlights gave out on us. I had to get out in all the torrent and spend half an hour taking the switch all apart. But I got them fixed and have been prouder than a peacock over it ever since. Some little chauffeur!! [63]

Here Luscomb was becoming a new kind of subject—not a separate human subject but a car driver—a new way of entering the public sphere through mobility where the driver, Luscomb, reimagines her relationship to the car as the car simultaneously remakes her. The reconfiguration of moral geographies can be intensely personal. Here, in Luscomb's act of learning to drive, we see the coming together of physical corporeal mobility, the mobility of ideas, and the fusion of person and technology. Luscomb was one of the early feminists who imported ideas from Britain to Boston. One of those ideas was the increasing use of mobility. Here she enacts this idea as she becomes a car driver. Luscomb was transgressing the masculine logic of mobility, which saw women as enclosed and homely beings. One of the unintended consequences of new technologies of mobility, such as the motorcar, was the opening up of the possibility of increased mobility for women and others. As Sidonie Smith has argued: "The technology of motion that the traveler chooses to carry her away from home affects the repertoire of identities available to her. Sometimes it offers her new identities; sometimes it forces her to new identities."[64]

## Conclusion

How do these different experiences of mobility connect with the politics of suffrage and with each other? That is the central question this chapter sought to address. Here I outline three answers.

First, the use of mobility as a deliberate political strategy was, in part, a result of the trip to Europe taken by Luscomb and Foley. There is no doubt that their transatlantic travels emboldened them. The connection between the visit to England and the new tactics were frequently made. On October 13, 1911, the *Boston Post* reported on divisions among suffragists concerning Foley's new public and mobile tactics. Under the heading "Made in England" the paper reported on how Foley's methods were "distinctly foreign." This was just one place where a connection was made between the trip to Europe and the new mobile campaigning strategies. Recall Foley's own response to Councilman Garland's claim that women should not be drivers—she referred to her experience in England to refute him.

Second, the journey across the ocean and drives through autumnal New England are both examples of Boston suffragists breaking out of the conventional spaces of suffrage activism to produce, through mobility, new spaces of interchange and confrontation. The SS *Bohemian* became a floating debating chamber as long as Foley and Luscomb were aboard. The use of cars allowed the suffragists to connect with audiences they would otherwise never have confronted. Regarding the tactic of turning up at Republican rallies in their car and making unannounced guerrilla speeches to the gathered crowds, Foley remarked:

> If we had announced a Votes for Women meeting for that place and hour how many of that big crowd would have been there? Not one. . . . They might be willing to listen to a gentle little talk on the subject in some lady's home over the afternoon tea cups, but to go to a public outdoor place with everybody else? Out of the question.[65]

Third, the corporeal mobilities of Luscomb and Foley were intertwined in contingent but important ways with the travels of things and ideas. They were prosthetic subjects both enabled and constrained by gendered ideologies of mobility and the technologies available to them. The principal idea that is traveling in this chapter is the idea of women's suffrage. It is an idea that travels in the words and actions of the two women, but also in the book lent out by Luscomb and, indeed, by the journal she wrote and kept. It is an idea that was part of the unrecorded cargo of the *Bohemian* and an idea that cut through the autumnal air of Massachusetts several months later. The ideas and practices of suffrage, at least for Luscomb and Foley, were transformed through mobility—mobility that produced new kinds of prosthetic subjectivity.

Luscomb and Foley were certainly not the first suffrage campaigners to harness the power of new technologies of mobility. There had been auto tours several years before their trip, and suffragists such as Susan B. Anthony had also used trains to go on speaking tours several decades earlier.[66] Mobility was not the only factor in the transformation of Luscomb and Foley's lives on the one hand, and the suffrage movement on the other. The period 1911 to 1915 was one marked by the advent of the "new woman."[67] New women were typically white, middle-class, and single. They were often involved in long-term friendships with other women, which may or may not have been lesbian relationships. Indeed, such relationships became known as "Boston marriages."[68] They characteristically engaged in the formation of new kinds of institutions outside of the home (such as suffrage associations) and practiced relatively poorly paid professional work such as social work. In addition to the new woman phenomenon, the changing gendered geographies of the city allowed many women new freedoms. These included the advent of spaces such as the department store, the café, and the restaurant, which allowed women a restricted but real public life.[69]

Despite these caveats, mobility was a key factor in the politics of women's suffrage in New England between 1911 and 1915. Luscomb and Foley played their roles in the history that was unfolding, but so did the SS *Bohemian* and the car that took them in pursuit of Frothingham. Luscomb and Foley were prosthetic subjects in that their mobility was not that of singular humanist agents, but that of humans in a world of things that together produced new effects. In Strom's account of the changing tactics of the suffrage movement in Boston she calls for a shift in attention from a few gifted leaders to the wider rank and file of the movement.[70] Here I have argued for a consideration of more actors—not just the people involved, but the relations between people and things that enabled a reconfiguration of the moral geography of gender at the time. The SS *Bohemian* and the car driven by Luscomb were just as much part of this reconfiguration as Luscomb and Foley were.

## CHAPTER 9

# The Production of Mobilities at Schiphol Airport, Amsterdam

Description is more valuable than metaphor.

**—Text on Jenny Holzer installation at Schiphol Airport,**
**Amsterdam**

It has been a central aim of this book to connect discussions of mobility from the blood cells coursing around the body to the movement of people across international boundaries. We have encountered a number of thinkers who have tried to enact just such an overarching story of mobility—from Etienne-Jules Marey in his Paris laboratory, to Thomas Hobbes pondering the definition of liberty, to spatial scientists equating the flow of rain into gutters with commuters entering a highway. These thinkers, in one way or another, have produced bodies of knowledge that have looked for similarities between moving things—to extract, if you like, an essence of mobility.

In this book I have had a slightly different aim. While I insist connections need to be made among mobilities at different scales, a central plank of my argument is that difference is an important but paradoxical theme connecting mobilities. A fully social notion of mobility, I have argued, is one that acknowledges the production of mobilities as an activity that occurs in a context of social and cultural difference within a systematically asymmetrical field of power. Mobility as a social and cultural resource gets distributed unevenly and in interconnected ways. One theme that connects mobilities, in other words, is not essential similarity, but the role mobility plays in the differentiation of society.

In this chapter, I make these connections-through-difference more concrete by exploring the way they are played out in the space par-excellence of postmodern, postnational flow—the international airport. In the airport, I argue, we can see a place where the micromanagement of human bodies extolled by Taylor and the Gilbreths meets the control and ordering of traffic from cars to planes—where the passenger standing in a line, moving slowly if at all, becomes the enactment of a discourse on mobility rights constructed at the transnational level. Mobilities from the body to the globe pulse and circulate through and around the airport. But before considering the production of corporeal mobilities in and around Schiphol Airport in Amsterdam, consider the role the airport-as -metaphor has performed in the emergent nomadic metaphysics of the late twentieth and early twenty-first centuries.

## The Airport as Metaphor

The airport has become something of an iconic space for discussions of modernity and postmodernity, and its central role in literature on mobility makes it an ideal place to consider the ways in which geographies of human mobility have developed.[1] As Mike Crang has recently suggested, in order to understand a globalized world of transitory experience, we need to understand the points and nodes at which mobilities are produced: "Of all the spaces of a globalised world," he writes, "airports may be the most emblematic."[2]

What, exactly, airports are emblematic of is a matter for debate. In one reading they are seen as the opposite of authentic, rooted, bounded place—as placeless places or non-places. Take Marc Augés discussion of *non-place* for instance.

> The multiplication of what we may call empirical non-places is characteristic of the contemporary world. Spaces of circulation (freeways, airways), consumption (department stores, supermarkets), and communication (telephones, faxes, television, cable networks) are taking up more room all over the earth today. They are spaces where people coexist or cohabit without living together.[3]

Augé's discussion of the "anthropology of super-modernity" starts from the perspective of an air traveler and flits in and out of airports throughout.

It asks anthropologists to come to terms with the reality of a mobile world. Other writers are even more enamored with the airport world. Consider the enthusiasm of the architect Hans Iberlings:

> Airports are to the 1990s what museums were to the postmodern 1980s: the arena where numerous contemporary themes converge and all kinds of interesting developments take place. . . . Mobility, accessibility and infrastructure are seen as fundamental themes of the age, unlimited access to the world as the ideal of the moment.[4]

Iberlings describes the airport as "an attractive model for the kind of existence that is nowadays associated with globalization, a world where 'jet lag' is built into everybody's biological clock and time and place have become utterly relative."[5] This enthusiasm is shared by cultural theorists, such as Iain Chambers, who sees a place such as the airport lounge as a contemporary symbol of flow, dynamism, and mobility. Chambers delights in a postmodern world that finds its ultimate expression in the international airport. "With its shopping malls, restaurants, banks, post-offices, phones, bars, video games, television chairs and security guards," he writes, "it is a miniaturised city. As a simulated metropolis it is inhabited by a community of modern nomads: a collective metaphor of cosmopolitan existence where the pleasure of travel is not only to arrive, but also not to be in any particular place."[6] This vision of the airport is shared by the feminist theorist Rosi Braidotti who writes:

> But I do have special affection for the places of transit that go with travelling: stations and airport lounges, trams, shuttle buses, and check-in areas. In between zones where all ties are suspended and time stretched to a sort of continuous present. Oases of nonbelonging, spaces of detachment. No-(wo)man's land.[7]

Much of the fetishization of speed and mobility comes from male commentators, and has more than a touch of "boys and their toys" about it. In this respect, Braidotti's "special affection" is unusual. But clearly the airport has become the site par excellence of musing about the world of flow.

Typical of the contemporary gloss on the significance of airports is the claim made by architectural critic Deyan Sudjic that airports are the contemporary substitute for the public square—a place where strangers come together and cross paths. Architectural consultant M. Gordon Brown clearly believes this. "Travel is no longer the special and liberating activity it once was," he writes, "it is becoming normalized as a part of everyday urban life for many people. . . . Airports have developed into self-contained cities that boast more activity and a greater diversity of people than most American downtowns."[8]

Travel writer Pico Iyer seems to agree with this diagnosis. Los Angeles International Airport (affectionately known as LAX by the people who pass through) is, he argues, a self-sufficient community complete with chapel, gym, and museum, Airports to him are "the new epicenters and paradigms of our dawning post-national age . . . bus terminals in the global village . . . prototype, in some sense, for our polyglot, multicoloured, user-friendly future."[9] Mobility, of course, plays a key role in the construction of these new public spaces, where they are "merely stages on some great global Circle Line, shuttling variations on a common global theme. Mass travel has made L.A. contiguous to Seoul and adjacent to Sao Paulo, and has made all of them now feel a little like bedroom communities for Tokyo."[10] Typical of the assumptions made by Western writers and academics jetting around the world, Iyer notes that: "We eat and sleep and shower in airports, we pray and weep and kiss there." Who *we* consists of is left to the reader's imagination.

Perhaps we can see the airport terminal as a specific kind of site from which global mobility is theorized. Kevin Hetherington has suggested that the airport may be the (post)modern equivalent of the coffee house of the eighteenth century or the street of the nineteenth century.

> Perhaps now we see a shift of site of intellectual endeavour to the kinds of non-places that Augé has associated with our future sense of solitary existence (we all know that intellectual writing is largely a solitary exercise): the airport lounge, Bonaventure hotels, conference centres, motorways and of course the aircraft itself.[11]

These are the spaces from which people write the postmodern global experience. Clearly, business people and intellectuals spend a lot of time in airport terminals between meetings and conferences. They are avatars of what Pico Iyer has called the "Global Soul."[12] Perhaps these members of the kinetic elite are mistaking their experience—their particular geographical trajectories—for a general global condition.

If the new airport boosterism is to be believed, a space such as Heathrow, Schiphol, Changhi, or LAX is a kind of transnational utopian space of flows where nationality has been abolished and class erased—where people are generally contented. While it is possible to see how these conclusions might have been arrived at, they are also somewhat surprising. They are surprising because they erase other features of the airport experience highlighted by an approach that takes the politics of mobility seriously. Clearly, not all passengers in terminals are mobile in quite the same way. As Mike Crang has argued, the image of the airport as global, transnational space "may speak to a globe-trotting semiotician, but says little to the family with overtired children delayed by lack of connecting buses in Majorca."[13] Indeed, as Jenny Holzer's art installation at Schiphol Airport suggests, perhaps description is sometimes better than metaphor.

Consider, for instance, the various mobilities that produce and are produced by the airport spaces around the world. First, consider the passengers waiting to board their planes. The airport lounge is indeed the space of the privileged business traveler, in addition to those who have recently purchased discount tickets on the Internet for an EasyJet flight. There is no system on Earth that quite so explicitly makes the existence of a kinetic hierarchy so clear. On Virgin Atlantic, those who travel in the most luxury are traveling "upper class." On other airlines, such travelers are classified as "connoisseur" or "elite." If you travel "upper class," a limousine can pick you up at home. Your mobility will be seamless. On arrival at Heathrow the Virgin upper-class traveler can take the fast lane through immigration. In the airport there are lounges for this kinetic elite. Many of the people traveling through airports are familiar with them. Others have never flown before and still find the very idea of flying miraculous. So the airport is the space of the global kinetic elite as well as occasional flyers, budget airline flyers, and charter flight package tourists, such as the family en route to Majorca, that Crang reminds us of. Also making their way through the airport are immigrants, refugees, and asylum seekers. People who have been forced to smuggle drugs with condoms full of cocaine filling their stomachs. Then there is the workforce of pilots, flight attendants, mechanics, check-in workers, janitors. Major airports support a huge workforce whose members commute in daily patterns to and from the airport and its suburbs. The already differentiated traveler, the immigrant workers, and the airport workers are all mobile. Their mobilities are all enabled by the construction of the airport as a node in a network, but their mobilities are brimming over with different forms of significance. The general observation that the world is a more mobile place does not do justice to this richness. The suggestion that airports erase class and nationality seem, frankly, bizarre in an instrumental space where you are literally divided into classes and so frequently asked to show your passports as evidence of where you come from and where you are allowed to go. In the airport the corporeality of mobility—the way the body feels—intersects with categorizations of types—citizen, alien, tourist, business traveler, commuter.

Now think of the division of spaces in an airport—spaces that are themselves increasingly the product of assumptions about mobility built into modeling software.[14] Think of the lines at check-in—the long line of economy check-in and the non-line at upper-class check-in. Then there are the departure lounges and shops catering to different travelers. Arrival halls (in Europe) are divided into European and non-European immigration lines traveling at different speeds. Not long ago I arrived in Bologna and was rushed through immigration without so much as a glance at my passport. A plane from Albania had arrived at the same time and the line of people at immigration was more or less stationary. My traveling companions were American citizens and therefore had to stand in line with the Albanians until a policeman noticed their passports and moved them through the "European" line. Here was the politics of mobility and immobility—the geopolitics of mobility at a microscale. Once immigration has been negotiated, there is customs. Who gets stopped and why? What kinds of immobility are imposed on those subjected to body cavity searches? Many people every year are sent on the next plane home.

In short, very few places are more finely differentiated according to a kinetic hierarchy than an international airport. The airport also illustrates how the politics of mobility draws our attention to interrelating scales of mobility. While airports are most often mobilized as symbols of globalization and transnational identity, they also illustrate the politics of mobility at the scale of the body. Airports and air travel in general are replete with stories of comfort and illness, pampering and torture—bodies stopped and examined interminably. Some glide through the fast lane and have complimentary massages in the business lounge. Some bodies are found frozen in undercarriage wells. Once on the plane, upper-class passengers get more oxygen and more toilets. Economy-class passengers are left with a full bladder and a headache.

Clearly then, the airport as a symbol of global, postmodern nomadism needs to be unpacked. Seeing it as a space where motion, meaning, and power come together enacts such an unpacking. A politics of mobility directs our attention to the relations among different experiences of mobility and the relations between mobility and obduracy. It recognizes the importance of mobility in the modern world, but does not mistake it for a techno-utopian general condition. It insists on the importance of particular contexts for the production and consumption of mobility.

## It All Comes Together in Schiphol—From Roots to Routes

Writing about the airport runs the risk of generalizing the airport experience in a way I would not want to repeat. Clearly, the experience of Singapore's Changhi or London's Heathrow is vastly different from that of Salisbury, Maryland, or Liverpool's John Lennon. The kind of airport that seems to frequent the writings of contemporary theorists is clearly an international hub. A place the world passes through. The following, then, is an account of one particular airport, Schiphol Airport in Amsterdam. In 2004 it was Europe's fourth busiest airport, and one of the world's two or three most popular if web polls are accurate.

Networks, nodes, and mobilities are often presented to us in abstract form as spatialities outside of history. It is as if they have suddenly appeared out of thin air. This ahistorical approach is partly behind the assumption made by theorists of the present that the world is more homogeneous than it once was. These networks, it is argued, make place and time less and less important. Manuel Castells, for instance, writes that for the global elite "there is the construction of a (relatively) secluded space across the world along the connecting lines of the space of flows: international hotels whose decoration, from the design of the room to the color of the towels, is similar all over the world to create a sense of familiarity with the inner world, while inducing abstraction from the surrounding world; airports' VIP lounges, designed to maintain the distance *vis-à-vis* society in the highways of the space of flows."[15] This space of flows is contrasted with traditional notions of place replete with a sense of history and bounded-ness within which the majority of people are said to live. On the one hand there is a largely ahistorical and non-placebound space of flows, and on the other there is the rooted and historical space of place. But, as we shall see, the space of flows that is Schiphol has a very clear history—a history that permeates the networks that pass through it.

Schiphol's origins lie in its use as a military airport during World War I. It was built in an area known as Haarlemmermeer, an arable area (polder) situated near Amsterdam, Rotterdam, the Hague, and Harlaam. The site had to be reclaimed from a 30,000 acre lake and is 13 feet below sea level. To the northeast was a funnel-shaped section of coastline that became very dangerous when gales blew in from the southwest. This was called Schipshol, or the ship's hole, in reference to the number of ships that sunk there. The lake was drained and dykes were built around it in the years leading up to 1848, the year the work was completed. The first structure there was a military garrison. Growers of root vegetables taking advantage of the fertile soil soon farmed it.

The first commercial flight was on May 17, 1920, and the first scheduled service was between London and Amsterdam on July 5, 1920. This was quickly followed by scheduled service between Amsterdam and Hamburg and Copenhagen (September 1920), Amsterdam and Paris (May 1921), and Amsterdam and Berlin (April 1923). Not surprisingly, given the origins of the area, the airport was frequently a quagmire and passengers were carried from plane to terminal. Occasionally local farmers, whose land was being progressively eaten up by the airport complex, would throw various root crop products at the passengers as they were transported.

On October 1, 1924 crowds gathered to watch the first occasional flight from Schiphol to the Dutch East Indies.[16] By 1929 four airlines flew out of Schiphol.

In 1920, 400 passengers passed through Schiphol. By World War II, when Schiphol was destroyed, the figure was close to 100,000. In 1938 Schiphol became the national airport of the Netherlands; Douglas DC 3s and DC 2s used the airport. They had a range of 1,000 kilometers and regularly took passengers to North Africa, and twice a week to the Batavia (Djakarta) in the Dutch East Indies. The trip took five and one-half days, but was no longer an occasion for large crowds to gather.[17] Up until World War II the Amsterdam–Batavia route was the longest timetabled commercial air voyage available in the world, and for a long time it was the only route from Schiphol to anywhere outside of Europe. The first Batavia flight left Schiphol on October 1, 1924; it was a Fokker F.VII. The flight was scheduled to take twenty-two days, but due to a crash landing and mechanical problems did not arrive in Batavia until November 25. Nevertheless the successful delivery of Dutch mail to the far reaches of empire was a cause for considerable celebration in the Netherlands. On May 23, 1935 the first Douglas DC2 flight to Batavia left Schiphol and landed on May 31, reducing the flight time to a mere eight days. A few weeks later, KLM started flying to Batavia twice a week, and within a year the flight time had decreased still further to five and one-half days, stopping overnight at Athens, Baghdad, Jodhpur, Rangoon, and Singapore. A ticket included all hotels and travel insurance as well as meals. The logistical challenge for KLM was extraordinary. They had to provide spare parts at all twenty-two airfields used by the aircraft, as well as deal with visas and overflight permission in eighteen countries. There were no international agreements on airspace or sophisticated air traffic control staff to help them out. The mere existence of this mammoth flight, however, encouraged the development of directional radio transmissions, night lighting at airfields, and speedy refueling drills. It was these developments, as much as innovations in aircraft manufacture, that led to the effective annihilation of distance.

The success of the Schiphol–Batavia route was celebrated iconographically in an array of publicity material for Schiphol Airport, for KLM and for a number of other companies attached to the endeavor, such as Shell—who provided the fuel at all the refueling stations along the way (see Figures 9.1 to 9.3). The ever expanding network of routes that centered on Schiphol was also represented in Schiphol publicity material (see Figures 9.4 and 9.5). After World War II there was again debate over where the national airport would be sited due to the bombing of Schiphol, but it rose from the ashes and in 1945 was referred to as the World Airport of the Netherlands. A series of runways at tangents to one another were built there. In 1958 it became a public limited company with 76 percent of the shares owned by the government. It was not until 1979 that the government completely gave up on building a national airport elsewhere.

In the 1960s the airport continued to grow, and by 1964 had two runways and a standard terminal. In addition to the passengers, 1.5 million sightseers visited the airport to watch the planes—the Boeing 707s and Douglas DC8s equipped with sophisticated instrument landing systems, which could fly from New York or Chicago. For the first time Schiphol was being referred to in its own promotional literature as an "Aviation City" complete with banks, rental car facilities, showers, and duty-free shopping. It was just fifteen minutes from Amsterdam and employed 15,000 people. Schiphol was beginning to advertise itself as a gateway to Europe. Most passengers do not begin or end a journey in Amsterdam. It is much more likely to serve as a hub or connection point between flights. Indeed,

**Figure 9.1** Advertisement for Shell noting the use of its fuels on KLM's 14,500 km flight.

WEEKLY SERVICE AMSTERDAM-BATAVIA (JAVA)

CONNECTION
WITH LONDON

K·L·M
ROYAL DUTCH AIR LINES

WINTER AND SPRING
1933 – 1934
Nov. Dec. Jan. Febr. March April

Dutch Guilders

PREVIOUS EDITIONS CANCELLED

**Figure 9.2** The autumn timetable for the route in 1934. The image emphasizes the vast distances traveled by superimposing the route on an image of the eastern hemisphere.

the local population on its own could never sustain a large airport. Realizing this, Schiphol pioneered a simplified system for transit passengers that eliminated passport checks and encouraged shopping at the proliferating duty-free outlets.

It was also in the 1960s that the new airport terminal was constructed. The major impetus for this was the invention of the Boeing 747 Jumbo Jet, which carried over 400 passengers and needed new terminal docking points to accommodate its massive bulk. The new terminal (1967) had twenty-five gates on three piers. In addition to the new terminal, four new runways were built swallowing up more and more of the polder, where the farmers continued to farm root vegetables. It was only recently, as David Pascoe points out, that "the justification for the polder's existence—farming as a stabilizing force on the landscape—has, to some extent, faded, thus providing new opportunities to reclaim the ground for transport."[18]

By the early 1970s the arrival of jumbo jets led to a further extension of the arrivals hall and the extension of the piers that were used to provide births for the new leviathan. In 1971 the handling capacity of the airport

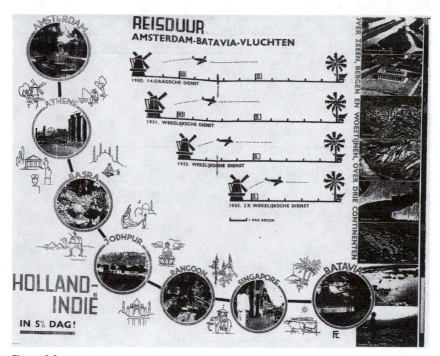

**Figure 9.3** A graphic depiction of time-space compression from a Schiphol Airport brochure of 1936.

was 8 million passengers a year. The new D pier was constructed specially for the new wider body jets. By 1974 the capacity had risen to 18 million passengers with 42 docking positions for aircraft, and a railway connection to the airport was developed for the first time. Over 350 businesses were located in and around the airport, and 24,000 people were employed there. By 1977, 9,114,974 passengers used Schiphol from all corners of the globe (See Table 9.1 and Table 9.2).

Schiphol had successfully made itself into a gateway to Europe—it had shifted from an airport to a *mainport*. By the 1990s it was Europe's fourth busiest airport servicing 18 million passengers on 350,000 flights; 508 companies were based at the airport employing 36,000 people.[19] It competes successfully with London, Frankfurt, and Paris for passenger traffic on the basis of transfer traffic (people who do not leave the airport as they change planes). It has been able to market itself as a hub because it only has one terminal building and the passengers only need 50 minutes between planes. Take away the transfer traffic and Schiphol would only rank tenth among Europe's airports. It has excellent transport connections to the rail network, which now has a station under the terminal. It is well known for

**Table 9.1** Schiphol Airport Statistics

|  | Passengers | Airlines | Connected Cities |
|---|---|---|---|
| 1929 | 14,000 | 4 | 18 |
| 1936 | 58,000 | 9 | - |
| 1964 | 2,141,000 | 26 | 115 |
| 1977 | 9,114,000 | 50 | 140 |
| 2003 | 40,000,000 | 102 | - |

**Table 9.2** Schiphol Airport Passenger Figures (1977)

| Origination Point | Number of Passengers |
|---|---|
| Europe | 6,823,459 |
| London | 1,023,570 |
| North America | 1,068,291 |
| Far East | 391,582 |
| Middle East | 333,673 |
| Africa | 264,716 |
| Mid and South America | 233,253 |

its retail outlets and duty-free shopping. As air traffic continues to grow, the terminal building evolves, growing new fingers to accommodate more planes. As the terminal expands its reach, so the air-traffic-control towers become higher and higher. Road networks and rail development occur to handle the traffic at Schiphol, and a kerosene pipeline from Rotterdam provides fuel for the planes.

Today's Schiphol is a truly remarkable kind of place. As well as being a very successful and extremely busy airport, it is also a retail space, place of entertainment, and office park. The Burger King at Schiphol is the world's busiest fast food outlet. Retail space in the airport can expect a turnover of ten times that of the most successful equivalent in downtown Amsterdam. The offices in the attached World Trade Centre can demand considerably higher rents than their downtown competitors. In addition to shops, restaurants, and offices, you can find a museum, a casino, hotels, a massage parlor, a conference center, and a place for children to play. There are areas where you can check out the Internet from your own laptop due to the provision of wireless Internet services (provided by the appropriately named Nomadix company). Below the airport is a rail station that can take you to Amsterdam in ten minutes or further afield.

Schiphol's place in the world can be read as a simple tale of expansion. It has certainly become one of the world's busiest and most successful

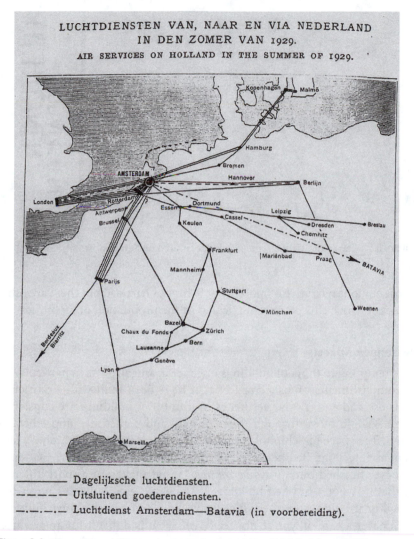

**Figure 9.4** Map of the airline route network centered on Schiphol from 1929.

airports. It is extremely popular with passengers and is often voted the world's best airport. One scale of mobility impacted (produced) by Schiphol then, is the global scale. It has been a place from which the process of time-space compression has been produced, just as time-space compression was producing this place. As early as 1936 the airport brochures were advertising this fact in very graphic form as they sought to advertise the possibility of travel to the Dutch East Indies in only five and one-half days. This is the

**Figure 9.5** Map of the airline route network centered on Schiphol from 1936.

most obvious narrative of mobility at Schiphol Airport, but there are other scales at which this place is implicated in the production of mobilities.

## Schengen Space(s)

It is tempting to think of buildings in general, and airports in particular, as accomplishments—finished spaces that have been built with a particular purpose and a particular aesthetics in mind. But buildings are constantly used. People move through them in new and sometimes unpredictable ways. The space of Schiphol is thus very much in process. Schiphol's current architect, Jan Benthem, described his vision of Schiphol as a place that is never finished but always *becoming*. "What makes an airport different is that it is not a finished building. It's always being built. It's never finished or it's always finished. It's always as it is. You are always building. It is never a case of 'you're not ready yet.'"[20] It is difficult for an architect like Benthem to plan the construction of the airport over the medium and long term, as "you will never know what it is going to be because it will always be something different." Benthem's experience of working with and on Schiphol underlines his conviction that airports are never finished. He started, twenty years previously, by designing a bicycle shed for one of the outbuildings; this was soon followed by a temporary bus station that was never used. By the time it was finished time had moved on.

> We started with small buildings and then got some bigger jobs. Our first involvement with the main terminal was building a temporary bus station. . . . The big architect was too involved with the extension

of the airport and they needed a bus station in five months time! It had to be there because of a certain growth in air traffic. We did that within cost and within time. . . . they never used it . . . they changed their minds so—they don't like to put people on buses they like to put people on planes and if things go well you don't need it. And in 1988 there was a large leap forward because, well, there was a sudden growth in air traffic and there was the problem of European unity and they had to solve in the medium and long time. In 1988 there was the decision that in 1993 there would be one control system and they had to change this airport—because basically it was an international airport—into an airport that has both [international and domestic] . . . and that was a very difficult situation and there was no scheme for the future and there was a need to build up the airport in four or five years. They wanted someone with a new vision for the airport as well.

Here the production of mobilities at Schiphol clashed; first, through the production of a never-to-be-used bus terminal, and second, through the rearrangement of space to make room for a new arrangement of mobilities at the continental scale.

Consider the scale of European mobility. Since its inception, the European Union (EU, formally the European Economic Community) has placed the right to mobility at the heart of its constitution. The development of the EU can be seen as the gradual reduction in barriers to the movement of people, goods, information, and capital.[21] Border controls were gradually abolished and replaced by more limited passport and document checks. This process was solidified in the Schengen Agreement, which was signed in 1985 and implemented in most states a decade later.[22] The purpose of the agreement was to stimulate free-market forces by reducing the time and effort needed to move. In this way, it was believed, Europe could compete with the United States and Japan. The Schengen Agreement was also underlined by an ideological commitment to a sense of European "community" that would transcend national allegiances and reduce the chance of conflict between member states.

But alongside this commitment to freedom of movement in "Schengen space," came an equal commitment of fortifying Europe's external borders against illegal immigrants, terrorists, and drug traffic. As Ginette Verstraete puts it, "new frontiers had to be implemented to be able to distinguish between Europeans and non-Europeans, and between (authorized) travel and (unauthorized) migration. The freedom of mobility for some (citizens, tourists, business people) could only be made possible through the organized exclusion of others forced to move around as illegal 'aliens', migrants, or refugees."[23] This differentiation of mobilities at a continental scale could only be operationalized through a multitude of local spatial reorganizations and practices of surveillance. The "external borders" of Schengen space in the age of hypermobility were not simply the land borders of the Schengen states but, clearly, the airports and seaports. Airports in particular are a strange kind of border marking a crossing point in vertical rather than horizontal space. Few would think of the borders of Europe as being in Manchester, Amsterdam, or Bologna, but there they are—a multitude of dispersed nodal borders. It is in these transport nodes that Schengen space was enacted and, indeed, materially produced.

The Schengen accords were represented as the abolition of borders, but they can also be seen as the multiplication of borders and the production of new kinds of borders. Just as the borders were being created, so were the mobilities. While it became easier for the Italian businesswoman to enter Germany or the Belgian tourist to backpack to Greece, it became significantly more difficult to enter from the outside.

The Schengen Agreement, an agreement about mobility and its control at the scale of Europe, produced Schengen space—the space of the states in Europe through which it was now possible to travel "freely." It also raised a series of issues that had to be dealt with at Schiphol Airport, as in other airports throughout Europe. Other kinds of Schengen space were produced at the local and micro scales. The agreement was made to allow freedom of movement between the Schengen states. For Schiphol this meant that there were now two distinct categories of flights and passengers—Schengen passengers and non-Schengen passengers. In the local context of Amsterdam's airport, this was a particularly significant moment in the production of mobilities. Pre-Schengen Schiphol was more or less an international airport with international passengers in transit. Unlike London's Heathrow or Paris's Charles de Gaulle, for instance, Schiphol never catered to a large number of domestic passengers—there are very few flights that operate within the Netherlands and Amsterdam is a relatively small source of outbound passengers. Schiphol had built its success on the basis of being a mainport or hub—an extremely successful node in a global network. Suddenly a large number of passengers effectively became "domestic" passengers, who would not have to pass through passport control on arrival. This was the problem that faced Jan Benthem as he became the lead architect at Schiphol:

> Well you have to change your structure because on the air side of your original airport you have the international and the European passengers mixed in one level . . . departure and arrivals mixed on one level . . . everybody is mixed there . . . and if you have to take one category of Schengen people out then you have to make

divisions somewhere or you have to make a second level and make every gate have the possibility of a switch and it was very difficult to solve the problem and of course it was very difficult if you don't know what your future is and you have to double the airport physically in five years time.

Part of the problem Benthem faced was due to the fact that Schiphol is different from other large airports in that it is based on the concept of a single terminal building. In practice this had given it the advantage of making the location of aircraft, in relation to the flows of passengers and baggage, relatively immaterial. It also had the advantage of being popular with passengers who could make quick connections between planes. The effect of the Schengen Agreement on the architectural space of Schiphol was to demand the separation of passenger streams for the first time. There was considerable debate about how to accomplish this. Although Schiphol has only one terminal building, it is split into three connected sections referred to as Terminals 1 to 3. The first plan was to designate Terminal 2 as a Schengen traffic space. This was resisted by the airport's home airline, KLM, which did not want its operations divided between terminals at great expense. In 1992 the airport directorate decided to divide space based on airlines rather than origins and destinations of passengers. Terminal 3 was allocated to airlines with few or no European routes, Terminal 2 to KLM, and all other airlines (operating in both Schengen space and non-Schengen space) to Terminal 1. Just as the terminal was divided in this way, so the piers became Schengen or non-Schengen; B and C piers became Schengen piers and E, F, and G piers were designated non-Schengen traffic spaces. The most difficult space was D pier, which marked the boundary between Schengen space and non-Schengen space. It also acts as a switch space between the two global spaces. Thus an aircraft arriving from the United States and flying on to Frankfurt would not have to switch piers between legs of the flight.

In order to accommodate both kinds of traffic, pier D had to be split both horizontally and vertically. Originally the pier corridor was divided horizontally by a vertical glass wall. In 1996 a second level was added to the pier thus dividing the space vertically (see Figure 9.6).

Finally the process of customs and immigration had to be divided in new ways. Where once there was simply a universal passport check procedure, there now had to be one set of lines for non-Schengen passengers and another set of lines for Schengen passengers, who would not have to have their passports checked. The production of space within the airport thus ensured the entanglement of bodies moving in lines with the structure of material space and European Union ideologies of free movement. In this

**Figure 9.6** Pier D at Schiphol. Note the horizontal division produced by the new top level in order to divide Schengen passengers from others. Photo courtesy of author.

way, the production of Schiphol Airport helped to ensure a space of flows for emerging European citizens.

These citizens, through the reiterative practice of mobility in airport space, were performing European identity. This has been made quite explicit in European Union documentation. The recent European Convention documents, for instance, confirmed the long-established idea that the right to mobility is perhaps the most significant fundamental right in Europe. European Commission documentation is quite clear about the significance of this right to mobility.

> The freedom to travel or to go about one's business throughout Europe as in one's own country is for the citizen the most potent symbol of the existence of the European Union.[24]

> Barriers to the free movement of people within the European Union have tumbled over the past 25 years. Queues of vehicles at borders between EU countries are a thing of the past. Citizens of the Union can now travel or go about their business throughout Europe almost as if it were one country.[25]

The promotion of mobility as a way of being a free European citizen extends well beyond formal rights. A pamphlet on European citizenship produced by the European Commission makes this clear:

> Everyone nowadays recognizes the sky-blue banner with 12 gold stars symbolizing European unification, which we see more and more often flying alongside national flags in front of public buildings .... What Community national does not enjoy following the "European Community" sign in airport arrival halls, and passing through simply by showing the uniform passport adopted in 1985?[26]

The pamphlet goes on to list the different technologies and practices of mobility that will ensure a feeling of European identity through constant reiterative use. These include common driving licenses, agreements for provision of health care, a frontier free mobile phone transmission zone, a lack of customs checks, the EU channel at airports and border crossings without passports. There is a clear sense here that it is the practice of mobility that will produce a feeling of freedom, citizenship, and European identity—that citizenship will be produced through the practice of freedom of/as mobility. Representations and ideologies of mobility pervade many aspects of European iconography. The Euro, for instance, features images of bridges and gateways—but not real bridges and gateways for fear of appearing to favor one country over others. Rather, they are made to represent a generic Europeanness.[27]

So as the creation of a space of mobility at a European level (and at an airport and pier level) was enacted, the final point of impact was the human body, which either had to wait in line or pass smoothly through. Suddenly a large number of passengers became "domestic" and could pass relatively smoothly through a non–passport check line while others had to wait in lines that moved slowly, if at all. The comfortable mobility of some, European, citizens is dependent on the establishment of new boundaries and frontiers between different kinds of space and different kinds of mobility.

## Managing Mobile Bodies

Clearly Schiphol, as a node in a network, is both produced by and productive of both global and continental forms of mobility. Indeed, they are the "customised spaces *par excellence* for organising and housing global flows."[28] But as anyone who has waited in line at immigration knows, it is at the scale of the body that the production of mobilities is brought home. In addition to being sites that enable global travel, airports are places where the motion of human bodies is finely managed. They are machines for mobility. There are few sites on earth where the individual motions of human bodies are so consistently monitored and micromanaged. Just as the ideology of mobility as a right of citizenship is reproduced in airport space, so the models of motion developed by Taylor, the Gilbreths, and others find their logical end-point in the management of mobile bodies in the airport. Consider the interconnected roles of information technology, signs, and architecture, and their impact on the body.

## Information Technology

Elaborate software programs are used to both design the architecture of airports and predict and manage the movement of passengers once they are built. Surveillance, simulation, and security are mingled into a hybrid space of code, people, and physical structures.[29] As Martin Dodge and Rob Kitchin put it, "Progress from buying a ticket, to moving through an airport, to travel on a plane is mediated through code/space—space produced through code."[30] In the airport, the construction of material space and the programming of software have become inseparable. The architecture itself is produced using software models: flows in and out of the airport space are modeled, and surveillance systems monitor the use of space in great detail. In addition, passports have become computer readable and tickets are more often than not e-tickets, for the most part unintelligible to the average passenger. As you move through the airport you are processed— you move through real space and code space simultaneously.[31] The use of modeling and surveillance is combined to both model future movement through the airport and monitor existing mobility. Trustworthy mobilities need to be differentiated from untrustworthy ones. Passenger profiling, for instance, uses complicated and increasingly biometric indicators to choose who should be searched when boarding the aircraft. Airport authorities, in the wake of 9/11, are increasingly looking for travelers who should be prevented from traveling. The new American system called CAPPS II (Computer Assisted Passenger Prescreening System) performs exactly this function. A system such as this "relies on stories about activities that are proper and ones that are improper, about activities that belong in particular places and activities that do not. Each in the end relies on a simple and unstable story, of the treacherous—or trusted—traveller."[32]

Modeling mobility has been central to the planning and engineering of airport environments. This has grown ever more sophisticated as computing power has increased. Peter Adey has shown how the use of modeling systems in airport environments has developed from simple generalized models of flow to complicated three-dimensional envisionings of passenger mobility. In the process, specific human bodies have been made to disappear and reappear at will.[33] To most people in airport management, passengers become mere PAX. PAX are passengers—generic passengers with no identifying marks. Once you have invented PAX, you can then produce models of PAX movements in airport space. PAX are a symptom of a synoptic perspective on space that enacts a transformation of mobile bodies into a legible record that can be analyzed by the panoptic gaze of the architect, planner, and engineer. The ways in which mobile bodies are made to disappear bring to mind the work of Muybridge, Marey, Taylor, and the Gilbreths. Indeed, there is a clear logic that links early efforts to make mobility legible with the models used by airport planners today. Again, movement is abstracted and standardized through the removal of the clumsy fleshiness of real bodies. Bodies are thus transformed "into a phantom in order to establish a space of reason."[34] The meaningful mobility of people is abstracted into the movement of PAX.

Airport managers used a model known as Critical Path Analysis (CPA) to model the movements of PAX in airport space. Passengers were given cards that could be punched at various points in the airport in order to log the time taken to travel between points. These times would then be used to record the longest time in which a sequence of events would occur. The term *critical path* referred to the longest path in a particular network—the longest time it took for particular events to occur. Architects and planners could then reengineer the space to shorten the critical path—to make things happen *faster* and more efficiently.[35] Contemporary airport modeling programs construct sophisticated 3-dimensional animated images of PAX wandering around beautiful and functional terminals as well as moving smoothly between exits, entrances, and check-in. Meanwhile the airplanes land and take off like clockwork in order to transport the animated PAX to their final destination.

While PAX enact abstract, disembodied movement within flow models, other forms of hardware and software rely on the very specificity of particular kinds of bodies in order to police mobility at various points within the airport. The airport enacts a series of thresholds for mobility allowing some (most) people to move on while effectively immobilizing others. Passports have to be shown and identities revealed. Codes have to match identities. Suspicious movements are watched and monitored. During a tour of Schiphol given to me by its chief architect, Jan Bentham, we were stopped on emerging from the baggage handling area. We both had passes (Bentham had arranged one for me), but were nevertheless recognized as unauthorized mobile bodies among the machines and luggage. Jan explained our interview and identified himself as the architect. We were allowed to proceed, but only after being told that even the building's architect did not have permission to take visitors into the baggage handling underworld. So much for architects as gods. There is nowhere in Schiphol where mobilities are not being monitored.

Schiphol is more advanced than most airports in that it has introduced a biometric monitoring scheme for frequent passengers willing to submit to it and pay an appropriate fee (about $100).[36] Starting in 2001 the scheme, called Privium, allows approved travelers to move at speed through immigration by simply submitting to an iris scan. Members not only travel through the airport more quickly, they are also allotted guaranteed parking at the closest car park and are provided with dedicated check-in services at certain airline check-in desks. The technique of iris scanning is explained on the Privium website:

> The technology used in the iris scan is based on the recognition of specific characteristics of the iris. The iris scan is more reliable and faster than other forms of biometric identification, such as fingerprint or hand palm recognition. This is because the iris never changes and irises are rarely damaged or injured. Just a tiny injury to the finger or to the palm of the hand can hamper biometric recognition.[37]

There are limits to membership in the scheme. You have to be a member of the European Economic Area (EU plus Iceland, Switzerland, and Norway) and over 1.5 meters tall. Images of people using the scheme on the web and in pamphlets available at the airport are all of smartly dressed white people—mostly men. Signing up for this form of voluntary surveillance is seen as a privilege that allows highly mobile (the literature states it is useful for people who enter Schiphol over eight times a year) business travelers to effectively bypass immigration. These members of the kinetic elite are granted what amounts to a fast lane from home to meeting and back again. The absence of people in the Privium line is very noticeable as you stand in line at passport control.

Biometric schemes for monitoring identities as they pass through mobility thresholds work on the basis of linking a particular unique body (more precisely—a metonymic part of it, such as the iris or a fingerprint) to an identity. So while closed circuit television monitors mobility everywhere through the logic of the gaze, biometrics works to track movement by logging identities at particular points or thresholds. What is at stake, at these thresholds, is the ability of particular bodies to move in speed and comfort. As one observer has put it, "[b]iometrics is concerned with keeping people in or out: of buildings; of websites; of countries. It is a method of controlling the chaos of movement, of protecting capital from contagion—the harmful touch of an unauthorized ingress—and streamlining the flow for those with the right password."[38] As acceptable passengers are allowed to enact their mobility unmolested, so human security officials are freed up to monitor life in the slow lane of non-Privium members. The speed of some is logically related to the slowness of others.

Biometric schemes like Privium are implicated in the construction of various forms of citizenship as particular types of passengers are separated from others. As the scheme's members are more than likely to be European business travelers, they fall neatly into established notions of what constitutes a citizen in Europe—bodies that are easily understood within liberal framings of mobility in a free-trade zone. The excluded are those who, to a greater or lesser degree, do not match such a framing—"[t]he improved mobility of these Privium cardholders is therefore paired with the promise that illegal aliens and potential terrorist threats will be deterred."[39] As Martha Rosler has argued, "information manipulation—which includes the construction and dissemination of social narratives as well as covert surveillance and other forms of data gathering and management—has come into focus as the most visible and consistent form of social control. This impulse to control is part and parcel of the air transport system."[40] Representation, ideology, and practice cohere around a scheme such as Privium and the mobilities it manages. As Rosler suggests, behind the seemingly neutral technology lie social narratives—ideologies—of mobility. These ideologies course through the mundane practices of passenger mobilities as they are practiced on a day-to-day basis in Schiphol. They connect the patterns of the Iris to notions of transnational citizenship.

## Signs

The sophisticated computational world of code space is not the only "code" in the airport. There is also the more familiar code of conventional directional signage. While these signs, which Schiphol is justly famous for, work because they are visible, their mundane obviousness makes them paradoxically just as invisible as the computational code space. Simple directional markers are rarely the subject of admiration. Most of us do not even notice them. When you arrive at Schiphol you enter a world full of signs letting you know how to get where you want to go. Similarly, once you are past the security check and have entered the departure lounge, you are surrounded by signs informing you of how to get to your gate and what you might want to buy along the way.

The vast majority of the signs you see in Schiphol were designed by Paul Mijksenaar. In 1963 Mijksenaar was an art student at the Gerrit Rietveld Academy in Amsterdam when he noticed the newly standardized British road signs designed by Jock Kinnear. He was impressed by their simplicity and their beauty. Previously he had thought of signs as the products of government officials rather than designers. Now, Mijksenaar is something of a global transport sign design guru. He has designed the signs for both Schiphol and the new Amsterdam Metro System. The success of the Schiphol sign system has led to him being commissioned to produce a standardized system for all of New York's airports. Heathrow has also copied Mijksenaar's system.

The spatial location of signs is calculated in relation to the patterns of flow in the airport. As the architect, Jan Benthem, told me: "[a] simple rule is that when you have commercial signs you put them parallel to the flows. And if you have a sign for directions you put it at right angle to the flows . . . . We try to put commercial messages on a lower level . . . when it is getting busier, commercial messages blend in with people and with all the excitement. The higher line is for the real signing messages."

The signs are colorful. The original interior designer employed at Schiphol was Kho Liang Ie, who believed that the interior spaces of airports should be largely neutral. In a busy and anxiety-provoking place, there would be more than enough color and excitement without adding to it. It is against this neutral backdrop that the colorful signs stand out. As Mijksenarr suggested to me. "Airport is a kaleidoscopic space already, so the architecture should be neutral and the signs should stand out from the architecture."[41]

All the signs are back-lit and carefully color coded. The most prominent are the yellow signs with black writing and symbols that Mijksenaar refers to as "primary process" signs (Figure 9.7). These are the signs that tell you where to go—they are signs for flow. Then there are the black signs with yellow writing that Mijksenaar refers to as the "secondary process"

**Figure 9.7** Directional (black on yellow) sign at Schiphol. Photo courtesy of author.

or "waiting/staying" signs. These mark the locations of things such as the museum, toilets, and chapel (Figure 9.8). Green signs refer to emergency exits and other important emergency functions (Figure 9.8). Finally, there are completely different blue signs that point to commercial enterprises (Figure 9.9). These are made to look like city street signs with many signs on a single pole. These remind passengers of the well-known tourist signs that tell you how many miles it is to Chicago or Tokyo. To Mijksenaar, the

**Figure 9.8** Sign for facilities (yellow on black). Photo courtesy of author.

**Figure 9.9** Sign for shops (blue). Photo courtesy of author.

yellow signs are the most important and therefore the most prominent. "[I]n the yellow sign the yellow background in itself is the main thing—it gives the signal "I'm a sign." These signs unconsciously direct the traveler and process him or her through the airport. The contrast of yellow and black has the highest measurable contrast (86 percent) against black and white, which is the next best (82 percent). Benthem told me that passengers are not supposed to notice this coding. It is supposed to work at an unconscious level—to become embodied. This confirms a point made by Gillian Fuller. "These signs don't merely represent the airport," she writes, "they create it. In other words, the textualised cartographies and myriad jurisdictions of the airport are to be obeyed, not believed."[42]

Signs are a central part of what the anthropologist Marc Augé calls non-place.[43] Non-places, often spaces of transit, refer to other places without taking you there. Schiphol Airport, read through its signs, is consumed by the need to keep moving. The combinations of letters, arrows, and (helpfully) times are part of the code that produces a space of incredibly intricate flows. They are built into the architecture of mobility. The sheer number of signs reaffirms the idea that the airport is a processing machine for mobile bodies. Ideally, Mijksenaar told me, there would be a one-to-one relationship between a sign and a location or thing it referred to. In the world of the airport, however, this is not possible.

> The ideal situation will be that you choose your destination and the signs will direct you to your destination—it's one to one. But of course that never happens. There are thousands of users and there are thousands of destinations—so it is impossible—so how can you approach this? It is a stop by stop—first you have to go there and then you have to . . . it is like a menu of information.

The signs at Schiphol are located at crucial decision points. You do not enter the front of the airport and see a sign directing you to your gate. You are given a choice between departure and arrivals. Then you are directed to your check-in desk, then to security, and so on. They form a set of nested categories at crucial decision points within the building. The passenger simply has to give in to the process and act accordingly. It is for this reason that there are few large maps on Schiphol signs—they tend to be hidden away or featured on handy little pocket pamphlets that are available widely in the airport. To Mijksenaar, maps are not useful technologies for way-finding in airports.

Cresswell:     You don't like maps do you?

Mijksenaar:    Maps are only for getting an idea of your topographical environment or how big it is . . . you shouldn't use it as a wayfinding instrument. It's more of an opening—a window.

Cresswell:    So in the kind of places we are talking about like airports and hospitals—places where I never know where I am—

Mijksenaar:    It is hard to make any sense of where you are—the place where you are is a non-place—you are somewhere in the lounge—what does it say? You only want to know where you are in the process. Am I before or after immigration? Is baggage claim after or before? What is between me and the gates?

Cresswell:    Don't you think that sometimes people in an airport might like to feel a sense of security about—more like a normal place? In a sense Schiphol is like a public square. And so it's more like a city space than most airports.

Mijksenaar:    In a city it is more stretched, there are more squares and there are neighborhoods. That's a difference. The difference is they call an airport city an airport city—that is how it is marketed—its more that it has one of everything—a square, a main street, a hospital—a real city has neighborhoods with different squares, different streets . . . Then it is important what this neighborhood is like compared to the other neighborhood . . . airports are more about process.

In Schiphol they hold meetings and use the hotel. They are not interested in where the hotel is—they want to know the direction and how far it is.

Developing signs that do the work they are supposed to in an international airport involves producing a universal language in a polyglot world. As it is impossible to write out directions in every language on earth, the signs have to work across differences. Like computer software, they have to become universal and ubiquitous. In addition to linguistic differences, there are all the other differences in modes of mobility that must be accounted for. Blind people, slow people, anxious people, and mobility-impaired people all have to find their way. The signs have to speak to all of them. Despite the ingenuity of the pictograms on Schiphol's signs, they remain firmly European in their origins, "restaurant pictograms display plates, knives and forks (not bowls and chopsticks, or hands), our universal female generally wears an a-line knee-length skirt (who herself is a sign for a toilet), and arrival and departure signs are designed to follow the vectoral logic of left to right literacy systems, such as English."[44]

Mijksenaar's Schiphol signs are all in English and are often combined with innovative pictograms depicting the function referred to by the sign—aircraft leaving and arriving, baggage, and so forth. The decision was made in 2001 that it was only necessary to use one language, as having Dutch on the signs simply made them more confusing. This says something about the expected PAX. As Mijksennar puts it, "the lingua franca of the international traveller is not Esperanto, but English—the language used at airports and railway stations worldwide."[45] All the signs were changed to English only.

There is no doubt that the sign system used at Schiphol is extremely efficient. In addition to directing PAX smoothly through the system, it produces a modernist uniform aesthetic against the neutral backdrop of the interior design. In addition, Mijksenaar's scheme has received the attention of numerous designers and been exported abroad. Heathrow was one of the first airports to import the color coding system, and Mijksenaar is now in the process of developing a similar standardized system for all the airports in New York. When he first examined the signage in and around JFK airport, Mijksenaar was perplexed by the idiosyncrasy of what he found. There were no signs to Manhattan—only to the Van Wyck Expressway—a meaningless piece of information for anyone who was not local. Even more confusing was the sign that read "W/B BQE Closed," which apparently meant that the Westbound Brooklyn Expressway was closed. Inside the seventeen terminals of New York's airports there are hundreds of directional signs, each with different styles. Individual airlines have frequently dominated the appearance of signs in the terminals they are associated with. The signs are often made up of white letters on dark backgrounds. Soon they will all look something like Schiphol. "Level A" will become "Ground Floor" and "Courtesy Vans" will become "Hotel Shuttles."[46] JFK is beginning to look a lot more like Schiphol. Thus an international aesthetic of air mobility is radiating out from Amsterdam.

*Architecture*

In Schiphol Plaza, mobility is subtly coded into the fabric of the architecture. As you enter the public square that forms the front entrance to the airport, there are surprisingly few obvious signs directing you one way or another. This was a deliberate decision by the architects. As Jan Bentham put it: "[i]n this area we tried to use all kinds of models for flow and we experimented with all kinds of signage and in the end we removed all signing from this area as we had to get used to the idea that this is a square and on a square you don't need signage—you need signage on street or on roads but on a square it is impossible to sign—it's much better to give names to the buildings around the square and to the different elements and find your own way because the traffic here has all kinds of directions." So while it is possible to see the entrances to different parts of the terminal (the buildings around the square) and the entrances descending into the rail station below, there are not arrows sending you one way or another. The space appears devoid of directional markings. Rather than signs, the architects built visual clues into the very structure of the plaza.

The floor of the plaza is made of a neutral colored grid that immediately indicates two directions for movement at ninety degrees to each other. One of these directions leads from the entrances and exits into the airport, and the other leads the passengers past the entrances to the rail terminal.

The columns supporting the roof also form passages and the roofing material is made of a striated material that runs diagonal to the flooring. Between them they indicate the "three main directions in the building in the construction because this is parallel with one terminal—this is parallel with the other terminal, and this is on a right angle with the railway track." To Bentham, the plaza is completely different from the terminal itself. While the terminal is marked by an overabundance of signs, the plaza is a space with flows coded directly into it. "An airport is an interior—it may be a building, but the passengers don't experience it as a building—they experience it as one large interior and that is a different problem because you have to find some kind of order in the interior to make it readable properly, and that is one of the reasons why we changed the atmosphere in this part of the building [the plaza]—almost completely opposite to the terminals upstairs. The common airline building—especially the departure check-in area—this is not so much the airport—the building of the airlines."

It has repeatedly been pointed out that airports are machines for mobility—spaces of process and becoming rather than location and identity. At Schiphol it is quite clearly the case that architecture, information technology, and signs form a seamless machine with each operating in coordination with the other.

## Inhabiting Space Otherwise

"Space is the ongoing possibility of a different inhabitation."

Elizabeth Grosz[47]

So Schiphol is both a node in the production of global mobilities and a place that frames and orders new hierarchies of mobility through the internal organization of its spaces of flow. It is designed to enable and constrain particular kinds of mobile practice by particular kinds of people. But there are other kinds of mobility we need to consider to properly describe Schiphol. Here I turn to the homeless and the taxi drivers.

## Homeless People

In his essay on Martha Rosler's images of airports, Anthony Vidler notes how airports are places where "all travellers are for a moment subject to the powerlessness of the unemployed, and a once excited thrill of spatial exploration has been regularized into a controlled mechanism of calculated flows and uneasy, unwanted delays."[48] The space of the airport, he argues, is an abstract, regulated space in which mobilities are closely and carefully channeled. In this sense the airport, with its security apparatus, "ensures that the airport, like the shopping mall, the theme park, and the new gambling palaces of multimedia combines, will remain free of the disturbing presence of the truly homeless, leaving them open to the vicarious and temporary homelessness of the privileged nomadism."[49] One of the most surprising things about Schiphol, therefore, is the number of homeless people that inhabit it. Within minutes of sitting down in the terminal, I was approached by a homeless man carrying a huge bag overflowing with bits and pieces. He asked me for a cigarette. "There's nowhere to buy cigarettes around here," he gestured, ignoring the many places that do, in fact, sell cigarettes. I did not have any to give. I could not recall seeing a homeless person in an airport before and his presence surprised me. Over the next few days I became accustomed to seeing some familiar faces. A black man with a green towel wrapped around his head rummaging through the bins. Four people sitting near one of the entrances. Several people talking to themselves and moving strangely—out of sync with the general sense of ordered movement that surrounded me. On the face of it, the airport was not designed for these people. I raised this with the architect, Jan Benthem. Benthem, it turns out, is quite proud of what he sees as the "public space" ambience of Schiphol Plaza. "We very much tried to give it the atmosphere of a public area," he insisted, "and this is how the front entrance to an airport should be—the public square of this city." When I mentioned the homeless people to him he smiled, adding, "yes, this is the city—it is a public square. The nice thing is that the airport authorities—they have already changed their business statement. Their business statement is not managing an airport—it is creating airport cities. They have changed not only an airport to an airport city, but they changed their own profession also from only managing an airport to creating this kind of urban quality and opportunities around the airport." Part of this urban quality, for Benthem, is the toleration of homelessness.

Nevertheless, the homeless experience of Schiphol as a place would be entirely different from the members of the kinetic elite the airport was designed to serve. So what do homeless people make of the airport?

As I sat in the Burger King seating area watching and writing, I began to see homeless people everywhere. One black, balding man sat in a public seating area marked "no smoking" and proceeded to light up nonchalantly. No one paid any attention. He seemed to be watching people as closely as I was. Occasionally he would stroll up and down and, at opportune moments, lift the top off the cylindrical bins and rummage through their contents. Once he found a magazine and sat reading it for over an hour as the world passed him by. A large white man with grey hair, dressed in an enormous bright orange coat, was sitting near me drinking cola and smoking cigarettes. He occasionally gestured to people and laughed loudly. He took a television remote control out of his green plastic bag and acted as though he was changing channels. Passengers waiting for planes looked past and through him. I offered him another drink and a burger and he talked to me as best he could in English. He said he frequently came to the airport as it was warm and easy to get to. He liked to watch the planes from the viewing platform. He gave me the name Nick. He looked about fifty years old. He had no socks and occasionally made sudden gestures with his head or hands that made little sense. At one point he suddenly started running his finger along the table as though drawing a map for me. The Burger King seating area was, it turns out, one of the favorite places for homeless people in the airport. People in a hurry leave drinks, fries, and burgers that can be picked up by a watchful homeless person before the Burger King employee who is paid to clean the tables and, presumably, police the activities of the homeless. Nick saw people leave at the other side of the seating area and ran over to rummage through the wrappers. He found a burger and more Pepsi and wolfed it down between sudden articulations in Dutch to no one in particular. Perhaps the caffeine was influencing him unduly, but his motions and speech were becoming more and more dramatic. The Burger King employee, a very young black man, approached him gingerly and began to clear up the litter around him quite deliberately. He went away and came back to sweep around Nick's feet. Nick was the only person who got this treatment—he occasionally waved his arms at the employee. His head movements became more and more dramatic, and he certainly seemed to be speaking to someone who no one else could see. Eventually a more senior employee arrived and told him to leave.

It strikes me that the airport has a fairly relaxed attitude to the obviously homeless people who inhabit it, but Nick's bodily movements exceeded some sort of pact between the authorities and the homeless allowing them to stay. It was Nick's sudden head movements and waving arms that crossed the line and brought the sanction of the Burger Kind hierarchy. These movements caused unease and anxiety.

Over another burger I spoke to James, a talkative and eloquent homeless black man who spoke excellent English. He had moved to Amsterdam from the former Dutch colony of Curaçao ten years earlier to live with some family members and attempt a new life. That was the first time he had seen Schiphol. Now James spends almost every day of the year in the airport. He had been separated from his wife and (grown-up) children and become homeless. He gets sleep during the day in an area of Terminal 2 near the viewing panorama platform. Between midnight and 4:00 A.M., when the building is closed to all those without tickets, he gets the train into Amsterdam and hangs out in the Red Light District "watching people having fun." It is easy to catch the train because no one ever checks tickets in the short time between the airport and the city. He told me the airport is a good place for him. Security guards don't bother him. He has friends to keep him company. There is plenty of food, warmth, shelter, and reading material left by people in a hurry. He said he felt free with no one telling him what to do or playing loud music. But, he admitted, his dreams are like those of anyone, a nice house and car and lots of money. He dreams of returning to Curaçao but dislikes hot weather. He asked me questions, too. He enquired about my children and asked what life in Britain is like. He was curious about why I should be so interested in airports and homeless people. It is obvious why the homeless like airports, he told me. They are warm, dry, and interesting. They are easy to sleep in. He came across as a man of the world.

The homeless feature in Michael Serres' haunting book *Angels*.

> Airports are built on the outskirts of cities, in the suburbs, what we call the *banlieue*: a place of banishment. Excluded and pushed out to the margins, the down and outs end up here. It's almost a law of nature. When they arrive, they're amazed to discover they can actually sleep here, in the dry, on benches, like ordinary travelers . . . their movement is like the movement of passengers arriving and departing—it never ceases. They stay for a while and then they move on, like everyone else.[50]

There are other reasons why a homeless person may be relatively comfortable in an airport terminal, other than the obvious benefits of shelter and warmth. No one looks twice at people carrying lots of bags around in airports, and it is not unusual to see people sleeping. It is possible to see airport space as a kind of liminal space where unusual activities (at least ones that do not threaten security) are allowed to occur—even expected. As Kim Hopper, an astute writer on homelessness, has observed, "airports occupy a singular place in the American night: Nowhere else may one observe, as accepted practice, ordinary citizens—some in quite casual attire, many with bags, and most looking a little worse for the wear—bedding down for the night in full public view. A reasonably clean and decently dressed homeless person has no trouble fitting in with the impromptu sleepers scattered about."[51] In addition, as Hopper notes, "legitimate" travelers, like the homeless, frequently need to go through their bags to reorganize their possessions, momentarily making their private belongings a public spectacle.

Accounts of the presence of homeless people at Schiphol are sketchy. Leon Deben has been researching homelessness in Amsterdam for many years. Every two years since 1995 he has conducted censuses of the homeless. There have, he notes, been stories circulating about a large number of homeless people sleeping in Schiphol Airport. In 1999, Schiphol was included in the census despite the fact that it lies outside the city. They counted fifteen to twenty homeless people—a number that led them to believe that homelessness was "not that bad" at the airport.[52] By 2001, however, a homeless man was able to point out forty or so homeless people who regularly slept in the terminal to Deben and his colleagues. News stories indicated numbers of between one and two hundred. Deben concurs with Hopper that airports are a logical place for homeless people to seek shelter and food. Even after 2001, when a homeless man was blamed for a small fire in one of the toilets in the arrival hall and the toilets were subsequently closed after midnight to anyone without a ticket, numbers of homeless people in the airport continued to rise. "Schiphol is an attractive place to stay for some of them," Deben writes, "as it is not only warm and dry; there are also lots of things to find there. Many travellers throw away their telephone cards, train tickets or even their weed . . . thus providing smart homeless people with something on the side. With a train ticket they can, for instance, legally make a round trip to Utrecht, Rotterdam, and the Hague (with coffee breaks) after midnight then resume their sleep to returning to Schiphol around 4 A.M."[53] A student of Deben's, Frank Groot, spent months undertaking participant observation at Schiphol. He made contact with twenty-eight homeless people who used the airport regularly. About half of these were there almost permanently. Twenty-three were male and five female.[54] He noted the use of innovative strategies to make do in the airport. One person would go to sleep with a large label attached to him reading "Please wake me up at 10:00 P.M.—I have a plane to catch."

*Taxi Drivers*

Homeless people are not the only unorthodox users of Schiphol Airport. As I sat in the terminal, I became aware of a repeated announcement made every fifteen minutes. "Disregard taxis offering unofficial services—use the official taxi rank," the recorded voice said. Intrigued by the possibility of unofficial taxi drivers, I decided to take some rides and ask the drivers about this. It did not take long to discover more.

My first ride was with a white, fifty-something driver who was more than happy to explain the situation to me. He explained to me that his taxi is a special "Schiphol Taxi," which means that his company pays about €400 a month for a licence that allows them to pick up people at Schiphol. I suggest that he probably doesn't have to wait long to pick up travelers at the airport:

Driver 1:     Sometimes you have to wait too long.

Cresswell :   Yes?

Driver 1:     Because there are too many taxis.

Cresswell:    Oh, right.

Driver 1:     We are an official Schiphol taxi but our government would like to see more competition in the trade.

Cresswell:    Right. So are there unofficial taxis?

Driver 1:     Uh yes—they call them "cockroach."

Cresswell:    Cockroach?

Driver 1:     Cockroach—they are not 100 percent qualified like Schiphol taxis.

Cresswell:    But are they legal?

Driver 1;     They are legal—yes, in a way you know.

Cresswell:    Right.

Driver 1: But we are paying an awful lot of contribution for the airport . . . and those people who are called the cockroach—they are paying just by passenger—and it is all organized by a transponder in the car.

Driver 1: Another problem that is very common is that we do have— we call them snorders.

Cresswell: Snorders?

Driver 1: And they are completely illegal—because they are going at the arrivals and trying to take some passengers in their cab or in their private cars I should say. You must have an expression in English for these kind of people. And they are completely illegal.

Cresswell: Pirates, maybe? That's interesting—at the airport there is an announcement that tells you to disregard people asking you for taxi rides.

Driver 1: And they are mainly from foreign nationalities—nationality of abroad—like Moroccans.

On another occasion—again with a white male taxi driver (I never met a female driver) I mentioned that I noticed an article in a local paper about a taxi war and asked him what that meant.

Driver 2: There is a taxi war coming up, yes.

Cresswell: What does that mean?

Driver 2: This is about—Snorders—too many taxis at Schiphol—more or less legal, illegal—so there must be a quality certificate— because it is very dishonest—we have to pay so much contribution to the airport we should be protected.

Cresswell: So how much do you pay Schiphol then?

Driver 2: I think it is about €400 a month.

Cresswell: Wow—that is a lot.

Driver 2:    To get license at Schiphol—and you have to have not less than Mercedes 200E.

Cresswell:    Yes, and that's the other thing that is amazing—the cars are so good—you don't get this in London.

Driver 2:    You cannot drive along in a fifteen-year-old Toyota or whatso-ever—it is crazy.

Cresswell:    No.

Driver 2:    Even when he has arrived and gets his certificate from the gov-ernment, you cannot do it—it is as simple as that—not very honest against the customer at all because the car is not clean and 100 percent safe car.

Cresswell:    Yes—that's true.

Driver 2:    But if you are taking a taxi in Amsterdam—8 of 10 times you will find there is people from abroad driving the taxi. And Amsterdam used to have 2,500 taxis driving around now there are 4,000—so you can imagine that.

Clearly there is a great deal of tension between these official Mercedes-driving, white, Schiphol taxi drivers and the incomers in their old Toyotas. The word *snorder* does not translate into English, but is a slang term used only among taxi drivers to refer to illegal (mostly migrant) drivers who have operated without a license. Eventually I managed to locate some immigrant taxi drivers who may or may not have been the so-called cockroaches or snorders. While not driving Mercedes cars, these drivers nevertheless offered a perfectly good service in reasonably clean and new cars. One such driver came to Amsterdam from Turkey eleven years earlier. He had driven taxis in Istanbul and moved to Amsterdam in order to marry his girlfriend—also a Turkish immigrant. He had help from within the Turkish community to find his job and set him up with a taxi. He could tell me about members of his family in the United Kingdom, the United States, and Spain who also drive taxis. Another Turkish driver I spoke to spoke Dutch, English, Turkish, and a little French. He had been in Amsterdam five years and planned to move to London in order to work in his uncle's restaurant. Clearly these drivers were part of fairly elabo-rate and extensive transnational family networks of taxi drivers and others. There also appeared to be a significant degree of mobility around this network as people moved from job to job and place to place.

So what do these accounts of homeless people and taxi drivers tell us about airports? The most important thing I think they point to is the way different networks and experiences of mobility intersect in this particular place. The metaphorical construction of airports as placeless places or non-places constitutes them as spaces of pure motion—uninhabited and inauthentic. Similarly, the celebration of airports as avatars of a brave new classless and postnational world feature a largely uncritical celebration of global nomadism, as if everyone were moving in more or less the same ways. Even when a difference is noted between those who move and those who do not move, it appears to miss the sheer variability of mobility experiences. Manuel Castells, in *The Network Society*, makes the following observation.

> In short elites are cosmopolitan, people are local. The space of power and wealth is projected throughout the world while people's life and experience is rooted in places, in their culture, in their history. Thus, the more a social organization is based upon ahistorical flows, superseding the logic of any specific place, the more the logic of global power escapes the socio-political control of historically specific local/national societies.[55]

This observation clearly indicates the link between the mobility of some and immobility of others. Its suggestion that only the elite are cosmopolitan, however, hides the considerable cosmopolitanism of the kinetic underclass. Everywhere that the kinetic elite travel, they are serviced by a mobile workforce who do not share in the luxury of the business travelers Castells writes of. They drive their taxis, clean their rooms, and look after their children. They, too, are mobile. They, too, are cosmopolitan. The general celebration of the nomadic in contemporary theory too often levels out agency so that these differences in the experience of mobility disappear. Not only are there snorders at the airport, driving Toyotas rather than Mercedes, there are also the truly homeless moving side by side with the kinetic elite. Zygmunt Bauman has metaphorically described the mobilities of globalization through the two mobile figures who mark the end points of a scale of mobilities—the vagabond and the tourist. He argues that the globalized society we inhabit is just as stratified as any other. The dimension along which we are plotted is our "degree of mobility."[56] It is not just the degree of mobility, however, it is the nature of the experience of mobility. Often those "high up" in a kinetic hierarchy "travel through life by their heart's desire and pick and choose their destinations according to the joys they offer. Those 'low down' happen time and again to be thrown out from the site they would rather stay in."[57] So while both the metaphorical vagrant and the metaphorical tourist are mobile, they are in different experiential worlds. The globally mobile kinetic elite inhabit a world in which space is less and less of a constraint, while the kinetic underclass are often thrown into a mobile world they did not choose or are tied to spaces which, in Bauman's terms, "close in on them." Space for them is not disappearing but has to be transcended painfully.

> For the inhabitants of the first world—the increasingly cosmopolitan, extraterritorial world of global businessmen, global culture managers or global academics, state borders are levelled down, as they are dismantled for the world's commodities, capital and finances. For the inhabitant of the second world, the walls built of immigration controls, of residence laws and of "clean streets" and "zero tolerance" policies, grow taller; the moats separating them from the sites of their desire and of dreamed of redemption grow deeper. . . . The first travel at will, get much fun from their travel . . . are cajoled or bribed to travel and welcomed with smiles and open arms when they do. The second travel surreptitiously, often illegally, sometimes paying more for the crowded steerage of a stinking unseaworthy boat than others pay for business-class gilded luxuries—and are frowned upon, and, if unlucky, arrested and promptly deported, when they arrive.[58]

The kinetic elite are voluntarily mobile. They take pleasure in their mobility and experience mobility as freedom, while the kinetic underclass—the vagabonds—are confined or forced to move out of necessity and experience mobility as survival. Bauman's point, however, is not just that these experiences of global mobility are different, but that they are tied up in the same logic. Globalization, he argues, is tied to the dreams and desires of the kinetic elite who inhabit the luxurious space of flows, and who need the kinetic underclass to service it. There are no *tourists* without *vagabonds*.

## Conclusions

In conclusion, there are five points to make about Schiphol. First, like Heathrow or Paris it is clearly an important node in a global network of air travel that has connected first world places to distant ex-colonies and effectively made them closer. Second, it is a local place that enacts the continental construction of a space of free mobility in most of Europe, while keeping a close eye on those who come from outside. Just as ancient Chinese cities were designed as scale models of the wider cosmos, so Schiphol has been designed as a map of continental and European distinctions between acceptable and unacceptable mobilities. Third, Schiphol has ghosts in its mobility machine. The homeless man from the Dutch Antilles once arrived in Schiphol on a flight and now lives there. The Turkish taxi driver also arrived at Schiphol in order to marry his sweetheart and become a taxi driver shuttling the kinetic elite to and from the airport.

Fourth, these nested mobilities take place in Schiphol. Schiphol is clearly a place of movement, but it is not a place that easily becomes a metaphor. It does not do justice to the many-layered complexity of the place to call it a non-place or a new transnational utopia. Paying attention to the politics of mobility begins to undo the equation that links a generalized celebration of mobility to sites such as the airport. Schiphol is a complicated kind of space on which an intricate "place-ballet" of multiple movements takes place on a daily basis. It is not simply a part of the life-world of the kinetic elite, but a place of shelter and livelihood. The people who service the kinetic elite are every bit as cosmopolitan as the jet-lagged business-class passengers who need their rooms tidied, their taxis driven, and their food cooked.

Finally, the fact that this is Schiphol and not Paris, London, or Chicago matters. Airports as metaphors appear as spaces of equivalence—places that could be anywhere—non-places. But clearly, Schiphol, like any other kind of place, is situated and has its own history and own sets of connections. Its geographical location makes a difference to the experience of the mobilities that are produced there. This can be seen in the connections between Schiphol and Batavia, in the mapping of Schengen space onto the airport, and in the fact that a homeless man from Curaçao inhabits it on a daily basis. Schiphol may be a node in a global space of flows, but it is still uniquely Schiphol—still a place.

All of these point to the incredibly complicated nature of mobility in the modern West. At various points in this book we have considered moving bodies, social narratives about mobility, arguments about meaning, domination, resistance, conformity, and transgression. All of these are jumbled up in a place like Schiphol where the movement of bodies is tied to notion of rights to mobility, social narratives of the acceptable and unacceptable, and increasingly sophisticated technologies of mobility.

In addition to all this, the experience of Schiphol makes it quite clear that people continue to be remarkably creative in mobile ways. The homeless people and semi-legal taxi drivers of Schiphol reveal the complex ways in which people can exercise power against the grain of the acceptable and expected. Workers, no doubt, continued to work in ways that deviated from the expectations of those studying their time and motion. Dancers continued to dance wildly in London despite the best efforts of Victor Silvester and others. Bus riders in Los Angeles continue to ask awkward questions about ideologies of mobility (public and otherwise) in urban America. Suffragists took to the road in automobiles, whether or not male observers were shocked by their actions. The story of mobility in modernity is one in which creativity continues to play an important role. Virtual, ideal, mobilities are still being produced and real, fleshy people continue to refuse to comply.

# Epilogue

## Hurricane

On August 29, 2005 a category four hurricane, Katrina, hit the Gulf Coast of Louisiana with 150-mile-per-hour winds and a huge tidal surge that broke the levees of New Orleans and flooded 80 percent of the city. Over one thousand people were killed and hundreds of thousands left homeless. New Orleans residents who could not find shelter and food with relatives and friends were evacuated to locations across the American south. The flooding had been foreseen and an evacuation of the city ordered. Along with the detritus of human life that came to the surface in the days of early September were issues of race, poverty, and mobility. Since Katrina struck, media viewers like myself have been inundated with images of predominantly poor black people stuck in an urban landscape that has had the majority of white people removed from it.

## The Mobility Poor

It is estimated that 85 percent of the population of New Orleans had left before the hurricane struck. This, it seems, included the vast majority of white residents. The evacuation order depended on people being able to move of their own free will, for the most part by car. Just as people were leaving en masse, bus and train services were being canceled. A popular image circulating in the media featured around one hundred school buses parked in orderly lines and up to their roofs in water. Radio reports on the BBC have featured interviews with (predominantly black) residents who stayed in the area during the hurricane. Again and again they are asked why they did not leave, and the residents have repeatedly informed the incredulous reporters that they could not afford to leave, did not have a car, and had nowhere to go. Automobility is, after all, central to American life and culture. To be American is to have a car. Public transport has consistently lost out in terms of subsidies and tax dollars to the automobile industry and its supporters.[1] As has been shown repeatedly throughout this book, the production of some kinds of mobility often effectively immobilizes others.

Before the hurricane, the issue of a low-mobility population had come up during disaster emergency plans as reported in the *New York Times*:

> Brian Wolshon, an engineering professor at Louisiana State University who served as a consultant on the state's evacuation plan, said little attention was paid to moving out New Orleans's "low-mobility" population—the elderly, the infirm and the poor without cars or other means of fleeing the city, about 100,000 people. . . . At disaster planning meetings, he said, "the answer was often silence."[2]

The vast majority of people immobilized in New Orleans were black. The politics of race and the politics of mobility, as so often before in American history, were joined at the hip. As a columnist for the progressive magazine, *Mother Jones*, put it:

> What many of those people shared that night was this: they didn't own a vehicle. They had no car, no truck, no SUV to point north or west, away from the storm and the flood waters. They had no "extra set of keys" to tuck into their "Disaster Supply Kit," as recommended by the New Orleans Emergency Preparedness Guide. They had no gas tank to keep half-full at all times, a key evacuation preparation step suggested by the Department of Homeland Security.[3]

There have been attempts to deracialize the crisis by dislocating issues of mobility from issues of race. Consider a news piece written for the *Hawaii Reporter* by Randal O'Toole of the American Dream Coalition—a right-wing/libertarian organization that opposes the development of light rail initiatives and supports automobility. In response to Hurricane Katrina, O'Toole writes:

> What made New Orleans more vulnerable to catastrophe than most U.S. cities is its low rate of auto ownership. According to the 2000 Census, nearly a third of New Orleans households do not own an automobile. This compares to less than 10 percent nationwide. There are significant differences by race: 35 percent of black households but only 15 percent of white households do not own

an auto. But in the end, it was auto ownership, not race, that made the difference between safety and disaster."[4]

According to the U.S. Census Bureau, over 77,000 households in New Orleans had no form of private transportation, leaving around 200,000 people without an immediate way out of the city when Katrina struck. The New Orleans city government knew this was the case. A year earlier the mayor, Ray Nagin, had explained that he could not order an evacuation of the city when threatened by a hurricane because he had no way to evacuate people who did not have access to cars. This is despite the sentence in the New Orleans Emergency Preparedness Guide that reads: "Local transportation will be mobilized to assist persons who lack transportation."[5] Evacuation plans, in New Orleans and elsewhere, simply assume that American citizens are car owners—that their mobility is automobility. The *Mother Jones* article reports Havidan Rodriguez, the director of the Disaster Research Center at the University of Delaware, as stating that car ownership data is simply not taken into account when considering evacuation plans. And yet it is precisely those people without cars who need to be at the center of emergency evacuation planning. To Rodriguez the most poignant image of the disaster in New Orleans was a widely circulated photograph of a hundred school buses with only their rooftops showing above the water. While the image was used to illustrate the depth of the flood waters, it represented a missed opportunity to Rodriguez. They could, after all, have been used for an evacuation. Evacuation plans included an assumed model of mobility based on privatized automobility, when instead they should have worked on a model of mobility as a public need.

The argument that those who suffered most from the effects of Hurricane Katrina were those without cars is often contrasted to the argument that there is a racial politics to the disaster. Mobility, in this formulation, is emptied of social content. Separating mobility from race (and class and age, in particular) is simply nonsensical. While speaking to members of the Bus Riders Union in Los Angeles (see chapter 6) it was frequently observed how transport planners sought to dissociate transit from race. The Bus Riders Union response was that they could not be so easily dissociated. In the United States the politics of race and the politics of mobility (particularly public transit provision) have moved side by side through the civil rights movement. Think of Jim Crow. Think of Rosa Parks. The population of New Orleans that was left behind were indeed the transit dependent, but they were overwhelmingly black. In the New Orleans metropolitan area, only 5 percent of non-Hispanic white people did not have access to an automobile. For the black population, the figure was 27 percent.[6] The elderly and the very young were similarly transit dependent. Some of the worst scenes from

New Orleans were of elderly hospital patients abandoned as the waters rose. Many died. To say that the human disaster that followed Hurricane Katrina was not about race or age or class, but instead about car ownership is to divert attention to how mobility is social through and through.

## Tourists/Refugees/Evacuees

The issue of the "mobility poor" was not the only way in which the politics of mobility came to the surface in the early days of September. They also arose in the accounts of some British tourists who had joined New Orleans residents in the Superdome as the floodwaters rose. The Superdome had been designated as a safe space for those many people who could not simply leave the city. Much of the media coverage following the hurricane focused on the dome as a Dante-like dystopia of death, rape, and filth. Numerous accounts tell of the U.S. military taking tourists out under cover of night to make sure they were safe and able to return home. Clearly the designation "tourist" merits special treatment. Every other person in the Superdome surely needed the same kind of help and also needed to be safe. Tourists, however, were separated out and taken over the road to what had previously been a luxury hotel before being flown to their home countries.

New Orleans is an important tourist destination. Its famous French Quarter provides an atmospheric backdrop to jazz and blues music and free-flowing alcohol. The tourist industry brought $4.9 billion to the city in 2004 and was the city's second largest employer.[7] In many ways, the city was dependent on mobility for its prosperity. It is perhaps unsurprising, therefore, that the biggest single investment in the urban public transport infrastructure in the years leading up to August 2005 was $160 million on a tourist-oriented streetcar line and a planned $120 million on another line. In May 2004, U.S. Secretary for Transportation Norman Mineta visited New Orleans to congratulate them on the opening of the Canal Street streetcar line; he applauded the public-private finance initiative that had brought the streetcar into being. The conversion of a bus line into a streetcar, he said, "will improve the environment, encourage economic development, and expand tourism."[8] He continued by stating that "Besides the advantages of moving people and attracting tourists, the streetcars behind me are important to building the economy of New Orleans, which will be dependent upon this city's ability to move people and goods, safely and efficiently. . . . The work that you do, every day, keeps New Orleans moving." Mineta could hardly have been more mistaken. While the streetcars certainly provide an attraction for tourists, and are convenient for those who live along it, they were woefully inadequate when it came to moving people safely when safety was at a premium. It was tourists and their mobility that benefited most from the new streetcar lines. As Mineta joyfully recounted: "the rebounding economy means that Americans are traveling again for both work and pleasure at record numbers, and New Orleans is one of the destinations to which they're headed." As Zygmunt Bauman has reminded us, the figure of the tourist can "travel at will, get much fun from their travel . . . are cajoled or bribed to travel and welcomed with smiles and open arms when they do."[9] Indeed, streetcars are made for them and, when disaster strikes, they can be rescued and flown home while the metaphorical vagabonds, many of whom work in the tourist industry, remain where they are, unable to escape.

Tourists were not the only mobile figures to become an issue following Katrina. In the days and weeks following Hurricane Katrina, stories began to emerge about the categorization of people who were displaced by the hurricane and the floods that followed it. These displaced people were increasingly upset about being referred to as refugees. Black New Orleans citizens displaced by the storm were featured on BBC news stating that they were not refugees. Soon it became a political issue, as Rev. Jesse Jackson claimed: "It is racist to call American citizens refugees."[10] The word *refugee*, it seems, was quickly associated with notions of race (the majority were black) and foreignness. Refugees were effectively second-class citizens—not quite American. Soon President Bush had joined the debate declaring: "The people we are talking about are not refugees.... They are Americans and they need the help and love and compassion of our fellow citizens."[11] Over the next few days, various media outlets in the United States stopped talking about refugees and started to refer to displaced people or evacuees. The *Washington Post* and the *Boston Globe* both banned the use of the word refugee, while the Associated Press and *New York Times* continued to use it when it seemed appropriate. The Associated Press executive editor stated, "Several hundred thousand people have been uprooted from their homes and communities and forced to seek refuge in more than 30 different states across America. Until such time as they are able to take up new lives in their new communities or return to their former homes, they will be refugees."[12] William Safire, the *New York Times* columnist, insisted that a refugee is simply someone looking for refuge and can be from any race or nation. Mike Pesca, a reporter for National Public Radio, went further in defense of the term refugee, focusing on a claim by the black activist, Al Sharpton, that the use of the term strips people of their dignity. "They are not refugees wandering somewhere looking for charity," he said. "They are victims of neglect and a situation they should have never been in in the first place."[13] While Sharpton made the claim that these people were not refugees because their plight was the product of politics, Pesca writes that perhaps the term refugee is appropriate for exactly that reason.

> They're refugees because circumstance is turning them into refugees. I was at one of the evacuation points the other day. Thousands of people were standing in mud. . . . If you watched this situation on television, you might not realize how dirty and foul-smelling these people were. There was a reluctance on the part of the rescuers to touch the people. There was a total unwillingness to walk among them.

Later in the article, Pesca makes the point that the contrast between armed men in fatigues on one side of a barricade and bedraggled survivors on the other brought to mind scenes from "Haiti or Kosovo, . . . The people who heeded warnings and had the wherewithal to leave town before Katrina hit were evacuees. These beleaguered people who had lost everything were something else."

The use of a term such as refugee highlights the entanglement of mobility with meaning and power. A whole host of mobile characters have inhabited the pages of social and cultural theorists of late. Nomads, travelers, tourists, vagabonds, and exiles have all been used to illustrate contemporary concerns with a world in motion. While each tells us something about mobility, each also tells us something about the social baggage that accompanies those on the move. The word refugee is no exception. There is no inherent reason why the use of this particular term should be deemed racist by Jackson, Sharpton, and others. What their criticism highlights, however, is how the history of the term has loaded it with connotations of subversive and threatening mobility. The word *crisis* often accompanies the word refugee, as do the words foreign and immigrant. A term first used to describe wealthy Protestants who had been forced to leave France has become a term of abuse. In Britain and the United States, refugees have been seen as people seeking to take advantage of the state's generosity. They are people who do not belong to a host nation and are therefore not entitled to the rights of citizenship. They are people without place who need to be regulated. While it is strictly true that a refugee must be "outside the country of his nationality" (according to the Geneva Convention), this ignores the wider use of the term to apply to anyone who has been displaced and is seeking refuge. Indeed, it is often the case that those who need the most help are those who cannot move. An event such as a hurricane, as we have seen, effectively immobilizes the most vulnerable.[14] Nevertheless the term refugee has become wrapped up in notions of being out of place, of being foreign and suspect. The term is, as Jackson and Sharpton indicate, heavily racialized because of a long history of negative representations of refugees as other, as being from somewhere else, as threateningly mobile.

Hurricane Katrina and its aftermath have highlighted the politics of mobility. The material infrastructure of mobility opportunities has been shown to serve some more than others. The term *mobility poor* has become a part of the media lexicon. A diverse array of mobile practices—driving, using public transport, going on holiday—have been shown to be related to each other in a myriad of ways. The meanings of mobility associated with tourists, drivers, refugees, and evacuees have been a matter of public debate. But New Orleans, in this instance, is but a metonym for an entire world on the move. In this world it is important to understand that mobility is more than about just getting from A to B. It is about the contested world of meaning and power. It is about mobilities rubbing up against each other and causing friction. It is about a new hierarchy based on the ways we move and the meanings these movements have been given.

# Notes

Chapter 1

. John Bale and Joe Sang, *Kenyan Running: Movement Culture, Geography, and Global Change* (London; Portland, OR: Frank Cass, 1996); Tim Cresswell, "Embodiment, Power and the Politics of Mobility: The Case of Female Tramps and Hobos," *Transactions of the Institute of British Geographers* 24 (1999): 175–92; Iris M. Young, *Throwing Like a Girl and Other Essays in Feminist Philosophy and Social Theory* (Bloomington: Indiana University Press, 1990).

2. Stephen Graham and Simon Marvin, Splintering Urbanism *Networked Infrastructures, Technological Mobilities and the Urban Condition* (London and New York: Routledge, 2001).

3. Arjun Appadurai, *Modernity at Large: Cultural Dimensions of Globalization* (Minneapolis, MN: University of Minnesota Press, 1996); Marc Augé, *Non-Places: Introduction to an Anthropology of Supermodernity* (London; New York: Verso, 1995); Iain Chambers, *Migrancy, Culture, Identity* (London: Routledge, 1994); James Clifford, *Routes: Travel and Translation in the Late Twentieth Century* (Cambridge, MA: Harvard University Press, 1997); Lawrence Grossberg, "Cultural Studies and/in New Worlds," *Critical Studies in Mass Communication* 10 (1993): 1–22; Akhil Gupta and James Ferguson, "Beyond Culture: Space, Identity and the Politics of Difference," *Cultural Anthropology* 7, no. 1 (1992): 6–22.

4. John Urry, *Sociology Beyond Societies: Mobilities for the Twenty-First Century*, (London; New York: Routledge, 2000).

5. Rosi Braidotti, *Nomadic Subjects: Embodiment and Sexual Difference in Contemporary Feminist Theory*, (New York: Columbia University Press, 1994); Gilles Deleuze and Felix Guattari, *Nomadology: The War Machine* (New York: Semiotext(e), 1986); Paul Virilio, *Speed and Politics: An Essay on Dromology*, (New York: Columbia University, 1986).

267

6. See, for instance, Henri Lefebvre, *The Production of Space* (Oxford: Blackwell, 1991); Robert David Sack, *Conceptions of Space in Social Thought: A Geographic Perspective*, (London: Macmillan, 1980); Edward W. Soja, *Postmodern Geographies: The Reassertion of Space in Critical Social Theory* (London; New York: Verso, 1989).

7. For a short introduction to *place*, see Tim Cresswell, *Place: A Short Introduction* (Oxford: Blackwell, 2004). For important discussions from the geographical tradition, see Tim Cresswell, *In Place/Out of Place: Geography, Ideology and Transgression* (Minneapolis: University of Minnesota Press, 1996); J. Nicholas Entrikin, *The Betweenness of Place: Towards a Geography of Modernity* (Baltimore, MD: Johns Hopkins University Press, 1991); Edward Relph, *Place and Placelessness* (London: Pion, 1976); Robert Sack, *Homo Geographicus* (Baltimore, MD: Johns Hopkins University Press, 1997); Yi-Fu Tuan, *Space and Place: The Perspective of Experience* (Minneapolis: University of Minnesota Press, 1977). For a philosophical perspective, see Edward S. Casey, *The Fate of Place: A Philosophical History* (Berkeley: University of California Press, 1998); J. E. Malpas, *Place and Experience: A Philosophical Topography* (Cambridge: Cambridge University Press, 1999).

8. David Delaney, "Laws of Motion and Immobilization: Bodies, Figures and the Politics of Mobility" (paper presented at the Mobilities Conference, Gregynog, Newtown, Wales, 1999).

9. See David Harvey, *The Condition of Postmodernity* (Oxford: Blackwell, 1989); Karl Marx, *Grundrisse. Foundations of the Critique of Political Economy* (New York: Vintage Books, 1973); Wolfgang Schivelbusch, *The Railway Journey: The Industrialization of Time and Space in the 19th Century* (Berkeley: University of California Press, 1986); Nigel Thrift, "Inhuman Geographies: Landscapes of Speed, Light and Power," in *Writing the Rural: Five Cultural Geographies*, ed. Paul Cloke (London: Paul Chapman, 1994), 191–250.

10. Mary Ann Doane, *The Emergence of Cinematic Time: Modernity, Contingency, the Archive* (Cambridge, MA: Harvard University Press, 2002); Mark Gottdiener, *The Social Production of Urban Space* (Austin: University of Texas Press, 1994); Stephen Kern, *The Culture of Time and Space 1880–1918* (Cambridge, MA: Harvard University Press, 1983); Lefebvre, *The Production of Space*; Neil Smith, *Uneven Development: Nature, Capital, and the Production of Space* (Oxford: Blackwell, 1991).

11. But also, importantly, by expectations about race and gender. See Doreen Massey, "A Global Sense of Place," in *Reading Human Geography*, ed. Trevor Barnes and Derek Gregory (London: Arnold, 1997), 315–23.

12. *Quarterly Review* 1839 quoted in Schivelbusch, *The Railway Journey: The Industrialization of Time and Space in the 19th Century*, 34.

13. For a detailed discussion of this process, see William Cronon, *Nature's Metropolis: Chicago and the Great West* (New York: Norton, 1991).

14. Ralph Harrington, "The Railway Journey and the Neuroses of Modernity," in *Pathologies of Travel*, ed. Richard Wrigley and George Revill (Amsterdam: Rodopi, 2000), 261–78, 241.

15. Daniel Miller, "Conclusion: A Theory of Virtualism," in *Virtualism: A New Political Economy,* ed. James G. Carrier and Daniel Miller (Oxford: Berg, 1998), 187–216.

16. Richard Sennett, *Flesh and Stone: The Body and the City in Western Civilization* (New York: W.W. Norton, 1994).

17. Ibid., 256.

18. Alain Corbin, *The Foul and the Fragrant: Odor and the French Social Imagination* (Cambridge, MA: Harvard University Press, 1986); Christopher Prendergast, *Paris and the Nineteenth Century* (Oxford: Blackwell, 1992); Sennett, *Flesh and Stone: The Body and the City in Western Civilization.*

19. Corbin, *The Foul and the Fragrant: Odor and the French Social Imagination,* 91.

20. Emily Martin, "Science and Women's Bodies: Forms of Anthropological Knowledge," in *Body/Politics: Women and the Discourses of Science,* ed. Mary Jacobus, Evelyn Fox Keller, and Sally Shuttleworth (London: Routledge, 1990), 69–82, 76.

21. Emily Martin, "The Egg and the Sperm: How Science Has Constructed a Romance Based on Stereotypical Male-Female Sex Roles," *Signs: Journal of Women in Culture and Society* 16, no. 3 (1991): 485–501.

22. Gerald and Helen Schatten quoted in Evelyn Scott Heller "Gender Language and Science." The 1996 Templeton Lecture, University of Sydney, Sydney, Australia. (http://www.scifac.usyd.edu.au/chast/templeton/1996templeton/1996lecture.html)

23. Norman Bryson, "Cultural Studies and Dance History," in *Meaning in Motion: New Cultural Studies of Dance,* ed. Jane Desmond (Durham, NC: Duke University Press, 1997), 55–80, 60.

24. Ibid., 71.

25. R. A. Dodgshon, *The European Past: Social Evolution and Spatial Order* (Basingstoke, Hampshire: Macmillan Education, 1987), chapter 6.

26. John C. Torpey, *The Invention of the Passport: Surveillance, Citizenship, and the State* (Cambridge: Cambridge University Press, 2000).

27. Zygmunt Bauman, *Legislators and Interpreters* (Oxford: Polity Press, 1987), 39.

28. Ibid., 40.

29. Lewis Mumford, *The City in History* (New York: Harcourt, Brace and World, 1961), 269.

30. Leslie Feldman, *Freedom as Motion* (Lanham, MD: University Press of America, 2001); John Rutherford, *The Troubadours: Their Loves and Their Lyrics: With Remarks on Their Influence, Social and Literary* (London: Smith Elder, 1873).

31. Zygmunt Bauman, *Life in Fragments: Essays in Postmodern Morality* (Oxford: Blackwell, 1995), 94.

32. For an account of this, see Norman Davies, *Europe: A History* (Oxford: Oxford University Press, 1996), 535–36.

33. For a detailed account to the legislative response to these "masterless men" see A. L. Beier, *Masterless Men: The Vagrancy Problem in England 1560–1640* (London: Methuen, 1985).

34. Mumford, *The City in History,* 277.

35. Bauman, *Legislators and Interpreters,* 40.

36. For the seminal account of the rise of institutionalized surveillance, see Michel Foucault, *Discipline and Punish: The Birth of the Prison* (New York: Vintage Books, 1979).
37. Torpey, *The Invention of the Passport: Surveillance, Citizenship, and the State*, 9.
38. Thomas A. Spragens, *The Politics of Motion; the World of Thomas Hobbes* (Lexington: University Press of Kentucky, 1973).
39. For a detailed account, see Roy Porter, *The Greatest Benefit to Mankind: A Medical History of Humanity* (New York: W.W. Norton, 1997).
40. Thomas Hobbes, *The English Works of Thomas Hobbes of Malmesbury* (London: J. Bohn, 1839), 407.
41. Spragens, *The Politics of Motion: The World of Thomas Hobbes*, 73–74.
42. Thomas Hobbes, *Leviathan* (London: Penguin, 1988), 261.
43. Ibid., 261–62.
44. Quoted in Nick Blomley, *Law, Space and the Geographies of Power* (New York: Guilford, 1994), 209.
45. Ibid.
46. For a classic account, see Dean MacCannell, *The Tourist: A New Theory of the Leisure Class* (New York: Schocken Books, 1989). See also James Buzard, *The Beaten Track: European Tourism, Literature, and the Ways to Culture, 1800–1918* (Oxford: Oxford University Press, 1992); Maxine Feifer, *Tourism in History: From Imperial Rome to the Present* (New York: Stein and Day, 1986); Paul Fussell, *Abroad: British Literary Traveling between the Wars* (New York: Oxford University Press, 1980).
47. For an account of the links between tourism and citizenship in Europe, see Ginette Verstraete, "Heading for Europe: Tourism and the Global Itinerary of an Idea," in *Mobilizing Place, Placing Mobility: The Politics of Representation in a Globalized World*, ed. Tim Cresswell and Ginette Verstraete (Amsterdam: Rodopi, 2002), 33–52.
48. Sennett, *Flesh and Stone: The Body and the City in Western Civilization*, 255–56.
49. N. J. Thrift, "Transport and Communication 1730–1914," in *An Historical Geography of England and Wales*, ed. Robert A. Dodgshon and Robin Butlin (London: Academic Press, 1990), 453–86.
50. See John Agnew, *The United States in the World Economy* (Cambridge: Cambridge University Press, 1987); Tim Cresswell, *The Tramp in America* (London: Reaktion, 2001); George H. Douglas, *All Aboard! The Railroad in American Life* (New York: Paragon House, 1992).
51. For a variety of perspectives, see Marshall Berman, *All That Is Solid Melts into Air: The Experience of Modernity* (Harmondsworth: Penguin, 1988); Paul Gilroy, *The Black Atlantic: Modernity and Double Consciousness* (Cambridge, MA: Harvard University Press, 1993); Miles Ogborn, *Spaces of Modernity: London's Geographies, 1680–1780* (New York: Guilford Press, 1998); James Scott, *Seeing Like a State: How Certain Schemes to Improve the Human Condition Have Failed* (New Haven, CT: Yale University Press, 1998); Peter J. Taylor, *Modernities: A Geohistorical Interpretation* (Cambridge: Polity Press, 1999); Thrift, "Inhuman Geographies: Landscapes of Speed, Light and Power."

52.  Ogborn, *Spaces of Modernity: London's Geographies, 1680–1780*, 2.

53.  Foucault, *Discipline and Punish: The Birth of the Prison*.

54.  Lefebvre, *The Production of Space*, 95–96.

55.  Scott, *Seeing Like a State: How Certain Schemes to Improve the Human Condition Have Failed*. For a similar argument on an urban scale, see M. Christine Boyer, *Dreaming the Rational City: The Myth of American City Planning* (Cambridge, MA: MIT Press, 1983).

56.  Scott, *Seeing Like a State: How Certain Schemes to Improve the Human Condition Have Failed*, 1.

57.  Georg Simmel, *The Sociology of Georg Simmel* (Glencoe, IL: Free Press, 1950), 409–24.

58.  George Beard, "Causes of American Nervousness," in *Popular Culture and Industrialism*, ed. Henry Nash Smith (New York: New York University Press, 1967), 57–70, 57.

59.  Ibid., 61.

60.  These two quotations are from Nels Anderson, "The Trends of Urban Sociology," 13. This manuscript can be found at the University of Chicago special collections department in the Ernest Burgess papers Box 126.

61.  Berman, *All That Is Solid Melts into Air: The Experience of Modernity*.

62.  Walter Benjamin, *The Arcades Project* (Cambridge, MA: Belknap Press of Harvard University Press, 1999).

63.  Susan Buck-Morss, "The Flâneur, the Sandwichman and the Whore: The Politics of Loitering," *New German Critique* 39 (1986): 99–141; Keith Tester, ed., *The Flâneur* (London: Routledge, 1994); Elizabeth Wilson, *The Sphinx in the City* (Berkeley: University of California Press, 1991).

64.  John Berger, *Into Their Labours: A Trilogy* (New York: Pantheon Books, 1991).

65.  For a persuasive account of the link between migration and modernity see Nikos Papastergiadis, *The Turbulence of Migration: Globalization, Deterritorialization, and Hybridity* (Cambridge: 2000).

66.  Zygmunt Bauman, *Modernity and Ambivalence* (Ithaca, NY: Cornell University Press, 1991). For a more recent diagnosis of modernity as mobile see Zygmunt Bauman, *Liquid Modernity* (Cambridge: Polity Press, 2000).

67.  Appadurai, *Modernity at Large: Cultural Dimensions of Globalization*, 3.

68.  Ibid., 4.

69.  Ibid.

70.  Taylor, *Modernities: A Geohistorical Interpretation*, 17.

71.  Harrington, "The Railway Journey and the Neuroses of Modernity," 229.

72.  J. K. Wright, "Terrae Incognitae: The Place of the Imagination in Geography," *Annals of the Association of American Geographers* 37 (1947): 1–15.

## Chapter 2

1.  David Atkinson, "Nomadic Strategies and Colonial Governance: Domination and the Resistance in Cyrenaice, 1923–1932," in *Entanglements of Power: Geographies of Domination/Resistance*, ed. Joanne Sharp, et al. (London: Routledge, 2000), 256–68; Tim Cresswell, *The Tramp in America* (London:

Reaktion, 2001); Kevin Hetherington, *New Age Travellers: Vanloads of Uproarious Humanity* (London: Cassell, 2000); David Sibley, *Outsiders in Urban Societies* (New York: St. Martin's Press, 1981).

2. Cited in Liisa Malkki, "National Geographic: The Rooting of Peoples and the Territorialization of National Identity among Scholars and Refugees," *Cultural Anthropology* 7, no. 1 (1992): 24–44, 32.

3. Peter Haggett, *Locational Analysis in Human Geography* (London: Edward Arnold, 1965), 31.

4. Doreen B. Massey and P. M. Jess, *A Place in the World? Places, Cultures and Globalization* (Oxford: Oxford University Press, 1995); Carl Ortwin Sauer, *Agricultural Origins and Dispersals* (New York: American Geographical Society, 1952).

5. See, for instance, Derek Gregory, *Geographical Imaginations* (Cambridge, MA: Blackwell, 1994); Derek Gregory, *Ideology, Science and Human Geography* (London: Hutchinson, 1978); Richard Peet, *Modern Geographical Thought* (Oxford: Blackwell, 1998).

6. For examples, see William Louis Garrison, *Studies of Highway Development and Geographic Change* (Seattle: University of Washington Press, 1959); Roger Robinson, *Ways to Move: The Geography of Networks and Accessibility* (Cambridge and New York: Cambridge University Press, 1977); Edward J. Taaffe and Howard L. Gauthier, *Geography of Transportation* (Englewood Cliffs, NJ: Prentice-Hall, 1973); Edward Ullman, "The Role of Transportation and the Bases for Interaction," in *Man's Role in Changing the Face of the Earth*, ed. William L. Thomas (Chicago, IL: University of Chicago Press, 1956), 862–80; H. P. White and M. L. Senior, *Transport Geography* (London; New York: Longman, 1983).

7. J. Lowe and S. Moryadas, *The Geography of Movement* (Boston: Houghton Mifflin, 1975), 2.

8. Ron Abler, John Adams, and Peter Gould, *Spatial Organization: The Geographer's View of the World* (Englewood Cliffs, NJ: Prentice Hall, 1971), 197.

9. Lowe and Moryadas, *The Geography of Movement*, 3.

10. Abler, Adams, and Gould, *Spatial Organization: The Geographer's View of the World*, 251.

11. See George Kingsley Zipf, *Human Behavior and the Principle of Least Effort: An Introduction to Human Ecology* (Cambridge, MA: Addison-Wesley Press, 1949).

12. Pip Forer, "A Place for Plastic Space?" *Progress in Human Geography* 2 (1978): 230–67.

13. See Susan Hanson and Geraldine J. Pratt, *Gender, Work, and Space* (London and New York: Routledge, 1995); Torsten Hägerstrand and Allan Pred, *Space and Time in Geography: Essays Dedicated to Torsten Hägerstrand* (Lund: CWK Gleerup, 1981); Allan Richard Pred, "The Choreography of Existence: Comments on Hagerstrand's Time-Geography and Its Usefulness," *Economic Geography* 53 (1977): 207–21; Allan Pred, "Power, Everyday Practice and the Discipline of Human Geography," in *Space and Time in Geography*, ed. Allan Pred (Lund: CWK Gleerup, 1981), 30–55.

14. Gillian Rose, *Feminism and Geography: The Limits of Geographical Knowledge* (Cambridge: Polity, 1993).

15. Yi-Fu Tuan, *Space and Place: The Perspective of Experience* (Minneapolis: University of Minnesota Press, 1977).

16. J. B. Jackson, *Landscape in Sight: Looking at America* (New Haven, CT: Yale University Press, 1997); David Seamon, "Body-Subject, Time-Space Routines, and Place-Ballets," in *The Human Experience of Space and Place*, ed. Anne Buttimer and David Seamon (London: Croom Helm, 1980), 148–65.

17. Yi-Fu Tuan, "A View of Geography," *Geographical Review* 81, no. 1 (1991): 99–107.

18. Edward Relph, *Place and Placelessness* (London: Pion, 1976), 1.

19. Ibid., 38.

20. Tuan, *Space and Place: The Perspective of Experience*, 179.

21. Ibid., 183.

22. Yi-Fu Tuan, *Morality and Imagination: Paradoxes of Progress* (Madison, WI: University of Wisconsin Press, 1989).

23. Matthew Arnold and John Dover Wilson, *Culture and Anarchy* (Cambridge: Cambridge University Press, 1935); T. S. Eliot, *Notes towards the Definition of Culture* (London: Faber and Faber, 1948); F. R. Leavis, *Mass Civilisation and Minority Culture* (Cambridge: Minority Press, 1930).

24. Eliot, *Notes towards the Definition of Culture*, 108.

25. Tuan, *Space and Place: The Perspective of Experience*, 183.

26. Eliot, *Notes towards the Definition of Culture*, 52.

27. Ibid., 62–63.

28. Raymond Williams, "Mining the Meaning: Keywords in the Miners Strike," in *Resources of Hope*, ed. Raymond Williams (London: Verso, 1989), 124.

29. For an account of this "militant particularism," see David Harvey, "From Space to Place and Back Again," in *Mapping the Futures*, ed. Jon Bird, et al. (London: Routledge, 1993), 3–29.

30. Richard Hoggart, *The Uses of Literacy* (London: Pelican, 1958), 20.

31. Ibid., 44.

32. Ibid., 45.

33. Ibid., 158.

34. Ibid.

35. Ibid., 205.

36. I am thinking here of Durkhiem's notions of organic and mechanical solidarity and Tönnies' gemeinschaft and gesellschaft. See Emile Durkheim, *The Division of Labour in Society* (Houndmills, Basingstoke, Hampshire: Macmillan, 1984); Ferdinand Tönnies, *Community & Society (Gemeinschaft Und Gesellschaft)* (New York: Harper & Row, 1963).

37. Ernest Burgess, "The Growth of the City: An Introduction to a Research Project," in *The City: Suggestions for Investigation of Human Behavior in the Urban Environment*, ed. Robert Park and Ernest Burgess (Chicago, IL: University of Chicago Press, 1925), 47–62, 59. For an extended discussion of mobility in the Chicago School, see Cresswell, *The Tramp in America*, 63–70.

38. Anderson, *The Trends of Urban Sociology*, 14.
39. Robert Park, "The Mind of the Hobo: Reflections Upon the Relation between Mentality and Locomotion," in *The City: Suggestions for Investigation of Human Behavior in the Urban Environment*, ed. Robert Park and Ernest Burgess (Chicago: University of Chicago Press, 1925), 156–60, 159.
40. Alvin Toffler, *Future Shock* (New York: Random House, 1970).
41. Ibid., 35.
42. Ibid., 75.
43. Ibid., 77.
44. Ibid., 90.
45. Marc Augé, *Non-Places: Introduction to an Anthropology of Supermodernity* (London; New York: Verso, 1995); Paul Virilio, *Speed and Politics: An Essay on Dromology*, Semiotext(e) (New York: Columbia University, 1986).
46. Robert Staughton Lynd and Helen Merrell Lynd, *Middletown: A Study in American Culture* (New York: Harcourt Brace, 1956); William Hollingsworth Whyte, *The Organization Man* (New York: Simon and Schuster, 1956).
47. Cited in Atkinson, "Nomadic Strategies and Colonial Governance: Domination and the Resistance in Cyrenaice, 1923–1932," 105.
48. Cited in Atkinson, "Nomadic Strategies and Colonial Governance: Domination and the Resistance in Cyrenaice, 1923–1932," 111.
49. Ibid., 113. Interestingly, the Italians were busy constructing their own "modern" form of mobility through the construction of clean straight highways dissecting the desert.
50. Roy Stryker Archives, Reel 6, Part C, Section 3a. The Stryker Archives are available in microfilm form at the New York Public Library.
51. An extended commentary on these images can be found in Cresswell, *The Tramp in America*.
52. Cited in S. Phillips, "Dorothea Lange: An American Photographer," in *Dorothea Lange: American Photographs*, ed. T. Heyman, S. Phillips, and J. Szarkowski (San Francisco, CA: Chronicle Books, 1994), 10–41, 24.
53. Dorothea Lange and Paul Schuster Taylor, *An American Exodus: A Record of Human Erosion* (New York: Reynal & Hitchcock, 1939), 67.
54. For fuller accounts of gypsy-travelers and reactions to them, see Angus M. Fraser, *The Gypsies* (Oxford: Blackwell, 1992); Judith Okely, *The Traveller-Gypsies* (Cambridge and New York: Cambridge University Press, 1983); Sibley, *Outsiders in Urban Societies*.
55. See George L. Mosse, *Nazi Culture: Intellectual, Cultural, and Social Life in the Third Reich* (New York: Grosset & Dunlap, 1966).
56. Martin Heidegger, *Poetry, Language, Thought* (New York: Harper & Row, 1971).
57. Sibley, *Outsiders in Urban Societies*.
58. John Urry, *Sociology Beyond Societies: Mobilities for the Twenty-First Century*, International Library of Sociology (London; New York: Routledge, 2000), 18. See also Vincent Kaufman, *Re-thinking Mobility* (London: Ashgate, 2002).

59. James Clifford, *Routes: Travel and Translation in the Late Twentieth Century* (Cambridge, MA: Harvard University Press, 1997); James Clifford, "Traveling Cultures," in *Cultural Studies*, ed. Lawrence Grossberg, Cary Nelson, and Paula Treichler (London: Routledge, 1992), 96–111; Marc Augé *Non-Places: Introduction to an Anthropology of Supermodernity*.

60. Clifford, "Traveling Cultures," 101.

61. Augé, *Non-Places: Introduction to an Anthropology of Supermodernity*, 44.

62. Ibid., 78.

63. Edward Said, *Culture and Imperialism* (London: Vintage, 1994), 402–03.

64. David Harvey, *The Condition of Postmodernity* (Oxford: Blackwell, 1989).

65. Iain Chambers, *Border Dialogues: Journeys in Postmodernity* (London; New York: Routledge, 1990), 57–58.

66. Said, *Culture and Imperialism*, 407–08.

67. Chambers, *Border Dialogues: Journeys in Postmodernity*, 11. This project has been enthusiastically taken up in anthropology and cultural studies. See Arjun Appadurai, *Modernity at Large: Cultural Dimensions of Globalization* (Minneapolis, Minn.: University of Minnesota Press, 1996); Paul Gilroy, *The Black Atlantic: Modernity and Double Consciousness* (Cambridge, MA: Harvard University Press, 1993); Lawrence Grossberg, "Cultural Studies and/ in New Worlds," *Critical Studies in Mass Communication* 10 (1993): 1–22; Akhil Gupta and James Ferguson, "Beyond Culture: Space, Identity and the Politics of Difference," *Cultural Anthropology* 7, no. 1 (1992): 6–22; Smadar Lavie and Ted Swedenburg, "Between and among the Boundaries of Culture: Bridging Text and Lived Experience in the Third Timespace," *Cultural Studies* 10, no. 1 (1996): 154–79.

68. Seamon, "Body-Subject, Time-Space Routines, and Place-Ballets."

69. Pred, "The Choreography of Existence: Comments on Hagerstrand's Time-Geography and Its Usefulness."

70. Gilles Deleuze and Felix Guattari, *Nomadology: The War Machine* (New York: Semiotext(e), 1986); Maurice Merleau-Ponty, *The Phenomenology of Perception* (London: Routledge and Kegan Paul, 1962). For a sympathetic geographical reading see Marcus A. Doel, *Poststructuralist Geographies: The Diabolical Art of Spatial Science* (Lanham, MD: Rowman & Littlefield, 1999).

71. M. Bakhtin, *Rabelais and His World* (Bloomington: Indiana University Press, 1984); Zygmunt Bauman, *Liquid Modernity* (Cambridge: Polity Press, 2000); Rosi Braidotti, *Nomadic Subjects: Embodiment and Sexual Difference in Contemporary Feminist Theory* (New York: Columbia University Press, 1994); Michel de Certeau, *The Practice of Everyday Life* (Berkeley, CA: University of California Press, 1984); Deleuze and Guattari, *Nomadology: The War Machine*; Said, *Culture and Imperialism*.

72. Gloria Anzaldua, *Borderlands: La Frontera = the New Mestiza* (San Francisco, CA: Aunt Lute Books, 1987); Augé, *Non-Places: Introduction to an Anthropology of Supermodernity*; Chambers, *Border Dialogues: Journeys in Postmodernity*; Saskia Sassen, *The Global City: New York, London, Tokyo* (Princeton, NJ: Princeton University Press, 2001).

73. Nigel Thrift, "Inhuman Geographies: Landscapes of Speed, Light and Power," in *Writing the Rural: Five Cultural Geographies*, ed. Paul Cloke (London: Paul Chapman, 1994), 191–250.

74. Ibid., 212–213.

75. de Certeau, *The Practice of Everyday Life*, 29.

76. Ibid., 31.

77. Ibid., 34.

78. Bakhtin, *Rabelais and His World*.

79. Ibid., 3.

80. Ibid., 9.

81. Ibid., 11.

82. For a pithy account of this, see Julian Holloway and James Kneale, "Mikhail Bakhtin: Dialogics of Space," in *Thinking Space*, ed. Mike Crang and Nigel Thrift (London: Routledge, 2000), 71–88.

83. See Deleuze and Guattari, *Nomadology: The War Machine*.

84. Ibid., 29.

85. Ibid.

86. Ibid., 50.

87. Ibid., 51.

88. Steven Best and Douglas Kellner, *Postmodern Theory: Critical Interrogations* (New York: Guilford Press, 1991), 103.

89. Gilles Deleuze and Félix Guattari, *A Thousand Plateaus: Capitalism and Schizophrenia* (Minneapolis: University of Minnesota Press, 1987), 481.

90. Ibid.

91. Gilles Deleuze, *On the Line* (Brooklyn, NY: Autonomedia, 1999), 10–11.

92. Robert Venturi, Denise Scott Brown, and Steven Izenour, *Learning from Las Vegas* (Cambridge, MA: MIT Press, 1972).

93. Institute for the City on the Move, *Architecture on the Move: Cities and Mobilities* (Paris: Institute for the City on the Move, 2003), 29–30.

94. Ibid., 30.

95. Bernard Tschumi, *Architecture and Disjunction* (Cambridge, MA: MIT Press, 1994), 195.

96. See Tschumi's website (www.tschumi.com) for a discussion of this project.

97. Bernard Tschumi and Robert Young, *The Manhattan Transcripts*, new ed. (London: Academy Editions, 1994), xxi

98. Ibid., xxiii.

99. Ronald Christ and Dennis Dollens, *New York: Nomadic Design* (Barcelona: Gustavo Gili, 1993).

100. Janet Wolff, "On the Road Again: Metaphors of Travel in Cultural Criticism," *Cultural Studies* 6 (1992): 224–39, 253.

101. Christopher Miller, "The Postidentitarian Predicament in the Footnotes of *a Thousand Plateaus*: Nomadology, Anthropology, and Authority," *Diacritics* 23, no. 3 (1993): 6–35, 11.

102. Ibid.

103. Ibid., 13.

104. I take this critique from Inge Boer, "No-Man's Land? Five Short Cases on Deserts and the Politics of Place," in *Mobilizing Place, Placing Mobility*, ed. Ginette Verstraete and Tim Cresswell (Amsterdam: Rodopi, 2002), 155–72. See also Caren Kaplan, *Questions of Travel: Postmodern Discourses of Displacement* (Durham, NC: Duke University Press, 1996).

105. This is the subject of Tim Cresswell, *In Place/Out of Place: Geography, Ideology and Transgression* (Minneapolis: University of Minnesota Press, 1996); Tim Cresswell, "Weeds, Plagues and Bodily Secretions: A Geographical Interpretation of Metaphors of Displacement," *Annals of the Association of American Geographers* 87, no. 2 (1997): 330–45.

106. J. D. Dewsbury, "Performativity and the Event: Enacting a Philosophy of Difference," *Environment and Planning D: Society and Space* 18 (2000): 473–96, 487.

*Chapter 3*

1. H. Gilpin, "Lifelessness in Movement, or How Do the Dead Move?" in *Corporealities: Dancing Knowledge, Culture and Power*, ed. S. Foster (London: Routledge, 1996), 106–28.

2. Liisa Malkki, "National Geographic: The Rooting of Peoples and the Territorialization of National Identity among Scholars and Refugees," *Cultural Anthropology* 7, no. 1 (1992): 24–44.

3. I am thinking here of the way of seeing described in James Scott, *Seeing Like a State: How Certain Schemes to Improve the Human Condition Have Failed* (New Haven, CT: Yale University Press, 1998).

4. Rebecca Solnit, *Motion Studies: Eadweard Muybridge and the Technological Wild West* (London: Bloomsbury, 2003), 23. See also Robert Bartlett Haas, *Muybridge: Man in Motion* (Berkeley: University of California Press, 1976); Gordon Hendricks, *Eadweard Muybridge: The Father of the Motion Picture* (New York: Grossman Publishers, 1975).

5. Cited in Solnit, *Motion Studies: Eadweard Muybridge and the Technological Wild West*, 184–85.

6. Noël Burch, *Life to Those Shadows* (Berkeley: University of California Press, 1990), 11.

7. Solnit, *Motion Studies: Eadweard Muybridge and the Technological Wild West*.

8. Ibid., 194.

9. Jonathan Crary, *Suspensions of Perception: Attention, Spectacle, and Modern Culture* (Cambridge, MA: MIT Press, 1999), 138–48.

10. Ibid., 140.

11. Karl Marx, *Grundrisse. Foundations of the Critique of Political Economy* (New York: Vintage Books, 1973), 539.

12. See David Harvey, *The Limits to Capital* (Oxford: Blackwell, 1982), 376–86.

13. Crary, *Suspensions of Perception: Attention, Spectacle, and Modern Culture*, 142.

14. Deborah Dixon and John Paul Jones, "My Dinner with Derrida: Or Spatial Analysis and Post-Structuralism Do Lunch," *Environment and Planning A* 30 (1998): 247–60.

15. Solnit, *Motion Studies: Eadweard Muybridge and the Technological Wild West,* 195.

16. Scott, *Seeing Like a State: How Certain Schemes to Improve the Human Condition Have Failed.*

17. Richard Sennett, *The Conscience of the Eye: The Design and Social Life of Cities* (New York: Knopf, 1990).

18. John Pultz, *Photography and the Body* (London: Weidenfeld & Nicholson, 1995), 30–31.

19. Huxley quoted in Frank Spencer, "Some Notes on the Attempt to Apply Photography to Anthropometry during the Second Half of the Nineteenth Century," in *Anthropology and Photography 1860–1920,* ed. Elizabeth Edwards (New Haven, CT: Yale University Press, 1992), 99–107, 99.

20. This line of thinking is most famously developed in Michel Foucault, *Discipline and Punish: The Birth of the Prison* (New York: Vintage Books, 1979). See also Scott, *Seeing Like a State: How Certain Schemes to Improve the Human Condition Have Failed.*

21. Sol LeWitt in conversation with Lucy Lippard, in Lucy R. Lippard, *Changing: Essays in Art Criticism* (New York: Dutton, 1971), 164. One of LeWitt's works is called Muybridge 1. The influence is obvious.

22. Crary, *Suspensions of Perception: Attention, Spectacle, and Modern Culture,* 142.

23. Ibid., 144.

24. *San Francisco Chronicle* quoted in Solnit, *Motion Studies: Eadweard Muybridge and the Technological Wild West,* 199.

25. It is ironic, given the nakedness of the subjects in Muybridge's paintings, that Eakin was expelled from the University of Pennsylvania for removing a loin cloth from a male model during a life-drawing class.

26. Emmanuel Cooper, *Fully Exposed: The Male Nude in Photography* (London; New York: Routledge, 1995).

27. Muybridge quoted in Solnit, *Motion Studies: Eadweard Muybridge and the Technological Wild West,* 222.

28. Eadweard Muybridge, *Muybridge's Complete Human and Animal Locomotion: All 781 Plates from the 1887 Animal Locomotion* (New York: Dover Publications, 1979), 1588.

29. I. M. Young, *Throwing Like a Girl and Other Essays in Feminist Philosophy and Social Theory* (Bloomington: Indiana University Press, 1990).

30. Marta Braun and Elizabeth Whitcombe, "Marey, Muybridge, and Londe: The Photography of Pathological Locomotion," *History of Photography* 23, no. 3 (1999): 218–24, 220, 222.

31. Elizabeth Edwards, *Anthropology and Photography, 1860–1920* (New Haven, CT: Yale University Press in association with the Royal Anthropological Institute London, 1992), 56.

32. Solnit, *Motion Studies: Eadweard Muybridge and the Technological Wild West*, 221.
33. George Miller Beard, *American Nervousness; Its Causes and Consequences, a Supplement to Nervous Exhaustion (Neurasthenia)* (New York: G. P. Putnam's Sons, 1881).
34. Beard, in Henry Nash Smith, *Popular Culture and Industrialism, 1865–1890, Documents in American Civilization Series* (New York: New York University Press, 1967), 64.
35. Jayne Morgan, "Edward Muybridge and W. S. Playfair: An Aesthetics of Neurasthenia," *History of Photography* 23, no. 2 (1999): 225–32.
36. Marey in Anson Rabinbach, *The Human Motor: Energy, Fatigue, and the Origins of Modernity* (New York: BasicBooks, 1990), 94.
37. Etienne-Jules Marey and Eric Pritchard, *Movement*, The International Scientific Series [Amer. Ed.] Vol. 73 (New York: D. Appleton and Company, 1895), 33.
38. For good accounts of Marey's work, see Marta Braun, *Picturing Time: The Work of Etienne-Jules Marey (1830–1904)* (Chicago: University of Chicago Press, 1992). and Rabinbach, *The Human Motor: Energy, Fatigue, and the Origins of Modernity*. I draw on their accounts as well as the writings of Marey himself, particularly Marey and Pritchard, *Movement*; Etienne Jules Marey, *Animal Mechanism: A Treatise on Terrestrial and Aerial Locomotion* (London: Henry S. King & Co., 1874).
39. This is persuasively argued in Braun, *Picturing Time: The Work of Etienne-Jules Marey (1830–1904)*.
40. Rabinbach, *The Human Motor: Energy, Fatigue, and the Origins of Modernity*, 92.
41. Marey and Pritchard, *Movement*, 33–34.
42. Ibid., 50–51.
43. Ibid., 57.
44. Marey, *Animal Mechanism: A Treatise on Terrestrial and Aerial Locomotion*, 9.
45. Braun, *Picturing Time: The Work of Etienne-Jules Marey (1830–1904)*, 14–15.
46. Ibid., xviii.
47. Ibid., 66.
48. Marey and Pritchard, *Movement*, 58.
49. Ibid., 145.
50. This has become an accepted method of modelling motion for both animation and sports science, as well as the development of prosthetic limbs.
51. Braun and Whitcombe, "Marey, Muybridge, and Londe: The Photography of Pathological Locomotion," 220.
52. For a longer discussion of the pathological, see Georges Canguilhem, *The Normal and the Pathological* (Cambridge, MA: Zone Books, 1989); Tim Cresswell, *The Tramp in America* (London: Reaktion, 2001), 111–14; Ian Hacking, *The Taming of Chance* (Cambridge: Cambridge University Press, 1990).

53. See Stephen Kern, *The Culture of Time and Space 1880–1918* (Cambridge, MA: Harvard University Press, 1983).

## Chapter 4

1. For biographies of Taylor, see Frank Barkley Copley, *Frederick W. Taylor, Father of Scientific Management* (New York: American Society of Mechanical Engineers, 1923); Robert Kanigel, *The One Best Way: Frederick Winslow Taylor and the Enigma of Efficiency* (New York: Viking, 1997). For critical accounts of Taylorism, see Harry Braverman, *Labor and Monopoly Capital* (New York: Monthly Review Press, 1974); Bernard Doray, *From Taylorism to Fordism: A Rational Madness* (London: Free Association, 1988); Judith A. Merkle, *Management and Ideology: The Legacy of the International Scientific Management Movement* (Berkeley: University of California Press, 1980); Ernest J. Yanarella and Herbert G. Reid, "From 'Trained Gorilla' to 'Humanware': Repoliticizing the Body-Machine Complex between Fordism and Post-Fordism," in *The Social and Political Body*, ed. Theodore Schatzki and Wolfgang Natter (New York: Guilford, 1996), 181–220.
2. Lenin cited in James Scott, *Seeing Like a State: How Certain Schemes to Improve the Human Condition Have Failed* (New Haven, CT: Yale University Press, 1998), 101.
3. Braverman, *Labor and Monopoly Capital*, 112.
4. Frederick Winslow Taylor, *The Principles of Scientific Management* (New York: Norton, 1967), 19.
5. Ibid., 21.
6. Ibid., 43.
7. Ibid., 45–46
8. Ibid., 59.
9. Frederick Taylor Archives, Special Collections, Stevens College, Hoboken, New Jersey, Box 106B, Legislation, Scientific Management, Henry Knolle.
10. Frederick Taylor Archives, Box 106B, Legislation, Scientific Management, Henry Knolle.
11. Letter to Mr. Cooke, December 6, 1913, Frederick Taylor Archives, Box 106B, Legislation, Scientific Management, Henry Knolle.
12. Letter to Mr. A. B. Wadleigh, December 22nd, 1913, Frederick Taylor Archives, Box 106B, Legislation, Scientific Management, Henry Knolle.
13. Report on Henry Knoll, January 3rd, 1914, Frederick Taylor Archives, Box 106B, Legislation, Scientific Management, Henry Knolle.
14. Martha Banta, *Taylored Lives: Narrative Productions in the Age of Taylor, Veblen, and Ford* (Chicago, IL: University of Chicago Press, 1993); Mark Seltzer, *Bodies and Machines* (New York: Routledge, 1992); Yanarella and Reid, "From 'Trained Gorilla' to 'Humanware': Repoliticizing the Body-Machine Complex between Fordism and Post-Fordism."
15. Antonio Gramsci, "Americanism and Fordism," in *Selections from the Prison Notebooks*, ed. Quintin Hoare and Geoffrey Smith (New York: International Publishers, 1971), 277–318, 298.

16. Yanarella and Reid, "From 'Trained Gorilla' to 'Humanware': Repoliticizing the Body-Machine Complex between Fordism and Post-Fordism."
17. Cited in *Congressional Record*, 63rd Congress, 3d. sess. Vol. 52, no. 69, 4905.
18. Cited in *Congressional Record*, 63rd Congress, 3d. sess. Vol. 52, no. 69, 4884.
19. Braverman, *Labor and Monopoly Capital*, 125.
20. Mark Bahnisch, "Embodied Work, Divided Labour: Subjectivity and the Scientific Management of the Body in Frederick W. Taylor's 1907 'Lecture on Management,'" *Body and Society* 6, no. 1 (2000): 51–68, 62.
21. Taylor, *The Principles of Scientific Management*, 77.
22. Ibid., 79.
23. Ibid., 117–18.
24. Marta Braun, *Picturing Time: The Work of Etienne-Jules Marey (1830–1904)* (Chicago, IL: University of Chicago Press, 1992), 321.
25. Bahnisch, "Embodied Work, Divided Labour: Subjectivity and the Scientific Management of the Body in Frederick W. Taylor's 1907 'Lecture on Management,'" 54.
26. Ibid., 63.
27. Taylor Archives. Letter from Taylor to Frank Copley, August 19, 1912.
28. David Harvey, *The Urban Experience* (Baltimore, MD: Johns Hopkins University Press, 1989); E. P. Thompson, "Time, Work Discipline, and Industrial Capitalism," *Past and Present* 38 (1967): 56–97.
29. Doray, *From Taylorism to Fordism: A Rational Madness*, 34.
30. Frank and Lillian Gilbreth worked together as Gilbreth Inc., but many of the papers and books published by them only feature Frank's name. Frank was responsible for most of the work done in factory spaces up to his death. The final section of this chapter deals with Lillian's work after Frank's death.
31. Frederick Taylor Archives. Letter from Gilbreth to Taylor April 18, 1912 (FBG Correspondance 1912–1915).
32. Frederick Taylor Archives. Letter from Gilbreth to Taylor July 29, 1912 (FBG Correspondance 1912–1915).
33. Frederick Taylor Archives. Letter from Taylor to Gilbreth August 24· 1912 (FBG Correspondance 1912–1915).
34. Gilbreth's copy of this book can be found in the Lillian M. Gilbreth Archives in Smith College Library, Northampton, Massachusetts. This annotation is on page 110.
35. Ibid., 130. The marginal notes become more extensive as the book progresses until Gilbreth sees fit to describe in all the detail the margins will allow the core difference between Taylor and himself.

    When Taylor says "motions" he means "elementary operations." His "elementary operations" should be called "sub-operations" because they are in no way elementary because they always consist of many motions—not the SAMPLE on this page.
    As a sample of these elementary operations which occur in all machine shops, I would cite picking up a bolt and clamp and putting the bolt head

into the slot of a machine, then placing a distance piece under the back end of the clamp and tightening down the bolt.

This shows that neither Copley nor the readers of his manuscript understand yet that "motion study" and "time study" are two entirely different things. (233).

36. Gilbreth Archives, Box 42, Folder 0265-3 NAPTM. The Frank Gilbreth Archives can be found in the Special Collections Department at Purdue University Library. The location codes (above) reflect exactly the idiosyncratic cataloguing of the archive by Gilbreth himself.

37. Ibid., 8.

38. Ibid., 9.

39. Ibid., 15.

40. Lillian Gilbreth. "Automation" Presented to the Logistics Systems Engineering Class 59B at Wright Patterson Air Force Base, Ohio, June 26, 1959 (Speeches of LMG, Lillian Gilbreth Archives, Smith College—Box 13, Folder 4).

41. Box 42, 0265-4 NAPTM Frank Gilbreth, "Motion Study as an Increase of National Wealth," *Annals of the American Academy of Political and Social Science*, Philadelphia, May 1915.

42. Frank Bunker Gilbreth and Lillian Moller Gilbreth, *Applied Motion Study: A Collection of Papers on the Efficient Method to Industrial Preparedness* (New York: Sturgis & Walton Company, 1917), 43.

43. Ibid., 3.

44. Ibid., 4.

45. Frank Bunker Gilbreth and Lillian Moller Gilbreth, *Motion Study for the Handicapped* (London: G. Routledge & Sons, Ltd., 1920), 5.

46. Frank Bunker Gilbreth and Lillian Moller Gilbreth, *Fatigue Study; the Elimination of Humanity's Greatest Unnecessary Waste, a First Step in Motion Study* (New York: The Macmillan Company, 1919), 181.

47. Gilbreth Archives, Box 46, Micro-Motion Study File 0265-20 NAPTM, 8–9.

48. A *grasp*, for instance, was defined as "The motion beginning at the time the hand or any part thereof comes into contact with the article being grasped, until the object starts to move in the performance of the following therblig." "*Assemble*", on the other hand, "[s]tarts the instant the hand begins to move an object or part of an object into or onto or together with another co-operating object of which it is an integral part or co-member and ends when the hand comes to rest, or goes on to another therblig." Ibid., 17.

49. Gilbreth Archives, Box 41 0265-1 NAPTM (June 19 1917).

50. Gilbreth Archives, Box 42 0265-2 NAPTM.

51. Ibid.

52. Ibid.

53. The descriptions above and the explanation of the mnemonic system all come from the Gilbreth Archives, Box 42, 0265-2 NAPTM.

54. Ibid.

55. Pierre Bourdieu, *The Logic of Practice* (Stanford, CA: Stanford University Press, 1990); Maurice Merleau-Ponty, *The Phenomenology of Perception* (London:

Routledge and Kegan Paul, 1962); David Seamon, "Body-Subject, Time-Space Routines, and Place-Ballets," in *The Human Experience of Space and Place*, ed. Anne Buttimer and David Seamon (London: Croom Helm, 1980), 148–65.

56. Frank Bunker Gilbreth and Robert Thurston Kent, *Motion Study, a Method for Increasing the Efficiency of the Workman* (New York: D. Van Nostrand Company, 1911), 8.

57. Ibid., 23.

58. Ibid., 67.

59. Gilbreth Archives, Box 41, 0265-1 NAPTM –8-30-1915. Seminar notes, page 27.

60. Ibid., 27.

61. Frank Gilbreth, "Likenesses as Demonstrated by Motion Study," January 1917, Gilbreth Archives, Box 42, 0265-4 NAPTM.

62. Letter from Mr. S. A. Whitaker to Gilbreth, December 6, 1915, Gilbreth Archives, Box 42, 0265-4 NAPTM.

63. Frank Bunker Gilbreth and Lillian Gilbreth, "Motion Models: Their Use in the Transference of Experience and the Presentation of Comparative Results in Educational Methods" (paper presented at the American Association for the Advancement of Science, Columbus, Ohio, December 27, 1915–January 1, 1916, 15.

64. Ibid., 16.

65. Pierre Bourdieu, *Distinction: A Social Critique of the Judgement of Taste* (Cambridge, MA: Harvard University Press, 1984); Iris M. Young, *Throwing Like a Girl and Other Essays in Feminist Philosophy and Social Theory* (Bloomington: Indiana University Press, 1990).

66. Bahnisch, "Embodied Work, Divided Labour: Subjectivity and the Scientific Management of the Body in Frederick W. Taylor's 1907 'Lecture on Management,'" 54.

67. See Brian Price, "Frank and Lillian Gilbreth and the Motion Study Controversy, 1907–1930," in *A Mental Revolution: Scientific Management since Taylor*, ed. Daniel Nelson (Columbus: Ohio State University Press, 1992), 58–76.

68. Gilbreth Archives, Box 41, 0265-1 NAPTM, August 6, 1914, 222–23.

69. Gilbreth Archives, Box 41, 0265-1 NAPTM, August 30, 1915.

70. See Brian Price, "Frank and Lillian Gilbreth and the Manufacture and Marketing of Motion Study, 1908–1924," *Business and Economic History* 18 (1989): 88–98.

71. Gilbreth Archives, Box 159, 0952-2 NZ610.

72. Ibid.

73. Gilbreth Archives , Letter of July 11, 1912, Box 159, 0952-2 NZ610.

74. Ibid.

75. Gilbreth Archives, Letter of July 30, 1912, Box 159 0952-2 NZ610.

76. Gilbreth Archives, Letter of August 8, 1912, Box 159 0952-2 NZ610.

77. Laurel Graham, "*Lillian Moller Gilbreth's Extensions of Scientific Management into Women's Work, 1924–1935*" (PhD diss., University of Illinois, 1992); Laurel Graham, *Managing on Her Own: Dr. Lillian Gilbreth and Women's Work in the Interwar Era* (Norcross, GA: Engineering & Management Press, 1998).

78. Graham, "Lillian Moller Gilbreth's Extensions of Scientific Management into Women's Work, 1924–1935," 2.

79. Phyllis M. Palmer, *Domesticity and Dirt: Housewives and Domestic Servants in the United States, 1920–1945* (Philadelphia, PA: Temple University Press, 1989).

80. Carolyn Goldstein, "From Service to Sales: Home Economics in Light and Power 1920–1940," *Technology and Culture* 38, no. 1 (1997): 121–52.

81. Ruth Schwartz Cowan, *More Work for Mother: The Ironies of Household Technology from the Open Hearth to the Microwave* (New York: Basic Books, 1983); Barbara Ehrenreich and Deirdre English, *For Her Own Good: 150 Years of the Experts' Advice to Women* (Garden City, NY: Anchor Press, 1978).

82. See, for instance, G. Weaver, *Our Home or Influences Emanating from the Hearthstone* (Springfield, MA, 1899).

83. Bettina Berch, "Scientific Management in the Home: The Empresses New Clothes," *Journal of American Culture* 3, no. 3 (1980): 440–45.

84. Graham, *Managing on Her Own: Dr. Lillian Gilbreth and Women's Work in the Interwar Era.*

85. Laurel Graham, "Domesticating Efficiency: Lillian Gilbreth's Scientific Management of Homemakers, 1924–1930," *Signs* 24, no. 3 (1999): 633–75, 641.

86. This argument has been made by Delores Hayden, who sees Lillian Gilbreth and Christine Frederick as explicitly antifeminist, pro-consumer, suburbanites. See Dolores Hayden, *The Grand Domestic Revolution: A History of Feminist Designs for American Homes, Neighborhoods, and Cities* (Cambridge, MA: MIT Press, 1981).

87. Archival material on Lillian Gilbreth can be found in the Lillian Gilbreth Archives at Smith College, Northampton, Massachusetts, and in the Frank Gilbreth Archives at Purdue University (files NF 87 NGH 0655-2, NF 3/ NAFDP 0030-20A, and NF 111/NHE 0809-1).

88. This poem can be found in the Frank Gilbreth Archives, Purdue University, file NF88/NGH 0655-7.

89. Lillian Gilbreth, "The Kitchen Practical," Lillian Gilbreth Archives, Series IV, Box 14, Smith College.

90. Lillian Gilbreth, "The Kitchen Practical," Lillian Gilbreth Archives, Series IV, Box 14, Smith College.

91. Similar charts were constructed in the United Kingdom by Jane Drew in order to construct similar "modern" kitchens. See Mark Llewelyn, "Designed by Women and Designing Women: Gender, Planning and the Geographies of the Kitchen in Britain 1917–1946," *Cultural Geographies* 10 (2004): 42–60.

92. The *New York Herald Tribune* Institute Presents Four Model Kitchens, October 1930, page 8, Lillian Gilbreth Archives, Series IV, Box 14, Smith College.

93. "Kitchen Practical: The Story of an Experiment. The Brooklyn Borough Gas Company," Lillian Gilbreth Archives, Smith College, Series IV, Box 14.

94. Gilbreth Management Desk brochure, Lillian Gilbreth Archives, Smith College, Series IV, Box 14.

95. A similar process was happening in 1940s Britain. See David Matless, *Landscape and Englishness* (London: Reaktion Books, 1998), 241–42.

96. See Graham, "Domesticating Efficiency: Lillian Gilbreth's Scientific Management of Homemakers, 1924–1930." Her argument here draws heavily on Foucault's conception of power as productive and distributed. See M. Foucault, *Power/Knowledge* (New York: Pantheon, 1980).

*Chapter 5*

1. Philip J. S. Richardson, *The History of English Ballroom Dancing 1910–1945* (London: Herbert Jenkins, n.d.), 41. I am indebted to the Imperial Society for Teachers of Dancing for the use of their archives. The following account is based on their archival material.
2. See, for instance, Nigel Thrift, "The Still Point: Resistance, Expressiveness Embodiment and Dance," in *Geographies of Resistance*, ed. S. Pile and M. Keith (London: Routledge, 1997), 124–51.
3. Jane Desmond, *Meaning in Motion: New Cultural Studies of Dance*, Post-Contemporary Interventions (Durham, NC: Duke University Press, 1997); G. Morris, ed., *Moving Words: Re-Writing Dance* (London: Routledge, 1996); C. Picart, "Dancing through Different Worlds: An Autoethnography of the Interactive Body and Virtual Emotion in Ballroom Dance," *Qualitative Inquiry* 8, no. 3 (2002): 348–61.
4. Margaret Lloyd cited in Richard G. Kraus and Sarah Chapman Hilsendager, *History of the Dance in Art and Education* (Englewood Cliffs, NJ: Prentice-Hall, 1981), 124.
5. Rudolf von Laban, *Laban's Principles of Dance and Movement Notation* (London: Macdonald & Evans, 1975), 5.
6. Rudolf von Laban and F. C. Lawrence, *Effort: Economy in Body Movement* (Boston: Plays, Inc., 1974), 73–74.
7. Ibid., 4.
8. Ibid., 12.
9. Ibid., 77–78.
10. J. Desmond, "Embodying Difference: Issues in Dance and Cultural Studies," *Cultural Critique* (winter 1993–94): 33–63, 58.
11. Ibid., 38–39; Marta Savigliano, *Tango and the Political Economy of Passion* (Boulder, CO: Westview Press, 1995).
12. Desmond, "Embodying Difference: Issues in Dance and Cultural Studies," 44.
13. M. Franko, "Five Theses on Laughter after All," in *Moving Words: Re-Writing Dance*, ed. G. Morris (London: Routledge, 1996), 43–62, 43–44.
14. This does not make such a process of mediation straightforward however. In dance, like all forms of movement, process and relation do not lend themselves "to fixity, abstraction or objectivity" (ibid., 46).
15. Sue Foster, "The Ballerina's Phallic Pointe," in *Corporealities: Dancing Knowledge, Culture and Power*, ed. S. Foster (London: Routledge, 1996), 1–24, 1–2.
16. Helen Thomas, *Dance, Modernity, and Culture: Explorations in the Sociology of Dance* (London; New York: Routledge, 1995), 170.
17. For examples, see J. Kaeli'inohomoku, "Cultural Change: Functional and Dysfunctional Expressions of Dance, a Form of Affective Culture," in

*The Performing Arts*, ed. J. Blacking and J. Kaeli'inohomoku (The Hague: Mouton, 1979); A. Kaeppler, "American Approaches to the Study of Dance," *Yearbook of Traditional Music* 23 (1991): 11–21; Susan Reed, "The Politics and Poetics of Dance," *Annual Review of Anthropology* 27 (1998): 503–32; D. Sklar, "On Dance Ethnography," *Dance Research Journal* 23, no. 1 (1991): 6–10; Paul Spencer, *Society and the Dance: The Social Anthropology of Process and Performance* (Cambridge: Cambridge University Press, 1985).

18. In geography this is connected to the observations made in Catherine Nash, "Performativity in Practice: Some Recent Work in Cultural Geography," *Progress in Human Geography* 24, no. 4 (2000): 653–64; George Revill, "Performing French Folk Music: Dance, Authenticity and Nonrepresentational Theory," *Cultural Geographies* 11 (2004): 199–209. For work on these themes elsewhere, see Desmond, "Embodying Difference: Issues in Dance and Cultural Studies."; Franko, "Five Theses on Laughter after All"; Savigliano, *Tango and the Political Economy of Passion.*

19. Derek P. McCormack, "The Event of Geographical Ethics in Spaces of Affect," *Transactions of the Institute of British Geographers* 28 (2003): 488–507, 488. For accounts of nonrepresentational theory, see J. D. Dewsbury, "Performativity and the Event: Enacting a Philosophy of Difference," *Environment and Planning D: Society and Space* 18 (2000): 473–96; Thrift, "The Still Point: Resistance, Expressiveness Embodiment and Dance."; Nigel Thrift, "Summoning Life," in *Envisioning Human Geographies*, ed. Paul Cloke, Philip Crang, and Mark Goodwin (London: Arnold, 2004), 81–103.

20. See James J. Nott, *Music for the People: Popular Music and Dance in Interwar Britain* (Oxford and New York: Oxford University Press, 2002).

21. Philip Richardson, "Can We Get Together and Raise the Standard of Ballroom Dancing? A Suggestion from Maurice," *Dancing Times*, April 1920, 526, 528.

22. Richardson, *The History of English Ballroom Dancing 1910–1945*, 42.

23. Edward Scott was a writer on dance and an influential figure in social dancing. For an account, see Theresa Buckland, "Edward Scott: The Last of the English Dancing Masters," *Dance Research* 21, no. 2 (2003): 3–35.

24. "Our Conference of Ballroom Teachers," *Dancing Times*, June 1920, 44.

25. "Paris Notes. The 'Shimmy' Once More," *Dancing Times* 125 (1921): 15.

26. See Sonny Watson's Streetswing.com, http://www.streetswing.com/histmain/z3shimy.htm (accessed March 26, 2004)

27. The *American Heritage Dictionary of the English Language*, 4th ed., (New York: Houghton Mifflin, 2000).

28. Richardson, *The History of English Ballroom Dancing 1910–1945*, 39.

29. "The Sitter Out," *Dancing Times*, June 1921, 703.

30. "Paris Notes. The 'Shimmy' Once More," *Dancing Times*, 129, 709.

31. Victor Silvester, *Dancing Is My Life: An Autobiography* (London: Heinemann, 1958), 89.

32. Richardson, *The History of English Ballroom Dancing 1910–1945*, 22–23.

33. Ibid., 23.

34. See Rob Shields, *Places on the Margin: Alternative Geographies of Modernity* (London: Routledge Chapman Hall, 1991); Victor Witter Turner, *The Ritual*

*Process: Structure and Anti-Structure*, Symbol, Myth, and Ritual Series (Ithaca, NY: Cornell University Press, 1977).

35. Richardson, *The History of English Ballroom Dancing 1910–1945*, 23.
36. For a wonderful account of the travels of tango, see Savigliano, *Tango and the Political Economy of Passion*.
37. Charles D'Albert, "The Evils of Imitative Teaching," *Dance Journal* 1, no. 2 (1907): 2–3, 3.
38. Gerald Butterfield, "The Degeneracy of Dancing," *Dance Journal* II, no. 3 (1908): 2.
39. "Is Dancing Degenerating?" *Dance Journal* II, no. 6 (1908): 8–9, 8–9.
40. "Decadent Dances: An American Woman's Denunciation of the New 'Freak' Dances," *Dance Journal* IV, no. 24 (1911): 15, 15.
41. "Degeneracy of Dancing. Ballroom Antics: Ragged Rag-Time in Two Steps," *Dance Journal* VI, no. 34 (1913), 7.
42. "The Sitter Out," 704–05.
43. Victor Silvester, *Modern Ballroom Dancing: History and Practice* (London: Barrie & Jenkins, 1974), 40.
44. Silvester, *Dancing Is My Life: An Autobiography*, 85.
45. Ibid., 86.
46. "Some Expressions of Opinion About the Conference," *Dancing Times*, June 1920, 709.
47. Richardson, *The History of English Ballroom Dancing 1910–1945*, 78.
48. Victor Silvester, "What Is Your Opinion?" *The Dance Journal* VIII, no. 2 (1935): 105–06 92, 105.
49. Ibid.
50. Richardson, *The History of English Ballroom Dancing, 1910–1945*, 37–38.
51. Quoted in Richardson, *The History of Ballroom Dancing, 1910–1945*, 38.
52. Jack Hylton, quoted in Nott, *Music for the People: Popular Music and Dance in Interwar Britain*, 201.
53. Ibid., 162.
54. Edward Scott "A Few Suggestions," *Dancing Times* 121 (October 1920): 17.
55. Frank Spencer and Peggy Spencer, *Come Dancing* (London: W. H. Allen, 1968), 14–15.
56. Silvester, *Modern Ballroom Dancing: History and Practice*, 41.
57. Richardson, *The History of English Ballroom Dancing 1910–1945*, preface.
58. Frank Gilbreth, "Likenesses as Demonstrated by Motion Study," Gilbreth Archives (Special Collections Department at Purdue University), January 1917, Box 42, 0265-4 NAPTM.
59. McCormack, "The Event of Geographical Ethics in Spaces of Affect," 489.
60. See Pierre Bourdieu, *The Logic of Practice* (Stanford, CA: Stanford University Press, 1990).

## Chapter 6

1. Notes of the Select Committee Investigating National Defense Migration, House of Representatives, Washington, DC, Monday, January 19, 1942, 9969.

2. Ibid., 9969.
3. Ibid., 10230.
4. Ibid., 10231.
5. Ibid., 10232.
6. David Delaney, "Laws of Motion and Immobilization: Bodies, Figures and the Politics of Mobility" (paper presented at the Mobilities Conference, Gregynog, Newtown, Wales, 1999), 3.
7. See, for instance, Jean Baudrillard, *America* (London: Verso, 1988); James M. Jasper, *Restless Nation: Starting Over in America* (Chicago: University of Chicago Press, 2000); John Kouwenhoven, *The Beer-Can by the Highway* (Baltimore, MD: Johns Hopkins University Press, 1961); Alexis de Tocqueville, *Democracy in America* (Chicago, IL: University of Chicago Press, 2000); Frederick Jackson Turner, *The Frontier in American History* (New York: Holt, Rinehart and Winston, 1947).
8. *Crandall v. State of Nevada*, 73 U.S. 35 (1867).
9. *Crandall v. State of Nevada*, 6 Wall. 35, 49.
10. *Kent v. Dulles*, 357 U.S. 116 (1958), 125–26.
11. Ibid., 126. Justice Douglas citing Zechariah Chafee, *Three Human Rights in the Constitution of 1787* (Lawrence: University of Kansas Press, 1956), 197.
12. Ibid., 127.
13. Louis Jaffe, *The Right to Travel: The Passport Problem*, 35 *Foreign Affairs* 17, 26. Cited in *Kent v. Dulles*, 357 U.S. 116 (1958), 141–42.
14. *United States v. Guest*, 383 U.S. 745 (1966), 748.
15. Ibid.
16. Ibid., 757.
17. Ibid.
18. Ibid., 758.
19. Ibid., 759.
20. *Corfield v. Coryell*, 4 Wash. C. C. 371 (1825) 380–81.
21. *United States v. Guest*, 383 U.S. 745 (1966) 767.
22. Ibid., 768.
23. *Kent v. Dulles*, 357 U.S. 116 (1958), 125.
24. Harlan citing Chafee, *Three Human Rights in the Constitution of 1787*, 192–93.
25. *Shapiro v. Thompson*, 394 U.S. 618 (1969), 636.
26. *Shapiro v. Thompson*, 394 U.S. 618 (1969), 629–30.
27. Ibid., 622.
28. Ibid., 643–43.
29. For a recent example citing *Crandall* and *Edwards*, for instance, see *Saenz v. Roe*. 526 U.S. 489 (1999).
30. I am drawing here on the law and geography interface developed in Nicholas K. Blomley, David Delaney, and Richard T. Ford, *The Legal Geographies Reader: Law, Power, and Space* (Oxford: Blackwell Publishers, 2001); Nick Blomley, *Law, Space and the Geographies of Power* (New York: Guilford, 1994); David Delaney, "The Boundaries of Responsibility: Interpretations of

Geography in School Desegregation Cases," in *The Legal Geographies Reader*, ed. Nicholas K. Blomley, David Delaney, and Richard T. Ford (Oxford: Blackwell, 2001), 54–68; David Delaney, *Law and Nature* (Cambridge: Cambridge University Press, 2003); David Delaney, *Race, Place and the Law* (Austin: University of Texas Press, 1998).

31. For a full account of these, see Tim Cresswell, *The Tramp in America* (London: Reaktion, 2001).

32. *United States v. Guest*, 383 U.S. 745 (1966), 767.

33. Orlando Lewis, *Vagrancy in the United States* (New York: Self-published, 1907), 13.

34. For interesting accounts, see A. L. Beier, *Masterless Men: The Vagrancy Problem in England 1560–1640* (London: Methuen, 1985); Ian Hacking, "Les Alienes Voyageurs: How Fugue Became a Medical Entity," *History of Psychiatry* 7 (1996): 425–49.

35. I am drawing here on the work of Engin Isin. See Engin F. Isin, *Being Political: Genealogies of Citizenship* (Minneapolis: University of Minnesota Press, 2002); Engin F. Isin and Patricia K. Wood, *Citizenship and Identity, Politics and Culture* (London: Sage, 1999).

36. Isin, *Being Political: Genealogies of Citizenship*, 3.

37. Ibid., 4.

38. For an account of legal rights, see Delaney, "The Boundaries of Responsibility: Interpretations of Geography in School Desegregation Cases."

39. Chafee, *Three Human Rights in the Constitution of 1787*.

40. Karl Marx, "On the Jewish Question," in *The Marx-Engels Reader*, ed. Robert C Tuckner (New York: Norton, 1978), 26–52, 35.

41. Ibid., 43.

42. Duncan Kennedy, "The Critique of Rights in Critical Legal Studies," in *Left Legalism/Left Critique*, ed. Wendy Brown and Janet Halley (Durham, NC: Duke University Press, 2002), 178–228, 214. Others are not so dismissive. They see rights as flawed but instrumentally useful for social movements in Western democracies. The legal scholar Patricia Williams has been particularly forceful in making these arguments on behalf of black people, and in particular black women, given their struggle for rights in the context of the United States. "Rights" she argues "feel new in the mouths of most black people." See Patricia J. Williams, *The Alchemy of Race and Rights* (Cambridge, MA: Harvard University Press, 1991), 164.

43. Mark Tushnet, "An Essay on Rights," *Texas Law Review* 62, no. 8 (1984): 1363–403, 1382.

44. Nicholas K. Blomley and Geraldine Pratt, "Canada and the Political Geographies of Rights," *Canadian Geographer* 45, no. 1 (2001): 151–66.

45. Ibid., 155.

46. Ibid., 163.

47. Audrey Kobayashi and Brian Ray, "Civil Risk and Landscapes of Marginality in Canada: A Pluralist Approach to Social Justice," *Canadian Geographer* 44 (2000): 401–17, 405.

48. Linda Peake and Brian Ray, "Racializing the Canadian Landscape: Whiteness, Uneven Geographies and Social Justice," *Canadian Geographer* 45, no. 1 (2001): 180–86, 184.

49. Ibid.

50. Vera Chouinard, "Legal Peripheries: Struggles over Disabled Canadians' Places in Law, Society and Space," *Canadian Geographer* 45, no. 1 (2001): 187–92; Rob Imrie, "Disability and Discourses of Mobility and Movement," *Environment and Planning A* 32, no. 9 (2000): 1641–56.

51. Vera Chouinard, "Legal Peripheries: Struggles Over Disabled Canadians' Places in Law, Society and Space," *Canadian Geographer* 45, no. 1 (2001): 187–92, 187.

52. Imrie, "Disability and Discourses of Mobility and Movement," 1641–42.

53. Ivan Illich, *Energy and Equity, Ideas in Progress* (New York: Harper & Row, 1974), 79.

54. Ivan Illich, *Toward a History of Needs* (New York: Pantheon Books, 1978), 119.

55. This idea is fully developed in Celeste Langan, "Mobility Disability," *Public Culture* 13, no. 3 (2001): 459–84.

56. Ibid., 465.

57. I am grateful to members of the Bus Riders Union for talking to me about these issues. I also acknowledge the assistance of Tom Rubin who spent several hours going over the history of Los Angeles transit and the BRU case against the MTA. Existing accounts of the Bus Riders Union can be found in Robert D. Bullard, Glenn S. Johnson, and Angel O. Torres, *Highway Robbery: Transportation Racism & New Routes to Equity* (Cambridge, MA: South End Press, 2004); Mike Davis, *Dead Cities, and Other Tales* (New York: New Press, distributed by W.W. Norton, 2002); Robert Garcia and Thomas A. Rubin, "Cross Road Blues: The MTA Consent Decree and Just Transportation," in *Running on Empty: Transport, Social Exclusion and Environmental Justice*, ed. Karen Lucas (London: Policy Press, 2004).

58. Blomley and Pratt, "Canada and the Political Geographies of Rights," 163.

59. I take this notion from Anna Bullen and Mark Whitehead, "Negotiating the Networks of Space, Time and Substance: A Geographical Perspective on the Sustainable Citizen," *Citizenship Studies* 9, no. 5 (2005): 499–516.

60. I am thinking here of Michael Brown, *Replacing Citizenship: Aids, Activism and Radical Democracy* (New York: Guilford, 1997); Bullen and Whitehead, "Negotiating the Networks of Space, Time and Substance: A Geographical Perspective on the Sustainable Citizen"; Luke Desforges, Rhys Jones, and Mike Woods, "New Geographies of Citizenship," *Citizenship Studies* 9, no, 5 (2005): 439–451; J. Painter and C. Philo, "Spaces of Citizenship: An Introduction," *Political Geography* 14, no. 2 (1995): 107–20; Susan Smith, "Society, Space and Citizenship: A Human Geography for New Times," *Transactions of the Institute of British Geographers* 14 (1990): 144–56.

61. Here I am following the development of the idea of spatial justice developed by Edward Soja, who mentions the work of the Bus Riders Union. See Edward W. Soja, *Postmetropolis: Critical Studies of Cities and Regions* (Oxford: Blackwell Publishers, 2000).

62. For a thorough account of the history of public transportation planning in Los Angeles and the particular problems of rail development, see William B. Fulton, *The Reluctant Metropolis: The Politics of Urban Growth in Los Angeles* (Point Arena, CA: Solano Press Books, 1997), chapter 5.

63. "Fighting for Equality in Public Transit: Labor Community Strategy Center v. MTA," Environmental Defense, http://www.environmentaldefense.org/article.cfm?contentid=2826 (accessed January 29, 2004).

64. *Labour Community Strategy Center v. MTA*: Case No.CV94-5936 TJH (MCX) Federal District Court, Los Angeles Summary of the Evidence, December 4, 1995, para 12a.

65. E. Bailey, "From Welfare Lines to Commuting Crush," *Los Angeles Times*, October 6, 1997.

66. Judge Hatter's Preliminary Injunction against the MTA, 1–2. *Labour Community Strategy Center v. MTA. Findings of Fact and Conclusions of Law re: Preliminary Injunction (Sept. 21, 1994)* Case No.CV94-5936 TJH (MCX) Federal District Court, Los Angeles.

67. Rita Burgos and Laura Pulido, "The Politics of Gender in the Los Angeles Bus Riders Union/Sindicato De Pasajaros," *Capitalism Nature Society* 9, no. 3 (1998): 75–82.

68. Ibid., 80–81.

69. Linda Peake and Brian Ray, "Racializing the Canadian Landscape: Whiteness, Uneven Geographies and Social Justice," *Canadian Geographer* 45, no. 1 (2001): 180–86, 184.

70. E. Balibar, "Ambiguous Universality," *Differences* 7 (spring 1995): 48–74, 65.

71. Iris Marion Young, *Justice and the Politics of Difference* (Princeton, NJ: Princeton University Press, 1990).

72. Eric Mann et al., "An Environmental Justice Strategy for Urban Transportation in Atlanta: Lessons and Observations from Los Angeles," (Los Angeles: Labor/Community Strategy Center, 2001), 25.

## Chapter 7

1. H. Mark Lai et al., *Island: Poetry and History of Chinese Immigrants on Angel Island, 1910–1940* (San Francisco; distributed by San Francisco Study Center, 1980), 102.

2. Ibid., 94.

3. Here we are building on Bonnie Honig, *Democracy and the Foreigner* (Princeton, NJ: Princeton University Press, 2001); Lisa Lowe, *Immigrant Acts: On Asian American Cultural Politics* (Durham, NC: Duke University Press, 1996).

4. Ian Hacking, "Making Up People," in *Reconstructing Individualism: Autonomy, Individuality, and the Self in Western Thought*, ed. T. Heller, M. Sosna, and D. Wellbery (Stanford, CA: Stanford University Press, 1986), 222–36.

5. Tim Cresswell, "The Production of Mobilities," *New Formations* 43 (spring 2001): 3–25; Jennifer Hyndeman, "Border Crossings," *Antipode* 29, no. 2 (1997): 149–76; Doreen Massey, "Power-Geometry and Progressive Sense of Place," in *Mapping the Futures: Local Cultures, Global Change*, ed. Jon Bird

et al. (London: Routledge, 1993), 59–69. Jean François Lyotard and Jean-Loup Thébaud, *Just Gaming, Theory and History of Literature* (Minneapolis: University of Minnesota Press, 1985); Iris Marion Young, *Justice and the Politics of Difference* (Princeton, NJ: Princeton University Press, 1990).

6.  Jean-Francois Lyotard, *The Postmodern Condition: A Report on Knowledge* (Minneapolis: University of Minnesota Press, 1984), 82.

7.  Ibid., 81.

8.  Lyotard and Thébaud, *Just Gaming*, 93.

9.  Ibid., 94.

10. Young, *Justice and the Politics of Difference*.

11. Ibid., 156.

12. Ibid., 157.

13. Ibid., 158.

14. Daniel Boorstin, *The Americans: The National Experience* (London: Weidenfeld and Nicholson, 1966); James M. Jasper, *Restless Nation: Starting Over in America* (Chicago, IL: University of Chicago Press, 2000); Frederick Jackson Turner, *The Frontier in American History* (New York: Holt, Rinehart and Winston, 1947); Wilbur Zelinsky, *The Cultural Geography of the United States* (Englewood Cliffs, NJ: Prentice Hall, 1973).

15. Alan M. Kraut, *Silent Travelers: Germs, Genes, and the "Immigrant Menace"* (Baltimore, MD: Johns Hopkins University Press, 1995); David Ward, *Poverty, Ethnicity and the American City, 1840–1925* (Cambridge: Cambridge University Press, 1989).

16. *The Chinese Exclusion Act 1882* Forty-Seventh Congress. Session I. 1882 Chapter 126 (http://www.ourdocuments.gov/doc.php?doc=47&page=transcript (accessed 1/4/06)

17. *The Chinese Exclusion Act 1882*.

18. Roger Daniels, *Not Like Us: Immigrants and Minorities in America, 1890–1924*, (Chicago, IL: Ivan R. Dee, 1997), 7.

19. Kay Anderson, *Vancouver's Chinatown: Racial Discourse in Canada, 1875–1980* (Montreal: McGill-Queen's University Press, 1991); Susan Craddock, *City of Plagues: Disease, Poverty, and Deviance in San Francisco* (Minneapolis: University of Minnesota Press, 2000).

20. Daniels, *Not Like Us: Immigrants and Minorities in America, 1890–1924*.

21. See Lucy E. Salyer, *Laws Harsh as Tigers: Chinese Immigrants and the Shaping of Modern Immigration Law* (Chapel Hill: University of North Carolina Press, 1995); John C. Torpey, *The Invention of the Passport: Surveillance, Citizenship, and the State*, (Cambridge: Cambridge University Press, 2000).

22. For accounts of this process, see Torpey, *The Invention of the Passport: Surveillance, Citizenship, and the State*; Aristide Zolberg, "Matters of State: Theorizing Immigration Policy," in *The Handbook of International Migration: The American Experience*, ed. Josh DeWind and Philip Kasinitz (New York: Russell Sage, 1999), 71–93.

23. I take this account from David Delaney, "Laws of Motion and Immobilization: Bodies, Figures and the Politics of Mobility" (paper presented at the Mobilities Conference, Gregynog, Newtown, Wales, 1999).

24. Mary Coolidge cited in Torpey, *The Invention of the Passport: Surveillance, Citizenship, and the State*, 99.
25. Ibid., 7.
26. *Peopling of America Theme Study Act 2000*, 106th Congress, 2nd Session, S.2478
27. *Peopling of America Theme Study Act 2000*, § 2,
28. Official Press Release, February 14th, 2001, (our emphasis).
29. Steven Hoelscher, "Conserving Diversity: Provincial Cosmopolitanism and America's Multicultural Heritage," in *Textures of Place: Exploring Humanist Geographies*, ed. Paul Adams, Steven Hoelscher, and Karen Till (Minneapolis: University of Minnesota Press, 2001), 375–402.
30. Honig, *Democracy and the Foreigner*.
31. Ibid., 74.
32. Ibid., 75.
33. Citing Ali Behdad, ibid., 77.
34. Ibid., 78.
35. Ibid., 97.
36. Engin F. Isin, *Being Political: Genealogies of Citizenship* (Minneapolis: University of Minnesota Press, 2002).
37. Lowe, *Immigrant Acts: On Asian American Cultural Politics*, 2.
38. Young, *Justice and the Politics of Difference*, 172.
39. *Peopling of America Theme Study Act 2000*, § 4B.
40. Wikipedia.com (http://en.wikisource.org/wiki/California_Proposition_187_ (1994)) (Accessed 5 January 2006).
41. For classic accounts, see Boorstin, *The Americans: The National Experience*; Turner, *The Frontier in American History*. In geography, claims for the unique and exceptional quality of American mobility have been made in J. B. Jackson, *Landscape in Sight: Looking at America* (New Haven, CT: Yale University Press, 1997); Zelinsky, *The Cultural Geography of the United States*.

## Chapter 8

1. Virginia Scharff, *Taking the Wheel: Women and the Coming of the Motor Age* (New York: Free Press, 1991).
2. Clay McShane, *Down the Asphalt Path: The Automobile and the American City* (New York: Columbia University Press, 1994).
3. Robert Sklar, *Movie-Made America: A Cultural History of American Movies* (London: Chappell and Company, 1978).
4. Jean Bethke Elshtain, *Public Man, Private Woman: Women in Social and Political Thought* (Princeton, NJ: Princeton University Press, 1993); Eleanor Flexner, *Century of Struggle: The Woman's Rights Movement in the United States* (Cambridge, MA: Belknap Press of Harvard University Press, 1975); Aileen S. Kraditor, *The Ideas of the Woman Suffrage Movement, 1890–1920* (New York: Columbia University Press, 1965); Mary P. Ryan, *Women in Public: From Banners to Ballots, 1825–1880* (Baltimore, MD: Johns Hopkins

University Press, 1989); Joan Wallach Scott, *Gender and the Politics of History* (New York: Columbia University Press, 1988).

5. Caren Kaplan, *Questions of Travel: Postmodern Discourses of Displacement* (Durham, NC: Duke University Press, 1996); Janet Wolff, "On the Road Again: Metaphors of Travel in Cultural Criticism," *Cultural Studies* 6 (1992): 224–39.

6. Susan Hanson and Geraldine J. Pratt, *Gender, Work, and Space* (London and New York: Routledge, 1995); Robin Law, "Beyond 'Women and Transport': Towards New Geographies of Gender and Daily Mobility," *Progress in Human Geography* 23, no. 4 (1999): 567–88. Susan Buck-Morss, "The Flâneur, the Sandwichman and the Whore: The Politics of Loitering," *New German Critique* 39 (1986): 99–141; Mona Domosh, "Those 'Gorgeous Incongruities': Polite Politics and Public Space on the Streets of Nineteenth-Century New York City," *Annals of the Association of American Geographers* 88, no. 2 (1998): 209–26; Janet Wolff, "The Invisible Flâneuse: Women and the Literature of Modernity," in *Feminine Sentences: Essays on Women and Culture*, ed. Janet Wolff (Oxford: Polity, 1990), 34–50. Alison Blunt, *Travel, Gender and Imperialism: Mary Kingsley and West Africa*, ed. Michael Dear, Derek Gregory, and Nigel Thrift, Mappings (New York: Guilford, 1994); Sara Mills, *Discourses of Difference* (London: Routledge, 1991); Benedicte Monicat, "Autobiography and Women's Travel Writings in Nineteenth-Century France: Journeys through Self-Representation," *Gender, Place and Culture* 1, no. 1 (1994): 61–70; Karen Morin, "A 'Female Columbus' in 1887 America: Marking New Social Territory," *Gender, Place and Culture* 2, no. 2 (1995): 191–208. Tim Cresswell, "Embodiment, Power and the Politics of Mobility: The Case of Female Tramps and Hobos," *Transactions of the Institute of British Geographers* 24 (1999): 175–92; Tim Cresswell, *The Tramp in America* (London: Reaktion, 2001).

7. Linda McDowell, "Off the Road: Alternative Views of Rebellion, Resistance, and the 'Beats,'" *Transactions of the Institute of British Geographers* 21, no. 2 (1996): 412–19; Geraldine Pratt, "Geographies of Identity and Difference: Marking Boundaries," in *Human Geography Today*, ed. Doreen Massey, John Allen, and Philip Sarre (Cambridge: Polity, 1999), 151–68.

8. John Urry, *Sociology Beyond Societies: Mobilities for the Twenty-First Century* (London; New York: Routledge, 2000).

9. Daniel T. Rodgers, *Atlantic Crossings: Social Politics in a Progressive Age* (Cambridge, MA: Belknap Press of Harvard University Press, 1998).

10. Celeste Langan, "Mobility Disability," *Public Culture* 13, no. 3 (2001): 459–84.

11. Catherine Hall, *White, Male and Middle-Class: Explorations in Feminism and History* (NY: Routledge, 1992).

12. Peter Linebaugh and Marcus Buford Rediker, *The Many-Headed Hydra: The Hidden History of the Revolutionary Atlantic* (Boston: Beacon Press, 2000); Hall, *White, Male and Middle-Class: Explorations in Feminism and History*; Paul Gilroy, *The Black Atlantic: Modernity and Double Consciousness* (Cambridge, MA: Harvard University Press, 1993).

13. Flexner, *Century of Struggle: The Woman's Rights Movement in the United States*; S. J. Kleinberg, *Women in the United States, 1830–1945* (New Brunswick, NJ: Rutgers University Press, 1999).

14. Sharon Strom, "Leadership and Tactics in the American Woman Suffrage Movement: A New Perspective from Massachusetts" *Journal of American History* 62, no. 2 (1975): 296–315.

15. See, for instance, Flexner, *Century of Struggle: The Woman's Rights Movement in the United States*; Kraditor, *The Ideas of the Woman Suffrage Movement, 1890–1920*.

16. Strom, "Leadership and Tactics in the American Woman Suffrage Movement: A New Perspective from Massachusetts," 304.

17. Flexner, *Century of Struggle: The Woman's Rights Movement in the United States*.

18. Ryan, *Women in Public: From Banners to Ballots, 1825–1880*.

19. Sarah Deutsch, *Women and the City: Gender, Space and Power in Boston, 1870–1940* (Oxford: Oxford University Press, 2002), 223.

20. Dennis Ryan, *Beyond the Ballot Box: Social History and the Boston Irish, 1845–1917* (Boston: University of Massachusetts Press, 1989).

21. Sharon Strom, *Political Woman: Florence Luscomb and the Legacy of Radical Reform* (Philadelphia, PA: Temple University Press, 2001).

22. Deutsch, *Women and the City: Gender, Space and Power in Boston, 1870–1940*, 223.

23. This clipping comes from Luscomb's archive and does not include the title of the publication or date. The column is headed "Suffragists Go to England."

24. Gilroy, *The Black Atlantic: Modernity and Double Consciousness*, 4.

25. Linebaugh and Rediker, *The Many-Headed Hydra: The Hidden History of the Revolutionary Atlantic*, 144.

26. Ibid., 151.

27. David Armitage, "Three Concepts of Atlantic History," in *The British Atlantic World 1500–1800*, ed. David Armitage and Michael Braddick (Basingstoke: Palgrave Macmillan, 2002), 11–27, 16.

28. Journal of Florence Luscomb, April 6, 1911 FHL, Box 206. This and following citations are taken from the travel journal of Florence Luscomb, which is held in Florence Hope Luscomb Collection (box 9 folder 206) in the Schlesinger Library, Radcliff College, Harvard University, Cambridge, Massachusetts.

29. Journal of Florence Luscomb, April 7, 1911, FHL Box 206.

30. Journal of Florence Luscomb, April 10, 1911, FLH Box 206.

31. Journal of Florence Luscomb, April 10, 1911, FHL Box 206.

32. Journal of Florence Luscomb, April 12, 1911, FHL Box 206.

33. Rodgers, *Atlantic Crossings: Social Politics in a Progressive Age*.

34. Gilroy, *The Black Atlantic*.

35. James Buzard, *The Beaten Track: European Tourism, Literature, and the Ways to Culture, 1800–1918* (Oxford: Oxford University Press, 1992); David Crouch, *Leisure/Tourism Geographies: Practices and Geographical Knowledge*, Critical Geographies; 3 (London; New York: Routledge, 1999); Eeva

Jokinen and Soile Veijola, "The Disorientated Tourist: The Figuration of the Tourist in Contemporary Cultural Studies," in *Touring Cultures*, ed. John Urry and Chris Rojek (London: Routledge, 1997), 23–51; Dean MacCannell, *The Tourist: A New Theory of the Leisure Class* (New York: Schocken Books, 1989); Urry, *Sociology beyond Societies: Mobilities for the Twenty-First Century*; John Urry, *The Tourist Gaze: Leisure and Travel in Contemporary Societies* (London and Newbury Park, CA: Sage Publications, 1990).

36. Cynthia H. Enloe, *Bananas, Beaches & Bases: Making Feminist Sense of International Politics* (London: Pandora, 1989), 28.

37. Jokinen and Veijola, "The Disorientated Tourist: The Figuration of the Tourist in Contemporary Cultural Studies"; Vivian Kinnaird and Derek R. Hall, *Tourism: A Gender Analysis* (New York: John Wiley & Sons, 1994); M. Swain, "Gender in Tourism," *Annals of Tourism Research* 22, no. 2 (1995): 247–66.

38. Journal of Florence Luscomb April 16, 1911, FHL Box 206.

39. Journal of Florence Luscomb April 17, 1911, FHL Box 206.

40. Journal of Florence Luscomb April 18, 1911, FHL Box 206.

41. Journal of Florence Luscomb April 30, 1911, FHL Box 206.

42. MacCannell, *The Tourist: A New Theory of the Leisure Class*, 61.

43. Piers Brendon, *Thomas Cook: 150 Years of Popular Tourism* (London: Secker & Warburg, 1991); John Pudney et al., *The Thomas Cook Story* (London: M. Joseph, 1953); Louis Turner and John Ash, *The Golden Hordes: International Tourism and the Pleasure Periphery* (London: Constable, 1975).

44. *Cook's Excursionist and Cheap Trip Advertiser*, August 20, 1855, 2, in Enloe, 28.

45. Journal of Florence Luscomb, June 10, 1911, FHL Box 206.

46. Walter Benjamin, *The Arcades Project* (Cambridge, MA: Belknap Press of Harvard University Press, 1999); Keith Tester, ed., *The Flâneur* (London: Routledge, 1994); Wolff, "The Invisible Flâneuse: Women and the Literature of Modernity."

47. Journal of Florence Luscomb May 6, 1911, FHL Box 206.

48. Journal of Florence Luscomb April 20, 1911, FHL Box 206.

49. Journal of Florence Luscomb June 3, 1911, FHL Box 206.

50. Journal of Florence Luscomb May 17, 1911, FHL Box 206.

51. Journal of Florence Luscomb May 17, 1911, FHL Box 206.

52. Marshall Berman, *All That Is Solid Melts into Air: The Experience of Modernity* (Harmondsworth: Penguin, 1988); Michel de Certeau, *The Practice of Everyday Life* (Berkeley, CA: University of California Press, 1984); Rebecca Solnit, *Wanderlust: A History of Walking* (New York: Viking, 2000); Tester, ed., *The Flâneur.*

53. de Certeau, *The Practice of Everyday Life*, 101.

54. Berman, *All That Is Solid Melts into Air: The Experience of Modernity.*

55. Wolff, "The Invisible Flâneuse: Women and the Literature of Modernity."

56. Domosh, "Those 'Gorgeous Incongruities': Polite Politics and Public Space on the Streets of Nineteenth-Century New York City."

57. Journal of Florence Luscomb, May 4, 1911, FHL Box 206.

58. These quotations are taken from an article titled "Women Defend Motorists of their Own Sex," which is a clipping in the Margaret Foley Collection

(Series III, File 60), Schlesinger Library, Radcliff College, Harvard University, Cambridge, Massachusetts.

59. *The Boston American*, Sunday, October 15, 1911.
60. *The Boston American*, Sunday, October 15, 1911.
61. This and the following quote are taken from newspaper clippings in the Margaret Foley collection (Series III, File 60), but do not include the source title or date.
62. Strom, *Political Woman: Florence Luscomb and the Legacy of Radical Reform*, 87.
63. Letter from Florence Luscomb to Hannah S. (Knox) Luscomb, summer 1915, FHL Box 93.
64. Sidonie Smith, *Moving Lives: Twentieth Century Women's Travel Writing* (Minneapolis: University of Minnesota Press, 2001), 26.
65. *Boston Post*, October 13, 1911.
66. Kathleen Barry, *Susan B. Anthony: Biography of a Singular Feminist* (New York: 1st Books, 2000).
67. Kleinberg, *Women in the United States, 1830–1945*; Carroll Smith-Rosenberg, *Disorderly Conduct: Visions of Gender in Victorian America* (New York: A. A. Knopf, 1985).
68. Deutsch, *Women and the City: Gender, Space and Power in Boston, 1870–1940*.
69. Margaret Mary Finnegan, *Selling Suffrage: Consumer Culture & Votes for Women* (New York: Columbia University Press, 1999); Elizabeth Wilson, *The Sphinx in the City* (Berkeley: University of California Press, 1991).
70. Strom, "Leadership and Tactics in the American Woman Suffrage Movement: A New Perspective from Massachusetts."

*Chapter 9*

1. For recent discussions of airports, see Mark Gottdiener, *Life in the Air: Surviving the New Culture of Air Travel* (Lanham, MD: Rowman & Littlefield, 2000); David Pascoe, *Airspaces* (London: Reaktion, 2001).
2. Mike Crang, "Between Places: Producing Hubs, Flows, and Networks," *Environment and Planning a* 34 (2002): 569–74, 571.
3. Marc Augé, *Non-Places: Introduction to an Anthropology of Supermodernity* (London; New York: Verso, 1995), 110. This idea of airports as a kind of nonplace is now commonplace. The artist Robert Smithson referred to the airport as a "non-site" in "Towards the Development of an Air Terminal Site," in Robert Smithson and Nancy Holt, *The Writings of Robert Smithson: Essays with Illustrations* (New York: New York University Press, 1979).
4. Hans Ibelings, *Supermodernism: Architecture in the Age of Globalization* (Rotterdam: NAi, 1998), 78–79.
5. Ibid., 80.
6. Iain Chambers, *Border Dialogues: Journeys in Postmodernity* (London; New York: Routledge, 1990), 57–58.
7. Rosi Braidotti, *Nomadic Subjects: Embodiment and Sexual Difference in Contemporary Feminist Theory* (New York: Columbia University Press, 1994), 18.

8. M. Brown, "A Flying Leap into the Future," *Metropolis*, July/August (1995): 50–79, 79.

9. Pico Iyer, "Where Worlds Collide," *Harper's Magazine*, August 1995, 51.

10. Ibid.

11. Kevin Hetherington, "Whither the World?—Presence, Absence and the Globe," in *Mobilizing Place, Placing Mobility: The Politics of Representation in a Globalized World*, ed. Tim Cresswell and Ginette Verstraete (Amsterdam: Rodopi, 2002), 173–88, 179.

12. Pico Iyer, *The Global Soul: Jet Lag, Shopping Malls, and the Search for Home* (New York: Knopf, 2000).

13. Crang, "Between Places: Producing Hubs, Flows, and Networks," 573.

14. See Peter Adey, "Secured and Sorted Mobilities: Examples from the Airport," *Surveillance and Society* 1, no. 4 (2004): 500–19.

15. Manuel Castells, *The Rise of the Network Society* (Oxford: Blackwell Publishers, 1996), 417.

16. This information is given in: Municipal Airport of Amsterdam, *Schiphol: Gemeente Luchthaven Amsterdam (Illustrated Guide of Municipal Airport of Amsterdam)* (1929). This and other guides to the airport are available in the Municipal Archives of Amsterdam.

17. This information is from: Municipal Airport of Amsterdam, *Gemeente Luchthaven Amsterdam (Illustrated Guide to Municipal Airport of Amsterdam)* (1936). Municipal Archives of Amsterdam.

18. Pascoe, *Airspaces*, 75.

19. This recent information is from Reinier Gerritsen and Luuk Kramer, *Schiphol Airport* (Rotterdam: NAi Publishers, 1999).

20. This and the following quotations are taken from an interview with Jan Benthem, November 18, 2003 at Schiphol Airport.

21. For a perceptive account of this, on which I draw here, see Ginette Verstraete, "Technological Frontiers and the Politics of Mobility in the European Union," *New Formations* 43 (spring 2001): 26–43.

22. The original signatories of the Schengen Agreement were Belgium, France, Germany, Luxemburg, and the Netherlands. These countries have been joined by Austria, Denmark, Finland, Greece, Iceland, Italy, Portugal, Norway, Spain, and Sweden.

23. Verstraete, "Technological Frontiers and the Politics of Mobility in the European Union," 29.

24. European Commission, *Freedom of Movement, Europe on the Move* (Brussels: Office for Official Publications of the European Communities, 1994), 3.

25. Ibid., 1.

26. Pascal Fontaine, *A Citizen's Europe* (Luxembourg: 1993), 7–8.

27. For insightful commentary on the role of mobility in European identity construction, see Ginette Verstraete, "Heading for Europe: Tourism and the Global Itinarary of an Idea," in *Mobilizing Place, Placing Mobility: The Politics of Representation in a Globalized World*, ed. Tim Cresswell and Ginette Verstraete (Amsterdam: Rodopi, 2002), 33–52; Verstraete,

"Technological Frontiers and the Politics of Mobility in the European Union."

28. Stephen Graham and Simon Marvin, *Splintering Urbanism Networked Infrastructures, Technological Mobilities and the Urban Condition* (London: Routledge, 2001), 364.

29. See Adey, "Secured and Sorted Mobilities: Examples from the Airport"; Peter Adey, "Surveillance at the Airport: Surveilling Mobility/Mobilising Surveillance," *Environment and Planning A* (2004); Michael Curry, "The Profiler's Question and the Treacherous Traveler: Narratives of Belonging in Commercial Aviation," *Surveillance and Society* 1, no. 4 (2004): 475–99; Martin Dodge and Rob Kitchin, "Flying through Code/Space: The Real Virtuality of Air Travel," *Environment and Planning A* 36 (2004): 195–211.

30. Dodge and Kitchin, "Flying through Code/Space: The Real Virtuality of Air Travel," 198.

31. For a wider interpretation of this phenomenon, see N. J. Thrift and S. French, "The Automatic Production of Space," *Transactions of the Institute of British Geographers* 27 (2002): 309–35.

32. Curry, "The Profiler's Question and the Treacherous Traveler: Narratives of Belonging in Commercial Aviation," 488.

33. Adey, "Surveillance at the Airport: Surveilling Mobility/Mobilising Surveillance."

34. Jonathan Crary, *Techniques of the Observer: On Vision and Modernity in the Nineteenth Century* (Cambridge, MA: MIT Press, 1990), 41.

35. Adey, "Surveillance at the Airport: Surveilling Mobility/Mobilising Surveillance"; Albert Battersby, *Network Analysis for Planning and Scheduling* (New York: Wiley, 1970).

36. A similar program (INSPASS) based on a scan of the hand is in operation in the United States with over 50,000 participants.

37. Privium website, http://www.schiphol.nl/schiphol/privium/privium_home.jsp (accessed June 14, 2004).

38. Gillian Fuller, "Perfect Match: Biometrics and Body Patterning in a Networked World," *Fibreculture Journal* 1 (2004). http://journal.fibreculture.org/issue1/issue1_fuller.html.

39. Adey, "Surveillance at the Airport: Surveilling Mobility/Mobilising Surveillance."

40. Martha Rosler, *Martha Rosler: In the Place of the Public: Observations of a Frequent Flyer* (New York: Cantz, 1998), 32.

41. This and all other quotations from Mijksenaar are taken from an interview conducted on November 20, 2003.

42. Gillian Fuller, "The Arrow-Directional Semiotics; Wayfinding in Transit," *Social Semiotics* 12, no. 3 (2002): 131–44, 131.

43. Augé, *Non-Places: Introduction to an Anthropology of Supermodernity.*

44. Fuller, "The Arrow - Directional Semiotics; Wayfinding in Transit," 135.

45. P. Mijksenaar, "Signs of the Times," *Airport World* 8, no. 4 (August–September 2003) http://www.mijksenaar.com/pauls_corner/index.html (accessed June 21, 2004).

46. For an account of this process see Patricia Leigh Brown, Fred Conrad, and Rebecca Cooney, "A Ray of Hope for Travellers Following Signs," *New York Times*, June 7, 2001. at http://www.mijksenaar.com/pauls_corner/index.html (accessed June 21, 2004).
47. Elizabeth Grosz, *Architecture from the Outside: Essays on Virtual and Real Space* (Cambridge, MA: MIT Press, 2001), 9.
48. Anthony Vidler, *Warped Space: Art, Architecture and Anxiety in Modern Culture* (Cambridge, MA: MIT Press, 2001), 185.
49. Ibid., 181.
50. Michel Serres, *Angels, a Modern Myth* (Paris: Flammarion, 1995), 19.
51. Kim Hopper, *Reckoning with Homelessness, The Anthropology of Contemporary Issues* (Ithaca, NY: Cornell University Press, 2003), 125.
52. Leon Deben, "Public Space and the Homeless in Amsterdam," in *Amsterdam Human Capital*, ed. Sako Musterd and Willem Salet (Amsterdam: Amsterdam University Press, 2003), 229–46, 238.
53. Ibid.
54. Personal communication with Leon Deben, February 25, 2004.
55. Castells, *The Rise of the Network Society*, 416.
56. Zygmunt Bauman, *Globalization: The Human Consequences* (New York: Columbia University Press, 1998), 86.
57. Ibid.
58. Ibid., 89.

## Epilogue

1. See Stephen Goddard, *Getting There: the Epic Struggle between Road and Rail in the American Century* (Chicago, IL: University of Chicago Press, 1994).
2. *New York Times*, http://www.nytimes.com/2005/09/02/national/national-special /02response.html?th=&emc=th&pagewanted=all (accessed October 5, 2005).
3. Alison Stein Wellner, "No Exit," September 13, 2005, *Mother Jones*, www.motherjones.com/news/update/2005/09/no_car_emergency.html (accessed October 5, 2005).
4. Randal O'Toole, *Hawaii Reporter*, http://www.hawaiireporter.com/story.aspx?0c98e6ee-047f-41cd-9f86-3e450a4391bf). (accessed October 5, 2005).
5. Wellner, "No Exit."
6. Alan Berube and Steven Raphael, "Access to Cars in New Orleans," Brookings Institution, http://www.brookings.edu/metro/20050915_katrinacarstables.pdf (accessed October 9 2005).
7. CNN "Mayor moves to heal New Orleans' lifeblood industry," http://www.cnn.com/2005/US/10/07/neworleans.casinos/ (accessed October 5 2005).
8. This and further quotes are from U.S. Department of Transportation, www.dot.gov/affairs/minetasp051804.htm (accessed October 5, 2005).
9. Zygmunt Bauman, *Globalization: The Human Consequences* (New York: Columbia University Press, 1988), 89.

10. Associated Press online at www.wwltv.com/stories/wwl090605refugees_.306635f1.html (accessed October 5, 2005).
11. Ibid.
12. Ibid.
13. This and the following quotations are from Mike Pesca, "Are Katrina's Victims 'Refugees' or 'Evacuees?'"National Public Radio, www.npr.org/templates/story/story.php?storyId=4833613 (accessed October 5, 2005).
14. See Patricia Tuitt, *False Images: Law's Construction of the Refugee* (London: Pluto, 1996).

# Bibliography

Abler, Ronald., John. Adams, and Peter Gould. *Spatial Organization: The Geographer's View of the World*. Englewood Cliffs, NJ: Prentice Hall, 1971.

Adey, Peter. "Secured and Sorted Mobilities: Examples from the Airport." *Surveillance and Society* 1, no. 4 (2004): 500–19.

———. "Surveillance at the Airport: Surveilling Mobility/Mobilising Surveillance." *Environment and Planning A* 36, no. 8 (2004): 1365–1380.

Agnew, John. *The United States in the World Economy*. Cambridge: Cambridge University Press, 1987.

Anderson, Kay. *Vancouver's Chinatown: Racial Discourse in Canada, 1875–1980*. Montreal: McGill-Queen's University Press, 1991.

Anzaldua, Gloria. *Borderlands: La Frontera = the New Mestiza*. San Francisco, CA: Aunt Lute Books, 1987.

Appadurai, Arjun. *Modernity at Large: Cultural Dimensions of Globalization*. Minneapolis, MN: University of Minnesota Press, 1996.

Armitage, David. "Three Concepts of Atlantic History." In *The British Atlantic World 1500–1800*, edited by David Armitage and Michael Braddick, 11–27. Basingstoke: Palgrave Macmillan, 2002.

Arnold, Matthew, and John Dover Wilson. *Culture and Anarchy*. Cambridge: Cambridge University Press, 1935.

Atkinson, David. "Nomadic Strategies and Colonial Governance: Domination and the Resistance in Cyrenaice, 1923–1932." In *Entanglements of Power: Geographies of Domination/Resistance*, edited by Joanne Sharp, Paul Routledge, Chris Philo and Ronan Paddison, 256–68. London: Routledge, 2000.

Augé, Marc. *Non-Places: Introduction to an Anthropology of Supermodernity*. London and New York: Verso, 1995.

Bahnisch, Mark. "Embodied Work, Divided Labour: Subjectivity and the Scientific Management of the Body in Frederick W. Taylor's 1907 'Lecture on Management.'" *Body and Society* 6, no. 1 (2000): 51–68.

Bailey, E. "From Welfare Lines to Commuting Crush." *Los Angeles Times*, October 6, 1997, 1.

Bakhtin, Mikhail. *Rabelais and His World*. Bloomington: Indiana University Press, 1984.

Bale, John, and Joe Sang. *Kenyan Running: Movement Culture, Geography, and Global Change*. London and Portland, OR: Frank Cass, 1996.

Balibar, Ettiene. "Ambiguous Univerality." *Differences* 7 (spring 1995): 48–74.

Banta, Martha. *Taylored Lives: Narrative Productions in the Age of Taylor, Veblen, and Ford*. Chicago, IL: University of Chicago Press, 1993.

Barry, Kathleen. *Susan B. Anthony: Biography of a Singular Feminist*. New York: 1st Books, 2000.

Battersby, Albert. *Network Analysis for Planning and Scheduling*. New York: Wiley, 1970.

Baudrillard, Jean. *America*. London: Verso, 1988.

Bauman, Zygmunt. *Globalization: The Human Consequences*. New York: Columbia University Press, 1998.

———. *Legislators and Interpreters*. Oxford: Polity Press, 1987.

———. *Life in Fragment: Essays in Postmodern Morality*. Oxford: Blackwell, 1995.

———. *Liquid Modernity*. Cambridge: Polity Press, 2000.

———. *Modernity and Ambivalence*. Ithaca, NY: Cornell University Press, 1991.

Beard, George. "Causes of American Nervousness." In *Popular Culture and Industrialism*, edited by Henry Nash Smith, 57–70. New York: New York University Press, 1967.

Beard, George Miller. *American Nervousness; Its Causes and Consequences, a Supplement to Nervous Exhaustion (Neurasthenia)*. New York: G. P. Putnam's Sons, 1881.

Beier, A. L. *Masterless Men: The Vagrancy Problem in England 1560–1640*. London: Methuen, 1985.

Benjamin, Walter. *The Arcades Project*. Cambridge, MA: Belknap Press of Harvard University Press, 1999.

Berch, Bettina. "Scientific Management in the Home: The Empresses New Clothes." *Journal of American Culture* 3, no. 3 (1980): 440–45.

Berger, John. *Into Their Labours: A Trilogy*. New York: Pantheon Books, 1991.

Berman, Marshall. *All That Is Solid Melts into Air: The Experience of Modernity*. Harmondsworth: Penguin, 1988.

Best, Steven, and Douglas Kellner. *Postmodern Theory: Critical Interrogations, Critical Perspectives*. New York: Guilford Press, 1991.

Blomley, Nicholas K. *Law, Space and the Geographies of Power*. New York: Guilford, 1994.

Blomley, Nicholas K., David Delaney, and Richard T. Ford. *The Legal Geographies Reader: Law, Power, and Space*. Oxford and Malden, MA: Blackwell Publishers, 2001.

Blomley, Nicholas K., and Geraldine Pratt. "Canada and the Political Geographies of Rights." *Canadian Geographer* 45, no. 1 (2001): 151–66.

Blunt, Alison. *Travel, Gender and Imperialism: Mary Kingsley and West Africa*. New York: Guilford, 1994.

Boer, Inge. "No-Man's Land? Five Short Cases on Deserts and the Politics of Place." In *Mobilizing Place, Placing Mobility*, edited by Ginette Verstraete and Tim Cresswell, 155–72. Amsterdam: Rodopi, 2002.

Boorstin, Daniel. *The Americans: The National Experience*. London: Weidenfeld and Nicholson, 1966.

Bourdieu, Pierre. *Distinction: A Social Critique of the Judgement of Taste*. Cambridge, MA: Harvard University Press, 1984.

———. *The Logic of Practice*. Stanford, CA: Stanford University Press, 1990.

Boyer, M. Christine. *Dreaming the Rational City: The Myth of American City Planning*. Cambridge, MA: MIT Press, 1983.

Braidotti, Rosi. *Nomadic Subjects: Embodiment and Sexual Difference in Contemporary Feminist Theory*. New York: Columbia University Press, 1994.

Braun, Marta. *Picturing Time: The Work of Etienne-Jules Marey (1830–1904)*. Chicago, IL: University of Chicago Press, 1992.

Braun, Marta, and Elizabeth Whitcombe. "Marey, Muybridge, and Londe: The Photography of Pathological Locomotion." *History of Photography* 23, no. 3 (1999): 218–24.

Braverman, Harry. *Labor and Monopoly Capital*. New York: Monthly Review Press, 1974.

Brendon, Piers. *Thomas Cook: 150 Years of Popular Tourism*. London: Secker & Warburg, 1991.

Brown, M. "A Flying Leap into the Future." *Metropolis*, July/August (1995): 50–79.

Brown, Michael. *Replacing Citizenship: Aids, Activism and Radical Democracy*. New York: Guilford, 1997.

Bryson, Norman. "Cultural Studies and Dance History." In *Meaning in Motion: New Cultural Studies of Dance*, edited by Jane Desmond, 55–80. Durham, NC: Duke University Press, 1997.

Buckland, Theresa. "Edward Scott: The Last of the English Dancing Masters." *Dance Research* 21, no. 2 (2003): 3–35.

Buck-Morss, Susan. "The Flâneur, the Sandwichman and the Whore: The Politics of Loitering." *New German Critique* 39 (1986): 99–141.

Bullard, Robert D., Glenn S. Johnson, and Angel O. Torres. *Highway Robbery: Transportation Racism & New Routes to Equity*. Cambridge, MA: South End Press, 2004.

Bullen, Anna, and Mark Whitehead. "Negotiating the Networks of Space, Time and Substance: A Geographical Perspective on the Sustainable Citizen." *Citizenship Studies* 9, no. 5 (2005): 499–516.

Burch, Noël. *Life to Those Shadows*. Berkeley: University of California Press, 1990.

Burgess, Ernest. "The Growth of the City: An Introduction to a Research Project." In *The City: Suggestions for Investigation of Human Behavior in the Urban Environment*, edited by Robert Park and Ernest Burgess, 47–62. Chicago, IL: University of Chicago Press, 1925.

Burgos, Rita, and Laura Pulido. "The Politics of Gender in the Los Angeles Bus Riders' Union/Sindicato De Pasajaros." *Capitalism Nature Society* 9, no. 3 (1998): 75–82.

Butterfield, Gerald. "The Degeneracy of Dancing." *Dance Journal* II, no. 3 (1908): 2–3.

Buzard, James. *The Beaten Track: European Tourism, Literature, and the Ways to Culture, 1800–1918*. Oxford: Oxford University Press, 1992.

Canguilhem, Georges. *The Normal and the Pathological*. Cambridge, MA: Zone Books, 1989.

Casey, Edward S. *The Fate of Place: A Philosophical History*. Berkeley: University of California Press, 1998.

Castells, Manuel. *The Rise of the Network Society*. Cambridge, MA: Blackwell Publishers, 1996.

Chafee, Zechariah. *Three Human Rights in the Constitution of 1787*. Lawrence: University of Kansas Press, 1956.

Chambers, Iain. *Border Dialogues: Journeys in Postmodernity*. New York: Routledge, 1990.

———. *Migrancy, Culture, Identity*. London: Routledge, 1994.

Chouinard, Vera. "Legal Peripheries: Struggles over Disabled Canadians' Places in Law, Society and Space." *Canadian Geographer* 45, no. 1 (2001): 187–92.

Christ, Ronald, and Dennis Dollens. *New York: Nomadic Design*. Barcelona: Gustavo Gili, 1993.

Clifford, James. *Routes: Travel and Translation in the Later Twentieth Century*. Cambridge, MA: Harvard University Press, 1997.

———. "Traveling Cultures." In *Cultural Studies*, edited by Lawrence Grossberg, Cary Nelson and Paula Treichler, 96–111. London: Routledge, 1992.

Cooper, Emmanuel. *Fully Exposed: The Male Nude in Photography*. 2nd ed. London and New York: Routledge, 1995.

Copley, Frank Barkley. *Frederick W. Taylor, Father of Scientific Management*. New York: American Society of Mechanical Engineers, 1923.

Corbin, Alain. *The Foul and the Fragrant: Odor and the French Social Imagination*. Cambridge, MA: Harvard University Press, 1986.

Cowan, Ruth Schwartz. *More Work for Mother: The Ironies of Household Technology from the Open Hearth to the Microwave*. New York: Basic Books, 1983.

Craddock, Susan. *City of Plagues: Disease, Poverty, and Deviance in San Francisco*. Minneapolis: University of Minnesota Press, 2000.

Crang, Mike. "Between Places: Producing Hubs, Flows, and Networks." *Environment and Planning A* 34 (2002): 569–74.

Crary, Jonathan. *Suspensions of Perception: Attention, Spectacle, and Modern Culture*. Cambridge, MA: MIT Press, 1999.

———. *Techniques of the Observer: On Vision and Modernity in the Nineteenth Century*. Cambridge, MA: MIT Press, 1990.

Cresswell, Tim. "Embodiment, Power and the Politics of Mobility: The Case of Female Tramps and Hobos." *Transactions of the Institute of British Geographers* 24 (1999): 175–92.

————. *In Place/Out of Place: Geography, Ideology and Transgression*. Minneapolis: University of Minnesota Press, 1996.

————. *Place: A Short Introduction*. Oxford: Blackwell, 2004.

————. "The Production of Mobilities." *New Formations* 43 (spring 2001): 3–25.

————. *The Tramp in America*. London: Reaktion, 2001.

————. "Weeds, Plagues and Bodily Secretions: A Geographical Interpretation of Metaphors of Displacement." *Annals of the Association of American Geographers* 87, no. 2 (1997): 330–45.

Cronon, William. *Nature's Metropolis: Chicago and the Great West*. New York: Norton, 1991.

Crouch, David. *Leisure/Tourism Geographies*. New York: Routledge, 1999.

Curry, Michael. "The Profiler's Question and the Treacherous Traveler: Narratives of Belonging in Commercial Aviation." *Surveillance and Society* 1, no. 4 (2004): 475–99.

D'Albert, Charles. "The Evils of Imitative Teaching." *Dance Journal* 1, no. 2 (1907): 2–3.

Daniels, Roger. *Not Like Us: Immigrants and Minorities in America, 1890–1924*. Chicago: Ivan R. Dee, 1997.

Davies, Norman. *Europe: A History*. Oxford; New York: Oxford University Press, 1996.

Davis, Mike. *Dead Cities, and Other Tales*. New York: New Press: Distributed by W.W. Norton, 2002.

de Certeau, Michel. *The Practice of Everyday Life*. Berkeley: University of California Press, 1984.

Deben, Leon. "Public Space and the Homeless in Amsterdam." In *Amsterdam Human Capital*, edited by Sako Musterd and Willem Salet, 229–46. Amsterdam: Amsterdam University Press, 2003.

Delaney, David. "The Boundaries of Responsibility: Interpretations of Geography in School Desegregation Cases." In *The Legal Geographies Reader*, edited by Nicholas K. Blomley, David Delaney and Richard T. Ford, 54–68. Oxford: Blackwell, 2001.

————. *Law and Nature*. Cambridge, U.K.; New York: Cambridge University Press, 2003.

————. "Laws of Motion and Immobilization: Bodies, Figures and the Politics of Mobility." Paper presented at the Mobilities Conference, Gregynog, Newtown, Wales 1999.

————. *Race, Place and the Law*. Austin: University of Texas Press, 1998.

Deleuze, Gilles. *On the Line*. Brooklyn, NY: Autonomedia, 1999.

Deleuze, Gilles, and Félix Guattari. *Nomadology: The War Machine*. New York: Semiotext(e), 1986.

Deleuze, Gilles, and Félix Guattari. *A Thousand Plateaus: Capitalism and Schizophrenia*. Minneapolis: University of Minnesota Press, 1987.

Desforges, Luke, Rhys Jones, and Mike Woods. "New Geographies of Citizenship." *Citizenship Studies* 9. no. 5 (2005): 439–451.

Desmond, Jane. "Embodying Difference: Issues in Dance and Cultural Studies." *Cultural Critique* (winter 1993–94): 33–63.

————. *Meaning in Motion: New Cultural Studies of Dance*. Durham, NC: Duke University Press, 1997.

Deutsch, Sarah. *Women and the City: Gender, Space and Power in Boston, 1870–1940*. Oxford: Oxford University Press, 2002.

Dewsbury, J. D. "Performativity and the Event: Enacting a Philosophy of Difference." *Environment and Planning D: Society and Space* 18 (2000): 473–96.

Dixon, Deborah, and John Paul Jones. "My Dinner with Derrida: Or Spatial Analysis and Post-Structuralism Do Lunch." *Environment and Planning A* 30 (1998): 247–60.

Doane, Mary Ann. *The Emergence of Cinematic Time: Modernity, Contingency, the Archive*. Cambridge, MA: Harvard University Press, 2002.

Dodge, Martin, and Rob Kitchin. "Flying through Code/Space: The Real Virtuality of Air Travel." *Environment and Planning A* 36 (2004): 195–211.

Dodgshon, Robert. A. *The European Past: Social Evolution and Spatial Order*. Basingstoke, Hampshire: Macmillan Education, 1987.

Doel, Marcus A. *Poststructuralist Geographies: The Diabolical Art of Spatial Science*. Lanham, MD: Rowman & Littlefield, 1999.

Domosh, Mona. "Those "Gorgeous Incongruities": Polite Politics and Public Space on the Streets of Nineteenth-Century New York City." *Annals of the Association of American Geographers* 88, no. 2 (1998): 209–26.

Doray, Bernard. *From Taylorism to Fordism: A Rational Madness*. London: Free Association, 1988.

Douglas, George H. *All Aboard! The Railroad in American Life*. New York: Paragon House, 1992.

Durkheim, Emile. *The Division of Labour in Society, Contemporary Social Theory*. Houndmills, Basingstoke, Hampshire: Macmillan, 1984.

Edwards, Elizabeth. *Anthropology and Photography, 1860–1920*. New Haven: Yale University Press in association with the Royal Anthropological Institute London, 1992.

Ehrenreich, Barbara, and Deirdre English. *For Her Own Good: 150 Years of the Experts' Advice to Women*. Garden City, NY: Anchor Press, 1978.

Eliot, T. S. *Notes towards the Definition of Culture*. London: Faber and Faber, 1948.

Elshtain, Jean Bethke. *Public Man, Private Woman: Women in Social and Political Thought*. Princeton, NJ: Princeton University Press, 1993.

Enloe, Cynthia H. *Bananas, Beaches & Bases: Making Feminist Sense of International Politics*. London: Pandora, 1989.

Entrikin, J. Nicholas. *The Betweenness of Place: Towards a Geography of Modernity*. Baltimore, MD: Johns Hopkins University Press, 1991.

Feifer, Maxine. *Tourism in History: From Imperial Rome to the Present*. New York: Stein and Day, 1986.

Feldman, Leslie. *Freedom as Motion*. Lanham, MD: University Press of America, 2001.

Finnegan, Margaret Mary. *Selling Suffrage: Consumer Culture & Votes for Women*. New York: Columbia University Press, 1999.

Flexner, Eleanor. *Century of Struggle: The Woman's Rights Movement in the United States*. Cambridge, MA: Belknap Press of Harvard University Press, 1975.

Fontaine, Pascal. *A Citizen's Europe, Europe on the Move.* Luxembourg: Office for Official Publications of the European Communities, 1993.

Forer, Pip. "A Place for Plastic Space?" *Progress in Human Geography* 2 (1978): 230–67.

Foster, Sue. "The Ballerina's Phallic Pointe." In *Corporealities: Dancing Knowledge, Culture and Power,* edited by S. Foster, 1–24. London: Routledge, 1996.

Foucault, Michel. *Discipline and Punish: The Birth of the Prison.* New York: Vintage Books, 1979.

———. *Power/Knowledge.* New York: Pantheon, 1980.

Franko, M. "Five Theses on Laughter after All." In *Moving Words: Re-Writing Dance,* edited by G Morris, 43–62. London: Routledge, 1996.

Fraser, Angus M. *The Gypsies.* Oxford: Blackwell, 1992.

Fuller, Gillian. "The Arrow - Directional Semiotics; Wayfinding in Transit." *Social Semiotics* 12, no. 3 (2002): 131–44.

———. "Perfect Match: Biometrics and Body Patterning in a Networked World." *Fibreculture Journal* 1 (2004): n.p.

Fulton, William B. *The Reluctant Metropolis: The Politics of Urban Growth in Los Angeles.* Point Arena, CA: Solano Press Books, 1997.

Fussell, Paul. *Abroad: British Literary Traveling between the Wars.* New York: Oxford University Press, 1980.

Garcia, Robert, and Thomas A. Rubin. "Cross Road Blues: The MTA Consent Decree and Just Transportation." In *Running on Empty: Transport, Social Exclusion and Environmental Justice,* edited by Karen Lucas. London: The Policy Press, 2004.

Garrison, William Louis. *Studies of Highway Development and Geographic Change.* Seattle: University of Washington Press, 1959.

Gerritsen, Reinier, and Luuk Kramer. *Schiphol Airport.* Rotterdam: NAi Publishers, 1999.

Gilbreth, Frank Bunker, and Lillian Moller Gilbreth. *Applied Motion Study; a Collection of Papers on the Efficient Method to Industrial Preparedness.* New York: Sturgis & Walton company, 1917.

———. *Fatigue Study; the Elimination of Humanity's Greatest Unnecessary Waste, a First Step in Motion Study.* 2d. rev. ed. New York: Macmillan Company, 1919.

———. "Motion Models: Their Use in the Transference of Experience and the Presentation of Comparative Results in Educational Methods." Paper presented at the American Association for the Advancement of Science, Columbus, Ohio, December 27, 1915– January 1, 1916.

———. *Motion Study for the Handicapped.* London: G. Routledge & Sons Ltd., 1920.

Gilbreth, Frank Bunker, and Robert Thurston Kent. *Motion Study, a Method for Increasing the Efficiency of the Workman.* New York: D. Van Nostrand Company, 1911.

Gilpin, H. "Lifelessness in Movement, or How Do the Dead Move?" In *Corporealities: Dancing Knowledge, Culture and Power,* edited by S Foster, 106–28. London: Routledge, 1996.

Gilroy, Paul. *The Black Atlantic: Modernity and Double Consciousness.* Cambridge, MA: Harvard University Press, 1993.

Goldstein, Carolyn. "From Service to Sales: Home Economics in Light and Power 1920–1940." *Technology and Culture* 38, no. 1 (1997): 121–52.

Gottdiener, Mark. *Life in the Air: Surviving the New Culture of Air Travel.* Lanham, MD: Rowman & Littlefield, 2000.

———. *The Social Production of Urban Space.* Austin: University of Texas Press, 1994.

Graham, Laurel. "Domesticating Efficiency: Lillian Gilbreth's Scientific Management of Homemakers, 1924–1930." *Signs* 24, no. 3 (1999): 633–75.

———. "Lillian Moller Gilbreth's Extensions of Scientific Management into Women's Work, 1924–1935." PhD diss., University of Illinois, 1992.

———. *Managing on Her Own: Dr. Lillian Gilbreth and Women's Work in the Interwar Era.* Norcross, GA: Engineering & Management Press, 1998.

Graham, Stephen, and Simon Marvin. *Splintering Urbanism Networked Infrastructures, Technological Mobilities and the Urban Condition.* New York: Routledge, 2001.

Gramsci, Antonio. "Americanism and Fordism." In *Selections from the Prison Notebooks,* edited by Quintin Hoare and Geoffrey Smith, 277–318. New York: International Publishers, 1971.

Gregory, Derek. *Geographical Imaginations.* Cambridge, MA: Blackwell, 1994.

———. *Ideology, Science and Human Geography.* London: Hutchinson, 1978.

Grossberg, Lawrence. "Cultural Studies and/in New Worlds." *Critical Studies in Mass Communication* 10 (1993): 1–22.

Grosz, Elizabeth. *Architecture from the Outside: Essays on Virtual and Real Space.* Cambridge, MA: MIT Press, 2001.

Gupta, Akhil, and James Ferguson. "Beyond Culture: Space, Identity and the Politics of Difference." *Cultural Anthropology* 7, no. 1 (1992): 6–22.

Haas, Robert Bartlett. *Muybridge: Man in Motion.* Berkeley: University of California Press, 1976.

Hacking, Ian. "Les Alienes Voyageurs: How Fugue Became a Medical Entity." *History of Psychiatry* 7 (1996): 425–49.

———. "Making Up People." In *Reconstructing Individualism: Autonomy, Individuality, and the Self in Western Thought,* edited by T. Heller, M. Sosna, and D. Wellbery, 222–236. Stanford, CA: Stanford University Press, 1986.

———. *The Taming of Chance.* Cambridge: Cambridge University Press, 1990.

Hägerstrand, Torsten, and Allan Richard Pred. *Space and Time in Geography: Essays Dedicated to Torsten Hägerstrand,* Lund Studies in Geography. Ser. B., Human Geography, No. 48. Lund: CWK Gleerup, 1981.

Haggett, Peter. *Locational Analysis in Human Geography.* London: Edward Arnold, 1965.

Hall, Catherine. *White, Male and Middle-Class: Explorations in Feminism and History.* NY: Routledge, 1992.

Hanson, Susan, and Geraldine J. Pratt. *Gender, Work, and Space.* New York: Routledge, 1995.

Harrington, Ralph. "The Railway Journey and the Neuroses of Modernity." In *Pathologies of Travel*, edited by Richard Wrigley and George Revill, 261–78. Amsterdam: Rodopi, 2000.

Harvey, David. *The Condition of Postmodernity*. Blackwell. Oxford, 1989.

———. "From Space to Place and Back Again." In *Mappiing the Futures*, edited by Jon Bird, Barry Curtis, Tim Putnam, George Robertson, and Lisa Tickner, 3–29. London: Routledge, 1993.

———. *The Limits to Capital*. Chicago, IL: University of Chicago Press.

———. *The Urban Experience*. Baltimore, MD: Johns Hopkins University Press, 1989.

Hayden, Dolores, and Cairns Collection of American Women Writers. *The Grand Domestic Revolution: A History of Feminist Designs for American Homes, Neighborhoods, and Cities*. Cambridge, MA: MIT Press, 1981.

Heidegger, Martin. *Poetry, Language, Thought*. Edited by Martin Heidegger. *Works*. New York: Harper & Row, 1971.

Hendricks, Gordon. *Eadweard Muybridge: The Father of the Motion Picture*. New York: Grossman Publishers, 1975.

Hetherington, Kevin. *New Age Travellers: Vanloads of Uproarious Humanity*. London: Cassell, 2000.

———. "Whither the World? Presence, Absence and the Globe." In *Mobilizing Place, Placing Mobility: The Politics of Representation in a Globalized World*, edited by Tim Cresswell and Ginette Verstraete, 173–88. Amsterdam: Rodopi, 2002.

Hobbes, Thomas. *The English Works of Thomas Hobbes of Malmesbury*. London: J. Bohn, 1839.

———. *Leviathan*. London: Penguin, 1988.

Hoelscher, Steven. "Conserving Diversity: Provincial Cosmopolitanism and America's Multicultural Heritage." In *Textures of Place: Exploring Humanist Geographies*, edited by Paul Adams, Steven Hoelscher, and Karen Till, 375–402. Minneapolis: University of Minnesota Press, 2001.

Hoggart, Richard. *The Uses of Literacy*. London: Pelican, 1958.

Holloway, Julian, and James Kneale. "Mikhail Bakhtin: Dialogics of Space." In *Thinking Space*, edited by Mike Crang and Nigel Thrift, 71–88. London: Routledge, 2000.

Honig, Bonnie. *Democracy and the Foreigner*. Princeton, NJ: Princeton University Press, 2001.

Hopper, Kim. *Reckoning with Homelessness, The Anthropology of Contemporary Issues*. Ithaca, NY: Cornell University Press, 2003.

Hyndeman, Jennifer. "Border Crossings." *Antipode* 29, no. 2 (1997): 149–76.

Ibelings, Hans. *Supermodernism: Architecture in the Age of Globalization*. Rotterdam: NAi, 1998.

Illich, Ivan. *Energy and Equity, Ideas in Progress*. New York: Harper & Row, 1974.

———. *Toward a History of Needs*. 1st ed. New York: Pantheon Books, 1978.

Imrie, Rob. "Disability and Discourses of Mobility and Movement." *Environment and Planning A* 32, no. 9 (2000): 1641–56.

Isin, Engin F. *Being Political: Genealogies of Citizenship*. Minneapolis: University of Minnesota Press, 2002.

Isin, Engin F., and Patricia K. Wood. *Citizenship and Identity, Politics and Culture*. London and Thousand Oaks, CA: Sage, 1999.

Iyer, Pico. *The Global Soul: Jet Lag, Shopping Malls, and the Search for Home*. New York: Knopf: Distributed by Random House, 2000.

Iyer, Pico. "Where Worlds Collide." *Harper's Magazine*, August 1995, 50–57.

Jackson, John. B. *Landscape in Sight: Looking at America*. New Haven, CT: Yale University Press, 1997.

Jasper, James M. *Restless Nation: Starting over in America*. Chicago, IL: University of Chicago Press, 2000.

Jokinen, Eeva, and Soile Veijola. "The Disorientated Tourist: The Figuration of the Tourist in Contemporary Cultural Studies." In *Touring Cultures*, edited by John Urry and Chris Rojek, 23–51. London: Routledge, 1997.

Kaeli'inohomoku, J. "Cultural Change: Functional and Dysfunctional Expressions of Dance, a Form of Affective Culture." In *The Performing Arts*, edited by J. Blacking and J. Kaeli'inohomoku. The Hague: Mouton, 1979.

Kaeppler, A. "American Approaches to the Study of Dance." *Yearbook of Traditional Music* 23 (1991): 11–21.

Kanigel, Robert. *The One Best Way: Frederick Winslow Taylor and the Enigma of Efficiency*, The Sloan Technology Series. New York: Viking, 1997.

Kaplan, Caren. *Questions of Travel: Postmodern Discourses of Displacement*. Durham, NC: Duke University Press, 1996.

Kennedy, Duncan. "The Critique of Rights in Critical Legal Studies." In *Left Legalism/Left Critique*, edited by Wendy Brown and Janet Halley, 178–228. Durham NC: Duke University Press, 2002.

Kern, Stephen. *The Culture of Time and Space 1880–1918*. Cambridge, MA: Harvard University Press, 1983.

Kinnaird, Vivian, and Derek R. Hall. *Tourism: A Gender Analysis*. Chichester [England]; New York: John Wiley & Sons, 1994.

Kleinberg, S. J. *Women in the United States, 1830–1945*. New Brunswick, NJ: Rutgers University Press, 1999.

Kobayashi, Audrey, and Brian Ray. "Civil Risk and Landscapes of Marginality in Canada: A Pluralist Approach to Social Justice." *Canadian Geographer* 44 (2000): 401–17.

Kouwenhoven, John. *The Beer-Can by the Highway*. Baltimore, MD: Johns Hopkins University Press, 1961.

Kraditor, Aileen S. *The Ideas of the Woman Suffrage Movement, 1890–1920*. New York: Columbia University Press, 1965.

Kraus, Richard G., and Sarah Chapman Hilsendager. *History of the Dance in Art and Education*. 2d ed. Englewood Cliffs, NJ: Prentice-Hall, 1981.

Kraut, Alan M. *Silent Travelers: Germs, Genes, and the "Immigrant Menace."* Baltimore, MD: Johns Hopkins University Press, 1995.

Laban, Rudolf von. *Laban's Principles of Dance and Movement Notation*. London: Macdonald & Evans, 1975.

Laban, Rudolf von, and F. C. Lawrence. *Effort: Economy in Body Movement.* 2d ed. Boston, MA: Plays Inc., 1974.

Lai, H. Mark, Genny Lim, Judy Yung, and Chinese Culture Foundation. *Island: Poetry and History of Chinese Immigrants on Angel Island, 1910–1940.* HOC DOI ; distributed by San Francisco Study Center, 1980.

Langan, Celeste. "Mobility Disability." *Public Culture* 13, no. 3 (2001): 459–84.

Lange, Dorothea, and Paul Schuster Taylor. *An American Exodus; a Record of Human Erosion.* New York: Reynal & Hitchcock, 1939.

Lavie, Smadar, and Ted Swedenburg. "Between and among the Boundaries of Culture: Bridging Text and Lived Experience in the Third Timespace." *Cultural Studies* 10, no. 1 (1996): 154–79.

Law, Robin. "Beyond 'Women and Transport': Towards New Geographies of Gender and Daily Mobility." *Progress in Human Geography* 23, no. 4 (1999): 567–88.

Leavis, F. R. *Mass Civilisation and Minority Culture.* Cambridge, U.K.: Minority Press, 1930.

Lefebvre, Henri. *The Production of Space.* Oxford: Blackwell, 1991.

Lewis, Orlando. *Vagrancy in the United States.* New York: Self-published, 1907.

Linebaugh, Peter, and Marcus Buford Rediker. *The Many-Headed Hydra: The Hidden History of the Revolutionary Atlantic.* Boston, MA: Beacon Press, 2000.

Lippard, Lucy R. *Changing: Essays in Art Criticism.* New York: Dutton, 1971.

Llewelyn, Mark. "Designed by Women and Designing Women: Gender, Planning and the Geographies of the Kitchen in Britain 1917–1946." *Cultural Geographies* 10 (2004): 42–60.

Lowe, J. and S. Moryadas. *The Geography of Movement.* Boston: Houghton Mifflin, 1975.

Lowe, Lisa. *Immigrant Acts: On Asian American Cultural Politics.* Durham, NC: Duke University Press, 1996.

Lynd, Robert Staughton, and Helen Merrell Lynd. *Middletown: A Study in American Culture.* New York: Harcourt Brace, 1956.

Lyotard, Jean-François. *The Postmodern Condition: A Report on Knowledge.* Minneapolis: University of Minnesota Press, 1984.

Lyotard, Jean François, and Jean-Loup Thébaud. *Just Gaming.* Minneapolis: University of Minnesota Press, 1985.

MacCannell, Dean. *The Tourist: A New Theory of the Leisure Class.* Rev. ed. New York: Schocken Books, 1989.

Malkki, Liisa. "National Geographic: The Rooting of Peoples and the Territorialization of National Identity among Scholars and Refugees." *Cultural Anthropology* 7, no. 1 (1992): 24–44.

Malpas, J. E. *Place and Experience: A Philosophical Topography.* Cambridge, U.K.; New York: Cambridge University Press, 1999.

Mann, Eric, Kikanza Ramsey, Barbara Lott-Holland, and Geoff Ray. "An Environmental Justice Strategy for Urban Transportation in Atlanta: Lessons and Observations from Los Angeles." Los Angeles: Labor/Community Strategy Center, 2001.

Marey, Etienne Jules. *Animal Mechanism: A Treatise on Terrestrial and Aerial Locomotion*. 2d. ed. London: Henry S. King & Co. 65 Cornhill and 12 Paternoster Row London, 1874.

Marey, Étienne-Jules, and Eric Pritchard. *Movement*. New York: D. Appleton and Company, 1895.

Martin, Emily. "The Egg and the Sperm: How Science Has Constructed a Romance Based on Stereotypical Male-Female Sex Roles." *Signs: Journal of Women in Culture and Society* 16, no. 3 (1991): 485–501.

———. "Science and Women's Bodies: Forms of Anthropological Knowledge." In *Body/Politics: Women and the Discourses of Science*, edited by Mary Jacobus, Evelyn Fox Keller, and Sally Shuttleworth, 69–82. London: Routledge, 1990.

Marx, Karl. *Grundrisse. Foundations of the Critique of Political Economy*. New York: Vintage Books, 1973.

———. "On the Jewish Question." In *The Marx-Engels Reader*, edited by Robert C. Tuckner, 26–52. New York: Norton, 1978.

Massey, Doreen. "A Global Sense of Place." In *Reading Human Geography*, edited by Trevor Barnes and Derek Gregory, 315–23. London: Arnold, 1997.

———. "Power-Geometry and Progressive Sense of Place." In *Mapping the Futures: Local Cultures, Global Change*, edited by Jon Bird, Barry Curtis, Tim Putnam, George Robertson, and Lisa Tickner, 59–69. London: Routledge, 1993.

Massey, Doreen B., and P. M. Jess. *A Place in the World?: Places, Cultures and Globalization, Shape of the World*. Oxford and New York: Oxford University Press, 1995.

Matless, David. *Landscape and Englishness*. London: Reaktion Books, 1998.

McCormack, Derek P. "The Event of Geographical Ethics in Spaces of Affect." *Transactions of the Institute of British Geographers* 28 (2003): 488–507.

McDowell, Linda. "Off the Road: Alternative Views of Rebellion, Resistance, and the 'Beats.'" *Transactions of the Institute of British Geographers* 21, no. 2 (1996): 412–19.

McShane, Clay. *Down the Asphalt Path: The Automobile and the American City, Columbia History of Urban Life*. New York: Columbia University Press, 1994.

Merkle, Judith A. *Management and Ideology: The Legacy of the International Scientific Management Movement*. Berkeley: University of California Press, 1980.

Merleau-Ponty, Maurice. *The Phenomenology of Perception*. London: Routledge and Kegan Paul, 1962.

Miller, Christopher. "The Postidentitarian Predicament in the Footnotes of a Thousand Plateaus: Nomadology, Anthropology, and Authority." *Diacritics* 23, no. 3 (1993): 6–35.

Miller, Daniel. "Conclusion: A Theory of Virtualism." In *Virtualism: A New Political Economy*, edited by James G. Carrier and Daniel Miller, 187–216. Oxford: Berg, 1998.

Mills, Sara. *Discourses of Difference*. London: Routledge, 1991.

Monicat, Benedicte. "Autobiography and Women's Travel Writings in Nineteenth Century France: Journeys through Self-Representation." *Gender, Place and Culture* 1, no. 1 (1994): 61–70.

Morgan, Jayne. "Edward Muybridge and W. S. Playfair: An Aesthetics of Neurasthenia." *History of Photography* 23, no. 2 (1999): 225–32.

Morin, Karen. "A 'Female Columbus' in 1887 America: Marking New Social Territory." *Gender, Place and Culture* 2, no. 2 (1995): 191–208.

Morris, Gail, ed. *Moving Words: Re-Writing Dance*. London: Routledge, 1996.

Mosse, George L. *Nazi Culture: Intellectual, Cultural, and Social Life in the Third
Reich*. New York: Grosset & Dunlap, 1966.

Mumford, Lewis. *The City in History*. New York: Harcourt, Brace and World, 1961.

Muybridge, Eadweard. *Muybridge's Complete Human and Animal Locomotion:
All 781 Plates from the 1887 Animal Locomotion*. New York: Dover Publications, 1979.

Nash, Catherine. "Performativity in Practice: Some Recent Work in Cultural
Geography." *Progress in Human Geography* 24, no. 4 (2000): 653–64.

Nott, James J. *Music for the People: Popular Music and Dance in Interwar Britain,
Oxford Historical Monographs*. Oxford and New York: Oxford University
Press, 2002.

Ogborn, Miles. *Spaces of Modernity: London's Geographies, 1680–1780*. New York:
Guilford Press, 1998.

Okely, Judith. *The Traveller-Gypsies, Changing Cultures*. Cambridge and New
York: Cambridge University Press, 1983.

Painter, Joe, and Chris Philo. "Spaces of Citizenship: An Introduction." *Political
Geography* 14, no. 2 (1995): 107–20.

Palmer, Phyllis M. *Domesticity and Dirt: Housewives and Domestic Servants in the
United States, 1920–1945*. Philadelphia, PA: Temple University Press, 1989.

Papastergiadis, Nikos. *The Turbulence of Migration: Globalization, Deterritorialization, and Hybridity*. Cambridge: Polity Press, 2000.

Park, Robert. "The Mind of the Hobo: Reflections Upon the Relation between
Mentality and Locomotion." In *The City: Suggestions for Investigation
of Human Behavior in the Urban Environment*, edited by Robert Park
and Ernest Burgess, 156–60. Chicago, IL: University of Chicago Press,
1925.

Pascoe, David. *Airspaces*. London: Reaktion, 2001.

Patton, Paul. "Conceptual Politics and the War-Machine in *Mille Plateaux*." *Sub-
Stance* 13, no. 3–4 (1984): 61–80.

Peake, Linda, and Brian Ray. "Racializing the Canadian Landscape: Whiteness,
Uneven Geographies and Social Justice." *Canadian Geographer* 45, no. 1
(2001): 180–86.

Peet, Richard. *Modern Geographical Thought*. Oxford: Blackwell, 1998.

Phillips, S. "Dorothea Lange: An American Photographer." In *Dorothea Lange:
American Photographs*, edited by T. Heyman, S. Phillips, and J. Szarkowski,
10–41. San Francisco, CA: Chronicle Books, 1994.

Picart, C. "Dancing through Different Worlds: An Autoethnography of the Interactive Body and Virtual Emotion in Ballroom Dance." *Qualitative Inquiry*
8, no. 3 (2002): 348–61.

Porter, Roy. *The Greatest Benefit to Mankind: A Medical History of Humanity*. New
York: W.W. Norton, 1997.

Pratt, Geraldine. "Geographies of Identity and Difference: Marking Boundaries." In *Human Geography Today*, edited by Doreen Massey, John Allen and Philip Sarre, 151–68. Cambridge: Polity, 1999.

Pred, Allan Richard. "The Choreography of Existence: Comments on Hagerstrand's Time-Geography and Its Usefulness." *Economic Geography* 53 (1977): 207–21.

———. "Power, Everyday Practice and the Discipline of Human Geography." In *Space and Time in Geography*, edited by Allan Richard Pred, 30–55. Lund: CWK Gleerup, 1981.

Prendergast, Christopher. *Paris and the Nineteenth Century*. Oxford: Blackwell, 1992.

Price, Brian. "Frank and Lillian Gilbreth and the Manufacture and Marketing of Motion Study, 1908–1924." *Business and Economic History* 18 (1989): 88–98.

———. "Frank and Lillian Gilbreth and the Motion Study Controversy, 1907–1930." In *A Mental Revolution: Scientific Management since Taylor*, edited by Daniel Nelson, 58–76. Columbus: Ohio State University Press, 1992.

Pudney, John. *The Thomas Cook Story*. London: M. Joseph, 1953.

Pultz, John. *Photography and the Body*. London: Weidenfeld & Nicholson, 1995.

Rabinbach, Anson. *The Human Motor: Energy, Fatigue, and the Origins of Modernity*. New York: BasicBooks, 1990.

Reed, Susan. "The Politics and Poetics of Dance." *Annual Review of Anthropology* 27 (1998): 503–32.

Relph, Edward. *Place and Placelessness*. London: Pion, 1976.

Revill, George. "Performing French Folk Music: Dance, Authenticity and Nonrepresentational Theory." *Cultural Geographies* 11 (2004): 199–209.

Richardson, Philip J. S. *The History of English Ballroom Dancing 1910–1945*. London: Herbert Jenkins, n.d.

Robinson, Roger. *Ways to Move: The Geography of Networks and Accessibility*. Cambridge, U.K.; New York: Cambridge University Press, 1977.

Rodgers, Daniel T. *Atlantic Crossings: Social Politics in a Progressive Age*. Cambridge, MA: Belknap Press of Harvard University Press, 1998.

Rose, Gillian. *Feminism and Geography: The Limits of Geographical Knowledge*. Cambridge: Polity, 1993.

Rosler, Martha. *Martha Rosler: In the Place of the Public: Observations of a Frequent Flyer*. New York: Cantz, 1998.

Rutherford, John. *The Troubadours: Their Loves and Their Lyrics: With Remarks on Their Influence, Social and Literary*. London: Smith Elder, 1873.

Ryan, Dennis. *Beyond the Ballot Box: Social History and the Boston Irish, 1845–1917*. Boston: University of Massachusetts Press, 1989.

Ryan, Mary P. *Women in Public: From Banners to Ballots, 1825–1880*. Baltimore, MD: Johns Hopkins University Press, 1989.

Sack, Robert David. ———. *Conceptions of Space in Social Thought: A Geographic Perspective*. London: Macmillan, 1980.

———. *Homo Geographicus*. Baltimore, MD: Johns Hopkins University Press, 1997.

Said, Edward. *Culture and Imperialism*. London: Vintage, 1994.

Salyer, Lucy E. *Laws Harsh as Tigers: Chinese Immigrants and the Shaping of Modern Immigration Law*. Chapel Hill: University of North Carolina Press, 1995.

Sassen, Saskia. *The Global City: New York, London, Tokyo*. 2nd ed. Princeton, NJ: Princeton University Press, 2001.

Sauer, Carl Ortwin. *Agricultural Origins and Dispersals*. New York: American Geographical Society, 1952.

Savigliano, Marta. *Tango and the Political Economy of Passion*. Boulder, CO: Westview Press, 1995.

Scharff, Virginia. *Taking the Wheel: Women and the Coming of the Motor Age*. New York: Free Press, 1991.

Schivelbusch, Wolfgang. *The Railway Journey: The Industrialization of Time and Space in the 19th Century*. Berkeley: University of California Press, 1986.

Scott, James. *Seeing Like a State: How Certain Schemes to Improve the Human Condition Have Failed*. New Haven, CT: Yale University Press, 1998.

Scott, Joan Wallach. *Gender and the Politics of History*. New York: Columbia University Press, 1988.

Seamon, David. "Body-Subject, Time-Space Routines, and Place-Ballets." In *The Human Experience of Space and Place*, edited by A. Buttimer and D. Seamon, 148–65. London: Croom Helm, 1980.

Seltzer, Mark. *Bodies and Machines*. New York: Routledge, 1992.

Sennett, Richard. *The Conscience of the Eye: The Design and Social Life of Cities*. New York: Knopf, distributed by Random House, 1990.

———. *Flesh and Stone: The Body and the City in Western Civilization*. 1st ed. New York: W.W. Norton, 1994.

Serres, Michel. *Angels, a Modern Myth*. Paris: Flammarion, 1995.

Shields, Rob. *Places on the Margin: Alternative Geographies of Modernity*. London: Routledge Chapman Hall, 1991.

Sibley, David. *Outsiders in Urban Societies*. New York: St. Martin's Press, 1981.

Silvester, Victor. *Dancing Is My Life: An Autobiography*. London: Heinemann, 1958.

———. *Modern Ballroom Dancing: History and Practice*. London: Barrie & Jenkins, 1974.

Simmel, Georg. *The Sociology of Georg Simmel*. Glencoe, IL: Free Press, 1950.

Sklar, D. "On Dance Ethnography." *Dance Research Journal* 23, no. 1 (1991): 6–10.

Smith, Henry Nash. *Popular Culture and Industrialism, 1865–1890*. New York: New York University Press, 1967.

Smith, Neil. *Uneven Development: Nature, Capital, and the Production of Space*. Oxford, UK ; Cambridge, MA, USA: B. Blackwell, 1991.

Smith, Sidonie. *Moving Lives: Twentieth Century Women's Travel Writing*. Minneapolis: University of Minnesota Press, 2001.

Smith, Susan. "Society, Space and Citizenship: A Human Geography for New Times." *Transactions of the Institute of British Geographers* 14 (1990): 144–56.

Smith-Rosenberg, Carroll. *Disorderly Conduct: Visions of Gender in Victorian America*. New York: A. A. Knopf, 1985.

Smithson, Robert, and Nancy Holt. *The Writings of Robert Smithson: Essays with Illustrations.* New York: New York University Press, 1979.

Soja, Edward W. *Postmetropolis: Critical Studies of Cities and Regions.* Oxford; Malden, MA: Blackwell Publishers, 2000.

———. *Postmodern Geographies: The Reassertion of Space in Critical Social Theory.* London ; New York: Verso, 1989.

Solnit, Rebecca. *Motion Studies: Eadweard Muybridge and the Technological Wild West.* London: Bloomsbury, 2003.

———. *Wanderlust: A History of Walking.* New York: Viking, 2000.

Spencer, Frank. "Some Notes on the Attempt to Apply Photography to Anthropometry during the Second Half of the Nineteenth Century." In *Anthropology and Photography 1860–1920,* edited by Elizabeth Edwards, 99–107. New Haven, CT: Yale University Press, 1992.

Spencer, Frank, and Peggy Spencer. *Come Dancing.* London: W. H. Allen, 1968.

Spencer, Paul. *Society and the Dance: The Social Anthropology of Process and Performance.* Cambridge: Cambridge University Press, 1985.

Spragens, Thomas A. *The Politics of Motion; the World of Thomas Hobbes.* Lexington: University Press of Kentucky, 1973.

Strom, Sharon. "Leadership and Tactics in the American Woman Suffrage Movement: A New Perspective from Massachusetts." *Journal of American History* 62, no. 2 (1975): 296–315.

———. *Political Woman: Florence Luscomb and the Legacy of Radical Reform.* Philadelphia, PA: Temple University Press, 2001.

Swain, M. "Gender in Tourism." *Annals of Tourism Research* 22, no. 2 (1995): 247–66.

Taaffe, Edward J., and Howard L. Gauthier. *Geography of Transportation.* Englewood Cliffs, NJ: Prentice-Hall, 1973.

Taylor, Frederick Winslow. *The Principles of Scientific Management.* New York: Norton, 1967.

Taylor, Peter J. *Modernities: A Geohistorical Interpretation.* Cambridge: Polity Press, 1999.

Tester, Keith, ed. *The Flâneur.* London: Routledge, 1994.

Thomas, Helen. *Dance, Modernity, and Culture: Explorations in the Sociology of Dance.* London and New York: Routledge, 1995.

Thompson, E.P. "Time, Work Discipline, and Industrial Capitalism." *Past and Present* 38 (1967): 56–97.

Thrift, Nigel. "Inhuman Geographies: Landscapes of Speed, Light and Power." In *Writing the Rural: Five Cultural Geographies,* edited by Paul Cloke, 191–250. London: Paul Chapman, 1994.

———. "The Still Point: Resistance, Expressiveness Embodiment and Dance." In *Geographies of Resistance,* edited by S. Pile and M. Keith, 124–51. London: Routledge, 1997.

———. "Summoning Life." In *Envisioning Human Geographies,* edited by Paul Cloke, Philip Crang and Mark Goodwin, 81–103. London: Arnold, 2004.

———. "Transport and Communication 1730–1914." In *An Historical Geography of England and Wales*, edited by Robert A. Dodgshon and Robin Butlin, 453–86. London: Academic Press, 1990.

Thrift, Nigel. J., and Sean French. "The Automatic Production of Space." *Transactions of the Institute of British Geographers* 27 (2002): 309–35.

Tocqueville, Alexis de. *Democracy in America*. Chicago, IL: University of Chicago Press, 2000.

Toffler, Alvin. *Future Shock*. New York: Random House, 1970.

Tönnies, Ferdinand. *Community & Society (Gemeinschaft Und Gesellschaft)*. New York: Harper & Row, 1963.

Torpey, John C. *The Invention of the Passport: Surveillance, Citizenship, and the State*. Cambridge: Cambridge University Press, 2000.

Tschumi, Bernard. *Architecture and Disjunction*. Cambridge, MA: MIT Press, 1994.

Tschumi, Bernard, and Robert Young. *The Manhattan Transcripts*. London: Academy Editions, 1994.

Tuan, Yi-Fu. *Morality and Imagination: Paradoxes of Progress*. Madison, WI: University of Wisconsin Press, 1989.

———. *Space and Place: The Perspective of Experience*. Minneapolis: University of Minnesota Press, 1977.

———. "A View of Geography." *Geographical Review* 81, no. 1 (1991): 99–107.

Turner, Frederick Jackson. *The Frontier in American History*. New York: Holt, Rinehart and Winston, 1947.

Turner, Louis, and John Ash. *The Golden Hordes: International Tourism and the Pleasure Periphery*. London: Constable, 1975.

Turner, Victor Witter. *The Ritual Process: Structure and Anti-Structure*. Ithaca, NY: Cornell University Press, 1977.

Tushnet, Mark. "An Essay on Rights." *Texas Law Review* 62, no. 8 (1984): 1363–403.

Ullman, Edward. "The Role of Transportation and the Bases for Interaction." In *Man's Role in Changing the Face of the Earth*, edited by William L. Thomas, 862–80. Chicago, IL: University of Chicago Press, 1956.

Urry, John. *Sociology beyond Societies: Mobilities for the Twenty-First Century*. London and New York: Routledge, 2000.

———. *The Tourist Gaze: Leisure and Travel in Contemporary Societies*. London and Newbury Park, CA: Sage Publications, 1990.

Venturi, Robert, Denise Scott Brown, and Steven Izenour. *Learning from Las Vegas*. Cambridge, MA: MIT Press, 1972.

Verstraete, Ginette. "Heading for Europe: Tourism and the Global Itinerary of an Idea." In *Mobilizing Place, Placing Mobility: The Politics of Representation in a Globalized World*, edited by Tim Cresswell and Ginette Verstraete, 33–52. Amsterdam: Rodopi, 2002.

———. "Technological Frontiers and the Politics of Mobility in the European Union." *New Formations* 43 (spring 2001): 26–43.

Vidler, Anthony. *Warped Space: Art, Architecture and Anxiety in Modern Culture*. Cambridge, MA: MIT Press, 2001.

Virilio, Paul. *Speed and Politics: An Essay on Dromology*, Semiotext(E) Foreign Agents Series. New York, NY, USA: Columbia University, 1986.

Ward, David. *Poverty, Ethnicity and the American City, 1840–1925*. Cambridge: Cambridge University Press, 1989.

Weaver, G. *Our Home or Influences Emanating from the Hearthstone*. Springfield, MA: King Richardson, 1899.

White, H. P., and M. L. Senior. *Transport Geography*. London and New York: Longman, 1983.

Whyte, William Hollingsworth. *The Organization Man*. New York: Simon and Schuster, 1956.

Williams, Patricia J. *The Alchemy of Race and Rights*. Cambridge, MA: Harvard University Press, 1991.

Williams, Raymond. "Mining the Meaning: Keywords in the Miners Strike." In *Resources of Hope*, edited by Raymond Williams. London: Verso, 1989.

Wilson, Elizabeth. *The Sphinx in the City*. Berkeley: University of California Press, 1991.

Wolff, Janet. "The Invisible Flaneuse: Women and the Literature of Modernity." In *Feminine Sentences: Essays on Women and Culture*, edited by Janet Wolff, 34–50. Oxford: Polity, 1990.

———. "On the Road Again: Metaphors of Travel in Cultural Criticism." *Cultural Studies* 6 (1992): 224–39.

Wright, John K. "Terrae Incognitae: The Place of the Imagination in Geography." *Annals of the Association of American Geographers* 37 (1947): 1–15.

Yanarella, Ernest J., and Herbert G. Reid. "From 'Trained Gorilla' to 'Humanware': Repoliticizing the Body-Machine Complex between Fordism and Post-Fordism." In *The Social and Political Body*, edited by Theodore Schatzki and Wolfgang Natter, 181–220. New York: Guilford, 1996.

Young, Iris Marion. *Throwing Like a Girl and Other Essays in Feminist Philosophy and Social Theory*. Bloomington: Indiana University Press, 1990.

———. *Justice and the Politics of Difference*. Princeton, NJ: Princeton University Press, 1990.

Zelinsky, Wilbur. *The Cultural Geography of the United States*. Englewood Cliffs, NJ: Prentice Hall, 1973.

Zipf, George Kingsley. *Human Behavior and the Principle of Least Effort; an Introduction to Human Ecology*. Cambridge, MA: Addison-Wesley Press, 1949.

Zolberg, Aristide. "Matters of State: Theorizing Immigration Policy." In *The Handbook of International Migration: The American Experience*, edited by Josh DeWind and Philip Kasinitz, 71–93. New York: Russell Sage, 1999.

# Index